War Law

War Law

*Understanding International Law
and Armed Conflict*

MICHAEL BYERS

GROVE PRESS
New York

First published in Great Britain in 2005 by Atlantic Books, an imprint of Grove Atlantic Ltd.

Printed in the United States of America

Library of Congress Cataloging-in-Publication Data

    Byers, Michael, 1966–
        War law : understanding international law and armed conflicts / Michael Byers.
          p. cm.
        Originally published: Great Britain : Atlantic Books, 2005.
        Includes bibliographical references and index.
        ISBN 978-0-8021-4294-8
        1. War (International law). 2. War—Causes. 3. Just war doctrine.
    I. Title.
    KZ6385.B94 2006
    341.6—dc22   2005045641

Grove Press
an imprint of Grove/Atlantic, Inc.
841 Broadway
New York, NY 10003

Distributed by Publishers Group West

www.groveatlantic.com

11 12 13 14 15   10 9 8 7 6 5 4 3 2

For Katharine

Contents

Foreword

The international law governing the use of military force has recently been the subject of intense public debate. Both the Kosovo War (1999) and the Iraq War (2003) sparked controversy as neither was expressly authorized by the United Nations Security Council. National leaders, including Bill Clinton, Tony Blair and George W. Bush, spoke openly about issues of international law. Pundits pontificated and millions of people marched in the streets, yet there was considerable confusion about the international rules of war.

This book aims to provide the interested non-lawyer with a readily comprehensible overview of the law governing the use of force in international affairs. It does so against the backdrop of recent political developments – including, most notably, the United States' rise to military predominance – in recognition of the intrinsic relationship between global politics and international law. Although this book is not intended for legal experts, references to further reading are provided for those who wish to delve more deeply into the issues.

Any book intended for a general readership will draw on diverse sources and experiences. Although more people deserve thanks than I could ever list here, I do wish to record my gratitude to certain individuals. Robert Byers, Michael Perry, Scott Silliman, Adriana Sinclair, Greta Smith and Nicholas Wheeler read and commented on the entire manuscript, while Kathy and Mike Edmunds provided the quiet English village environment in which most of the writing was done. The editors of the *London Review of Books* have long encouraged my efforts to explain the complexities of international law and politics to non-specialist audiences: portions of this book consolidate and expand upon some of the essays that I have written for them. And I am indebted to the many excellent students, from many countries, who have taken my courses on international law and the use of military force. Although we often disagreed, our lively discussions have greatly enriched my perspective on these controversial issues. In this sense, my students helped me write this book.

MB
Blewbury, Oxfordshire
20 December 2004

Introduction

During the lead-up to the Iraq War, on 6 February 2003, BBC *Newsnight* host Jeremy Paxman asked Prime Minister Tony Blair: 'Will you give an undertaking to this audience and indeed to the British people that before any military action you will seek another UN resolution specifically authorizing the use of force?'

Blair replied, 'Those are the only circumstances in which we would agree to use force, except for one caveat' – which, he explained, was if a veto was 'unreasonably' exercised by one of the five permanent members of the UN Security Council, thus blocking the adoption of a further resolution.

As the Prime Minister recognized, there are rules governing how countries behave. Most of the rules, concerning matters such as international postal services, air travel and trade, are obeyed almost all of the time; as a consequence, they are rarely noticed and generally uncontroversial. Other rules, such as those governing the use of military force, are highly politicized and the subject of frequent dispute. Blair, by introducing the concept of an 'unreasonable veto', was advancing a hotly contested – even bizarre – understanding of those rules. The United Nations Charter does not even hint at the concept of an unreasonable veto, nor have countries ever treated Security Council vetoes in this way. But Blair, torn between his personal commitment to join President George W. Bush's invasion of Iraq, and widespread domestic concern about the wisdom and legality of that action, was not above grasping at legal straws.

It should come as no surprise that the law on the use of force is politicized. Prussian military philosopher Carl von Clausewitz famously wrote that 'war is politics by other means'. And the stakes are particularly high in this particular sphere of politics, since war constitutes a direct challenge to the sovereignty, territorial integrity and political independence of nation-states. Nevertheless, governments pay considerable attention to the rules on the use of force – indeed, most governments, including the British and US governments, take these rules very seriously – since they directly protect and support *their* sovereignty, and not just the sovereignty of other countries. Tony Blair, even when advancing the novel concept of an 'unreasonable veto', neither rejected the existence of rules nor argued that none were applicable in the circumstances.

Historically speaking, legal rules on the use of military force are a relatively recent development. Prior to the adoption of the UN Charter in 1945, international law imposed few constraints on the recourse to arms. International law was conceived in strictly consensual terms during the nineteenth and early twentieth centuries: countries were only bound by those rules to which they had agreed, either through the conclusion of a treaty or through a consistent pattern of behaviour that, over time, gave rise to what is referred to as 'customary international law'. This consent-based conception of law is often referred to as 'positivism' to distinguish it from earlier conceptions of 'natural law' based on intuitions and interpretations of divine will. Today, consent remains central to international law. Although ethicists and scholars of canon law draw on natural law to distinguish between 'just' and 'unjust' wars, their thinking exists in a sphere that is separate from the rules regarded as binding by national governments.

Since governments had not agreed otherwise, military aggression was left largely unregulated until the UN Charter was adopted in 1945. Until this time, conquest gave good title to territory, as was demonstrated by the British acquisition of the Falkland Islands in 1833. The only rule concerning recourse to force was the right of self-defence, which, when properly exercised, enabled a country to use force without provoking all-out conflict. The introduction of legal limits on the use of force through the UN Charter was a transformative moment in international affairs, and it was entirely consensual. As US President

Harry Truman explained at the conference that founded the United Nations: 'We all have to recognize – no matter how great our strength – that we must deny ourselves the licence to do always as we please.'

Since 1945, governments that use force have almost always sought to justify their actions in legal terms, however tenuously. The United States advanced two legal arguments for the invasion of Iraq in March 2003: an extended right of pre-emptive self-defence and the enforcement of UN Security Council resolutions. Other countries, as they deliberated how to respond, assessed the merit of the legal claims. In some cases, their willingness to send troops, contribute financially, or at least provide access to military bases and airspace, was clearly influenced by their understanding of international law. In Britain, Attorney General Lord Goldsmith's public pronouncement on the legality of the war was a political prerequisite for Tony Blair's decision to take the country into the conflict. Similarly, the Turkish parliament's concerns about the illegality of the war resulted in the denial of Turkish territory for the deployment of US tanks into northern Iraq.

Illegal recourses to force will sometimes prompt countries to take forceful action in response. The invasion of Kuwait by Iraq in August 1990 was a clear violation of international law. Five months later, the Iraqi army was expelled from Kuwait by a coalition of approximately thirty countries expressly authorized to use force by the UN Security Council. In other instances, responses to illegal uses of force will be limited to economic sanctions or diplomatic measures against the law-breaking state. The refusal of many countries to aid the United States and Britain in and after the 2003 Iraq War can be explained, in part, by the profound difference of opinion on the legality of Operation Iraqi Freedom.

It is clear that the international rules on the use of force matter. But what exactly is international law, where does one find it, and how does one determine its rules?

There are two principal sources of international law, the first of which is customary international law, an informal, unwritten body of rules deriving from a combination of 'state practice' and *opinio juris*. State practice is what governments do and say; *opinio juris* is a belief, on the part of governments, that their conduct is obligated by international law.

Most rules of customary international law apply universally: they bind all countries and all countries contribute to their development and change. When a new rule of customary international law is being formed, every country has a choice: support the developing rule through its actions or statements, or actively and publicly oppose the rule. A new rule will not come into force until it receives widespread support.

Support for a customary rule does not need to be actively expressed. Acquiescence by a country in the face of a developing rule is sufficient. A country may thus be bound to a new rule as a result of doing nothing – a possibility that entails certain risks for unwary or understaffed governments. Most countries monitor the international legal system carefully to avoid becoming unwittingly bound by new customary rules.

Treaties are the second main source of international law. Treaties are contractual, written instruments entered into by two or more countries with the intent of creating binding rights and obligations and registered with a third party, nowadays usually the UN Secretary General. Treaties may be referred to by any number of different names, including 'charter', 'convention', 'covenant', 'exchange of notes' or 'protocol'.

Entering into – or concluding – a treaty typically requires a two-step process: 'signature' indicates a country's intention to assume obligations and 'ratification' is the point at which the obligations are formally undertaken. Non-lawyers often fail to distinguish between these two phases – which can lead to confusion when a country has signed, but not yet ratified, a treaty that would otherwise be relevant to a particular dispute. Complicating things further, the act of ratifying a treaty that has already entered into force between other countries is referred to as 'accession' rather than 'ratification'!

Countries ratify treaties in accordance with constitutional processes. In Britain, Canada and Australia, treaty ratification is an executive act by the government that does not require parliamentary approval. In the United States, a treaty cannot be ratified until the president receives the 'advice and consent' of two thirds of the members of the Senate. As a result, it is more difficult for the United States to ratify treaties, especially if the president and the majority of senators belong to different political parties. Republican Jesse Helms, a fierce opponent of international law, chaired the Senate Foreign Relations Committee during the last six years of the administration of President Bill Clinton, a Democrat. Politics in the process helps explain why some important treaties, such as the Comprehensive Test Ban Treaty (CTBT) on nuclear weapons, have not yet been ratified by the United States. Helms postponed bringing the CTBT to a vote until the height of the Monica Lewinsky scandal, when Clinton's influence was at its nadir.

Treaties are interpreted on the basis of agreed rules conveniently set out in a treaty of their own: the 1969 Vienna Convention on the Law of Treaties. The Vienna Convention is widely accepted – even by non-parties – as an accurate codification of the customary international law governing treaties. Accordingly, the rules set out in the Vienna Convention are binding on all countries. The most important rule concerning treaty interpretation is found in Article 31(1):

A treaty shall be interpreted in good faith in accordance with the ordinary meaning to be given to the terms of the treaty in their context and in the light of its object and purpose.

Giving words their *ordinary meaning* is the guiding principle of treaty interpretation. Treaties mean what they say. Yet in some instances the same word, or combination of words, can reasonably be understood to mean different things. In some instances, treaty interpretation requires a consideration of *context*, which generally involves reading the treaty as a whole. This process is frequently facilitated by 'preambles': non-binding paragraphs at the beginning of treaties that are meant to indicate their *object and purpose*. For example, when interpreting the UN Charter's provisions on the use of force, it is relevant that the preamble to the treaty expresses a determination to 'save succeeding generations from the scourge of war'.

A treaty provision prevails over any conflicting rule of customary international law. For this reason, countries sometimes conclude treaties in order to exempt aspects of their relations from otherwise applicable customary rules. For example, a government sending troops abroad will sometimes enter into a 'status of forces agreement' that exempts its soldiers from customary rules that would otherwise give the country to which they are being deployed jurisdiction over criminal and civil matters involving them.

Many rules of customary international law have been 'codified' into treaty provisions, while other customary practices have 'crystallized' into rules as a result of treaties replicating and thus reinforcing them. The UN Charter goes even further. In addition to codifying and crystallizing a number of customary rules, including a prohibition on the use of force and the right of self-defence, the Charter explicitly states that it prevails over all other treaties. Accordingly, countries cannot exempt themselves from the provisions of the UN Charter, which include the authority of the UN Security Council and the international rules governing recourse to military force.

This admittedly complex picture is rendered more complex by the existence of a few non-treaty rules of a 'peremptory' character. These special rules – called *jus cogens* rules – override conflicting rules, including conflicting treaty provisions. *Jus cogens* rules include the prohibitions on genocide, slavery and torture. The customary rule prohibiting the use of force, crystallized in the UN Charter, is also widely regarded as having achieved *jus cogens* status.

The UN Charter is thus the starting point for most issues

concerning international law and the use of force. Adopted in the immediate aftermath of the Second World War, the primary goal of the Charter was to provide clear rules on recourse to force, along with an institutional framework for enforcing the rules. The Charter has since been ratified by 192 countries.

The UN Charter's central provision is Article 2(4):

> All Members shall refrain in their international relations from the threat or use of force against the territorial integrity or political independence of any state, or in any other manner inconsistent with the Purposes of the United Nations.

The ordinary meaning of Article 2(4) is clear: the use of force across borders is not permitted. This meaning is supported by the Charter's context, object and purpose.

The UN Charter provides two exceptions to the prohibition set out in Article 2(4): authorization by the Security Council and self-defence. The Security Council, an executive body made up of fifteen countries, may authorize the use of force by adopting resolutions to that effect under a section of the Charter referred to as 'Chapter VII'. The central role of the Security Council in matters concerning recourse to force is the focus of the first three chapters of this book.

As for self-defence, Article 51 of the UN Charter stipulates:

> Nothing in the present Charter shall impair the inherent right of individual or collective self-defence if an armed attack occurs against a Member of the United Nations, until the Security Council has taken measures necessary to maintain international peace and security.

Article 51 is the focus of several debates. The first concerns whether one country may use force within the territory of another country against terrorists located there. In 1998 and 2001, the United States invoked self-defence to justify military action in

Afghanistan following terrorist attacks against US targets, first in Nairobi and Dar es Salaam, and then in New York City and Washington, DC. Similarly, Israel claims self-defence when engaging in the 'targeted killing' of Palestinian leaders in the Gaza Strip and West Bank. The Bush Administration has accepted the Israeli claim, while European governments regard the same acts as 'extrajudicial killings', which are illegal under international law.

Another debate over self-defence concerns whether, and to what degree, the exception includes a right of pre-emptive or anticipatory military action. Prior to 1945, countries were widely considered to have a right of pre-emption if there was a 'necessity of self-defence, instant, overwhelming, leaving no choice of means, and no moment of deliberation'. The adoption of Article 51 of the UN Charter, permitting self-defence only 'if an armed attack occurs', would then seem to have rendered pre-emptive action illegal (that is, unless it has been authorized by the UN Security Council).

Since 2002, the United States has sought to develop a right of pre-emptive self-defence that extends to more distant and uncertain challenges, most notably those arising out of the combined threat of weapons of mass destruction and global terrorism. Although the so-called 'Bush Doctrine' remains highly controversial, it has been endorsed by several other countries, notably Israel and Russia. The right of self-defence is the focus of the fourth, fifth and sixth chapters of this book.

Two further, unwritten exceptions to the prohibition on the use of force may have developed in recent decades. The first is a right to intervene militarily to promote or restore democracy. Proponents of this exception point to the US-led interventions in Grenada in 1983 and Panama in 1989 as precedents. They also claim that advancements in international human rights have displaced sovereignty away from governments and into the hands of ordinary people; consequently, governments that deny the popular will are no longer sovereign and cannot benefit from the prohibition on the use of force.

The second possible additional exception involves a right to intervene on humanitarian grounds in the event of heinous abuses such as genocide, mass expulsion or systematic rape. Proponents of this right of unilateral humanitarian intervention – 'unilateral' because the interventions are not authorized by the UN Security Council – point to the creation of 'no-fly' zones in Iraq in 1991 and the 1999 Kosovo War as precedents. And like the proponents of a right of pro-democratic intervention, they argue that developments in international human rights favour the use of force against abusive governments. The seventh, eighth and ninth chapters of this book consider pro-democratic intervention, unilateral humanitarian intervention, and the related concept of a 'responsibility to protect'.

In addition to rules governing recourse to force, there are rules concerning how soldiers behave once armed conflict has begun. The four Geneva Conventions of 1949 are treaties that set out a body of law referred to as the 'laws of war', 'law of armed conflict' or 'international humanitarian law'. The latter term (also known as *jus in bello*) is preferred because it indicates that the rules protect individuals rather than nation-states.

Any armed conflict involves two broad categories of individuals: combatants and non-combatants (who are also referred to as civilians). International humanitarian law protects both categories of persons, though non-combatants are shielded more than those who take up arms. The most important protection for non-combatants is a requirement that the risk to them be factored into all military decisions. Purely civilian targets cannot be selected, while the targeting of 'dual-use facilities' such as electrical grids and sewage treatment plants must be assessed very carefully on a case-by-case basis. During the Kosovo War, the destruction of water filtration plants and a television station by the North Atlantic Treaty Organization (NATO) caused considerable controversy, though the prosecutor for the International Criminal Tribunal for the former Yugoslavia did not subsequently indict any NATO personnel.

Combatants are protected from weapons and means of warfare that cause unnecessary suffering, including chemical and biological weapons and bullets designed to explode on impact. Soldiers are entitled to surrender and receive a range of protections as prisoners of war (POWs). POWs may not be punished for having taken up arms and are entitled to be treated with dignity; they must also be released once the hostilities have come to an end. Yet the mistreatment of POWs is far too common. During the 2003 Iraq War, some captured US troops were mistreated by their Iraqi captors. After the invasion, many Iraqis in US custody were also abused.

Individuals who break the rules may be tried for war crimes before national courts or international tribunals. The Nuremberg and Tokyo Tribunals, established following the Second World War, have served as models for international tribunals for the former Yugoslavia and Rwanda. In 1998, negotiators from 120 countries established a permanent International Criminal Court (ICC). The ICC has been the subject of considerable controversy, largely because the United States has actively sought to undermine it. At the same time, the trials of Slobodan Milošević before the Yugoslav tribunal in The Hague and of Saddam Hussein before an Iraqi court in Baghdad have demonstrated the relative strengths of international and national proceedings. International humanitarian law and war crimes tribunals are dealt with in the tenth, eleventh and twelfth chapters of this book.

Much of this book refers to actions by the United States, which, in relative terms, is militarily more powerful than any political entity since the Roman Empire. Thanks to its massive defence spending – as much as the next twenty countries combined – the United States is also the only country that regularly makes major advances in military technology. It backs up its hardware and budget with an aggressive policy of forward staging: US troops are now based in more than 140 countries.

The United States has long demonstrated a willingness to use its military power in legally questionable circumstances, most recently in Kosovo and Iraq. The United States also consciously seeks to modify international law in accordance with its interests, for instance, by pushing for a right of self-defence against terrorism, and for the Bush Doctrine of pre-emptive self-defence. Over time, the combination of predominant military power and the deliberate pursuit of normative change will test, stretch and sometimes alter the limits of international law. Yet the existence of a militarily dominant, legally entrepreneurial state does not necessarily spell the end of the global rules on the use of force. International law is made and changed by all of the nearly 200 countries in this world and is indirectly influenced by an even larger number of non-governmental actors, such as international organizations and human rights groups.

The United States itself needs international law, if sometimes only to persuade other countries of the legitimacy of its actions and to secure their participation and support. As the high costs of the occupation of Iraq demonstrate, America pays a price for ignoring world opinion. Even in the highly politicized sphere of military action, and even for the single superpower, the question is not whether international law exists, but how and when it matters. The epilogue to this book considers the unique position of the United States – and of committed allies such as Tony Blair – as they shape, break and attempt to remake the international rules on the use of military force.

Part One

United Nations Action

Security Council Authorization

In 1945, representatives from fifty countries gathered in San Francisco to create a new international organization: the United Nations. The negotiations took place in the aftermath of the Second World War with its tens of millions of casualties, including the millions of civilians slaughtered during the Holocaust and the hundreds of thousands who were to die as a result of the atomic bombings of Hiroshima and Nagasaki. The diplomats sought an institution and set of rules that would, in their words, 'save succeeding generations from the scourge of war'. The treaty they negotiated – the Charter of the United Nations – focused on preserving the peace and empowering multilateral responses to threats or breaches of the peace. One hundred and ninety-two countries have since ratified the UN Charter and are thereby 'member states' of the United Nations with all the rights and obligations that entails.

Again, the central obligation of membership is set out in Article 2(4) of the UN Charter:

All Members shall refrain in their international relations from the threat or use of force against the territorial integrity or political independence of any state, or in any other manner inconsistent with the Purposes of the United Nations.

Interpreted according to the 1969 Vienna Convention on the Law of Treaties, the ordinary meaning of Article 2(4) is clear: the use of force across borders is categorically prohibited. This interpretation is supported by the Charter's context, object and purpose. The preamble to the UN Charter states that it is designed to 'ensure by the acceptance of principles and the institution of methods, that armed force shall not be used, save in the common interest'. The Charter sets out only two exceptions to the prohibition on the use of force. The first exception empowers the UN Security Council, a specialized decision-making body made up of representatives from fifteen member states of the United Nations, to authorize the use of force 'to maintain or restore international peace and security'.

Of the fifteen countries on the Security Council, five – Britain, China, France, the United States and the Soviet Union (now Russia) – are designated as 'permanent members'. Each permanent member has the power to veto any proposed resolution. Sometimes the mere threat of a veto is enough to prevent a resolution from being put to a vote. In the absence of a veto, nine votes are required for a resolution to pass. This requirement means that the support of at least four non-permanent members is needed for any resolution to be adopted, and more than four in the event that one or more permanent members choose to abstain from voting. In early 2003, the British government's decision not to put its so-called 'second resolution' on Iraq to a vote was conditioned as much by opposition from non-permanent members as it was by the threat of a French or Russian veto.

Under Chapter VII of the UN Charter, the Security Council has a broad authority to 'determine the existence of any threat to the peace, breach of the peace, or act of aggression'. The Council has an equally broad authority to decide which measures shall be taken to 'maintain or restore international peace and security'. Such measures can include imposing economic sanctions and, even more significantly, authorizing the use of military force against disobedient countries.

During the Cold War, the UN Security Council's power to authorize the use of force went largely unexercised, apart from an ambiguous, possible authorization in Korea and a clear but very constrained authorization to the United Kingdom with regard to Southern Rhodesia.

*

North Korea's invasion of South Korea in 1950 prompted the newly created Security Council to 'recommend' that UN member states 'furnish such assistance to South Korea as may be necessary to repel the armed attack and to restore international peace and security in the area'. The resolution was highly controversial. First, the Soviet Union boycotted the Council meeting at which the resolution was passed. According to an ordinary meaning interpretation of Article 27(3) of the UN Charter, which stipulates that substantive resolutions must receive the 'concurring votes' of all the permanent members, the Soviet Union's absence should have prevented adoption of the resolution. Nevertheless, most governments treated the resolution as valid. Second, since the resolution was recommending – rather than expressly authorizing – the use of force, it was questionable whether the Security Council was actually using its Chapter VII powers.

The Korean War had an important consequence for the international law on the use of force. Today, it is widely accepted that absences or abstentions by one or more permanent members of the Security Council are not fatal to resolutions under vote. If a permanent member wishes to block a resolution, it must actually cast a negative vote. Permanent members are now careful to attend all Security Council meetings lest their absence facilitate the lawmaking efforts of states whose policies they oppose.

In 1964, Ian Smith, the leader of the Rhodesian Front, became prime minister of the British colony of Southern Rhodesia. After failing to persuade London to set the colony free, Smith and his government made a 'unilateral declaration of independence' – under white minority rule – on 11 November 1965.

The UN General Assembly, a body made up of all UN member states, had adopted its first resolution on Rhodesia in 1961. The resolution deplored 'the denial of equal political rights and liberties to the vast majority of the people of Southern Rhodesia'. However, the General Assembly can only recommend – and not authorize – economic sanctions or military action. Accordingly, the Assembly responded to the 1965 Rhodesian declaration of independence by condemning it as a 'rebellion' by 'unlawful authorities' and a 'racialist minority' and recommending that the Security Council consider the situation 'as a matter of urgency'.

The Security Council condemned 'the usurpation of power by a racist settler minority', stating that the declaration of independence had 'no legal validity'. The Council also called upon countries to break all economic ties with Rhodesia, but neither imposed legally binding sanctions nor authorized the use of force.

Five months later, the Security Council learned that substantial quantities of oil were about to reach landlocked Rhodesia from tankers offloading oil into a pipeline that ran from the Mozambique port of Beira. The Council responded with Resolution 221, which deemed the situation a 'threat to the peace'. Most importantly, the resolution called upon the United Kingdom 'to prevent, by the use of force if necessary, the arrival of vessels reasonably believed to be carrying oil destined for Southern Rhodesia'.

Although the language of Resolution 221 did not expressly refer to the Security Council's powers under Chapter VII, the resolution was probably the first occasion on which that part of the UN Charter was used. That the resolution was adopted at all is remarkable, given the intense Cold War rivalry between the two veto-holding superpowers. The specific nature of the Rhodesian situation – a white racist minority rebellion in a part of the world where the Soviet Union and United States were competing for influence over newly independent black governments – helps explain its adoption, as do the narrowly defined limits of the apparent authorization given to the UK.

Eight months later, in December 1966, the Security Council imposed the first mandatory economic sanctions in UN history. In Resolution 232, the Council again determined that the situation in Rhodesia constituted a threat to international peace and security. Using the words 'all State Members of the United Nations shall prevent' to avoid any ambiguity, the resolution prohibited the import of any of Rhodesia's principal products, as well as the export of arms, oil or oil products to the country. The mandatory embargo was later broadened to sever air links, ban the acceptance of Rhodesian passports, withdraw all consular and trade representatives from the country and break off diplomatic relations and ground transportation links.

It took almost a decade, but these external pressures eventually led to all-party talks at Lancaster House in London in 1979. The talks produced a peace agreement and a new constitution for the country that guaranteed minority rights. In 1980, Robert Mugabe and his Zanu Party won British-supervised elections. Mugabe was named prime minister and, on 18 April 1980, the colony of Southern Rhodesia became the independent country of Zimbabwe. Although the Security Council's authorization of the use of force played only a minimal role in the international effort that ultimately led to a sovereign Zimbabwe, Resolution 221 is a milestone in the ongoing development of international rules on the use of force, and of Chapter VII of the UN Charter in particular.

The Security Council's period of general inactivity, coinciding with the Cold War, ceased after the Iraqi army invaded and seized the small neighbouring country of Kuwait on 2 August 1990. The invasion was a blatant violation of the UN Charter and its prohibition in Article 2(4) on the use of force against the 'territorial integrity and political independence' of any UN member state. The Security Council responded the very next day, adopting Resolution 660. Acting expressly under Chapter VII, the Council condemned the invasion and demanded Iraq's immediate withdrawal from Kuwait. A few days later, the Council imposed stringent mandatory economic sanctions on Iraq.

Four months of intense diplomatic activity followed as world leaders sought to persuade Iraqi president Saddam Hussein to comply with international law and the orders of the Security Council. When Saddam refused, the Security Council increased its pressure. On 29 November 1990, the Council adopted Resolution

678 in which it 'decided to allow Iraq one final opportunity' to remove its forces from Kuwait, and set a deadline of 15 January 1991. This was not an empty gesture. Resolution 678, which like Resolution 660 was expressly adopted under Chapter VII, went on to authorize countries co-operating with the government of Kuwait to 'use all necessary means' to remove the Iraqi forces and 'restore international peace and security in the area' – in the event that Iraq failed to withdraw its troops. The phrase 'use all necessary means' was clearly intended to authorize the use of military force.

By the time the deadline arrived, the US-led coalition had deployed nearly 700,000 troops to the region; they subsequently needed little time to remove Saddam's forces from Kuwait. Operation Desert Storm was a resounding success, not only militarily, but also for the authority of the Security Council and the broader UN. President George H. W. Bush spoke proudly of the 'new world order' that was reflected in this exercise in global multilateralism. Unfortunately, Bush's new order was remarkably fragile, as events in the Balkans soon demonstrated.

War consumed Bosnia-Herzegovina from April 1992 to November 1995, following the collapse of the Federal Republic of Yugoslavia and the eruption of ethnic tensions that since the Second World War had been largely suppressed by totalitarian rule. A defining feature of the conflict was the prevalence of ethnically motivated killings, rapes and expulsions, primarily involving Muslim victims. During the first five months of the conflict, more than 700,000 people were driven from an area covering 70 per cent of Bosnia-Herzegovina. The atrocities committed fell within the scope of the 1948 Convention on the Prevention and Punishment of the Crime of Genocide (the Genocide Convention), Article 2 of which states:

> In the present Convention, genocide means any of the following acts committed with intent to destroy, in whole or in part, a national, ethnical, racial or religious group, as such:

(a) Killing members of the group;

(b) Causing serious bodily or mental harm to members of the group;

(c) Deliberately inflicting on the group conditions of life calculated to bring about its physical destruction in whole or in part;

(d) Imposing measures intended to prevent births within the group;

(e) Forcibly transferring children of the group to another group.

During the Bosnian War, most journalists and state officials too readily adopted the Serbian euphemism 'ethnic cleansing' to describe the horrors that were taking place. The use of this label enabled Western governments to avoid the groundswell of public opinion that would likely have arisen had they invoked the more accurate, morally resonant word 'genocide'. It may even have been an attempt by those same governments to shirk their responsibility 'to prevent and to punish' genocide under Article 1 of the Genocide Convention. However, evasive terminology did not prevent public evocations of the Holocaust in describing the situation in Bosnia. Some 250,000 people were killed, thousands more were tortured and starved in concentration camps, millions lost their homes and countless women were raped and forcibly impregnated – and all this in a rapidly unifying, post-Cold War Europe that had as one of its central missions the promotion of human rights.

Shortly after the war began, the UN Security Council passed Resolution 713. Adopted expressly under Chapter VII of the UN Charter, the resolution imposed an arms embargo on all of the former Yugoslavia. The embargo arguably did more harm than good because it preserved a military imbalance between the Serbian forces, who had acquired most of the heavy weapons of the previous Yugoslav army, and the less well-armed Bosnian Muslims. The United States later sought to rescind the resolution and lift the embargo, but was unable to do so because of opposition by Russia, which was concerned about US influence in the region and identified religiously with the Eastern Orthodox Serbs. The arms embargo against the former Yugoslavia remained in force until the Dayton Accords brought an end to the conflict in November 1995, though weapons were smuggled into the country, some with the assistance of the United States.

In 1992, the UN Security Council, acting under Chapter VII, established the United Nations Protection Force (UNPROFOR) to provide peacekeeping – the non-violent monitoring of ceasefires, including by providing a neutral presence in buffer zones – in the former Yugoslavia. In 1993, the Security Council extended the force's mandate to include the creation and protection of 'safe havens' in Bosnia. The same year, again acting under Chapter VII, the Council took the novel step of creating an international tribunal to prosecute individuals who had allegedly committed atrocities and to deter further violations of international law. The International Criminal Tribunal for the former Yugoslavia (ICTY), located in The Hague, is a subsidiary organ of the UN Security Council. The ICTY has jurisdiction to investigate and prosecute war crimes and crimes against humanity committed in the former Yugoslavia since 1991. This jurisdiction continued through the 1999 Kosovo War and remains in place today. Moreover, since the ICTY was created by a Chapter VII resolution and not by a treaty, the tribunal's jurisdiction took effect immediately – without the need for the consent of individual countries. Slobodan Milošević, the former President of Yugoslavia, was thus unable to avoid the tribunal, and has been on trial in The Hague since 2001. In 1994, the UN Security Council followed the model of the ICTY in creating the International Criminal Tribunal for Rwanda, though the jurisdiction of this tribunal is limited to events occurring during 1994, the year the genocide took place. Both tribunals served as influential models for the International Criminal Court, a permanent institution with much broader jurisdiction, the treaty for which was adopted in 1998 and entered into force in 2002. They have also obtained a number of convictions, generated valuable precedents on questions of international criminal law, and generally helped advance international justice elsewhere.

In 1993, NATO, embarrassed by massacres in the UN 'safe havens' in the former Yugoslavia, and Europe's failure to stop them, bombed Serbian weapons and supply lines in Bosnia. The bombing was conducted under a complex mandate, provided through UN Security Council Resolution 836 of 4 June 1993, which required close cooperation on targeting decisions between NATO and then UN Secretary General Boutros Boutros-Ghali. The agreement proved unwieldy and ineffective. In July 1995, more than 7,000 Muslim men and boys were slaughtered in the 'safe haven' of Srebrenica as 400 Dutch peacekeepers stood by, their pleas for NATO air support unanswered. In 2001, the ICTY confirmed that the massacre was an act of genocide when it convicted Radislav Krstic, the Yugoslav general in charge, and sentenced him to forty-six years in prison.

International efforts to restore peace to the former Yugoslavia were, on the whole, embarrassingly ineffective, not due to any lack of international law but because of a near absence of international political will. The lack of political will continues today: in December 2004, Carla del Ponte, the ICTY prosecutor, publicly chided NATO governments for having done little over the course of a decade to bring two of the principal alleged perpetrators of the atrocities in Bosnia-Herzegovina, Radovan Karadzic and Ratko Mladic, to justice. That the two indicted men remain at liberty in the eastern mountains of Bosnia is chilling evidence of the transitory and opportunistic character of most international efforts to prevent or punish international crimes.

That said, the four situations discussed in this chapter – Korea (1950), Southern Rhodesia (1966), Iraq (1990–91) and Bosnia-Herzegovina (1992–5) – saw the UN Security Council exercise its Chapter VII powers to authorize force in new and quite different ways. With the exception of Iraq, however, the consistent theme of this period was one of hesitation, as the politics of the Council, an inherently political body, prevented it from acting decisively and expansively to maintain and restore the peace. This disappointing picture began to change in the 1990s, as the next chapter explains.

2

Expanding Reach of the Security Council

Chapter VII of the UN Charter empowers the Security Council to authorize the use of force in response to threats and breaches of international peace. Yet the definition of this role – and therefore the scope of Security Council action – has expanded in recent years.

The Security Council's actions in Korea and Iraq were directed at cross-border military conflicts of the kind originally associated with Chapter VII. The Council's involvement in the domestic affairs of Southern Rhodesia departed from that model but was not considered a precedent because of the unusual mix of legalized racism, stymied self-determination of the black population, and superpower rivalry involved in the situation. The Council's actions in Bosnia-Herzegovina, driven by a combination of traditional inter-state security concerns and not-so-traditional worries about human rights atrocities, were of greater legal significance. The use of Chapter VII to create 'safe havens' and an international criminal tribunal was part of a broader move by the Council to include internal humanitarian crises within the concept of 'threats to international peace and security'.

During the 1990s, the UN Security Council determined that a number of domestic humanitarian and human rights crises constituted 'threats to international peace and security', justifying the use of its Chapter VII powers to impose mandatory sanctions or authorize the use of military force. In doing so, the Security Council went beyond the traditional conception of threats, though not in a manner that violated the UN Charter – since the Charter grants the Council broad discretion to determine the scope of its own legal competence. In several instances, notably Haiti in 1994 and East Timor in 1999, Chapter VII was more important in providing legitimacy than legality, as the actions there occurred at the invitation of the country that was subject to the intervention. In other instances, such as Somalia, Rwanda, and more recently Darfur, Sudan, there has been insufficient political will either to intervene promptly, or to persevere when the going gets tough.

In January 1992, the UN Security Council determined that the combination of widespread civil strife and devastating famine in Somalia constituted a threat to international peace and security. Although the Security Council spoke of the consequences of the strife and famine for 'stability and peace in the region', the determination extended the Council's reach under international law. In the 'new world order' that still seemed possible following the fall of the Berlin Wall and the 1991 Iraq War, the Security Council was asserting a scope of competence that stretched security into humanitarian and human rights concerns. Having determined the existence of a threat, the Council imposed a mandatory arms embargo on Somalia, but did not, at this early stage, authorize military action.

Three months later, with the chaos growing worse and hundreds of thousands of people starving, the Council inched towards the deployment of troops, requesting that the UN Secretary General, Boutros Boutros-Ghali, deploy fifty UN observers to monitor the situation. This operation, referred to as the United Nations Operations in Somalia (UNSOM), was expanded in August of 1992. Yet it remained a lightly armed peacekeeping operation, despite the fact that the Somali government had collapsed and warlords ran rampant. In recognition of this, the Security Council in December 1992 adopted a further resolution that led to two UN-authorized deployments: an additional 3,500 soldiers for the UNSOM force, and a second, US-led multinational force with a broad mandate to 'use all necessary means to establish as soon as possible a secure environment for humanitarian relief operations'. Unlike UNSOM, the US-led force was empowered to engage in 'peacemaking' rather than 'peacekeeping'; in other words, it had wide discretion to use military force.

In March 1993, the UN Security Council changed the name of the first deployment from UNSOM to UNSOM II, increased its size, and extended its mandate to include the disarmament of local militia groups and repatriation of refugees. The UN commander of the operation was also directed 'to assume responsibility for the consolidation, expansion and maintenance of a secure environment throughout Somalia'. This task was too much for a force lacking heavy weapons and air support. On 5 June 1993, twenty-three Pakistani peacekeepers were ambushed and killed by members of a Somali militia. The Security Council responded to the attack by increasing the size of UNSOM II to 28,000 soldiers, affirming its mandate to 'arrest and detain' the individuals responsible for the killings, and urging UN member states – and the parallel US-led operation by implication – to provide UNSOM II with military support and transportation.

On 3 October 1993, eighteen US Army Rangers were killed while attempting to apprehend Somali militia leaders. Television footage of a Ranger's body being dragged through the streets of Mogadishu prompted a public outcry in the United States that soon led to the withdrawal of all US forces from Somalia and the subsequent collapse of both the US- and UN-led operations. One American officer commented during the ignominious retreat that US soldiers would again operate under foreign command 'as soon as it snows in Mogadishu'. Ironically, the US troops had remained under US command and control at all times. The United Nations had simply provided a legal basis for their presence in Somalia and legitimized their actions.

Although the Somalia experience substantially diminished political will in the United States and elsewhere to engage in military interventions for purely humanitarian purposes, it constituted an important precedent for the international rules on the use of force. For the first time, the UN Security Council had deemed a human rights crisis a threat to the peace and used its Chapter VII powers to authorize military intervention for the sole purpose of preventing further suffering.

Rwanda suffered for the sins of the Somali warlords. 'Genocide', defined in the 1948 Genocide Convention as the 'intent to destroy, in whole or in part, a national, ethnical, racial or religious group', is more than a crime against humanity prohibited by a *jus cogens* rule. The term has acquired enormous moral approbation, to the point that, during a 1994 Security Council meeting on Rwanda, the British ambassador cautioned against designating the ethnically motivated massacre of 800,000 Tutsis as genocide because the Council might then be compelled to act. Not until Mary Robinson broke the taboo, shortly after her appointment as UN High Commissioner for Human Rights in 1997, did the term achieved common usage in contemporary international affairs. This paradigm shift facilitated the subsequent creation of the International Criminal Court, and influenced NATO's decision to intervene in Kosovo.

As the mass slaughter of Tutsi men, women and children by Hutus began, General Roméo Dallaire, the Canadian commander of the small UN operation in Kigali, pleaded for 5,000 additional troops. Bizarrely, the UN Security Council responded by reducing Dallaire's force from 2,500 to 270 peacekeepers. It was not until the bloodbath was nearly over that France announced it would send forces into the country whose Hutu militia it had armed and trained. Seized with misgivings, but knowing that no other country was prepared to act, and that an intervention without UN authorization could create an awkward precedent, the Security Council ultimately adopted a Chapter VII resolution that authorized *Opération Turquoise*. The resolution, and the French intervention that followed, came too late to do more than protect the Hutu *génocidaires* from Tutsi retribution. But the adoption of the resolution, scandalously inadequate though it was, constituted another instance of the Council authorizing military action to address a purely internal crisis.

The only other action taken by the UN Security Council was to create the International Criminal Tribunal for Rwanda (ICTR), which has since convicted more than twenty high-level perpetrators and further developed international criminal law – for example, by expanding the scope of the crime of genocide to include the incitement of genocide. In September 1998, Jean Kambanda, the former prime minister of Rwanda, was convicted of genocide by the ICTR for having encouraged a radio station to promote the extermination of Tutsis in 1994. That same month, the Rwandan tribunal gave another boost to international criminal law by convicting a former mayor, Jean-Paul Akayesu, of genocide for inciting others to systematically rape Tutsi women.

Like Rwanda, the Caribbean country of Haiti has a turbulent history. Achieving independence in 1804 after a slave rebellion against French colonialism, Haiti became the first post-colonial country in the Western hemisphere to be governed by non-whites. The United States occupied the country between 1915 and 1934, concerned that civil unrest was threatening its foreign investments. But Haiti suffered its worst period from 1956 to 1986 when it was governed by two brutal dictators, first François 'Papa Doc' Duvalier, and then his son Jean-Claude 'Baby Doc'. Two military coups in quick succession subsequently led to the creation of a civilian government under military control, though it took four years and repeated urgings from the Organization of American States (OAS) before democratic elections were held.

International monitors certified the 1990 election as free and fair and Jean-Bertrand Aristide, a Roman Catholic priest of humble origins, was elected president. But a *coup d'état* soon led to the resumption of military rule; Aristide was sent into exile in the United States in September 1991.

The OAS promptly condemned the coup and recommended economic and diplomatic sanctions. The UN General Assembly likewise quickly criticized the 'illegal replacement of the constitutional President of Haiti' and affirmed the unacceptability of 'any entity resulting from that illegal situation'. However, the UN Security Council failed to respond with comparable speed, reportedly because China, a veto-holding permanent member, had reservations about the Council's increasing involvement in areas traditionally considered within the domestic jurisdiction of states.

The Haitian military, undeterred by the harsh words of toothless international bodies, refused to reinstate the Aristide government. The refusal, along with reports of the widespread persecution of Aristide's supporters, eventually prompted the Security Council to exercise its Chapter VII powers. In June 1993, the Council imposed a mandatory economic embargo on Haiti. The resolution reflected China's concerns, listing specific factors that had led the Council to determine 'that, in these unique and exceptional circumstances, the continuation of this situation threatens international peace and security in the region'. The factors included 'the incidence of humanitarian crises, including mass displacements of population', and the 'climate of fear of persecution and economic dislocation which could increase the number of Haitians seeking refuge in neighbouring Member States'.

The reference to Haitian refugees was prompted by thousands of people who were escaping the country on rickety boats and rafts, many of them setting out for Florida. These refugees were of concern to the United States, but they were also important to China because they brought an international dimension to the situation that could justify Security Council action on more traditional, state-to-state security grounds. In practical terms, the international element of the crisis was barely significant. The number of refugees was relatively small and the US Coast Guard was already reducing that number to pre-coup levels through an aggressive interdiction and return programme. Chinese protestations aside, the Security Council had again departed from the traditional conception of what constituted a threat to 'international peace and security'.

The mandatory economic embargo had almost immediate effect, prompting the Haitian *junta* to accept terms – set out in the 'Governors Island Agreement' – whereby Aristide would be returned to power and the sanctions lifted. However, the agreement quickly collapsed when violence against Aristide supporters resumed one month later. The Security Council responded by reimposing sanctions and authorizing a naval blockade.

On 29 July 1994, nearly three years after the coup, Aristide himself requested 'prompt and decisive action' by the United Nations. Two days later, the Security Council again invoked Chapter VII. Resolution 940 'authorized Member States to form a multilateral force' and 'use all necessary means' to remove the *junta*, restore the legitimate government and 'establish and maintain a secure and stable environment' in Haiti.

Within six weeks, the United States had formed an 'international force' composed primarily of its own soldiers. Only a last-minute agreement secured by former President Jimmy Carter prevented a forceful invasion. By the end of September 1994, over 17,000 US troops were peacefully deployed in Haiti and Aristide had returned to Port-au-Prince. International reaction to the events was generally positive – as indeed it should have been. Only a handful of countries expressed reservations about the behaviour of the Security Council and the United States.

The Security Council's actions on Haiti confirm that the Council considers itself legally competent to impose mandatory sanctions and authorize military force in response to internal humanitarian crises that pose little, if any, threat to other countries. This self-assignment of competence is difficult to challenge because nothing in the UN Charter limits the Council's capacity to determine if and when a situation constitutes a threat to international peace and security. As the UN Secretary General's High Level Panel on Threats, Challenges and Change reported in December 2004, 'the Council and the wider international community have come to accept that, under Chapter VII . . . it can always authorize military action to redress catastrophic internal wrongs if it is prepared to declare that the situation is a "threat to international peace and security", not especially difficult when breaches of international law are involved.'

Some academics point to the Security Council actions in Haiti as an example of growing recognition of a right to 'pro-democratic intervention' in international law, as is discussed in Chapter 7 of this book. Yet the invocation of Chapter VII of the UN Charter deprived the incident of any value as a precedent for a right to unilateral intervention. A careful reading of Resolution 940 also reveals that the disruption of democracy was referred to as only one of several factors – together with the 'systematic violations of civil liberties' and 'desperate plight' of the refugees – that contributed to the finding of a threat to international peace and security. Moreover, the resolution was the direct result of the Aristide government-in-exile's request for UN action. Although the Security Council, acting under Chapter VII, is legally competent to authorize interventions without an invitation from a legitimate government, such an invitation – even from a government in exile – is widely acknowledged as a sufficient basis for the deployment of military assistance. And the legitimacy of governments, and thus the legal justification of intervention by invitation, is not dependent on the democratic character of the inviting state.

Nor does the democratic character of a government necessarily provide protection against unwanted intervention, as Jean-Bertrand Aristide himself discovered in 2004. Aristide's peaceful return to Haiti ten years earlier had brought some hope to that beleaguered country. In 1995, his supporters won parliamentary elections; in 1996, he resigned as president, abiding by a constitutional provision prohibiting two consecutive terms in office. Aristide's elected successor, René Preval, proved less than effective: at one point he desperately declared that the Haitian parliament's term had expired, and began ruling by decree. Preval stood down at the end of his term in 2001, at which point Aristide was re-elected president.

Meanwhile, Haiti – already the poorest country in the Western hemisphere – was subjected to stringent US sanctions and a sharp decline in foreign aid that together brought it to the edge of economic collapse and civil chaos. An attempted *coup d'état* in 2001 was followed in 2004 by a violent uprising of disgruntled ex-soldiers and gang members headed by Butteur Metayer, the former leader of a gang known as the 'Cannibal Army'. Dozens of people were killed, and, on the night of 28–29 February 2004, Aristide was flown to the Central African Republic on a plane chartered by the US military. Although the United States claimed he had left the country voluntarily, Aristide insisted that he had been forced out at gunpoint, an assertion given greater credibility when the Caribbean Community (CARICOM) refused to recognize the government of the new president. Aristide later travelled to Jamaica before moving on to South Africa, where the government of President Thabo Mbeki accorded him sanctuary.

The day after Aristide's flight from Haiti, the UN Security Council unanimously adopted Resolution 1529, which authorized a multilateral force to restore law and order to the country. Within days, soldiers from the United States, Canada and France were patrolling the streets of Port-au-Prince. This action by the Security Council was widely interpreted as endorsing whatever role the United States may have played in the removal of the former president. Yet the resolution was carefully worded to be entirely neutral on the issue. Although it expressly invoked Chapter VII, the resolution simply 'took note' of Aristide's resignation, 'acknowledged' the new president's request for urgent assistance and 'determined' that the situation 'constituted a threat to international peace and security, and to stability in the Caribbean especially through the potential outflow of people to other States in the subregion'. The invocation of Chapter VII conveniently circumvented any need to determine whether the new president was in fact legally capable of inviting an intervention.

A similar overlap of Chapter VII authorization and an invitation to intervene had occurred five years earlier in East Timor. Indonesia, under the dictatorship of President Suharto, had invaded and occupied the neighbouring Portuguese colony in December 1975. Some 200,000 East Timorese – one quarter of the population – died as a result of the invasion. The UN Security Council responded by unanimously adopting Resolution 384, in which it recognized the 'inalienable right of the people of East Timor to self-determination and independence' and deplored the 'intervention of the armed forces of Indonesia'. The Security Council called upon Indonesia to withdraw its forces and refused to recognize its claims to sovereignty over the territory. At the same time, however, the Council refused to categorize the invasion as a violation of the UN Charter, impose economic sanctions, or authorize the use of military force. Indonesia was simply too strategically important to the United States and its allies during the Cold War to be subjected to the full range of Security Council pressures.

The Suharto regime finally collapsed in 1998, and B. J. Habibie was appointed president of Indonesia. In January 1999, Habibie, in response to international pressure and in order to consolidate his power, announced a referendum whereby East Timor would choose between independence and a largely autonomous position within Indonesia. In May 1999, Indonesia and Portugal, with help from UN Secretary General Kofi Annan, concluded an agreement on the logistics of the vote, which inadvisably assigned responsibility for security during the referendum to Indonesia rather than the United Nations.

In June 1999, the Security Council dispatched an election-monitoring mission to East Timor. The mission was subsequently expanded and its mandate strengthened after disturbances by members of the pro-Indonesian militia delayed the vote. The referendum was finally held on 30 August 1999. An overwhelming majority of East Timorese – 78.5 per cent of them, out of a 97.5 per cent voter turnout – cast ballots in favour of independence. In response, the pro-Indonesian militia turned increasingly violent, killing more than a thousand people and driving hundreds of thousands from their homes. United Nations officials also came under attack and were evacuated to Australia.

Two weeks later, the United States persuaded Habibie to accept international peacekeepers. On 15 September 1999, the UN Security Council adopted Resolution 1264, a Chapter VII resolution that identified the situation in East Timor as a 'threat to peace and security'. The resolution authorized the establishment of a 9,000-strong multinational force under Australian command to 'take all necessary measures' to restore peace and security and protect and support the monitoring mission. Later, the Security Council again exercised its Chapter VII powers to establish a United Nations Transition Administration in East Timor (UNTAET) to exercise full executive and legislative authority over the territory. This was the first time the United Nations had assumed complete control over the sovereign functions of a country. Thanks to the Council's willingness to interpret its own powers broadly, and the Australian-led intervention it had authorized, East Timor achieved independence on 20 May 2002, one month after former rebel leader Xanana Gusmao was elected its first president.

From a strictly legal perspective, Habibie's consent to the peacekeeping operation meant that the Security Council's authorization was unnecessary. United Nations peacekeeping often occurs with the consent of the host country and at the initiative of the General Assembly rather than Security Council. Still, the invocation of Chapter VII meant that the legitimacy of Australia's deployment of troops into a neighbouring developing country was beyond question. The Security Council's involvement in East Timor in 1999 also closed an important circle, for the crisis was as much about Indonesia's 1975 invasion and occupation of the territory – a classic violation of Article 2(4) of the UN Charter – as it was about self-determination, human rights and democracy. Although the international community took much longer to react to the Indonesian invasion than to Iraq's seizure of Kuwait in 1990, both outcomes confirm that the conquest of territory remains intolerable both politically and in law.

*

The most recent challenge facing the UN Security Council concerns Sudan, Africa's largest country, where a major humanitarian crisis arose in 2004. In the western region of Darfur (which is roughly the size of France), some 1.8 million people were forced from their homes and villages. More than 130,000 people fled across the border into Chad and, as of December 2004, more than 70,000 people had died, with hundreds of thousands more facing disease and possible starvation.

The agents of this disaster were the 'Janjaweed', which translates roughly as 'devils on horseback with guns'. These men are members of nomadic Arab tribes that, in recent decades, have come into conflict with Darfur's black (though also Muslim) agricultural tribes as drought and growing populations increased competition for water and pasture. After some of the black tribes attempted to rise up against the Sudanese government in February 2003, Khartoum armed the Janjaweed and delegated them the task of suppressing the rebellion.

The Arabs took up their mission with a vengeance, pillaging and burning villages, shooting the men and boys and systematically beating and raping the women. The atrocities violated international humanitarian law, as codified in Common Article 3 of the 1949 Geneva Conventions (see Chapter 5). They were also actively supported by the government in Khartoum: Sudanese soldiers often accompanied the Janjaweed and military planes bombed the villages in advance of the attacks. The government also seized every opportunity to impede any significant humanitarian response, denying the seriousness of the problem and delaying supplies and entry papers for aid workers.

In June 2004, US Secretary of State Colin Powell visited a refugee camp in Darfur. At the time, Powell said that his trip was intended to prompt the international community into increasing pressure on Khartoum. The following month, the US Congress passed a resolution that identified the atrocities being committed in Darfur as 'genocide'. However, the credibility of the United States had been compromised by its actions elsewhere. When

Sudan was re-elected as a member of the UN Commission on Human Rights in May 2004, the US representative declared that an 'absurdity' had occurred and walked out of the meeting. The Sudanese representative countered that America was simply shedding 'crocodile tears', pointing to an apparent revenge attack by US forces against civilians in Fallujah, Iraq, in April 2004, and the Abu Ghraib prisoner abuse scandal. There may be some truth in this characterization of the US position as both hypocritical and insincere. In July 2004, reports surfaced that British Prime Minister Tony Blair had ordered his officials to begin planning for an armed intervention in Darfur, until Secretary of State Powell deemed the idea 'premature'.

Instead, on 30 July 2004, the UN Security Council adopted Resolution 1556. The Council began by expressing its 'grave concern at the ongoing humanitarian crisis and widespread human rights violations' as well as its 'determination to do everything possible to halt a humanitarian catastrophe'. The Council deemed the situation a 'threat to international peace and security', explicitly invoked Chapter VII, and imposed an arms embargo on the Janjaweed – a move destined to be ineffective, given that the region was already awash with small arms and has porous borders with Libya, Chad and the Central African Republic, where such weapons are readily available.

In the most important paragraph of Resolution 1556, the Council:

> *Demands* that the Government of Sudan fulfil its commitments to disarm the Janjaweed militias and apprehend and bring to justice Janjaweed leaders and their associates who have incited and carried out human rights and international humanitarian law violations and other atrocities, and *further requests* the Secretary-General to report in 30 days, and monthly thereafter, to the Council on the progress or lack thereof by the Government of Sudan on this matter and *expresses its intention* to consider further actions, including measures as provided for

in Article 41 of the Charter of the United Nations on the Government of Sudan, in the event of non-compliance.

Although the word 'sanctions' was dropped from the resolution under pressure from China, Pakistan and Russia, the resolution did refer to Article 41, which gives the UN Security Council authority to order a 'complete or partial interruption of economic relations'. Yet most economic measures would not have much effect against Khartoum, which is already subject to US sanctions as an alleged state sponsor of terrorism. An oil embargo could have a significant impact, but China and Russia would block any attempt to impose this particular penalty. Both these veto-holding permanent members of the Security Council invested heavily in Sudan's oil industry after Western companies withdrew their operations when Khartoum's human rights record came under public scrutiny. For this reason, there is also little prospect that the Security Council will use Chapter VII to authorize the use of military force in Sudan.

The only international organization to have taken significant action in the region has been the African Union (AU), which in August 2004 sent a force of 300 Rwandan and Nigerian troops to protect 100 peace-observers already in Darfur. The AU subsequently prepared to send some 3,000 additional soldiers, while the United States, Canada and European Union indicated their willingness to provide logistical and financial support. But in the absence of authorization by the UN Security Council, the deployment of these forces is dependent on Khartoum's co-operation and consent, which has only reluctantly been forthcoming.

France, concerned about the destabilizing effect on neighbouring Chad of hundreds of thousands of refugees and cross-border incursions by the Janjaweed, sent 200 soldiers to the eastern territory of the former French colony with the consent of the government in N'Djaména. In early September 2004, the United States submitted a draft resolution to the UN Security Council that would have imposed an oil embargo on Sudan, while

Secretary of State Colin Powell and President George W. Bush both declared that genocide had occurred there. But there was still no agreement within the Security Council, or any willingness on the part of the US government to intervene militarily. The only country ready to stand up directly to the Janjaweed, and through them Sudan, was Rwanda. Although Rwandan troops are currently committing their own atrocities in the eastern Congo, Kigali still carries considerable moral weight on the issue of genocide. As he inspected the 155 Rwandan soldiers before their departure for Darfur in August 2004, President Paul Kagame said:

> Our forces will not stand by and watch innocent civilians being hacked to death like was the case here in 1994. I have no doubt that they certainly will intervene and use force to protect civilians. In my view, it does not make sense to provide security to peace observers while the local population is left to die.

If only the permanent members of the UN Security Council had displayed similar candour and courage. On 18 November 2004, during a special meeting of the Council in Nairobi, Kenya, UN Secretary General Kofi Annan reported that 'the security situation in Darfur continues to deteriorate'. The Council responded by adopting a third resolution that, again, only hinted at unspecified action if the hostilities in Darfur continued.

The extension of the Security Council's competence to authorize mandatory sanctions and forceful action for humanitarian purposes has changed international law for the better, providing for the possibility of humanitarian intervention in a manner that is consistent with the existing rules on recourse to force. Yet the Security Council remains a political body that cannot itself be forced to act. Frequently, it will not take action, even when – as in Darfur – the moral case is overwhelming. This raises the question of what, if anything, should be done in such circumstances – a question that is considered at length in Part III of this book.

3

Implied Authorization and Intentional Ambiguity

In April 1991, Saddam Hussein's forces began a campaign of retribution in northern Iraq, after the Kurds of that region – at the apparent encouragement of President George H. W. Bush – had attempted an uprising during the 1991 Gulf War. In response, the United States, Britain, France, Italy and the Netherlands deployed forces and established so-called 'safe havens' for civilians in northern Iraq. The five intervening countries sought to justify their action – codenamed 'Operation Provide Comfort' – on the basis of a UN Security Council resolution adopted on 5 April 1991. In Resolution 688, the Security Council expressed grave concern at 'the repression of the Iraqi civilian population ... including most recently in Kurdish-populated areas, which led to a massive flow of refugees towards and across international frontiers and to cross-border incursions, which threaten international peace and security'. The Council also called on countries to aid humanitarian relief efforts to be organized by then UN Secretary General Javier Perez de Cuellar.

Resolution 688 did not expressly authorize the use of force. China, concerned about the Security Council reaching into the domestic affairs of sovereign states, had reportedly threatened to veto any resolution that would authorize military action to protect the Kurds. Within a few weeks, more than a million refugees had either crossed, or were attempting to cross, from Iraq into Iran and Turkey. Television footage of hundreds of thousands of desperate people trapped in frigid mountain passes resonated with the Western public, and this in turn prompted the governments of the United States, Britain, France, Italy and the Netherlands to declare all Iraqi territory north of the 36th parallel out of bounds to Iraqi armed forces. They argued that this move was 'in support of' Resolution 688.

Later, the United States, Britain and France transformed the northern exclusion zone into two 'no-fly' zones: one north of the 36th parallel, the other south of the 32nd parallel. The southern 'no-fly' zone was created to protect Shiites who had similarly attempted an uprising against Saddam Hussein. Both 'no-fly' zones were justified primarily on the basis of Security Council Resolution 688, again despite the apparent absence of any words of authorization in the resolution. The justification was properly questioned by other countries and, in 1996, France pulled out of the operation after the United States and Britain extended the southern zone northwards to just south of Baghdad. But, given the power and influence of the United States and the unpopularity of Saddam Hussein, there was little more that other governments could – or wished to – do. At least Washington and London were advancing a legal argument based tenuously on Resolution 688, rather than simply disregarding the law.

Only some UN Security Council resolutions authorize the use of force unequivocally. Resolution 678, adopted in November 1990 following the Iraqi invasion of Kuwait, was one such resolution, authorizing UN member states 'to use all necessary means...to restore international peace and security to the area'. Other resolutions, such as Resolution 688, are considerably less clear. Security Council resolutions are sometimes worded ambiguously as a result of rushed negotiations; in other instances, the ambiguity is the result of deliberate compromise. In either case, some countries will sometimes argue that force has implicitly been authorized, while others will adamantly maintain the opposite view.

In 1997, the Federal Republic of Yugoslavia, headed by President Slobodan Milošević, launched a brutal crackdown on a rebel militia army and its supporters in the primarily Muslim province of Kosovo. Within a year, UN Secretary General Kofi Annan reported that force was being used in an 'indiscriminate and disproportionate' manner against civilians and that 'appalling atrocities' were being committed.

The UN Security Council responded on 23 September 1998 by adopting Resolution 1199. Acting expressly under Chapter VII, the Council demanded that the Milošević government cease its 'repressive actions against the peaceful population' of Kosovo and resolve the situation by non-forceful means. The Council also warned that, if Milošević failed to comply, it would 'consider further action and additional measures to maintain or restore peace and security in the region'.

One month later, the Security Council adopted Resolution 1203 in which it welcomed an agreement between Belgrade and the Organization for Security and Cooperation in Europe (OSCE) that provided for the establishment of a peace verification mission in Kosovo. The Security Council emphasized the need to ensure the safety and security of the members of the OSCE mission and affirmed that the situation in Kosovo remained a threat to peace and security. Then, acting expressly under Chapter VII, the Council stated that 'in the event of an emergency, action may be needed to ensure their [the members of the mission's] safety and freedom of movement'. The Council hinted at a possible need to intervene to rescue the OSCE personnel but said nothing more that could be construed as authorizing military action. The Council also decided to 'remain seized of the matter'.

On 24 March 1999, without the adoption of a further UN Security Council resolution, NATO began an air campaign against targets, not only in Kosovo but also in Serbia and Montenegro. Very little was advanced in the way of legal justification for the air strikes, though most of the countries involved considered it relevant that the Security Council had identified the situation in Kosovo as a threat to peace and security in both Resolutions 1199 and 1203. To the degree most of the intervening powers provided a justification at all, they argued that, once the Security Council has identified a threat and demanded action from a 'problem' state, the members of the United Nations are implicitly entitled to ensure that the Council's will is carried out. The Kosovo War was condemned as illegal by Russia, China and a large number of developing countries. And so, while an implied authorization argument was floated during the Kosovo War, very few people – even those who advanced the argument – took it all that seriously.

The march towards removing Saddam Hussein from power began shortly after George W. Bush entered the White House in January 2001. There were multiple, overlapping motivations for going to war, including concerns about Iraqi weapons of mass destruction, political instability in the Middle East, access to oil, and a personal vendetta arising from Saddam's failed attempt to assassinate the president's father, former president George H. W. Bush, in Kuwait in 1993.

Two legal justifications were advanced for the 2003 invasion. The sole argument advanced by Britain and Australia, and the main argument advanced by the United States, is examined here. The second justification, an extended claim to pre-emptive self-defence, is considered at length in Chapter 6.

The first justification for the military intervention in Iraq returns to Resolution 678, adopted by the UN Security Council following Iraq's invasion of Kuwait in 1990, whereby it authorized UN member states to 'use all necessary means . . . to restore peace and security to the area'. The argument claims, essentially, that the authorization provided by Resolution 678 was suspended – not terminated – by the ceasefire imposed by Resolution 687 in April 1991. This suspended authorization could be reactivated – so the argument goes – if and when Iraq engaged in a 'material breach' of its ceasefire and disarmament obligations. The concept of material breach, drawn from the law of treaties, had been expressly endorsed by the Security Council in the context of Iraq, most notably in the unanimously adopted Resolution 1441 of 8 November 2002, which found Iraq in material breach. This resolution gave Iraq 'a final opportunity to comply with its disarmament obligations' and warned that non-compliance would have 'serious consequences'. Iraq's failure to cooperate fully, including during February and March 2003, when it refused to allow weapons scientists to be interviewed outside the country, was argued to constitute a further material breach of Resolution 687, thereby permitting enforced compliance. The argument concludes with the assertion that, had the Security Council thought that an additional resolution was necessary before military action could be taken, it would have spelled out this requirement in Resolution 1441.

This approach, coupling the concept of material breach with that of implied authorization, is countered by several good arguments. For example, the 1991 ceasefire resolution is clearly worded to terminate – not suspend – the previous year's authorization of military force. In any event, since the parties to the ceasefire were the UN Security Council and Iraq, the coalition countries involved in the ejection of the Iraqis from Kuwait were not parties to the ceasefire (though they were bound by it). Any material breach could not have reactivated a right for the coalition members to use force independently. Moreover, Resolution 1441 neither specified the legal consequences of material breach nor expressly authorized military action. Indeed, following its adoption, all the Security Council's members, including the United States and Britain, confirmed publicly that the resolution provided no 'automaticity' – by which they presumably meant that force could not be used until a further resolution was adopted.

Disagreements over the legality of the Iraq War attracted unprecedented media attention, especially in the United Kingdom. Breaking with tradition, the holders of the Cambridge and Oxford chairs in international law, James Crawford and Vaughan Lowe, took a public stance against the British government. Even more telling was the resignation of Elisabeth Wilmshurst, the deputy legal adviser to the British Foreign Office. Her boss, Michael Wood, stoically remained in place and subsequently received a knighthood.

But the fact of the matter is that the members of the UN Security Council had agreed to disagree when, in November 2002, they adopted Resolution 1441. Different provisions of that resolution provided support to both sides of the debate over the legality of going to war against Iraq. By carefully balancing the arguments, the Security Council succeeded in effectively de-legalizing the situation, and thus protecting the international legal system from the damage that would otherwise have resulted when politics prevailed. In particular, the inclusion of language in favour of a right to go to war provided the United States with an argument – the material breach argument – that was more legally tenable than its parallel claim of a extended right of pre-emptive self-defence. And that more tenable argument then had the effect of absorbing much of the impact that the pre-emption claim might have had as a precedent in customary international law – a precedent that, had it been established, would have been of great concern to European and developing states. Most journalists, and many international lawyers, were woefully inattentive to this crucial context to the legal debate.

Yet the debate over the legality of the 2003 Iraq War went deeper than contesting political positions supported by an intentionally ambiguous UN Security Council resolution. At a more fundamental level, the debate concerned competing methods of legal interpretation and, more specifically, which particular approach should be taken to interpreting Security Council resolutions.

Most international lawyers regard the law through a judicial prism; courts must render a clear decision on the arguments presented. International lawyers therefore tend to believe that a right answer is always to be found. For their answers, they look to the 'sources' of international law, including treaties, customary international law and, since 1945, UN Security Council resolutions adopted under Chapter VII of the UN Charter. Where gaps exist, either in the source material or the application of the material to a specific dispute, international lawyers seek to fill them through analogies to established precedents, rules and principles.

But the analogies chosen and the weight accorded to source materials remain somewhat discretionary and, as a result, different international lawyers may assess the sources slightly differently. Nowhere was the impact of such subtle differences of approach more apparent than during the debates in early 2003 over the interpretation of UN Security Council Resolution 1441.

Although the members of the Security Council were aware that the ambiguities of Resolution 1441 provided room for argument on both sides of the debate over whether war would be legal, each believed that their particular understanding of the resolution was legally correct. Compared to most other countries, the United States tends to place more weight on the 'object and purpose' of international documents and less weight on their actual terms. This tendency dates back to at least 1968 when the US delegation to the Vienna Conference on the Law of Treaties proposed a purposive approach to treaty interpretation that emphasized a comprehensive examination of the context of any particular treaty, so as to ascertain the common will of the parties – as that will evolved over time. This approach was rejected overwhelmingly by the other countries at the conference. Accordingly, Article 31(1) of the Vienna Convention stipulates: 'A treaty shall be interpreted in good faith in accordance with the ordinary meaning to be given to the terms of the treaty in their context and in the light of its object and purpose', with the emphasis being on ordinary meaning. As importantly, Article 32 of the Vienna Convention restricts consideration of the 'preparatory work of the treaty... to determine the meaning' to situations where 'the interpretation according to Article 31' has left the meaning 'ambiguous or obscure' or led to a result 'which is manifestly absurd or unreasonable'. In other words, preparatory documents and records of negotiations cannot generally be used for interpretive purposes.

Despite Articles 31 and 32, the United States continues to prefer a more purposive, less textually oriented approach, most notably when interpreting the UN Charter. An extreme example of this tendency arose during the 1999 Kosovo crisis. As former State Department spokesman James Rubin explained:

> There was a series of strained telephone calls between [US Secretary of State Madeleine] Albright and [UK Foreign Secretary Robin] Cook, in which he cited problems 'with our lawyers' over using force in the absence of UN endorsement. 'Get new lawyers,' she suggested. But with a push from prime minister Tony Blair, the British finally agreed that UN security council approval was not legally required.

Unlike the UN Charter, Security Council resolutions are not treaties. Treaties resemble contracts whereas Security Council resolutions resemble executive orders, so the applicable interpretive rules may differ somewhat. Relatively little academic writing has been directed to this issue – perhaps because the Security Council was inactive for decades due to the Cold War rivalry between two veto-wielding superpowers – and those scholars who have studied it favour divergent approaches.

Before he became the Legal Adviser to the British Foreign Office, Michael Wood advanced an approach to interpreting UN Security Council resolutions that takes into account the full background of the Security Council's involvement with an issue, in order to determine the result the Council was seeking to achieve. Such a purposive approach leads relatively easily to a presumption in favour of an authorization to use force when: (1) a resolution is adopted; (2) the Security Council has previously identified a threat to international peace and security; (3) strict conditions have been placed on the threatening state, and; (4) the state has conspicuously failed to meet the conditions. Although the presumption may be countered by clear evidence to the contrary, textual ambiguities are read, where possible, in a manner consistent with the view that the Security Council intends its demands to be met and enforced. This approach was used by the United States and Britain to interpret Resolution 1441 on Iraq, as well as the resolutions adopted with regard to north-ern Iraq in 1991 and Kosovo in 1998.

In sharp contrast, Jochen Frowein, the recently retired director of the Max Planck Institute for International Law in Heidelberg, Germany, has advocated an interpretive approach to Security Council resolutions that is more restrictive than the approach taken to treaties. Frowein discounts the relevance of the subjective intentions of Security Council members, since any country against which Chapter VII power is wielded is unlikely to have contributed to the resolution's formulation. This means that: 'As far as they are concerned the resolution has the same sort of objective existence as laws or administrative acts in a specific legal system. Therefore, the objective view of the neutral observer as addressee must be the most important aspect for the interpreta-tion.' Frowein even suggests that the non-participation of the countries subject to resolutions, when combined with the Security Council's capacity to interfere with the territorial integrity and political independence of those same countries, requires a presumption that sovereign rights have neither been surrendered nor removed. The result is an approach to the interpretation of Security Council resolutions that focuses narrowly on the ordi-nary meaning of the terms.

The disagreement over the legality of the 2003 Iraq War indi-cated that many governments subscribe to the more textually oriented approach advanced by Frowein. The approach, modelled on Article 31 of the Vienna Convention of the Law of Treaties, correctly holds that the UN Security Council only means what it specifically says. There is, consequently, an interpretive presump-tion against the authorization of military force.

In the aftermath of the Iraq War, the damning failure of US-led weapons inspectors to find evidence that Saddam Hussein posed an imminent threat weakened the claim, not that Resolution 1441 authorized the use of force, but that any such authorization was appropriately relied upon by the United States and Britain. Similarly, the reluctance of many countries to support the US-led occupation and reconstruction of Iraq confirms that Washington and London's interpretation of Resolution 1441 was not widely shared. That said, governments are now exercising greater caution when negotiating and adopting UN Security Council resolutions. Resolution 1483 on Iraq, adopted in May 2003, was worded very tightly in order to leave little room for arguments that it provided retroactive authorization for the war. The same is true of Resolution 1511, adopted in October 2003, even though this resolution authorized a US-led multilateral force to provide 'security and stability' in Iraq. The attempt to advance a purposive approach to the interpretation of Security Council resolutions has backfired, prompting clarity in drafting and objectivity in interpretation. As a result, the textual approach to the interpretation of Security Council resolutions is well on its way to achieving the status of widely accepted, universally binding customary international law.

This does not mean, however, that the United States has given up on this legal battle. In a September 2004 interview with the BBC World Service, Secretary General Kofi Annan expressed the opinion that the Iraq War was 'illegal' since 'it was up to the Security Council to approve or determine' what the 'consequences should be' for Iraq's non-compliance with previously adopted resolutions. The White House immediately expressed its strong disagreement with this influential assessment. It then stood quietly by while a group of Republican Congressmen demanded Annan's resignation over the 'oil-for-food' scandal, whereby Saddam Hussein had abused an UN-run programme designed to provide humanitarian essentials to civilians in Iraq while the country was subject to Security Council sanctions. When pressed by reporters about the matter in November 2004, John Danforth, the US ambassador to the United Nations, pointedly declined to express confidence in the Secretary General's leadership. In the world of diplomatic protocol, this amounted to a powerful attack; it also suggested that, behind closed doors, the United States was pressing for Annan's departure before the end of his second term in 2006. Such is the extent of the Bush Administration's intolerance of dissent about the wisdom and legality of its actions.

Part Two

Self-defence

4

'Inherent Right' of Self-defence

In 1837, the British were crushing a rebellion in Upper Canada (now Ontario). The United States, while unwilling to antagonize a superpower by supporting the rebels directly, did not prevent a private militia from being formed in upstate New York. The 'volunteers' used a steamboat, the *Caroline*, to transport arms and men to the rebel headquarters on Navy Island, on the Canadian side of the Niagara River. The British responded with a night raid, capturing the vessel as it was docked at Fort Schlosser, New York. They set the boat on fire and sent it over Niagara Falls. Two men were killed as they fled the steamer and two prisoners were taken back to Canada but later released.

The incident caused disquiet in Washington. British forces, having torched the White House and Capitol Building in 1814, were again intervening on US territory. Secretary of State Forsyth wrote a letter to the British minister at Washington, one Mr Fox, asserting that the incident had produced 'the most painful emotions of surprise and regret'. The minister responded that the destruction of the *Caroline* was an act of 'necessary self-defence' – though probably all he meant by this statement was that the act was justified on political grounds. Historically, self-defence had been a political justification for what, from a legal perspective, were ordinary acts of war. The consent-based international law of the early nineteenth century rejected natural law distinctions between just and unjust wars.

The dispute over the destruction of the *Caroline* was settled in 1842 following a change of administration in Washington and the delegation of a new British minister, Lord Ashburton, to the

United States. Lord Ashburton was extremely well connected in Washington – his wife was the daughter of a US senator – and the diplomacy that followed was carefully managed on both sides.

Daniel Webster, the new Secretary of State, began by conceding that the use of force in self-defence could be justified in some circumstances:

> Undoubtedly it is just, that, while it is admitted that exceptions growing out of the great law of self-defence do exist, those exceptions should be confined to cases in which the necessity of that self-defence is instant, overwhelming, leaving no choice of means, and no moment of deliberation.

Webster then added, importantly, that nothing 'unreasonable or excessive' could be done in self-defence.

Other governments subsequently accepted these criteria – 'necessity and proportionality' – as the parameters of a new customary international law right of self-defence. Thus, while the case of the *Caroline* did nothing to prevent further aggression, it did lead to a legal distinction between war and self-defence. As long as a military response met the 'necessity and proportionality' criteria and the act defended against was not an act of war, peace would be maintained; a matter of considerable importance to relatively weak countries, as the United States then was.

Another century and the First World War were required to convince statesmen of the need for legal constraints on military aggression. A first effort was made in 1919 when the Covenant of the League of Nations was adopted at Versailles. Under the Covenant, the Council of the League could issue recommendations to countries that seemed to be heading for war. But if the members of the Council failed to agree, the disputing governments were free to take whatever action they considered 'necessary for the maintenance of right and justice'. The League of Nations also lacked the capacity to enforce its recommendations. Any hope that the League would coordinate enforcement action among its members disappeared in 1920, when the US Senate withheld its consent to the ratification of the Covenant of the League of Nations.

The Kellogg–Briand Pact of 1928 prohibited 'recourse to war for the solution of international controversies'. The Pact, named after US Secretary of State Frank Kellogg and French Foreign Minister Aristide Briand, was initially signed by fifteen countries and eventually ratified by sixty-two. However, like the League of Nations Covenant, the Kellogg–Briand Pact lacked an enforcement mechanism and had little practical effect. Some countries, such as Italy when it invaded Abyssinia and Japan when it invaded Manchuria, evaded their obligations under the Pact simply by avoiding formal declarations of war.

The Kellogg–Briand Pact also included a side agreement between the United States and France that provided an exception for self-defence. Neither the nature of the right nor the instances in which it could be invoked were defined. When the US Senate voted 85–1 in favour of ratifying the Pact, it did so on the explicit understanding that it did not imperil the Monroe Doctrine: President James Monroe's 1823 declaration that any European interference in the Western hemisphere would be regarded as a threat to the security of the United States. Given these complexities, the customary international law criteria established during the *Caroline* incident remained the only discernible legal constraints on the recourse to force in international affairs.

In 1945, the UN Charter required all countries to 'refrain...from the threat or use of force'. By using the general term 'use of force', the Charter extended the prohibition on war to include undeclared armed conflicts. The Charter also created the UN Security Council and gave it authority to determine 'the existence of any threat to the peace, breach of the peace or act of aggression', impose sanctions, and 'take such action by air, sea or land forces as may be necessary'. But the drafters of the Charter were hardly naive. Recognizing that the existence of the United Nations could be imperilled if powerful countries were subjected to the threat of collective action, they granted permanent membership on the Security Council and a veto over its resolutions to Britain, China, France, the Soviet Union and United States. Mindful that the Security Council could never respond promptly to every act of aggression, they also included an exception for force used in self-defence. This time, the exception was not left undefined. In addition to the customary international law criteria of 'necessity and proportionality', three further restrictions were introduced: 1) a state could act in self-defence only if subject to an 'armed attack'; 2) acts of self-defence had to be reported immediately to the Security Council; and 3) the right to respond would terminate as soon as the Council took action. The relevant provision of the UN Charter is Article 51:

> Nothing in the present Charter shall impair the inherent right of individual or collective self-defence if an armed attack occurs against a Member of the United Nations, until the Security Council has taken measures necessary to maintain international peace and security. Measures taken by Members in the exercise of this right of self-defence shall be immediately reported to the Security Council and shall not in any way affect the authority and responsibility of the Security Council under the present Charter to take at any time such action as it deems necessary in order to maintain or restore international peace and security.

Despite this careful attempt at definition, the content of Article 51 is greatly informed by customary international law, in part because of the explicit reference to the 'inherent' character of the right of self-defence. And so, while the right is codified in an almost universally ratified treaty, its contours have gradually evolved – or at least become more easily discernible – as the result of state practice and expressions of *opinio juris* since 1945. For example, it is not clear from the ordinary meaning or context of Article 51 that armed attacks against a country's citizens *outside* its territory constitute attacks against a 'Member of the United

Nations' sufficient to trigger the right to self-defence. This particular ambiguity was resolved in 1976.

On 27 June 1976, an Air France jet left Israel for France with 251 passengers and a crew of twelve on board. After a brief stop in Athens, pro-Palestinian hijackers seized control of the plane and forced it to land in Entebbe, Uganda. The hijackers threatened to kill the hostages unless 53 pro-Palestinian terrorists were released from jails in France, Israel, Kenya, Switzerland and West Germany. On the third day of the hijacking, forty-seven non-Jewish passengers were released. On the fourth day another 100 were let go. The Government of Uganda, led by the dictator Idi Amin, took no apparent steps to secure the release of the remaining, mostly Israeli, passengers or the crew.

On 3 July 1976, shortly before the deadline set by the hijackers, Israeli commandos conducted an audacious and highly successful rescue operation. Without notifying the Ugandan government, a small force landed at Entebbe airport, stormed the plane and killed the hijackers. They saved the lives of all but three of the hostages and flew them back to Israel. Jonathan Netanyahu, the leader of the commando unit and the brother of Israeli politician Binyamin Netanyahu, was the only Israeli soldier to die in the raid. A number of Ugandan soldiers were also killed and several Ugandan military aircraft destroyed.

Israel claimed that international law allowed it to use force to protect its nationals abroad when the country in which they had fallen into danger was unable or unwilling to do so. Two draft resolutions were introduced in the UN Security Council. The first, prepared by Britain and the United States, condemned the hijacking and called on states to prevent and punish all such terrorist attacks. This resolution was put to a vote but failed to obtain the nine out of fifteen votes necessary. Two countries (Panama and Romania) formally abstained from the vote, while seven (Benin, China, Guyana, Libya, Pakistan, the Soviet Union and Tanzania) refused even to participate.

The second draft resolution, submitted by Benin, Libya and Tanzania, condemned the violation of Uganda's sovereignty and territorial integrity and demanded that Israel pay compensation for all damage caused. The resolution was never put to a vote. The response of countries outside the Security Council was similarly mixed and muted, signalling widespread, tacit acceptance of the Israeli claim. Today, the Entebbe incident is regarded as having decisively contributed to a limited extension of the right of self-defence in international affairs to include the protection of nationals abroad. When civil strife threatens foreign nationals, whether in Haiti, Liberia or Sierra Leone, sending soldiers to rescue them has become so commonplace that the issue of legality is rarely raised. When controversy does arise, as when France intervened to rescue nationals in Mauritania (1977), Gabon (1990), Rwanda (1990), Chad (1992) and the Central African Republic (1996), concerns usually focus on whether the intervening government has exceeded the criteria of necessity and proportionality – for example, by using the protection of nationals as a pretence for intervening in a civil war.

If the right of self-defence extends to the protection of nationals abroad, what then of situations where an armed attack has occurred but the immediate threat has passed? In other words, is self-defence limited to the warding off of attacks-in-progress or does the right extend to action taken in response to a recent attack? If so, what, if any, line is to be drawn between defensive and punitive armed responses?

In April 1993, an attempt to assassinate former US President George H. W. Bush was thwarted when a sophisticated car bomb was discovered in Kuwait. Two months later, the United States fired twenty-three Tomahawk cruise missiles at the Iraqi Military Intelligence Headquarters in Baghdad. Sixteen of the missiles hit the target. Some six to eight people were killed.

Madeleine Albright, who was the US ambassador to the United Nations at the time, presented evidence of the Iraqi government's involvement in the assassination attempt to the UN Security Council. She asserted that the attempt to kill the former president was 'a direct attack on the United States, an attack that required a direct United States response'. Moreover, Albright claimed, the response was permitted under Article 51 of the Charter.

The US claim was unusual in several respects. First, the United States had not been attacked, nor was the assassination attempt aimed at a group of Americans. The car bomb was directed against a single citizen while he was outside the United States. Of course, George H. W. Bush is no ordinary citizen: even the Democrat Clinton Administration of the day regarded the former Republican president as a symbol and projection of US sovereignty when he travelled abroad.

Second, the armed response took place two months after the assassination attempt had been foiled and the threat to the former president eliminated. The response, rather than being an act of self-defence as such, was directed at the dual goals of punishing Iraq and deterring future plots. The missile strike therefore seemed more in the nature of a reprisal than an act of self-defence. But reprisals have been illegal under international law since the adoption of the UN Charter of 1945. In 1964, the UN Security Council went so far as to adopt a resolution that condemned armed reprisals as 'incompatible with the purposes and principles of the United Nations'. In response, some countries, including the United States, have persistently sought to extend the right of self-defence to include acts designed more to punish than defend.

In this instance, the members of the Security Council responded favourably to the US action and its claim of self-defence. Japan said that the use of force was an 'unavoidable situation'. Germany described the strike as a 'justified response'. Outside the Security Council, overall reaction was less favourable. Iran and Libya condemned the strike as an act of aggression, while the Arab League expressed 'extreme regret' and said that force should only have been used if authorized by the Security Council.

Determining whether an action falls within the rubric of self-defence will usually turn on the facts of the specific situation. In the case of the foiled 1993 assassination attempt, the US government explained that it had taken two months to gather conclusive evidence of Iraqi involvement in the plot and, once it was certain that Iraq was responsible, it had wasted no time in acting. The British found themselves in a similar situation in 1982, when an immediate response to Argentina's invasion of the Falklands was precluded by the time it took to assemble and send a naval task force from the United Kingdom to the South Atlantic, though the continued Argentine occupation of the islands could also have been considered an ongoing armed attack.

Still, once an armed attack has come and gone and there is no continuing or immediate threat, there is nothing to stop the country that has been attacked from asking the UN Security Council to respond. In most domestic legal systems, the right of self-defence terminates the moment an attack has ceased and there is time to call the police. However, since the Security Council is a political body, the country that has been attacked cannot be certain that the Council will respond to its pleas. The extension of the right of self-defence to the period following an attack represents a pragmatic response, not just to the prohibition of reprisals in international affairs but also to the unreliability of the Security Council as a policing mechanism for the international rules on the use of military force.

That said, this pragmatic extension of self-defence to the period following an attack exacerbates the very obstacle it seeks to overcome. By expanding the scope of situations where countries can use force without Security Council authorization, any extension to the right of self-defence necessarily decreases the frequency with which the Council is called upon to act. The United States, by pushing for this and other extensions to the right of self-defence, not only increases its own freedom to act, it diminishes the role and authority of the United Nations. Pragmatism can be attractive, but it carries a price.

5

Self-defence against Terrorism

On 11 September 2001, nineteen al-Qaeda operatives seized four passenger jets, crashing two of them into the World Trade Center and another into the Pentagon; the fourth plane was brought down in a field in Pennsylvania after the passengers revolted against the hijackers. Nearly 3,000 people were killed in the attacks. Almost immediately, the US government declared that it would respond militarily on the basis of self-defence. But as a legal justification for the use of force in Afghanistan – the country harbouring and supporting the al-Qaeda leadership – the right of self-defence was not as suitable as it might at first have seemed.

Even when countries are directly implicated in terrorism, acts of self-defence directed against them have not attracted much international support. In April 1986, a terrorist bomb exploded in a West Berlin nightclub crowded with US servicemen. Two soldiers and a Turkish woman were killed and 230 people were wounded, including fifty US military personnel. Ten days later, the United States responded by bombing a number of targets in Tripoli. More than fifteen people were killed, including an adopted daughter of Libyan leader Muammar Qaddafi.

The US government claimed the strike on Tripoli was legally justified as an act of self-defence. As then Secretary of State George P. Shultz said:

[T]he Charter's restrictions on the use or threat of force in international relations include a specific exception for the right of self-defence. It is absurd to argue that international law prohibits us from capturing terrorists in international waters or airspace; from attacking them on the soil of other nations, even for the purpose of rescuing hostages; or from using force against states that support, train, and harbour terrorists or guerrillas.

Yet the US claim was widely rejected, with many governments also expressing doubt as to whether the attack on Libya met the 'necessity and proportionality' requirements for self-defence. The most significant evidence of state practice and *opinio juris* in this instance was the refusal of France and Spain – both NATO allies of the United States – to allow their airspace to be used by the bombers that conducted the raid. As a result, the pilots, who began their mission at a US airbase in Britain, had to fly westwards around the Iberian Peninsula. The detour necessitated the heightened risk of mid-air refuelling. Denying the use of airspace is highly unusual, especially among allies. Canada, France and Germany opposed the 2003 Iraq War but left their airspace open to US military aircraft – including ultra long-range B-2 bombers – flying to and from the Middle East.

Today, the additional question arises as to whether the right of self-defence extends to situations where military responses take place on the territory of countries not directly implicated in the terrorist acts. For decades, the United States, Israel and apartheid South Africa advanced precisely this claim. Israel, for instance, claimed to be acting in self-defence when it attacked the headquarters of the Palestine Liberation Organization in Tunisia in 1985. The UN Security Council condemned the action, with the United States, unusually, abstaining rather than vetoing the resolution. A number of governments expressed concern that the territorial integrity of a sovereign state had been violated in an attempt to target, not the state itself, but alleged terrorists present there.

On 7 August 1998, powerful bombs exploded outside the US embassies in Nairobi, Kenya and Dar es Salaam, Tanzania. Twelve Americans and more than 200 Kenyans and Tanzanians were killed; thousands more were injured. United States intelligence sources indicated that Osama bin Laden and his al-Qaeda organization were responsible for the attacks. Two weeks later, the United States fired seventy-nine Tomahawk cruise missiles at six terrorist training camps around the town of Khowst, Afghanistan, and at a pharmaceutical plant on the outskirts of Khartoum, Sudan. At the time, the Central Intelligence Agency (CIA) was convinced that the plant was producing precursors to chemical weapons; it subsequently emerged that the intelligence was flawed.

The US government justified its actions on the basis of self-defence. As then National Security Adviser Sandy Berger said: 'I think it is appropriate, under Article 51 of the UN Charter, for protecting the self-defence of the United States . . . for us to try and disrupt and destroy those kinds of military terrorist targets.' Since propriety does not necessarily coincide with legality, Berger's choice of words may indicate that he recognized the tenuous nature of the claim. The United States was not asserting that it had been attacked by Afghanistan and Sudan; instead, it was claiming the right to fire missiles into those countries in response to the actions of a group that was not a state.

In an attempt to dampen international criticism, and perhaps modify the law, President Bill Clinton telephoned Tony Blair, Jacques Chirac and German Chancellor Helmut Kohl shortly before the strikes and asked for their support. Without having time to consult their lawyers, all three leaders agreed – and subsequently made concurring public statements immediately following the US action. As a result of the timely expressions of support, other countries were more restrained in their response than they might have been. Pakistan protested strongly, which was understandable given that its airspace had been used without permission and a stray cruise missile had landed on its territory. Cuba also denounced the raid, as did Iran, Iraq, Libya and Russia, and UN Secretary General Kofi Annan diplomatically expressed 'concern'. But most governments and international organizations remained silent; indeed, the incident never even made it on to the agenda of the UN Security Council. This broad lack of response probably contributed to obfuscating the limits of self-defence, if not to changing the law as it governs recourse to force against countries that harbour or otherwise support international terrorists.

It would serve the United States' interests to have the right of self-defence extend to the use of force against terrorists abroad, there being no prospect that another country would exercise self-defence against terrorists on US territory. At the same time, however, the United States has to regularly depend on allies who value and abide by international law. On other occasions, the United States finds it convenient to deploy legal arguments when seeking to persuade other countries not to use force themselves. It is this combined need for flexibility, compliance and constraint that motivates the law-making and law-changing efforts of the United States. Whenever the US government wishes to act in a manner that is inconsistent with existing international law, its lawyers regularly and actively seek to change the law. They do so by provoking and steering changing patterns of state practice and *opinio juris*, with a view to incrementally modifying customary rules and accepted interpretations of treaties such as the UN Charter.

Bill Clinton's telephone calls to close allies immediately prior to the 1998 missile strikes on Sudan and Afghanistan are one example of an attempt to promote support and acquiescence in a US legal position, and thus to change international law. A better example, directed at generating the exact same legal change, is found in the US government's approach to international law in the aftermath of 11 September 2001. At the time, there were several legal justifications available to the United States for the use of military force in Afghanistan. First, the United States could have argued that it was acting at the invitation of the Northern Alliance, a group which still controlled a portion of the country's territory and could have been cast – albeit tenuously – as the legitimate government of Afghanistan. Invitation is widely accepted as a legal basis for intervention under customary international law, since the UN Charter's prohibition on the use of force is only directed at non-consensual interventions. Second, the United States could have sought explicit authorization for military action from the UN Security Council. Such authorization would certainly have been granted, given the widespread sympathy that existed for the United States at the time as well as the heightened concern about terrorism felt by governments everywhere. The request was never made. Even then, the United States could have argued that Security Council Resolution 1373, adopted on 28 September 2001 and directed primarily at the freezing of terrorist assets, contained language that authorized the use of military force. Third, the United States could have claimed a right of humanitarian intervention based, in part, on the precedent of the 1999 Kosovo War, because millions of Afghan lives were at risk from famine during the winter of 2001–2002.

Yet the United States chose to focus on a single justification: a right of self-defence against terrorism. In doing so, it found itself in somewhat of a legal dilemma, though not an entirely unhelpful one. In order to maintain the coalition of countries willing to use force against terrorism, the response to the 11 September 2001 attacks had to comply with the criteria of necessity and propor-tionality. The military action therefore had to be focused on those individuals believed responsible for the deaths of the nearly 3,000 US citizens. But if the United States had singled out bin Laden and al-Qaeda as its targets, it would have run up against the widely held view that terrorist attacks, in and of themselves, do not justify military responses within the territory of sovereign coun-tries. Even today, most countries are wary of a rule that could expose them to attack whenever terrorists were thought to operate from within their territory. Consider, for instance, the position of Germany after 11 September 2001: although the city of Hamburg had unwittingly harboured several of the terrorists, few people would maintain that this fact alone could justify a US attack.

In response to this dilemma, the United States adopted a two-pronged legal strategy. First, it implicated the Taliban. By giving refuge to bin Laden and al-Qaeda and refusing to hand them over, the Taliban was alleged to have directly facilitated and endorsed their actions. The United States even gave the Taliban a deadline for surrendering bin Laden, a move that served to ensure their complicity. Moreover, the Taliban's continued control over Afghanistan was viewed as a threat, in and of itself, of even more terrorism. As John Negroponte, the US ambassador to the United Nations, explained in a letter to the President of the Security Council on 7 October 2001:

The attacks on 11 September 2001 and the ongoing threat to the United States and its nationals posed by the al-Qaeda organization have been made possible by the decision of the Taliban regime to allow the parts of Afghanistan that it controls to be used by this organization as a base of operation. Despite every effort by the United States and the international community, the Taliban regime has refused to change its policy. From the territory of Afghanistan, the al-Qaeda organization continues to train and support agents of terror who attack innocent people throughout the world and target United States nationals and interests in the United States and abroad.

In this way, the United States broadened its claim of self-defence to necessitate action against the state of Afghanistan. Although still contentious, this claim was much less of a stretch from pre-existing international law than a claimed right to attack terrorists who simply happened to be within the territory of another country. Subsequent statements by the Taliban that endorsed the terrorist acts further raised the level of their alleged responsibility. For these reasons, the claim to be acting in self-defence against the country of Afghanistan – and the modification of customary international law that claim entailed – had a much better chance of securing the expressed or tacit support of other countries.

As the second part of its legal strategy, the United States worked hard to secure widespread support in advance of military action. The formation of a coalition, including the invocation of the collective self-defence provisions of the 1949 North Atlantic Treaty and the 1947 Inter-American Treaty of Reciprocal Assistance, helped smooth the path for the claim of self-defence. Both NATO and the Organization of American States formally deemed the events of 11 September 2001 an 'armed attack'. Similarly, UN Security Council resolutions adopted on 12 and 28 September 2001 were carefully worded to affirm the right of self-defence in customary international law, within the context of the terrorist attacks on New York and Washington, DC.

As a result of the law-making strategies adopted by the United States and heightened concern about terrorism worldwide, the right of self-defence now includes military responses against countries that willingly harbour or support terrorist groups, provided that the terrorists have already struck the responding state. And in accordance with a longstanding consensus – and Article 51 of the UN Charter – self-defence can be either individual or collective, so states that have been attacked by terrorists can call on other countries to assist them in their military response.

The long-term consequences of the US approach to self-defence and terrorism may be significant. Under the circumstances, had the Bush Administration relied on arguments of invitation, Security Council authorization, or even humanitarian intervention, few governments would have objected. But acting alone might have been made more difficult for the United States in future. Although previous attempts to establish a right of self-defence against terrorism had failed to attract widespread international support, the situation in the aftermath of 11 September 2001 was considerably more conducive. Having now seized the opportunity to establish self-defence as a basis for military action against terrorism, the United States, and other countries, will be able to invoke it again in circumstances which are less grave, and where the responsibility of the targeted state is less clear. This raises the question: where, then, are the limits of this new extension to the right of self-defence? The importance of the question is highlighted by the international debate over Israel's policy of 'targeted killing'.

Although it had been shaped by 11 September 2001, endorsed after action in Afghanistan, and honed in Iraq, the 'special relationship' between Britain and the United States was tested in 2004 as the governments of Tony Blair and George W. Bush disagreed publicly on a major issue of foreign policy. In mid-March, Hamas leader Sheikh Ahmad Yassin was killed by an Israeli missile as he left a mosque in his wheelchair. One month later his successor, Abdel-Aziz al-Rantissi, was killed in a similar attack. Jack Straw, the British Foreign Secretary, condemned the killings as 'unlawful'. In contrast, White House spokesman Scott McClellan asserted that 'Israel has the right to defend itself'. That the two principal partners in the 'war on terrorism' presented such starkly different conclusions on the legality of the Israeli action reflected their dissimilar perspectives on the Israeli-Palestinian situation, and on the relevant rules of international law.

From a European perspective, the Israeli missile strikes were 'extra-judicial killings' that violated fundamental principles of international human rights and humanitarian law. Global standards of due process require that suspected criminals be apprehended, prosecuted and convicted before being punished. Capital punishment is permitted, but death sentences can only be imposed by duly constituted courts. Yassin and Rantissi may well have incited and organized suicide bombings, but they should have been captured and prosecuted rather than simply killed.

Moreover, European governments consider the struggle between the Israelis and Palestinians to be primarily an 'occupation-gone-wrong', and view Israel, as an occupying power, as legally constrained by the rules set out in the Fourth Geneva Convention of 1949, the Convention relative to the Protection of Civilian Persons in Time of War. In support of this position, they point out that Jordan had administered the West Bank and East Jerusalem, and Egypt the Gaza Strip, prior to the seizure of these territories by Israel during the 1967 Six Day War. They also cite the encompassing language of Article 4(1): 'Persons protected by the Convention are those who, at a given moment and in any manner whatsoever, find themselves, in case of a conflict or occupation, in the hands of a Party to the conflict or Occupying Power of which they are not nationals.' Finally, European governments take the view that, at a minimum, Article 3 of the Geneva Convention applies to Israel, both as a treaty provision and as a codification of customary international law. The same Article 3 is found in all four of the 1949 Geneva Conventions; it is therefore referred to as 'Common Article 3'. Its first part is of relevance here:

> In the case of armed conflict not of an international character occurring in the territory of one of the High Contracting Parties, each Party to the conflict shall be bound to apply, as a minimum, the following provisions:

> 1. Persons taking no active part in the hostilities, including members of armed forces who have laid down their arms and those placed hors de combat by sickness, wounds, detention, or any other cause, shall in all circumstances be treated humanely, without any adverse distinction founded on race, colour, religion or faith, sex, birth or wealth, or any other similar criteria.

> To this end, the following acts are and shall remain prohibited at any time and in any place whatsoever with respect to the above-mentioned persons:

> (a) Violence to life and person, in particular murder of all kinds, mutilation, cruel treatment and torture;
> (b) Taking of hostages;
> (c) Outrages upon personal dignity, in particular humiliating and degrading treatment;
> (d) The passing of sentences and the carrying out of executions without previous judgment pronounced by a regularly constituted court, affording all the judicial guarantees which are recognized as indispensable by civilized peoples.

From the US government's perspective, Israel's actions were legal because the killings were aimed at preventing further terrorist attacks. The international law of self-defence – as opposed to that of human rights – provides the framework for this analysis. The policy of 'targeted killing' is seen as part of the global war on terrorism. In this respect, it is comparable to the 2001 invasion of Afghanistan, which the United States similarly justified as an act of self-defence.

The Israeli government, for its part, claims that the Fourth Geneva Convention is not applicable because the West Bank and Gaza Strip were not part of any state prior to being occupied by Israel. This view was firmly rejected by the International Court of Justice in a July 2004 advisory opinion on Israel's so-called 'security fence', though Israel has rejected the decision as biased. Israel also argues that, by the time suicide bombers reach its territory, it is too late to stop them; consequently, the only way to prevent attacks is to target pre-emptively the individuals responsible for planning them. In this sense, Yassin and Rantissi were actively engaged in hostilities. The Israeli position acquires a degree of credibility from the fact that both men publicly took credit for organizing suicide bombings in Israel, and threatened to conduct more.

As is so often the case, where one stands on this issue depends on where one sits. From the perspective of Jerusalem or Tel Aviv, suicide bombers pose a definite threat. Having lost more than 900 of their fellow citizens to Palestinian attacks since September 2000, Israelis believe they are at war. But how far might Prime Minister Ariel Sharon take the policy of targeted killing?

Following the Yassin and Rantissi killings, Sharon unilaterally 'released' himself from a pledge to President George W. Bush that Israel would not physically harm Yasser Arafat. At the time, the threat to the beleaguered Palestinian leader had to be taken seriously. And had he been openly harmed, the argument of self-defence would, almost certainly, again have been deployed.

The United States would have had difficulty opposing such an action, and not just because the Bush Administration repeatedly expressed support for Israel's prior targeted killings. Three days before Rantissi was killed, Bush endorsed Sharon's plan to retain the major Jewish settlements in the West Bank while pulling the Israeli army out of Gaza. Bush at the same time agreed to alter US policy concerning Palestinian refugees, accepting Israel's position that the refugees have no right to return to lands within Israel. With these two moves, the president abandoned any pretence that the United States could serve as an objective mediator in the Israel–Palestine conflict. Ariel Sharon now had the backing of the White House as he sought to impose – rather than negotiate – an outcome on Palestine. Yasser Arafat was written out of the script. Had he not died of other causes – and poison will never be ruled out – his 'targeted killing' might only have been a matter of time. His successor will live under the same threatening shadow.

Yet Arafat, unlike Yassin and Rantissi, was the democratically elected leader of a quasi-nation-state that has concluded treaties with Israel and holds observer status at the United Nations. He had not, during his time as leader of the Palestinian Authority, publicly claimed responsibility for or endorsed terrorist acts. Instead of hiding in the dangerous warren of Gaza City, Arafat was closely surrounded by Israeli forces in a readily identified location in Ramallah, and thus was easy to apprehend. His assassination, had it occurred, would have been a clear and egregious violation of international law, and properly criticized as such by the international community. His death in a Paris hospital was therefore the optimal outcome, at least for Ariel Sharon, and perhaps for the United States.

6

Pre-emptive Self-defence

On 7 June 1981, eight Israeli air force pilots conducted a bold and dangerous raid deep into hostile territory. Hugging the ground to avoid detection, they flew more than 600 miles before dropping their bombs on a nuclear reactor under construction at Osirak, on the outskirts of Baghdad. The reactor was badly damaged, Iraq's nuclear programme was severely impaired, and none of the attacking planes were lost. The pilots became national heroes. One of them, Ilan Ramon, was again a hero twenty-two years later when he became the first Israeli to journey into space on the ill-fated mission of the space shuttle *Columbia*.

Israel claimed pre-emptive self-defence for the strike on the basis that a nuclear-armed Iraq would constitute an unacceptable threat, especially given Saddam Hussein's overt hostility towards the Jewish state. Israel also claimed to have met the traditional requirement of proportionality, having bombed the construction site on a Sunday in order to lessen the risk to foreign workers. The Osirak reactor bombing thus involved an explicit claim to pre-emptive self-defence coupled with decisive military action. In the language of international law, both *opinio juris* and state practice were clearly present. But not only the state practice and *opinio juris* of the acting country matter in these situations; the responses of other governments are equally crucial.

Immediately after the attack on Osirak, the UN Security Council unanimously adopted a resolution condemning the Israeli action as illegal. This condemnation was even stronger because the United States joined in the vote rather than abstaining. That said, it is not entirely clear that all the members of the UN

Security Council voted for the condemnatory resolution because they were categorically opposed to pre-emptive self-defence. Because the Iraqi reactor was nowhere close to functioning at the time of the attack, some governments may have been more concerned about the fact that the traditional requirement of necessity had not been fulfilled. The important point, however, is that Israel expressly claimed the right to engage in pre-emptive military action against a possible, future threat and the international community resoundingly rejected the claim. In the British House of Commons, then Prime Minister Margaret Thatcher said that an 'armed attack in such circumstances cannot be justified. It represents a grave breach of international law.' Other governments were equally critical. Considered in its entirety, the state practice and *opinio juris* generated by the Israeli raid was against – rather than for – a right of pre-emptive self-defence.

This was not simply an issue of customary international law, since the first sentence of Article 51 of the UN Charter reads:

> Nothing in the present Charter shall impair the inherent right of individual or collective self-defence if an armed attack occurs against a Member of the United Nations, until the Security Council has taken measures necessary to maintain international peace and security.

The rules of treaty interpretation, as codified in the 1969 Vienna Convention on the Law of Treaties, require that provisions be interpreted in accordance with the 'ordinary meaning of the terms'. When this approach is applied to Article 51, any pre-existing right of pre-emptive self-defence is apparently superseded by the requirement 'if an armed attack occurs'.

However, reference in Article 51 to the 'inherent' character of the right complicates the analysis by implicitly incorporating the pre-existing customary international law of self-defence into the treaty provision. Consequently, it is sometimes argued that pre-emptive action is justified if there is a 'necessity of self-defence, instant, overwhelming, leaving no choice of means, and no moment of deliberation'. These were the criteria set out by Daniel Webster after the 1837 *Caroline* incident, as discussed in Chapter 4. Until the adoption of the UN Charter in 1945, they were widely accepted as delimiting a narrow right of pre-emptive self-defence in customary international law. Today, with the Charter in force, these criteria can only succeed if Article 51 is ignored, re-read, or viewed as having been modified by subsequent state practice. Yet most of the state practice, including the widespread condemnation of the 1981 Israeli attack on the Osirak nuclear reactor, cuts the other way.

Indeed, since 1945, most governments have refrained from claiming pre-emptive self-defence. Israel, concerned not to be seen as an aggressor state, justified the strikes that initiated the 1967 Six Day War on the basis that Egypt's blocking of the Straits of Tiran constituted a prior act of aggression. The United States, concerned about establishing a precedent that other countries might employ, implausibly justified its 1962 blockade of Cuba as 'regional peace-keeping'. And in 1988, the United States similarly eschewed a claim of pre-emptive self-defence when it argued that the shooting down of an Iranian civilian Airbus by the USS *Vincennes*, although mistaken, had been in response to an ongoing attack by Iranian military helicopters and patrol boats. Even the most hawkish leaders baulked at a right of pre-emptive action during the Cold War, at a time when both the world's principal disputants possessed armadas of nuclear missile submarines designed to survive first strikes and ensure 'mutually assured destruction'.

Today, as seen from the White House, the situation looks quite different. Relations with Russia have improved dramatically, no other potential enemy has submarine-based nuclear missiles, and the first phase of a missile defence system has become operational (even though the technology is largely untested). When President George W. Bush announced an expansive new policy of pre-emptive military action on 1 June 2002, he clearly did not feel deterred by the prospect of Armageddon.

During a commencement speech at West Point, Bush addressed the threat of weapons of mass destruction (WMD) in association with international terrorism. The president advocated a degree of pre-emption that extended towards the preventive – or even precautionary – use of force: 'We must take the battle to the enemy, disrupt his plans, and confront the worst threats before they emerge.' Even if the threats are not imminent, 'if we wait for threats to fully materialize, we will have waited too long.' The new policy – now widely referred to as the 'Bush Doctrine' – made no attempt to satisfy the *Caroline* criteria. There was no suggestion of waiting for a 'necessity of self-defence' that was 'instant, over-whelming, leaving no choice of means, and no moment of deliberation'. The new policy is questionable on several levels.

Is unilateral military action the best way to deal with WMD? Weapons of mass destruction are hardly a new problem. The first treaty on poison gas dates back to 1899. For decades the United Nations has led efforts to control the development and spread of such weapons while, ironically, the United States has dragged its feet. The Bush Administration, shortly after coming to power, refused to ratify enforcement protocols to the Chemical and Biological Weapons Conventions. The Bush Administration pressured 139 countries into dismissing José Bustani, the highly regarded director-general of the Organization for the Prohibition of Chemical Weapons, in the middle of his term; it is now pushing for the removal of Mohamed ElBaradei, the head of the International Atomic Energy Agency. The Bush Administration, in violation of its obligations under the Nuclear Non-Proliferation Treaty, has accelerated efforts to develop battlefield nuclear weapons designed to penetrate deep bunkers and destroy dangerous chemicals and pathogens. And the Bush Administration actively opposes the International Criminal Court, which could prosecute individuals for using WMD. All of this could reasonably lead one to question whether George W. Bush has really provided leadership on the weapons of mass destruction issue.

A broad right of pre-emptive self-defence would also introduce dangerous uncertainties into international relations. Who would decide that a potential threat justifies pre-emptive action? How does one protect against opportunistic military interventions justified under the guise of pre-emptive self-defence? Do we wish to accord the same extended right to India, Pakistan or Israel – all nuclear powers with a history of engaging in cross-border interventions – as the equal applicability of customary international law would require us to do? Could the development of such a right prompt potential targets into striking first, using rather than losing their biological, chemical and nuclear weapons? Governments are intensely aware of the potentially dangerous consequences of the Bush Doctrine and most have been cautious about giving it their support.

Their concerns are heightened by the fact that the UN Charter already provides an answer to these questions: in the absence of an attack, only the UN Security Council can act. Provided with clear evidence of an imminent biological, chemical or nuclear attack, there is little doubt that the Security Council would act, since the effects of weapons of mass destruction are unlikely to be confined within a discrete geographical area. In recent years, the Security Council has repeatedly authorized military action in situations where there has been no direct or immediate threat to its fifteen members: in Iraq, Somalia, Bosnia-Herzegovina, Haiti and elsewhere. After the terrorist attacks of 11 September 2001, it took the Council only one day to affirm the right of the United States to engage in self-defence in that instance.

Only countries with no reason to fear countervailing military forces can contemplate a world without the combined protections of the UN Charter and the customary law of the *Caroline* incident. President Bush feels able to claim a broad right of pre-emptive action because other states do not have the capacity to retaliate against the United States. What the Bush Administration apparently fails to realize is that its actions might well provide incentives – perversely based on self-defence – for others to acquire the very weapons that the United States purports to abhor.

The staff lawyers and diplomats in the US State Department were undoubtedly aware of the potentially negative consequences of the President's words at West Point; words intended to convey a policy decision that had, in all likelihood, been made with little consideration of international law. The State Department lawyers had the task of justifying the new policy in legal terms. They would have soon realized that, as expressed, the new policy was not only ill-advised and unprecedented, but had little chance of becoming customary international law. Simply put, most countries do not stand to benefit from an extended right of pre-emptive self-defence because it would give all states – including every state's potential enemies – an almost unlimited discretion to use force. The absence of widely reciprocal benefits is usually fatal to the development of customary international law, which, as we have seen, requires not only the advancement of a claim but also widespread support or acquiescence.

Accordingly, the Bush Doctrine was reformulated to make it more acceptable to other countries, and thereby more effective in promoting legal change. The National Security Strategy of the United States, released on 20 September 2002, explicitly adopted – and then sought to extend – the criteria for self-defence articulated by Daniel Webster following the *Caroline* incident:

> For centuries, international law recognized that nations need not suffer an attack before they can lawfully take action to defend themselves against forces that present an imminent danger of attack. Legal scholars and international jurists often conditioned the legitimacy of preemption on the existence of an imminent threat – most often a visible mobilization of armies, navies, and air forces preparing to attack.
>
> We must adapt the concept of imminent threat to the capabilities and objectives of today's adversaries.

The National Security Strategy made no mention of the UN Charter, implicitly asserting by omission that the pre-1945 customary right of self-defence remained the applicable law. By glossing over the normally contentious issue of the relationship between the *Caroline* criteria and Article 51, the document strategically sought to establish a new baseline for the discussion of self-defence. Only then did it go further, asserting that the criterion of imminence now extends beyond threats which are 'instant, overwhelming, leaving no choice of means, and no moment of deliberation' to include more distant and uncertain challenges.

This claim was made within a context that at least suggested the need for legal change. Few would contest that terrorism and WMD are serious problems. As significantly, other governments were not asked to agree on an actual change to the rule. Instead, all that was proposed in the National Security Strategy was an adaptation of how the (supposed) existing rule is applied in practice. The claim thus appears patently reasonable and, as such, well suited to generate widespread support and acquiescence. Such support and acquiescence, once combined with military action justified on the basis of the claim, could quickly generate new customary international law.

Yet the reformulated doctrine of pre-emptive self-defence is not as innocuous as it first appears. By adopting and stretching the pre-1945 criterion of imminence, the approach advocated in the National Security Strategy could introduce much more ambiguity into the law. This ambiguity could, in turn, allow power and influence to play a greater role in the application of the law. In future, whether the criterion of imminence is fulfilled would depend in large part on the factual circumstances – as assessed by individual states and groups of states. And the ability of the powerful to influence these assessments could be considerable, given the various forms of political, economic and military pressure that can be brought to bear in international affairs. In addition, powerful countries sometimes have special knowledge based on secret intelligence, or at least claim such knowledge in an attempt to augment their influence, as occurred in the lead-up to the 2003 Iraq War. As a result, the criterion of imminence would more likely be regarded as fulfilled when the United States wished to act militarily than when other countries wished to do the same. The law on self-defence would remain generally applicable – available as a diplomatic tool to be deployed against weak states – while the most powerful of countries would have more freedom to act as they chose.

Fortunately, the US government does not have a monopoly on good international lawyers. A few regional powers, such as India, Israel and Russia, did respond favourably to the claim set out in the National Security Strategy, as did Australian Prime Minister John Howard, who suggested that the UN Charter be amended to allow for a right of unilateral pre-emptive action. But Howard's comments sparked angry protests from other Southeast Asian states – protests which could themselves constitute state practice and evidence of *opinio juris* against a right of pre-emptive self-defence. Other countries, including France, Germany and Mexico, expressed concern in more moderate terms, while Japan voiced support for a right of pre-emptive self-defence but was careful to confine its claim to the *Caroline* criteria.

As the Iraq crisis escalated, this at-best mixed reaction contributed to bringing the United States to the UN Security Council where, on 8 November 2002, it obtained Resolution 1441. As was explained in Chapter 3, the resolution did not expressly authorize the use of force against Iraq but did provide some support for an argument that a previous authorization, accorded in 1990, had been revived as a result of Iraq's 'material breaches' of the 1991 ceasefire resolution. The Bush Administration relied on both this argument and the pre-emptive self-defence claim to justify the 2003 Iraq War, while its two principal allies, Britain and Australia, relied solely on the Security Council resolutions. The advancement of two distinct arguments, with the latter receiving broader support, reduced any effect that the claim to an extended right of pre-emptive self-defence might have had on customary international law.

Following the war, widespread opposition to the Bush Doctrine was evident in the opening speeches of the 58th session of the UN General Assembly in September 2003. Hidipo Hamutenya, the Foreign Minister of Namibia, observed that 'the central theme, that runs through nearly all the speeches at this Session, is the call for a return to multilateral dialogue, persuasion and collective action, as the only appropriate approach to resolving many conflicts facing the international community'.

In light of this and other negative reactions, it is difficult to argue that the claim to an extended right of pre-emptive self-defence has obtained the widespread support necessary to change customary international law or, perhaps, Article 51 of the UN Charter. Yet the claim continues to be made. In a television interview on 7 February 2004, President Bush went so far as to say: 'I believe it is essential – that when we see a threat, we deal with those threats before they become imminent. It's too late if they become imminent. It's too late in this new kind of war.'

In December 2004, the UN Secretary General's High Level Panel on Threats, Challenges and Change, a group of sixteen former prime ministers, foreign ministers and ambassadors (including Brent Scowcroft, who served as National Security Adviser to President George H. W. Bush), presented its highly authoritative response to the US president's claim:

> The short answer is that if there are good arguments for preventive military action, with good evidence to support them, they should be put to the Security Council, which can authorize such action if it chooses to. If it does not so choose, there will be, by definition, time to pursue other strategies, including persuasion, negotiation, deterrence and containment – and to visit again the military option.
>
> For those impatient with such a response, the answer must be that, in a world full of perceived potential threats, the risk to the global order and the norm of non-intervention on which it continues to be based is simply too great for the legality of

unilateral preventive action, as distinct from collectively endorsed action, to be accepted. Allowing one to so act is to allow all.

The report was a stinging rebuke to the Bush Administration, and intended to be understood as such. The goal was not to change the president's mind (it will not), but to rally and reinforce international opposition to his dangerously destabilizing doctrine of pre-emptive war.

Part Three

Humanitarian Intervention

7

Pro-Democratic Intervention

United Nations Security Council authorization and the right of self-defence are written exceptions to the prohibition on the use of force and expressly set out in the UN Charter. Two further, unwritten exceptions may have developed in recent decades: a right to intervene militarily to promote or restore democracy, and a right to intervene to prevent serious human rights abuses or violations of international humanitarian law such as genocide, mass expulsion or systematic rape. This chapter considers 'pro-democratic intervention'. Chapter 8 examines 'humanitarian intervention'.

One year after the 2003 Iraq War, President George W. Bush and Prime Minister Tony Blair began speaking passionately about the importance of bringing 'democracy and freedom' to Iraq and the Middle East. The implication was obvious: the promotion of democracy was an after-the-fact justification for the war. Yet the democracy argument was not invoked until Iraq's alleged weapons of mass destruction – the principal justification for the war both under Resolution 1441 and the Bush Doctrine of pre-emptive self-defence – proved more elusive than expected. Credible legal justifications cannot be made retroactively. The failure to advance the democracy argument at the time of the invasion of Iraq suggests, among other things, an absence of belief (*opinio juris*) in the legality of the claim.

There are no credible precedents for the claim of pro-democratic intervention. In the absence of precedents, there is no supporting state practice or *opinio juris* and, therefore, no possible rule of customary international law. The UN Security Council could authorize an intervention for the purposes of supporting or restoring democracy, as it arguably did in Haiti in 1994, but individual countries or groups of countries cannot legally take such action on their own. Even the two possible precedents cited by some academics – the invasions of Grenada (1983) and Panama (1989) – do not provide assistance here. Closer scrutiny of these interventions reveals that, if anything, they reinforce the contrary rule: that the use of force to promote democracy is prohibited under customary international law unless expressly authorized by the Security Council.

Four hundred US marines and 1,500 paratroopers landed on the Caribbean island nation of Grenada on 25 October 1983, together with 300 soldiers from neighbouring Caribbean countries. The invasion came in response to a violent *coup d'état* by radical Marxist opponents of the democratically elected government of Maurice Bishop. It took just three days for the invading soldiers to depose the newly self-appointed Revolutionary Military Council. The US troops were home within eight weeks. Casualties numbered just over 100: 18 Americans, some 45 Grenadines (including 21 civilians killed in the accidental bombing of a hospital) and 34 Cuban soldiers (who were supporting the Marxists).

The Reagan Administration offered several justifications for the invasion. First, the United States cited an invitation from the Governor-General of Grenada received the day before the invasion was launched. However, evidence of the actual invitation is elusive. *The Economist*, which strongly supported the invasion, reported that the 'request was almost certainly a fabrication concocted between the OECS [Organization of Eastern Caribbean States] and Washington to calm the post-invasion diplomatic storm'. Moreover, the invasion was already in an advanced stage of implementation by the time the request would have been received. Although the timing of the request does not touch on the legality of the invasion, it does indicate that the invitation was not considered decisive by the United States.

Second, the United States cited a request to intervene from the OECS and claimed that the request was of legal import under Article 52 of the UN Charter. However, Article 52 deals solely with the 'pacific settlement of local disputes'. Forceful actions by regional organizations are dealt with under Article 53, where it is made clear that 'no enforcement action shall be taken under regional arrangements or by regional agencies without the authorization of the Security Council'. Authorization had not been provided with regard to Grenada.

Finally, the United States advanced a claim of self-defence for the protection of nationals, a specific rule discussed in Chapter 4. Yet the facts supporting the claim have been disputed. The United States asserted that Grenadine officials had refused to allow its citizens to leave the island, while Canada claimed to have flown a chartered plane to and from Grenada on the day of the invasion. In any event, David Robinson, the Legal Adviser at the US State Department at the time, subsequently admitted that the scale of the operation exceeded the limits of this 'well-established, narrowly drawn ground for the use of force'.

The United States never claimed that it was intervening in Grenada to restore democracy. In fact, David Robinson went so far as to stress the grounds on which it did *not* rely: an expanded view of self-defence, 'new interpretations' of Article 2(4) of the UN Charter, or 'a broad doctrine of "humanitarian intervention"'. The same is true of the Caribbean states involved, who claimed that the action was 'to help stabilize the country', 'restore law and order' and, above all, 'block the Russians and the Cubans'. Even if the United States and its allies had invoked the restoration of democracy to justify the intervention, the most relevant state practice and evidence of *opinio juris* would be the negative reactions of other governments. A UN Security Council resolution that would have condemned the invasion was vetoed by the United States. The General Assembly, free of such constraints, 'deeply deplored' the US-led action as a flagrant violation of international law. Rather than providing support for a right of pro-democratic intervention, the invasion of Grenada helped strengthen the rule against such actions.

On 20 December 1989, the United States deployed 26,000 troops to overthrow the government of Panama and capture its head of state, General Manuel Noriega. President George H. W. Bush justified the action on four grounds: 'to safeguard the lives of Americans, to defend democracy in Panama, to combat drug trafficking, and to protect the integrity of the Panama Canal Treaty'. Having captured Noriega, the United States recognized the 'rightful leadership' of the likely victors of elections that had been held earlier that year. Diplomatic relations would resume immediately, steps would be taken to lift the economic sanctions imposed against the Noriega regime, and US forces would be withdrawn 'as quickly as possible'. Apparently oblivious to the irony, Bush added that he would 'continue to seek solutions to the problems of this region through dialogue and multilateral diplomacy'. Analysis of the legal basis for the action – optimistically codenamed 'Just Cause' – is made difficult by the conflation of policy and legal reasoning in such statements.

Of the four grounds outlined above, the protection of nationals most closely resembled a legal argument. During the UN Security Council debate on the matter, the US ambassador stated: 'I am not here today to claim a right on behalf of the United States to enforce the will of history by intervening in favour of democracy where we are not welcomed. We are supporters of democracy but not the gendarmes of democracy, not in this hemisphere or anywhere else...We acted in Panama for legitimate reasons of self-defence and to protect the integrity of the Canal Treaties.'

While the right of self-defence in protection of nationals was the primary legal justification advanced by Washington, the defence of democracy claim garnered the most support from academics. Professor Anthony D'Amato of Northwestern University described US actions in Panama (and previously Grenada) as 'milestones along the path to a new nonstatist conception of international law'. Professor Michael Reisman of Yale University heralded a new era in which 'the people, not governments, are sovereign'. In a remarkably isolationist conception of customary international law, each scholar ignored – or at least discounted as irrelevant – the broad condemnation of the Panama intervention by the international community. A strongly condemnatory draft UN Security Council resolution was vetoed by the United States and Britain, while similar resolutions were adopted by the General Assembly – where all UN members are represented – and the Organization of American States.

The US government invoked democracy to support the invasion of Panama in two ways: as the exercise of a right to act unilaterally to promote democracy in other countries, and as the provision of assistance to a democratically elected head of state, Guillermo Endara, who had ostensibly consented to the action. But the United States never claimed that Endara had requested the invasion. Although Bush stated that Endara 'welcomed the assistance' of the United States and there was some reference to him having been 'consulted', Endara was not informed of the invasion until the troops were in the air. Journalist Bob Woodward reported that Bush had decided this was the point of no return and that, if Endara refused to 'play ball', Secretary of Defense Dick Cheney and General Colin Powell – who were overseeing the operation – were to check with Bush personally. Endara was sworn in as President of Panama at Fort Clayton, a US military base in the US-controlled Canal Zone, less than an hour before the invasion began.

There is, in fact, evidence that Endara was not entirely pleased with the operation, having later described it as a 'kick in the head'. In any event, most Latin American countries withdrew their ambassadors from Panama after the invasion and refused to recognize the Endara government, stating that diplomatic relations would be normalized only when the number of US troops in the country returned to pre-invasion levels and a plebiscite demonstrated popular support for the new regime. The Permanent

Council of the Organization of American States initially refused to accept the credentials of the ambassador dispatched by Endara. Noriega's ambassador remained at the organization's headquarters in Washington and participated in the vote that criticized the invasion. Some months passed before most countries recognized Panama's new government. This widespread reluctance to recognize the Endara government, coupled with strong objections from many states in the UN Security Council, the condemnatory resolution adopted by the UN General Assembly, and the fact that the restoration of democracy was only one of four justifications advanced by the United States, are further evidence that pro-democratic intervention remains prohibited under international law. George Bush and Tony Blair can talk all they want about the need to bring 'democracy and freedom' to the Middle East, but they cannot, by themselves, create a new right to military action.

The UN Charter's prohibition on the use of force also bars the provision of forceful assistance to opposition groups, even those seeking to bring democracy to their country. In 1970, the UN General Assembly adopted a 'Friendly Relations Resolution' that encapsulated the rule:

> Every State has the duty to refrain from organizing, instigating, assisting or participating in acts of civil strife or terrorist acts in another State or acquiescing in organized activities within its territory directed towards the commission of such acts, when the acts referred to in the present paragraph involve a threat or use of force.

The International Court of Justice reaffirmed the rule in 1986, in the *Nicaragua Case*, where the government of Nicaragua successfully sued Washington for using force, and particularly for training and equipping the Contras, the right-wing opposition forces operating out of neighbouring Honduras. The only exception to the rule – and it remains controversial – concerns support for national liberation movements seeking to expel colonial powers. Financial assistance to opposition groups is likewise permitted because no force is used.

If pro-democratic intervention and forceful assistance to opposition groups are both prohibited, what then of interventions, not authorized by the UN Security Council, that are aimed at preventing governments from committing mass atrocities against their own citizens? This issue – unilateral humanitarian intervention – is the subject of the next chapter.

8

Unilateral Humanitarian Intervention

The prohibition on the use of force has increasingly been challenged by scholars, politicians and commentators who believe that national governments that systematically murder, rape or expel their own citizens should not be shielded against military intervention. Convinced that the UN Security Council cannot be relied upon to address these problems, and that the United Nations – rather than its member states – is somehow to blame, they argue for a right of 'unilateral humanitarian intervention', that is, a right to intervene for humanitarian purposes without the authorization of the Security Council.

Advocates of such a right cite a handful of possible precedents, including India's intervention in East Pakistan (1971), Vietnam's intervention in Cambodia (1978), Tanzania's intervention in Uganda (1979) and the intervention in Northern Iraq (1991) by Britain, France, Italy, the Netherlands and the United States. A brief examination of these four instances reveals that none of the intervening countries, apart from Britain in 1991, advanced an argument of humanitarian intervention. Even then, Britain quickly abandoned its claim in favour of arguing that it had the implied authorization of the UN Security Council, as discussed in Chapter 3. Overall, this near absence of *opinio juris* deprived the state practice of any capacity to change international law to allow a right of unilateral humanitarian intervention.

The Kosovo War (1999) is frequently cited as having changed this calculus in favour of a new rule, though in the end only two NATO countries claimed a legal right to humanitarian intervention. And, as was the case when India invaded East Pakistan in 1971, most countries publicly opposed the war.

A largely Muslim country comprising East and West Pakistan was created as a result of the decolonization and partition of India in 1947. Although Bengali-speaking East Pakistan was separated from Urdu-speaking West Pakistan by more than 1,000 miles of Indian territory, the western province dominated political, economic and military affairs. In 1970, the Awami League, a political party that advocated autonomy for East Pakistan, won the majority of seats – and all but two of East Pakistan's seats – in the Pakistani National Assembly. Pakistan's military president, General Yahya Khan, responded by refusing to convene the Assembly. Widespread demonstrations then broke out, and Khan invoked martial law. In March 1971, the leader of the Awami League, Sheikh Mujibur Rahman, was arrested and taken to West Pakistan. On 26 March, his party issued a 'Declaration of Emancipation'. General Khan immediately sent the Pakistani army into Dacca.

At least one million people were killed in the following nine months, many of them children and most of them Hindu. The ethnic dimension of the conflict led the International Commission of Jurists, a widely respected non-governmental organization, to identify the campaign of violence as an apparent genocide. Awami League members were arrested, tortured and killed, as were countless community leaders. Women were systematically raped, villages looted and destroyed, and up to ten million people fled across the border into India.

The vast number of refugees caused massive social, economic and administrative problems for India and relations between New Delhi and Islamabad declined sharply. India provided refuge and air support for the Mukti Bahini, an armed Bengali liberation movement, and border incidents multiplied. War broke out on 3 December 1971 when Pakistan bombed ten Indian military airfields. Within days, India had occupied most of East Pakistan and recognized the province as the sovereign and independent country of Bangladesh. The Pakistani Army surrendered after just twelve days of fighting and Sheikh Mujibur returned to Dacca to become prime minister. Three years later, the new country was admitted to the United Nations.

Professor Fernando Tesón of Florida State University has described the Indian action as 'an almost perfect example' of humanitarian intervention. The use of force did stop a horrific campaign of repression. Yet the India government advanced a very different legal claim. Although humanitarian grounds figured prominently in the political justifications that were advanced initially, this rhetoric was soon replaced by a legal argument of self-defence. As India's representative on the UN Security Council explained, 'We decided to silence their guns, to save our civilians.'

Even the use of humanitarian crisis as political justification was opposed strongly by other countries. During the UN Security Council debate following the intervention, the US representative said: 'The fact that the use of force in East Pakistan in March can be characterized as a tragic mistake does not, however, justify the actions of India in intervening militarily and placing in jeopardy the territorial integrity and political independence of its neighbour Pakistan.' Even Sweden, a notably progressive country on international human rights issues, emphasized that 'the Charter of the United Nations forbids the use of force except in self-defence. No other purpose can justify the use of military force by States.' A Security Council resolution calling for a ceasefire and the immediate withdrawal of Indian troops from the country was vetoed by the Soviet Union, which at the time was a close ally of India. The UN General Assembly adopted essentially the same resolution in a 104–11 vote, with ten abstentions. Most importantly, not one country endorsed India's humanitarian intervention claim, so no *opinio juris* was expressed in its favour.

In the period between 1975 and 1978, the Khmer Rouge government of Cambodia (Kampuchea) murdered hundreds of thousands of its own citizens and implemented policies that killed millions more through starvation and disease. Under the leadership of General Pol Pot, the Khmer Rouge also launched a series of cross-border attacks on Vietnam. Vietnam responded by invading Cambodia on 25 December 1978. Fighting alongside Cambodian opposition forces, Vietnamese troops quickly established control over most of the country, capturing Phnom Penh on 7 January 1979.

Vietnam claimed that it was acting solely to defend itself against Cambodian aggression, and that the overthrow of Pol Pot's regime was the result of an internal uprising. The self-defence argument was widely rejected by other countries, apart from Vietnam's closest allies: the Soviet Union and its satellite states. However, since the invasion ended the humanitarian crisis, and since the suffering involved had been of such huge dimension, most governments felt it necessary to go further and address the possibility that stopping the atrocities might somehow have legitimized the use of military force. For example, the French representative to the UN Security Council said:

> The notion that because a regime is detestable foreign intervention is justified and forcible overthrow is legitimate is extremely dangerous. That could ultimately jeopardize the very maintenance of international law and order and make the continued existence of various regimes dependent on the judgement of their neighbours.

Similar emphatic statements were made by Australia, Britain, France, Indonesia, Malaysia, Nigeria, Norway, the Philippines, Portugal, Singapore and Yugoslavia. Even Bangladesh, the beneficiary of India's 1971 invasion of East Pakistan, reaffirmed the principle of non-intervention in domestic affairs. A resolution to the same effect was introduced in the Security Council by seven of its developing country members. The document also called on all foreign forces – Vietnamese forces – to withdraw. Thirteen countries voted in favour of the resolution, and only two – the Soviet Union and Czechoslovakia – voted against it, with the Soviet vote acting as a veto.

The UN General Assembly was equally unsupportive of what Vietnam had done. In September 1979 it rejected a demand for accreditation from the new, Vietnamese-sponsored government in Phnom Penh and instead accepted the credentials of a Khmer Rouge delegation. General Pol Pot's regime, confined to a remote area near the border with Thailand, represented Cambodia in the General Assembly for nine more years. In November 1979, the General Assembly voted 91–21, with 29 abstentions, in favour of a resolution that demanded the immediate withdrawal of all foreign forces and an end to interference in the domestic affairs of Southeast Asian states.

A handful of countries did support the Vietnamese action on humanitarian grounds. For example, the East German representative to the UN General Assembly asserted that 'the assistance of Vietnam in the struggle for a new Kampuchea was primarily a humanitarian matter. It rescued the Kampuchean people from total destruction.' Such expressions of support, however, were not only in the minority, but came from countries that had less-than-stellar human rights records. Democratic, human rights-respecting countries condemned unanimously both the Vietnamese intervention and the atrocities committed by Pol Pot's regime. As the Norwegian representative to the United Nations explained:

The Norwegian Government and public opinion in Norway have expressed strong objections to the serious violations of human rights committed by the Pol Pot Government. However, the domestic policies of that Government cannot – we repeat, cannot – justify the actions of Vietnam over the last days and weeks. The Norwegian Government firmly rejects the threat or use of force against the territorial integrity or political independence of any State.

The 1978 Vietnamese invasion of Cambodia provides no support for a right of unilateral humanitarian intervention in international law. During the Cold War, geopolitical competition between the United States and the Soviet Union precluded any new exception to the prohibition of the use of force in international affairs.

Idi Amin served as president of Uganda for eight bloodstained years. He and his henchmen murdered some 300,000 of their fellow citizens and countless more were tortured, raped or otherwise brutalized. Although many countries condemned the Ugandan regime for these human rights violations, no significant action was taken until 1978 when Amin sent troops into neighbouring Tanzania and declared that he was annexing the northwest corner of that country. Julius Nyerere, the President of Tanzania and one of Africa's most respected heads of state, responded that the purported annexation was 'tantamount to an act of war'. Nyerere ordered his troops to push Amin's forces back into Uganda. The Ugandan dictator made a plea for reinforcements and Libya's Colonel Muammar Qaddafi obliged, sending 2,500 troops. In March 1979, Tanzania launched a full-fledged counter-attack. With the help of Ugandan rebels, the Tanzanian troops soon overwhelmed the Ugandan army, gained control of the country and installed Yusufu Lule as president. Amin fled into exile, first to Libya and later to Saudi Arabia, where he lived in luxury until his death in August 2003.

Despite Amin's atrocious human rights record, Tanzania never sought to justify its intervention on humanitarian grounds, relying instead on a claim of self-defence. As Nyerere explained:

The war between Tanzania and Idi Amin's regime in Uganda was caused by the Ugandan Army's aggression against Tanzania and Idi Amin's claim to have annexed part of Tanzania. There was no other cause for it.

Tanzania also asserted, much as Vietnam had done eight years earlier, that a domestic uprising had led to the overthrow of the opposing government. In this instance, most countries accepted the self-defence claim, some of them – including Angola, Botswana, Mozambique and Zambia – expressly, but most tacitly. When Amin asked that the UN Security Council meet to discuss the situation, the request fell on deaf ears. The UN General Assembly accredited the new Ugandan government less than six months after Amin was ousted from power. Tanzanian forces were out of the country within two years.

A few academic international lawyers have invoked Tanzania's actions as a precedent for a right of unilateral humanitarian intervention. The atrocities committed by the Amin dictatorship could have provided a strong factual basis, but only if Tanzania had chosen to make the claim. Even then, the weight of the precedent would depend on the reaction of other countries. But Tanzania never claimed a humanitarian motivation, let alone a right to intervene for humanitarian purposes. This absence of *opinio juris* on the part of the acting power renders the intervention in Uganda irrelevant to legal discussions concerning unilateral humanitarian intervention, except as a reflection of the general awareness that no such right could plausibly be claimed.

Some of the geopolitical constraints on a possible right of unilateral humanitarian intervention changed after the collapse of the Soviet Union and the end of the Cold War, though widespread support for a change in international law has yet to appear.

During the 1991 Gulf War, the United States encouraged the Kurds of northern Iraq and the Shiites of southern Iraq to rebel against Saddam Hussein's regime. Yet Resolution 687, adopted by the UN Security Council to secure and regulate the ceasefire between Iraq and the coalition forces, did nothing to protect the Kurds and Shiites from the violent retribution that followed. As news of the horrors reached Western capitals and hundreds of thousands of desperate refugees appeared on television screens, the Security Council begrudgingly passed Resolution 688. This resolution identified the situation as a threat to international peace and security, called on the Iraqi government to end the repression and demanded access to northern Iraq for international humanitarian organizations. On this basis, in April 1991, American, British, Dutch, French and Italian forces were deployed in northern Iraq as part of 'Operation Provide Comfort', establishing so-called 'safe havens' to protect Kurdish civilians.

Resolution 688 did not expressly authorize the use of force against Iraq. The intervening countries weakly suggested that the Security Council's determination of a threat to international peace and security constituted implicit authority for their actions. One country – the United Kingdom – used the occasion to advance a doctrine of unilateral humanitarian intervention when the British Foreign and Commonwealth Office said:

> We believe that international intervention without the invitation of the country concerned can be justified in cases of extreme humanitarian need. This is why we were prepared to commit British forces to *Operation Haven*, mounted by the coalition in response to the refugee crisis involving the Iraqi Kurds.

The Foreign Office proceeded to suggest that the doctrine should be limited to situations where: 1) there is a compelling and urgent situation of extreme humanitarian distress; 2) the state targeted by the intervention is unable or unwilling to act; 3) there is no practical alternative; and 4) the intervention is limited in time and scope. Although the claim was unprecedented among governments, it was also deliberately restrained. The British government never specifically claimed a 'legal' right, speaking instead of 'justification', which could refer to moral, political or legal grounds. And the United Kingdom did not advance the claim in the United Nations, probably out of concern that it would be badly received.

Even if there were considerable state practice and *opinio juris* in favour of a right of unilateral humanitarian intervention, the international law on this issue might remain unchanged. Since clear treaty provisions prevail over customary international law, a customary rule allowing intervention would be insufficient to override Article 2(4) of the UN Charter. Nor could deficiencies in the United Nations system enable countries to fall back on a customary rule allowing intervention on humanitarian grounds. When, in the 1949 *Corfu Channel Case*, Britain sought to justify an intervention in Albanian territorial waters on the basis that no one else was prepared to deal with the threat of mines laid in an international strait, the International Court of Justice ruled:

> The Court cannot accept this line of defence. The Court can only regard the alleged right of intervention as the manifestation of a policy of force, such as has, in the past, given rise to the most serious abuses and such as cannot, whatever be the present defects in international organization, find a place in international law.

Accordingly, in light of Article 2(4) of the UN Charter, any right of unilateral humanitarian intervention could have effect only if it achieved the status of *jus cogens*, a peremptory rule that overrides conflicting treaty provisions. This clearly had not occurred before 1999, but what then of the Kosovo War? Did the state practice and *opinio juris* associated with that intervention constitute the broad consensus necessary to generate a new customary rule with the capacity to override the UN Charter?

Albanian and Slavic peoples have coexisted in Kosovo since the eighth century. Initially part of the Serbian Empire, Kosovo became part of the Ottoman Empire in 1389. Serbia regained control in 1913 and in 1946 Kosovo became part of the Federal Republic of Yugoslavia. When Slobodan Milošević became president of Yugoslavia in 1989, one of his first acts was to strip Kosovo of its status as an autonomous province. Following the break-up of Yugoslavia in the early 1990s, and facing increasingly frequent attacks on Serb targets by an ethnic Albanian guerrilla movement, the Kosovo Liberation Army (KLA), President Milošević initiated a brutal crackdown that provided all the indications of a genocide in the making. The United States and its European allies, embarrassed by their failure to stop the earlier atrocities in Bosnia-Herzegovina, warned that such acts would not be tolerated. The UN Security Council twice deemed the situation a threat to 'international peace and security' before Milošević – now being threatened with war by NATO (a regional *defence* alliance) – agreed to internationally brokered negotiations with the KLA at Rambouillet, France. The negotiations came close to securing a peace agreement, until Milošević baulked at a patently unreasonable provision that would have granted NATO forces unrestricted access to all Yugoslav territory, not just in Kosovo.

Although the numbers of Kosovo-Albanians killed, raped or expelled up to this point were low, the credibility of NATO's threats was at issue. On 24 March 1999, the United States and a number of other NATO countries inaugurated a long campaign of air strikes against Serbian forces in Kosovo and government targets in Serbia and Montenegro. They did so without attempting, in the couple of months before the attack, to discuss the matter in the UN Security Council. A Security Council resolution condemning the attack was quickly proposed by Russia, but defeated, in large part because the five NATO countries then on the Council voted against it.

In the end, only two NATO countries – initially the United Kingdom and later Belgium – sought to justify the Kosovo War on the basis of a legal right to unilateral humanitarian intervention. NATO Secretary General Javier Solana confined himself to saying, 'We must halt the violence and bring an end to the humanitarian catastrophe now unfolding.' There was thus a remarkable absence of *opinio juris* to accompany the state practice involved in the intervention. Russia, China and India spoke out strongly against the war, as did Namibia (which had voted in the Security Council to condemn the bombings), Belarus, Ukraine, Iran, Thailand, Indonesia and South Africa. Following the intervention, the 133 developing countries of the 'Group of 77' twice adopted declarations unequivocally affirming that unilateral humanitarian intervention was illegal under international law.

Shortly after the war ended, the UN Security Council adopted Resolution 1244, which gave the United Nations a central role in Kosovo's reconstruction. Although the resolution was carefully worded to preclude any argument that it retroactively authorized the war, some academics have argued that it did so. Similar arguments have been made about the defeat of the Russian-proposed resolution condemning the intervention. These arguments ignore the fact that the UN Charter requires a positive rather than negative authorization, and the possibility that a less angrily worded draft might have attracted more support.

The Kosovo War was neither consistent with international law nor effective in changing the law in favour of a right of unilateral humanitarian intervention. As the International Court of Justice indicated in the 1986 *Nicaragua Case*, international rules usually continue in force despite the occasional violation:

> It is not to be expected that in the practice of States the application of the rules in question should have been perfect, in the sense that States should have refrained, with complete consistency, from the use of force or from intervention in each other's internal affairs. ... In order to deduce the existence of customary rules, the Court deems it sufficient that the conduct of States should, in general, be consistent with such rules, and that instances of State conduct inconsistent with a given rule should generally be treated as breaches of that rule, not as indications of the recognition of a new rule.

Much more state practice and *opinio juris* would be needed before a right of unilateral humanitarian intervention, as an exception to the well-established prohibition of the use of force, could reasonably be considered to have acquired legal force. Even then, any new rule of customary international law would not – unless it somehow achieved *jus cogens* status – override Article 2(4) of the UN Charter. For these reasons, the significance of humanitarian concerns to the international law on the recourse to force remains at the level of political will – and moral and political justification, including what is now called the 'responsibility to protect'.

9

Responsibility to Protect

Following the 1999 Kosovo War, the British Foreign Office submitted a proposal to the United Nations for a carefully defined, limited right of unilateral (i.e. not Security Council authorized) humanitarian intervention – one that 1) would only be available as a last resort; 2) addressed an overwhelming humanitarian catastrophe which the territorial government was unable or unwilling to prevent; 3) involved force that was both proportionate and in accordance with international law; and 4) was exercised by a group of states rather than an individual state. The proposal was attacked on so many fronts that it was quickly withdrawn.

United Nations Secretary General Kofi Annan found himself in a difficult position. His initial reaction to the Kosovo War was to say: 'Emerging slowly, but I believe surely, is an international norm against the violent repression of minorities that will and must take precedence over concerns of State sovereignty.' Later in 1999, however, Annan acknowledged that this norm had not yet achieved legal status and, moreover, that its development could have undesirable consequences for the international order. Annan said: 'What is clear is that enforcement action without Security Council authorization threatens the very core of the international security system founded on the Charter of the UN. Only the Charter provides a universally accepted legal basis for the use of force.' People who, like the Ghanaian-born Secretary General, seek a more peaceful world immediately encounter the dilemma that the constraints imposed by the existing rules on the use of force may – by preventing an unknown number of armed conflicts – already be saving many lives, and that this benefit could be compromised by any attempt to create a new right of unilateral humanitarian action.

To address this dilemma, Canada established an independent body – the International Commission on Intervention and State Sovereignty – and charged it with finding 'some new common ground'. The commissioners, who included former Australian Foreign Minister Gareth Evans, former Philippine President Fidel Ramos, former US Senator Lee Hamilton and the Canadian author Michael Ignatieff, would seem to have disagreed on some of the issues. The resulting report, entitled 'The Responsibility to Protect', contains some passages that favour a right of unilateral humanitarian intervention:

> Based on our reading of state practice, Security Council prece-
> dent, established norms, emerging guiding principles, and
> evolving customary international law, the Commission believes
> that the Charter's strong bias against military intervention is not
> to be regarded as absolute when decisive action is required on
> human protection grounds.

But in their chapter on 'The Question of Authority', the commissioners come to a final conclusion that cuts against this analysis and is distinctly unhelpful to proponents of unilateral humanitarian intervention:

> As a matter of political reality, it would be impossible to find
> consensus... around any set of proposals for military interven-
> tion which acknowledged the validity of any intervention not
> authorized by the Security Council or General Assembly.

Consensus – or at least very widespread agreement – is a necessary condition for the making or changing of international rules on the use of military force.

Three years later, the commissioners' conclusion was confirmed by another leading group of experts, the UN Secretary

General's High Level Panel on Threats, Challenges and Change. Although the High Level Panel endorsed the concept of the responsibility to protect, it also made clear that, when it comes to the use of military force, the responsibility to protect may only be exercised by the UN Security Council. The Panel proceeded to propose its own series of guidelines, or 'criteria of legitimacy', concerning when force should be used: seriousness of intent, proper purpose, last resort, proportional means and balance of consequences. But the promotion of these criteria was in no way intended to limit the discretionary power of the Council – and only the Council – to deploy force for humanitarian ends.

Although the report of Canada's International Commission was the result of a painful compromise between moral aspiration and political reality, many proponents of unilateral humanitarian intervention – including Lloyd Axworthy, the foreign minister who provided the impetus for the formation of the group – rely upon it readily. Axworthy, in his book *Navigating a New World: Canada's Global Future*, describes the 'gist of the report' as follows:

> [S]overeignty is not a prerogative but a responsibility. It is a way of coming both at the tyrants who hide behind the walls of sovereignty and at those states that can't or won't protect their citizens, without usurping the right of those states that exercise their sovereign duty to care for their people.

Axworthy and most other proponents of the 'responsibility to protect' are motivated by a desire to prevent human suffering. However, by arguing for a new and largely self-judging exception to the UN Charter's prohibition on the use of force, they play into the hands of those who would seek exemption for less benevolent ends.

British Prime Minister Tony Blair has provided the most worrying example of the potential for politically motivated abuse of a right to unilateral humanitarian intervention. In a speech in his Sedgefield constituency in March 2004, he explained how:

[B]efore September 11th, I was already reaching for a different philosophy in international relations from a traditional one that has held sway since the treaty of Westphalia in 1648; namely that a country's internal affairs are for it and you don't interfere unless it threatens you, or breaches a treaty, or triggers an obligation of alliance.

This passage would likely be endorsed by Axworthy and other well-intentioned proponents of the responsibility to protect – were its application left abstract. But Blair proceeded to apply the concept retroactively to Iraq, stating specifically and emphatically: '[W]e surely have a responsibility to act when a nation's people are subjected to a regime such as Saddam's.'

Suddenly, a highly contentious war – justified ostensibly on the basis of a series of UN Security Council resolutions – was being rationalized, one year after the fact, with a doctrine that had already been widely rejected by most of the world's governments. Blair's invocation of a responsibility to protect undoubtedly related back to the all-too-apparent absence of weapons of mass destruction in Iraq, but it was also forward-looking. For Blair – who in his Sedgefield speech claimed almost in passing that existing international law allows for unilateral humanitarian intervention in situations of genocide, mass expulsion and systematic rape – also indicated explicitly a desire to change international law to extend the responsibility to protect to a broader range of circumstances, including tyranny and famine.

The problem with such an objective, of course, is that the many countries that currently oppose a limited right of unilateral humanitarian intervention will oppose, even more strongly, any claim that seeks to go further. Blair, in a truly audacious move, responded to this challenge by seeking to substitute the traditional requirement of state consent in international law-making with the concept of community: 'The essence of a community is common rights and responsibilities. We have obligations in relation to each other. ... And we do not accept in a community that others have a right to oppress and brutalize their people.' As morally appealing as this approach may be, Blair seemed unable to grasp what it means to live under the rule of law, particularly when the community subject to that law – the international community, in this case – has already established clear and firm rules. In Sedgefield, he went on to say, with no apparent sense of irony:

> I understand the worry the international community has over Iraq. It worries that the US and its allies will, by sheer force of their military might, do whatever they want, unilaterally and without recourse to any rule-based code or doctrine. But our worry is that if the UN – because of a political disagreement in its Councils – is paralysed, then a threat we believe is real will go unchallenged.

This is a vision of power without accountability, exercised by supposedly benevolent leaders with the best interests of their subjects in mind. At the same time, it is reminiscent of a much earlier natural law approach to international law – one that did not require broad-based consent and was instead imposed by the so-called 'civilized'. The prime minister, by reaching for the concept of community, was in fact relying on the international law of the crusaders and conquistadors – which, in essence, was no law at all. Were Blair truly concerned about the plight of the world's oppressed, he would have done better to focus on the other, non-military aspects of the responsibility to protect.

Like the British prime minister, most proponents of the responsibility to protect focus on the concept's potential implications for military intervention. But despite its title, the 'Report of the International Commission on Intervention and State Sovereignty' makes clear that military intervention will only ever be appropriate in 'extreme cases' and that the responsibility to protect encompasses a far broader range of options and obligations. Notable among these is a 'responsibility to prevent' by addressing the 'root causes' of internal conflicts and other threats to civilian populations caused by humans. As the report explains:

> This Commission strongly believes that the responsibility to protect implies an accompanying responsibility to prevent. And we think that it is more than high time for the international community to be doing more to close the gap between rhetorical support for prevention and tangible commitment. The need to do much better on prevention, and to exhaust prevention options before rushing to embrace intervention, were constantly recurring themes in our worldwide consultations, and ones which we wholeheartedly endorse.

The report identifies numerous dimensions to the prevention of root causes. These include support for democratic institutions, press freedom and the rule of law, provision of development assistance and improved terms of trade, and the promotion of arms control, disarmament and nuclear non-proliferation regimes. The overwhelming focus of the responsibility to protect is thus the prevention of conflict through a range of non-military measures that would entail significantly larger transfers of wealth, expertise and opportunity from developed to developing countries. The responsibility to protect entails taking Third World development seriously. From this perspective, any perceived need to engage in humanitarian intervention will usually result from a failure to live up to the responsibility to protect on the part of those who wish to intervene.

It is a reflection of the lack of commitment to this original, broader conception of the responsibility to protect that in April 2004, ten years after the 1994 Rwanda genocide, UN Secretary General Kofi Annan felt it necessary to release a five-point plan for the prevention of similar atrocities in future. The plan emphasizes the main point of the 2001 Report of the International Commission on Intervention and State Sovereignty: that the key to preventing armed conflict and mass atrocities lies in addressing root causes. The Secretary General also recommended that more be done to protect civilians during armed conflict, support the International Criminal Court, and ensure 'early and clear warning' of potential genocides. In July 2004, Annan appointed Argentine law professor Juan Méndez as his Special Adviser on the Prevention of Genocide, assigning him the task of reporting to the Security Council and the General Assembly on unfolding or potential genocides. Finally, as the International Commission on Intervention and State Sovereignty had done, Annan specified that force should only be used as a last resort, and that the instrument for humanitarian intervention must remain the Security Council. He stressed: 'Anyone who embarks on genocide commits a crime against humanity. Humanity must respond by taking action in its own defence. Humanity's instrument for that purpose must be the United Nations, and specifically the Security Council.' This latter point was further reinforced in December 2004, in the Report of the Secretary General's High Level Panel on Threats, Challenges and Change.

In a world where the use of force remains governed by the UN Charter and most countries still believe that the Security Council is functioning appropriately, conflict prevention is the only area where the responsibility to protect could add something new and useful. If developed countries were to redirect just a portion of their current military budgets to foreign aid and development, it should be possible to prevent most armed conflicts and humanitarian crises. In 2003, the United States spent $417 billion on its military, the United Kingdom $37 billion, and the fifteen leading spenders a staggering $723 billion combined. In comparison, the total amount spent on foreign aid by *all* of the world's countries during the same period came to $60 billion, with much of that aid being linked to the purchase of goods and services from donor states, or involving the suspension or cancellation of longstanding foreign debts.

Preventive action taken early will almost always be less expensive than military action taken later. As the International

Commission on Intervention and State Sovereignty explained with regard to the intervention that prompted its own creation and thus the development of the concept of responsibility to protect: 'In Kosovo, almost any kind of preventive activity... would have had to be cheaper than the $46 billion the international community is estimated to have committed at the time of writing in fighting the war and following up with peacekeeping and reconstruction.' The Commission's report was written during the summer and autumn of 2001. Today, the UN Interim Administration Mission in Kosovo retains full authority over the territory with the support of 18,000 NATO-backed peacekeepers and at a massive, ongoing cost to developed states. Worse yet, additional costs are borne indirectly by distressed populations in other needy countries and territories, which, as a result of the redirection of peacekeeping, aid and development budgets to Kosovo, have for five years been deprived essential support. The subsequent interventions in Afghanistan and Iraq have only exacerbated the problem of a seemingly limited pool of money being siphoned from one crisis to another in response to the shifting attentions of Western governments and media. Proponents of the responsibility to protect who focus on military intervention are participating in a terrible charade.

Part Four

International Law during Armed Conflict

Protection of Civilians

More than 300 Iraqi civilians died on 13 February 1991 when two
US F-117 stealth bombers targeted the Al'Amiriya bunker in
Baghdad. Photographs of the charred and twisted bodies of
women and children shocked a world which, thanks to General
Norman Schwarzkopf and CNN, had seen little of the horrors of
the Gulf War. Pentagon officials, who claimed to have intelligence
indicating the bunker was a command and control centre, denied
knowledge of the civilian presence. Had they known, the attack
would probably have been a war crime.

International humanitarian law – the *jus in bello* – governs *how*
wars may be fought. It is distinct from the law governing *when*
wars may be fought: the *jus ad bellum* of the UN Charter and self-
defence, as discussed in Chapters 1 to 9. Also known as the 'laws
of war' or the 'law of armed conflict', international humanitarian
law seeks to limit the human suffering that is the inevitable consequence of war. As a body of law, it traces its origins to 1859, when
the Swiss businessman Henri Dunant witnessed the aftermath of
the Franco-Austrian Battle of Solferino – in which 40,000 men
died, many as the result of untreated wounds – and initiated a
movement that became the International Committee of the Red
Cross (ICRC).

Today, the rules of international humanitarian law are found
primarily in the four Geneva Conventions of 1949 (and the prede-
cessor Hague Conventions of 1907). The Geneva Conventions are
aimed at protecting, respectively: the wounded and sick on land;
the wounded, sick and shipwrecked at sea; prisoners of war; and
civilians (who are technically referred to as 'non-combatants').

The protections guaranteed under these treaties are replicated and elaborated in two Additional Protocols of 1977, a multitude of more specific treaties and a parallel body of unwritten customary international law.

A key principle of international humanitarian law prohibits the direct targeting of civilians, as Article 51(2) of Additional Protocol I explains:

> The civilian population as such, as well as individual civilians, shall not be the object of attack. Acts or threats of violence the primary purpose of which is to spread terror among the civilian population are prohibited.

In addition to its presence in this widely ratified treaty, the rule against the direct targeting of civilians during armed conflict is generally considered to have achieved the status of customary international law, and therefore binds all countries, including those that have not ratified the relevant conventions, treaties and protocols.

It follows that civilians cannot be collectively punished. The actions of US forces in Fallujah, Iraq, in April 2004, following the killing and mutilation of four US contractors, certainly looked like war crimes from afar. Hundreds of civilians were killed, many of them with apparent indiscrimination, as US marines fought their way into the densely populated city – before retreating out of concern about US public opinion, and popular uprisings around Iraq provoked by Arab news reports of the many innocents killed. Immediately after the US presidential election on 2 November 2004, the marines moved back into Fallujah with a vengeance. Howitzers and 2000-pound bombs, neither of which are particularly precise weapons, were used to soften up the city. Fuel-air explosives were dropped on residential neighbourhoods and virtually every house was struck by US tank, machine-gun or rifle fire.

Even if the assault on Fallujah was not motivated by revenge, it appears to have been an illegally indiscriminate attack – because all reasonable measures were not taken to avoid harming civilians. The 'carpet bombing' of North Vietnam in the early 1970s was a violation of international humanitarian law, as were moves to designate certain villages as 'free-fire zones', as was famously the case at the village of My Lai in 1968 when 300 civilians were massacred by US soldiers. Iraq violated the same rule when it fired eleven Scud missiles at Israel during the 1991 Gulf War. The Scuds, notoriously inaccurate to begin with, were rendered even more inaccurate by modifications that were designed to extend their range. They were aimed at the general vicinity of Tel Aviv, rather than at specific military targets, and their use justifiably provoked outrage. The use of B-52 bombers to lay down swathes of destruction in the Basra area of Iraq in 1991 was probably not a war crime because the bombing was directed solely against the Iraqi Republican Guard, though the International Committee of the Red Cross and Human Rights Watch have concluded otherwise.

Given the indiscriminate character of the assault on Fallujah, the duty to protect civilians was probably also violated when US forces refused to allow men between the ages of fifteen and forty-five to leave the city before the attack. Hundreds if not thousands of innocents may have perished as a result, not just of the attacks, but of the discrimination on the basis of sex and age that put them in harm's way. The United States continued to violate international humanitarian law, as it and its allies have done throughout the Iraq War and occupation, by refusing to count and document the Iraqi dead. According to the *New York Times*, the first goal of the November 2004 assault on Fallujah was to capture the city's general hospital because 'the American military believed that it was the source of rumours about heavy casualties' and 'this time around, the American military intends to fight its own information war, countering or squelching what has become one of the insurgents' most potent weapons'. Article 16 of the First Geneva Convention of 1949 is categorical with regard to the relevant obligation: 'Parties to the conflict shall record as soon as possible, in respect of each wounded, sick or dead person of the adverse Party falling into their hands, any particulars which may assist in his identification...[and] shall prepare...certificates of death or duly authenticated lists of the dead.' The same rule exists as part of customary international law. Here, and in too many other circumstances, the United States, Britain and Australia are committing war crimes that they could easily avoid.

Civilians are neither members of the armed forces of a 'belligerent' (that is to say, a party to the conflict), nor do they play a direct or active part in the hostilities. A contractor who delivers ammunition to combatants is actively taking part in hostilities, but what about one who is merely delivering food, water or sanitary supplies? If the same contractor is alternating between delivering ammunition and delivering food, he or she is not a civilian, just like the person who fights by night and pretends to be a non-combatant by day.

International humanitarian law seeks to draw the clearest possible distinction between combatants and civilians. In order to be considered soldiers, individuals should be in a chain of command, wear identifiable insignia, carry their weapons openly, and act in accordance with the laws of war. The sanction for non-compliance with these requirements is the loss, if captured, of 'prisoner of war' status and the standards of treatment it requires. The rationale is that individuals who do not fight fairly – wearing uniforms, carrying their weapons openly, etc. – do not deserve the protection of the rules. The distinction simultaneously rewards soldiers for being readily identifiable and deters civilians from entering the fray, thereby keeping the line between combatants and civilians as discernible as possible and maximizing civilian safety.

Mercenaries – persons who fight solely for financial gain – are not entitled to be treated as prisoners of war. The increasing use of private contractors by the US military, in some cases very near or even in combat zones, raises questions as to what, if any, rights – beyond international human rights – these individuals have if captured by opposing armies. At the same time, the extended involvement of these contractors in activities traditionally reserved to military personnel is obfuscating the all-important distinction between combatants and civilians, with potentially serious consequences. Journalists, for instance, are considered civilians even when 'embedded' within armed units, provided they do not themselves take up arms. Journalists may not be targeted by military forces, though they put themselves at risk of being accidentally or incidentally harmed whenever they approach or enter a combat zone. The risk to journalists has increased in proportion to the growth in numbers of militarily active contractors wearing civilian clothes, since enemy forces cannot readily distinguish one group from the other.

Balancing 'military necessity' against the protection of civilians is seldom easy, either for targeting or choosing weapons. However, some general constraints remain: attacks must be deliberate and tend towards the military defeat of the enemy; they must not cause harm to civilians or civilian objects that is excessive in relation to the direct military advantage anticipated; and military necessity does not justify violating other rules of international humanitarian law. Usually, the boundary between acceptable and unacceptable targets will depend on the facts of the specific situation. For example, the tower of a mosque is normally inviolable, since places of worship and cultural property enjoy special protection, but may become a legitimate target if used by a sniper. Although balancing military necessity against risks to civilians is always required, international humanitarian law accepts that wars are fought to be won, while containing belligerents within a sphere of (relatively) civilized behaviour.

During the 1991 Gulf War, these obligations were taken seriously. Desert Storm was the first major combat operation undertaken by the United States after the Vietnam War. Fearful of another domestic backlash if things went wrong, the politicians left the conduct of hostilities to professional soldiers – who are trained to fight by the book. Adherence to the rule of law was further aided by the fact that the United States was part of a substantial coalition. Some allies of the United States accord considerable importance to the requirements of international humanitarian law, and so, in order to maintain the coalition, the United States had to fight according to the rules.

Some 200 US military lawyers were dispatched to the Gulf. Legal experts vetted every targeting decision. A strike on a statue of Saddam Hussein in Baghdad was ruled out on the basis that only targets that contribute to the war effort are permissible under international humanitarian law. Those legal controversies that arose stemmed from differing interpretations of the law, rather than any desire to ignore legal constraints. At least five British officers resigned their commissions after the United States used cluster bombs and fuel-air explosives to attack Iraqi weaponry, with devastating effects on enemy soldiers. A similar divergence of views arose over the use of earthmovers and tank-mounted ploughs to bury Iraqi soldiers alive in their trenches, thus avoiding the dangers of hand-to-hand combat. International humanitarian law forbids methods of warfare that cause 'unnecessary suffering or superfluous injury', but where one sets the balance between military necessity and humanitarian concerns also depends, perhaps inevitably, on where one is coming from – during the 1990s, the US government was particularly concerned to avoid American casualties.

After decades of massive defence spending, the United States is today assured of victory in any war it chooses to fight. High-tech weaponry has reduced the dangers to US personnel, making it easier to sell war to domestic constituencies. As a result, some US politicians had begun – at least until the quagmire in Iraq – to view armed conflict as an attractive foreign policy option in times of domestic scandal or economic decline, rather than the high-risk recourse of last resort. This change in thinking has led to a more cavalier approach to the *jus ad bellum*, as exemplified by the Bush Doctrine of pre-emptive self-defence, and is beginning to have a similar effect on the *jus in bello*. When war is seen as a tool of foreign policy – Clausewitz's 'politics by other means' – political and financial considerations may distort the balance between military necessity and humanitarian concerns.

In Washington, it has become accepted wisdom that future opponents are unlikely to abide by international humanitarian law. This assumption has been fuelled by events. During the 1991 Gulf War, captured American pilots were brutalized in several ways, some having been raped. The September 2001 attacks on the Twin Towers breached international humanitarian law as 'crimes against humanity', a category of international criminal law that concerns violent acts committed as part of systematic attacks on civilian populations. And during the 2003 war, Iraqi soldiers committed the war crime of 'perfidy' by using civilian clothes and white flags to trick and then kill opposing forces. If your enemy is going to cheat, why bother playing by the rules?

No love has been lost between Defense Secretary Donald Rumsfeld and his military lawyers. In October 2002, CIA operatives used an unmanned Predator reconnaissance aircraft to track the Taliban leader Mullah Omar to a building in a residential area of Kabul. The air strike to kill Omar was called off because a lawyer at US Central Command was concerned about the risk of disproportionate civilian casualties. According to a report in the *New Yorker*, the incident left Rumsfeld 'kicking a lot of glass and breaking doors'. The Secretary sought – unsuccessfully – to reduce the number of lawyers in uniform.

Rumsfeld also encouraged a re-evaluation of the prohibition on targeting civilians, particularly with regard to actions directed at shattering support for opponent regimes. This kind of thinking was popular during the Second World War – as evidenced by the firebombing of Dresden, Hamburg and several cities in Japan – but was subsequently rejected during the negotiation of the 1949 Geneva Conventions. In the last several years, a theory claiming that every regime has 'five strategic rings' has attracted adherents in Washington. According to this view, each ring represents a different facet of a society: political leadership, economic system, supporting infrastructure, population and military forces. Air power is supposed to enable the United States to target opponents from the 'inside out', bypassing military forces and attacking the political leadership directly. In this context, the indirect harm caused to civilians – through the destruction of bridges, electrical grids, oil refineries and water-filtration plants – is considered justified because it promotes dissatisfaction within the regime and thus hastens the course of the conflict (while, incidentally, reducing the cost of victory).

During the 1991 Gulf War, the United States targeted the Iraqi national electrical grid, shutting down hospitals as well as water and sewage stations. The health consequences for civilians were severe, but the strikes were legal because Iraqi military communications depended heavily on the grid. In 1999, when Slobodan Milošević's forces proved much more resilient than expected, the United States pushed for the adoption of a looser approach, which led to the use of more questionable military tactics. Electrical grids and water-filtration plants in Serbia were targeted, not to disrupt the actions of the Yugoslav Army in Kosovo but to provoke domestic opposition to Milošević's government in Belgrade.

Equally problematic was the targeting of the State Serbian Television and Radio station in April 1999, as well as the Iraqi State Television station in March 2003. The two stations were legitimate targets if they had been integrated into military communications networks, but not if they were simply being used for propaganda. Again, applying the rules often has as much to do with finer points of fact as it does with those of law.

In 1991, a number of coalition warplanes (especially British Tornados) were lost to Iraqi anti-aircraft fire because they were bombing from low altitudes in order to reduce civilian casualties. Less accurate high-altitude strikes by B-52s were restricted to targets well clear of civilian areas. Almost all the bombing during the Kosovo War was carried out above the reach of Serbian air defences. As a result of the high altitudes, NATO pilots were sometimes unable to distinguish between military and civilian targets, with disastrous results for several refugee convoys. Again, as a result of the United States taking a somewhat different approach to these issues, there is now a different reckoning of the balance between military necessity and humanitarian concerns.

The Kosovo War was complicated by the fact that Yugoslavia had ratified Additional Protocol I, which imposes stricter protections for civilians than the Geneva Conventions. Since the United States was the only member of NATO not to have ratified the Protocol, and therefore not bound to uphold its standards reciprocally vis-à-vis Yugoslavia, certain types of missions were allocated only to US pilots. Canadian pilots, who train with their American counterparts, were not assigned as wingmen to US pilots in missions over the former Yugoslavia: the Canadian pilots could not be relied upon to respond to some threats, such as anti-aircraft fire coming from a school or hospital, in the same way that US pilots would. Whether countries such as Canada and Britain are collectively liable under Protocol I for the actions of US pilots operating under NATO targeting procedures remains an open question. Carla Del Ponte, the prosecutor for the International Criminal Tribunal for the former Yugoslavia, chose not to investigate any of NATO's alleged war crimes. The issue did not arise in Iraq in 2003, since Saddam never ratified Protocol I.

Precision-guided missiles give rise to a further complication. When civilians are present, international humanitarian law requires belligerents to use weapons that can distinguish between civilians and combatants; it follows that they should usually use the most accurate weapons available to them. In another instance of political and financial cost-benefit analysis intruding into international humanitarian law, the United States argues that this requirement imposes an unfair burden on it, given the substantial production costs of smart bombs. Extending the same logic, it could be argued that, because precision-guided weapons reduce the number of civilian casualties across a campaign, attacking forces using them may exercise less concern for the protection of civilians when making individual targeting decisions, since the overall collateral damage will still be less than in a low-tech war.

Applying such calculations to rules designed to protect human beings is not only inappropriate, but also immoral.

The use of weapons that cause superfluous injury or unnecessary suffering is also prohibited under international humanitarian law. Explosive or expanding ('dum-dum') bullets, booby-traps and blinding laser weapons are banned outright on the basis that the military benefits of their use can never be proportionate to the suffering they cause. A special treaty – the 1925 Geneva Protocol – unequivocally prohibits the use of poisonous gas and biological weapons. These prohibitions have achieved the status of customary international law, as was confirmed by the harshly negative reaction of other countries to the use of nerve and mustard gas during the Iran–Iraq War of the 1980s. Other weapons have been banned by most but not all countries. The United States' refusal to ratify the 1997 Ottawa Landmines Convention can create awkward situations for its allies. In 2001, Canadian soldiers operating in Afghanistan were ordered by their US commander to lay mines around their camp. When the Canadians refused to do so, US soldiers, who were not subject to the same restrictions, laid the mines. Depleted uranium, cluster bombs and fuel-air explosives are among the weapons whose use remains legally uncertain. Favoured for their armour-piercing abilities, depleted uranium shells leave radioactive residues that can pose health problems for civilians and combatants alike. Given the scientific uncertainty as to the extent of the risk, humanitarian concerns should prevail – though depleted uranium was used extensively in Iraq in 2003 (as, indeed, were cluster bombs). Again, political and financial expediency have seemingly influenced the balance between humanitarianism and military necessity, at least for the United States.

Nuclear weapons are not banned but their use is subject to the constraints of international humanitarian law. Although it is difficult to envision how the use of nuclear weapons could not cause suffering disproportionate to military gain, the Pentagon in March 2002 issued a *Nuclear Posture Review* that cited the need for new nuclear weapons specifically designed to destroy deeply buried command centres and biological weapon facilities. In February 2003, the British Defence Secretary Geoff Hoon stated that Britain reserved the right to use nuclear weapons against Iraq in 'extreme self-defence'. Hoon sought to justify his assertion on the basis of a 1996 advisory opinion of the International Court of Justice in which the Court could not 'conclude definitively whether the threat or use of nuclear weapons would be lawful or unlawful in an extreme circumstance of self-defence, in which the very survival of a state would be at stake'. But Hoon omitted to mention the latter part of this passage, which (as quoted here) clearly shows that his reliance on the opinion was misplaced. The only state whose survival was at stake in February 2003 was Iraq.

Hoon's advisers would have done better to direct him to the rules concerning belligerent reprisals. Actions that violate international humanitarian law (though not acts that violate the *jus ad bellum*) can become legally justifiable when taken in response to violations of the law by the other side. The purpose of belligerent reprisals is to deter further violations, and the possibility of reprisal is often cited as the reason countries comply with international humanitarian law. But belligerent reprisals must be proportionate to the original violation and cannot be directed towards civilians or objects indispensable to the survival of civilians. The apparently indiscriminate targeting of civilians in Fallujah, Iraq, in April 2004 – after the killing and mutilation of four US contractors – could not be legally justified, even as a belligerent reprisal.

No treaty specifically prohibits belligerent reprisals carried out with otherwise prohibited weapons. This raises the possibility that it might be legal to use nuclear weapons in response to the use of chemical or biological weapons. In 1991, then US Secretary of State James Baker privately warned Saddam Hussein that any recourse to chemical or biological weapons would result in a tactical nuclear response by the United States. More recently, the Bush Administration has shown no compunction about making the threat publicly. *The National Strategy to Combat Weapons of*

Mass Destruction, released in December 2002, 'reserves the right to respond with overwhelming force – including through resort to all of our options – to the use of WMD against the United States, our forces abroad, and friends and allies'. But the use of any nuclear weapon, even as a belligerent reprisal, would almost certainly cause disproportionate civilian suffering and thus violate international humanitarian law.

The military power of the United States prevailed in the Iraq War. A number of reluctant allies were pressured into providing practical and political support. Many critics of the invasion – and of the United States' conduct during it – were initially silenced, not just by the victory but because only a few thousand civilians had been killed. But balancing military necessity and humanitarian concerns was never the exclusive province of Donald Rumsfeld and like-minded advisers such as Paul Wolfowitz. Most international humanitarian law treaties contain something called the Martens Clause, which in its original form was drafted by the Russian delegate to the conferences that produced the Hague Conventions of 1907:

> Until a more complete code of the laws of war is issued, the high contracting Parties think it right to declare that in cases not included in the Regulations adopted by them, populations and belligerents remain under the protection and empire of the principles of international law, as they result from the usages established between civilized nations, from the laws of humanity, and the requirements of the public conscience.

International humanitarian law is, in part, what you and I and the rest of the people on this planet determine it to be. In the lead-up to future wars – and throughout the ongoing occupation of Iraq – we should insist that all countries uphold the strict standards of international humanitarian law, not because it is expedient but because it is right.

Protection of Combatants and Prisoners of War

Soldiers are legitimate targets during armed conflict. Killing members of the enemy's armed forces is one of the goals of military action. Still, soldiers – referred to under international humanitarian law as 'combatants' – benefit from some protections, including the prohibition on the use of certain types of weapons discussed in the previous chapter. The proscription of chemical and biological weapons benefits combatants as well as civilians, as does the ban on booby-traps, the developing ban on anti-personnel landmines set out in the 1997 Ottawa Landmines Convention, and the limitations on the use of nuclear weapons. The prohibitions on explosive or expanding bullets and blinding laser weapons are directed more specifically at protecting soldiers, as is the requirement that soldiers who have been wounded or wish to surrender must be captured rather than killed.

Soldiers who have been wounded are deemed *hors de combat* (out of combat) and accorded protections similar to those that apply to civilians. Soldiers who lay down their arms or otherwise clearly express 'an intention to surrender' become prisoners of war. Wounded soldiers and prisoners of war cannot be killed, used as human shields, held hostage, or used to clear landmines. The execution-style shooting of a wounded and unarmed Iraqi in Fallujah in November 2004, as captured on tape by an embedded television cameraman, was almost certainly a war crime.

Medical personnel benefit from similarly strict protections, while medical facilities, ambulances and hospital ships are off-limits as targets unless used as locations from which to launch attacks. As with many rules of international humanitarian law, this rule is sometimes honoured in the breach. In 1992 and early 1993, the main hospital in Sarajevo, Bosnia-Herzegovina, was hit by no less than 172 mortar shells while full of patients.

Civilians can be protected in time of armed conflict only if a distinction is maintained between combatants and non-combatants. This differentiation is achieved by offering combatants the protection of prisoner of war status if captured, as long as they are in a chain of command, wearing a fixed distinctive emblem (usually a shoulder patch), carrying their arms openly and acting in accordance with international humanitarian law. These incentives are not always effective, especially in conflicts involving irregular forces in poorer countries, and some experts argue that the distinctive emblem requirement is inconsistent with modern forms of war. Apart from their turbans, the armed forces of the Taliban government did not wear anything approaching uniforms during the 2001 Afghanistan War, though they were in a chain of command, carried their arms openly and, for the most part, abided by international humanitarian law.

The distinction between combatants and non-combatants is most severely threatened by the practice of US special forces, who constitute an increasingly important part of the US military yet have – with the apparent support of Secretary of Defense Donald Rumsfeld – taken to wearing civilian clothing. The practice has been challenged. When the New Zealand government sent a contingent of commandos to fight in Afghanistan, it refused to allow the soldiers to wear civilian clothes, a decision that created some friction with the United States. The decision was correct: if special forces – indeed, any soldiers – are captured operating out of uniform, they are not entitled to the protections owed to prisoners of war regardless of the country for which they fight. Although this consequence may seem unduly harsh, it is based on the rationale that soldiers who do not wear their uniforms are not fighting fairly, and are needlessly endangering civilians, and consequently do not deserve the full protections of international humanitarian law. The policy of allowing US special forces to wear civilian clothes entails unnecessary risks for individual soldiers and civilians; perhaps in recognition of this, the practice – at least in Afghanistan – has since been reversed.

Rumsfeld's disdain for international humanitarian law became blatantly apparent in January 2002 when suspected Taliban and al-Qaeda members were transported to the US naval base in Guantánamo Bay, Cuba. Ignoring public criticism from a number of European leaders, the UN High Commissioner for Human Rights and even the normally neutral and extraordinarily discrete International Committee of the Red Cross, the Secretary of Defense insisted the detainees were not prisoners of war and refused to convene the tribunals required under Article 5 of the Third Geneva Convention relative to the Treatment of Prisoners of War to determine their status. Rumsfeld also ignored advice from the Pentagon's own lawyers, the 'judge advocates', and based his decision on an analysis of international humanitarian law by then White House Counsel (now Attorney General) Alberto Gonzales, a former corporate lawyer from Texas. Three years after the war in Afghanistan, nearly 600 suspects remain at Guantánamo Bay despite having never been charged or granted access to counsel. Only forty-two detainees have been released, including five Saudis who were traded for six Britons (and one Belgian) who had been arrested and tortured in Riyadh. More than thirty detainees have attempted suicide.

In November 2002, the English Court of Appeal correctly described the position of the Guantánamo Bay detainees as 'legally objectionable'; it was as if they were in a 'legal black hole'. The situation has improved marginally since then. On 29 June 2004, the US Supreme Court finally addressed the matter. On behalf of a 6–3 majority of judges, Justice John Paul Stevens wrote:

> Executive imprisonment has been considered oppressive and lawless since John, at Runnymede, pledged that no free man should be imprisoned, dispossessed, outlawed, or exiled save by

the judgment of his peers or by the law of the land. The judges of England developed the writ of habeas corpus largely to preserve these immunities from executive restraint.

Stevens went on to hold that anyone detained by the US government outside the United States has the right to have the legal basis for his detention reviewed by a US federal court. Just one week later, the Pentagon announced that it would in fact convene the status determination tribunals required by Article 5 of the Third Geneva Convention.

These Article 5 tribunals are not courts, but rather panels of three US military officers who review the facts pertaining to each detainee and determine whether he or she is a prisoner of war. The detainees are not provided access to lawyers. Instead, military officers are assigned as their 'personal representatives'. The absence of legal counsel and the non-judicial nature of the process probably fail to meet the standards of due process envisaged by the Supreme Court in its June 2004 decision. The matter is now the subject of a new round of litigation and the Supreme Court may eventually rule further. The Bush Administration's belated move to respect the Third Geneva Convention is nothing more than an attempt to buy more time to interrogate the Guantánamo Bay detainees outside the constraints of domestic and international law.

The Article 5 status determination tribunals are different from the military commission concurrently established to criminally prosecute three of the detainees at Guantánamo Bay. This military commission, and other commissions to come, are the result of a November 2001 presidential order. The order permits the US military to create the commissions to try detainees and authorizes the imposition of the death penalty when all three of the military officers who serve like judges agree. The commissions apply procedures similar to regular military courts, albeit with tighter controls on the release of evidence to defence counsel and journalists. The accused is provided with lawyers, or may engage his own. The presumption of innocence applies, as does the usual burden of proof, namely 'guilty beyond a reasonable doubt'. However, the Third Geneva Convention stipulates that POWs must, if charged with crimes, be tried in the regular military courts of the detaining country. The operation of the status determination tribunals could thus, by determining that individual detainees are POWs, remove them from the purview – and relative secrecy – of the military commissions. This possible consequence helps explain Rumsfeld's refusal to create such tribunals in January 2002. How one views the situation will depend on whether one trusts the US government to play it straight with intelligence, and treat detainees fairly, even behind closed doors.

Widespread violations of international humanitarian law have been committed against detainees in Afghanistan and Iraq. In November 2001, a prisoner revolt at Mazar-i-Sharif was put down with air-to-surface missiles and B-52 launched bombs. More than 175 detainees were killed; fifty died with their hands tied behind their backs. In December 2002, the *Washington Post* reported on the use of 'stress and duress' techniques during interrogations at Bagram air base in Afghanistan. In March 2003, the *New York Times* reported that, while in custody over a three-month period, a suspected member of al-Qaeda was 'fed very little, while being subjected to sleep and light deprivation, prolonged isolation and room temperatures that varied from 100 degrees to 10 degrees'. Ten degrees Fahrenheit is easily cold enough to kill. Also in March 2003, the *New York Times* reported that a death certificate, signed by a US military pathologist, stated the cause of death of a twenty-two-year-old Afghan detainee at Bagram air base in December 2002 as 'blunt force injuries to lower extremities complicating coronary artery disease'. The form gave the pathologist four choices for 'mode of death': 'natural, accident, suicide, homicide'. She marked the box for homicide. A week earlier, another Afghan detainee – just thirty years old – had reportedly died of a pulmonary embolism.

In July 2003, UN Secretary General Kofi Annan reported to the Security Council that his Special Representative for Iraq, the late Sergio Vieira de Mello, had expressed concern to the United States and Britain about their treatment of thousands of detained Iraqis. One week later, Amnesty International claimed that US forces in Iraq were resorting to 'prolonged sleep deprivation, prolonged restraint in painful positions – sometimes combined with exposure to loud music, prolonged hooding and exposure to bright lights'.

Regrettably, the reports failed to attract widespread media attention until March 2004, when it became known that the *New Yorker* was about to publish photographs of prisoner abuse at Abu Ghraib prison near Baghdad, together with a damning report by investigative journalist Seymour Hersh. At this point, CBS television decided to air photographs it had been suppressing for several weeks, reportedly at the behest of the Bush Administration. The photographs showed detainees stripped naked, ridiculed, piled on top of each other, being raped, forced to masturbate, bitten by dogs, and terrorized with the threat of electrocution. The actions were blatant violations of both international humanitarian law and the detainees' international human rights.

Given the proximity to the 2003 Iraq War, it is likely that some of the detainees at Abu Ghraib were prisoners of war. If so, the captors who abused them violated the Third Geneva Convention, Article 13 of which provides that POWs 'must at all times be protected, particularly against acts of violence or intimidation and against insults and public curiosity'. To reinforce the point, Article 14 stipulates that prisoners of war 'are entitled in all circumstances to respect for their persons and their honour'.

Any of the captives at Abu Ghraib who were not prisoners of war were probably still protected by Common Article 3 of the Geneva Conventions. This provision requires that, even in armed conflicts not of an international character (as, arguably, the situation in Iraq had become), persons taking no part in the hostilities are protected absolutely from 'violence to life and person, in particular murder of all kinds, mutilation, cruel treatment and torture' as well as 'outrages upon personal dignity, in particular, humiliating and degrading treatment'. (The first part of Common Article 3 is reproduced in Chapter 5.)

Regardless of the status of the detainees, some of the outrages committed against them were violations of the 1984 Convention against Torture and Other Cruel, Inhuman or Degrading Treatment or Punishment, a treaty ratified by the United States and universally regarded as codifying customary international law. Article 1 of the Convention defines torture as:

> [A]ny act by which severe pain or suffering, whether physical or mental, is intentionally inflicted on a person for such purposes as obtaining from him or a third person information or a confession, punishing him for an act he or a third person has committed or is suspected of having committed, or intimidating or coercing him or a third person, or for any reason based on discrimination of any kind, when such pain or suffering is inflicted by or at the instigation of or with the consent or acquiescence of a public official or other person acting in an official capacity.

A confidential memorandum, prepared for Secretary of Defense Rumsfeld by a group of Bush Administration lawyers in March 2003 and obtained by the *Washington Post* in June 2004, argued that the President was not bound by the provisions of the Third Geneva Convention or the Convention against Torture, at least insofar as these international rules are implemented in US domestic law. The analysis was based on an earlier Department of Justice memorandum that made a series of dubious assumptions – including that none of the detainees were prisoners of war and that customary international law and US federal law are hermetically sealed from each other – that together transformed legal analysis into an exercise in politically motivated justification. That memorandum was written by John Yoo, a political appointee who has since returned to his regular position as a law professor at the University of California, Berkeley. The *New York Times* reported that the State Department Legal Adviser, William Taft IV, dissented from the group's analysis and its conclusions, 'warning that such a position would weaken the protections of the Geneva Conventions for American troops'.

The abuse of detainees engages the responsibility not only of individual soldiers. Under a principle of international criminal law known as 'command responsibility', individuals higher in the chain of command – including defence secretaries and presidents who serve as commanders-in-chief – may also commit war crimes if they know, or have reason to know, that their subordinates are committing or are about to commit crimes and fail to take all feasible steps to prevent or stop the violations. Article 12 of the Third Geneva Convention provides but one articulation of the principle:

> Prisoners of war are in the hands of the enemy Power, but not of the individuals or military units who have captured them. Irrespective of the individual responsibilities that may exist, the Detaining Power is responsible for the treatment given them.

Additional violations of international humanitarian law were committed when the International Committee of the Red Cross was denied access to some parts of Abu Ghraib prison, and to some detainees, as reportedly occurred early in 2004. Under the 1949 Geneva Conventions and the 1977 Additional Protocols, the ICRC is mandated to visit and register prisoners of war. This right of access is essential because it promotes the good treatment of prisoners of war and ensures they do not disappear. Although the ICRC traditionally does not publicly denounce governments that fail to uphold international humanitarian law – in order to preserve its neutrality, thereby ensuring future access to prisoners and civilians in need – it has, on several occasions since 2001, openly expressed concern about the actions of the United States.

Many of the ICRC's concerns persist today with regard to persons detained by the United States or its allies in a variety of known and unknown locations, including in Afghanistan and at a US airbase on the British-owned Indian Ocean island of Diego Garcia. The ICRC has not been provided access to these individuals – itself a violation – and there is no way of knowing whether they are being tortured, otherwise mistreated, or killed.

In the same context, a second confidential memorandum obtained by the *Washington Post* in October 2004 was reportedly used to justify a related war crime: the transfer of detainees out of occupied Iraq for interrogation elsewhere. Article 49 of the Fourth Geneva Convention protects civilians during an occupation by unambiguously prohibiting 'individual or mass forcible transfers, as well as deportation of protected persons from occupied territory … regardless of their motive'. Indeed, one of the principal purposes of the Fourth Geneva Convention is to prevent persons from being moved out of an occupied territory and thus out of the oversight of the International Committee of the Red Cross. The memorandum, which strains legal credulity, was written by Jack Goldsmith, who served as a political appointee at the Pentagon and Department of Justice, and is now a professor of law at Harvard University.

Even alleged terrorists are protected by the ban on extra-judicial killing found in numerous human rights treaties and customary international law. When it comes to extra-judicial killings, George W. Bush's State of the Union address in January 2003 included a damning admission: 'All told, more than 3,000 suspected terrorists have been arrested in many countries. Many others have met a different fate. Let's put it this way – they are no longer a problem to the United States and our friends and allies.' Previous administrations at least paid lip service to the existence of normative constraints by concealing and denying their covert operations. The Bush Administration, during its more arrogant moments, lets the mask slip – to the discredit of the nation and, by undermining the already fragile edifice of international humanitarian law, at the peril of the individual soldiers whom so many of the rules are designed to protect.

War Crimes Courts and Tribunals

'This is theatre. Bush is the real criminal.'

With a smile, Saddam Hussein, looking fit and well groomed despite nearly seven months of interrogations and solitary confinement, condemned the Iraqi Special Tribunal established to try him and senior members of his regime for alleged atrocities. Saddam's allegations of political bias resonate deeply. During a television interview shortly after his capture, President George W. Bush stated: 'He is a torturer, a murderer, and they had rape rooms, and this is a disgusting tyrant who deserves justice, the ultimate justice.'

Dishevelled, confused and compliant when captured in December 2003, Saddam must have seemed the perfect puppet for an election-year show trial. Salem Chalabi, the nephew of the once omnipresent and now discredited Iraqi opposition leader Ahmad Chalabi, was handpicked by US envoy L. Paul Bremer to direct the production. A statute for the tribunal was quickly drafted, drawing heavily on the Rome Statute of the International Criminal Court; a slate of safely anti-Saddam judges was rubber-stamped by Bremer's Iraqi Governing Council. The FBI was assigned to gather evidence; twenty US lawyers were dispatched to support the prosecution. After the Governing Council had been hastily transformed into a supposedly sovereign interim government in June 2004, one of its first acts was to reintroduce the death penalty. Only the resurgent and all-too-predictable resilience of Saddam, the hardened dictator, frustrated the careful preparations.

Saddam's transfer to Iraqi authorities and his first court appearance on 1 July 2004 were small concessions to international law: the Third Geneva Convention requires that prisoners of war be either charged or released at the end of hostilities. Bush, citing security concerns, initially resisted transferring custody over Saddam to the Iraqi interim government, but was soon reminded that unnecessary violations of the Geneva Conventions can lead to diplomatic trouble – not to mention judicial review by the newly vigilant US Supreme Court. And so Saddam and eleven other senior Iraqi officials were handed over, though, as with the transfer of sovereignty, the transfer was formal rather than practical. Saddam and his henchmen remain under US lock and key. The only print journalists allowed to attend the hearing were American. Al-Jazeera and CNN were permitted to film the event – carefully timed to coincide with prime-time breakfast television stateside – but had to block out the sound of Saddam's voice.

At first it seemed that Saddam might be denied the right to choose his own lawyers, especially after his senior wife, Sajidah, assembled a multinational legal defence team, some of whom wanted to put the United States on trial. There were no defence lawyers in the courtroom during Saddam's first appearance before the tribunal. The president of the tribunal, Salem Chalabi, even raised the possibility of holding the trial in secret, but this measure would have too clearly exposed the bias of the proceedings. The impropriety of the Iraqi court is not its capacity to determine and apply the law, as international human rights organizations were quick to assert. Not only does the statute of the new tribunal take the bulk of its provisions directly from the governing instrument of the International Criminal Court; international experts could be provided to assist the judges, prosecution and defence. Carefully selected Iraqi jurists could, with time and patience, grasp the intricacies of international criminal law and apply them to complex facts. Rather, the problems with using an Iraqi tribunal to try the former dictator concern inadvertent bias, the likelihood of rushed procedures, and the absence of international legitimacy.

As with most members of the Iraqi Governing Council and interim government, the judges of the tribunal will have suffered as a result of Saddam's actions; few Iraqis escaped the shadow of his rule. The inexorable conflict between judicial functions and personal interests has led most of the world's legal systems to preclude victims acting as judges or jurors. While we grieve with victims and families, we would not wish them to determine guilt.

As for speed, one member of the Iraqi Governing Council indicated initially that Saddam's trial might start within weeks of his capture. At the time, others spoke of a conviction in June 2004. It now seems likely that proceedings will begin in 2005. Iraqis are accustomed to swift justice. During Saddam's rule, trials – if held at all – rarely took more than a day. Yet the evidence against Saddam is voluminous. The final charge sheet could contain tens of thousands of crimes, including murder, torture, mass rape, armed aggression, using chemical weapons, mistreating prisoners of war, and perhaps even genocide. Some 50,000 people died in Saddam's 1988 campaign against the Kurds, during which chemical weapons were used on at least sixty occasions. Rooms full of documents will need to be read and a multitude of victims and witnesses will wish to testify. Mounting a rigorous defence will be an awesomely difficult, time-consuming task. Yet a rigorous defence there must be. By providing due process to those individuals accused of the most heinous crimes, societies demonstrate their adherence to the rule of law and the rightness of the punishments they mete. Establishing Saddam's guilt beyond a reasonable doubt also serves an important policy purpose, in that an undeniably fair trial might help sway people whose sympathy he would otherwise attract. Countless dissatisfied young men and women across the Islamic world will be watching the proceedings closely; if the trial were patently fair, they might be less inclined towards violent acts.

The most significant problem with the Iraqi tribunal is that it lacks the legitimacy of an international court. International criminal law is designed to provide accountability for particularly grave offences – and access to justice for the victims – when national legal systems are unable or unwilling to act. The potential charges against Saddam are proscribed by treaty and custom. They are international crimes in both severity and scope: the victims of his regime include the thousands of people tortured and killed during the Iraqi occupation of Kuwait, and the hundreds of thousands who died or were maimed during Iraq's decade-long war with Iran. These are crimes giving rise to universal jurisdiction in the national courts of other countries, and, on the basis of treaties or resolutions of the UN Security Council, to the jurisdiction of international courts and tribunals.

The higher the office of the alleged offender, and the more serious his crimes, the more appropriate an international judicial forum becomes. The multinational Nuremberg Tribunal was used for senior members of the Nazi regime only, with lower ranking offenders tried in national courts. The ad hoc international tribunals for the former Yugoslavia and Rwanda, based in The Hague and Arusha, Tanzania, respectively, have likewise focused their attention on senior officials, with national courts dealing with subordinates. The Statute of the International Criminal Court, adopted in 1998, foresees that national courts will hear most cases involving international crimes – as British Foreign Minister Jack Straw was at pains to point out following Saddam's arrest. But the ICC statute allows the court to determine whether a fair and genuine prosecution will take place at the national level, and to insist that the case be transferred in the event of domestic failings. Most importantly, the UN Security Council has the legal authority to order that any particular situation involving international crimes be dealt with at the international level.

Saddam Hussein could easily have been tried in a special international court created by the UN Security Council, providing that its veto-holding permanent members agreed. Agreement was achieved with regard to ad hoc tribunals for Yugoslavia, Rwanda and, most recently, Sierra Leone, with considerable dividends in international legitimacy.

The Sierra Leone court is a particularly useful model. A hybrid institution, the court in Freetown includes international judges appointed by the United Nations and local judges appointed by the government of Sierra Leone. A similar court, authorized by both the UN Security Council and the Iraqi Governing Council, would have ensured the highest standards of due process for Saddam's trial. Most importantly, the involvement of the United Nations and judges who are neither Iraqi nor from coalition countries would have guaranteed objectivity, while sending a powerful message that the evils perpetrated under Saddam's regime were crimes against humanity, that his trial and sentence was not simply 'victor's justice', and that the reconstruction of Iraq had become a global responsibility. Simultaneously, an Iraqi-international court would have given the Iraqi people a sense of ownership in the process while remaining global in scope. After twelve long years of UN sanctions, a purely UN process would have been regarded with as much scepticism by Iraqis as a court appointed by the United States. Instead, we have the worst of both worlds: a court run and staffed by Iraqis thirsty for revenge that, behind the scenes, is dependent on – and responsive to – the foreign government that engineered Saddam's downfall for its own ends.

In The Hague, another tough and cagey former dictator is causing difficulties. More than three years into his detention, Slobodan Milošević has outlived his nemesis, the presiding judge in his trial at the International Criminal Tribunal for the former Yugoslavia, Richard May. Milošević has also, through fierce determination and cross-examination, exposed the case against him to be less solid than first appeared. Command responsibility – ordering a crime, or failing to stop a crime that a commander knows or should know is about to occur – is notoriously difficult to prove.

Milošević began his defence in August 2004, after his fragile health had repeatedly delayed the proceedings. With high blood pressure putting him at risk of a heart attack or stroke, Milošević continually demands more time to rest. Court-appointed lawyers were assigned to represent him, but they then asked to be relieved of their duties after he refused to co-operate. In any event, the trial will continue until Milošević is acquitted, convicted or dies. The judges, who are insulated from political pressure by their diverse origins, high salaries and pending retirements, can be expected to show more resilience on this issue than did British Prime Minister Tony Blair and then Home Secretary Jack Straw when dealing with the ageing former Chilean dictator Augusto Pinochet (who they released because of his ostensible dementia, only to have him ruled fit to stand trial in Chile). They might even grant Milošević his rightful wish and call Blair and other NATO leaders – past and present – as witnesses. In principle, this order would have to be obeyed, since the Yugoslav tribunal is a creation of the UN Security Council.

Milošević, who faces charges of crimes against humanity, war crimes and genocide against Bosnian and Kosovar Muslims, claims that he was defending his country against illegal interventions by the United States and NATO. But his allegations of 'victor's justice' ring hollow in a court that was approved by Russia and China, is staffed by lawyers and judges from around the world, and has provided him with seemingly endless opportunities to speak and cross-examine witnesses. It is difficult to imagine the authorities in Belgrade conducting a similarly unbiased prosecution, or one that so carefully protects Milošević's right to a full and rigorous defence.

Moreover, Slobodan Milošević's alleged crimes are international in scope. Bosnia-Herzegovina and Croatia were independent countries during part of the conflict, and the allegations against Milošević are crimes under international law. International criminal courts are needed most when the objectivity of a purely national process would be suspect, and there is an international dimension to the crimes themselves. International courts can be remarkably fair. In 2004, the Special Court for Sierra Leone ruled that its president, Geoffrey Robertson QC, could not participate in cases concerning the Sierra Leone rebels because of condemnations he had published prior to becoming a judge. It is difficult to imagine the Iraqi special tribunal taking similar steps to ensure the appearance and reality of objectivity. The problem with the Milošević trial is not the considerable time it has taken or the grandstanding opportunities provided for the accused, but rather that we are simply not accustomed to seeing former heads of state being prosecuted – and prosecuted properly at that.

Take Ariel Sharon, for example. There is no shortage of allegations against the current Israeli prime minister and former army officer, starting with the 1953 massacre of sixty-nine civilians in the Jordanian village of Qibya, the 1982 slaughter of a thousand Palestinians in the Lebanese refugee camps of Sabra and Shatila, and, in 2004, the 'targeted killings' of the Hamas leaders Sheikh Ahmad Yassin and Abdel-Aziz al-Rantissi. Even the ever-cautious Jack Straw, now the British Foreign Secretary, described the latter acts as 'unlawful'.

Nor is there any shortage of law. In 1951, Israel ratified all four of the 1949 Geneva Conventions. The Israeli government, aware that many of its actions are inconsistent with the Conventions, argues that they do not apply to the Occupied Territories because there was no prior sovereign. But this hair-splitting argument does not circumvent the now accepted status of the Geneva Conventions as customary international law, or the fact that some of the allegations against Sharon concern crimes in Jordan and Lebanon.

The challenges in the case of Sharon, and many others, concern issues of custody, immunity and jurisdiction. Many legal systems require accused individuals to be physically present at their trials. Sharon keeps well clear of countries where he might be arrested and any country that dared to detain him would likely have to reckon with the Israeli Defence Force. Even trials in absentia can be subject to political pressure. In Brussels, an investigative judge had to abandon an attempt to try Sharon in 2003 after the Belgian government succumbed to Israeli and US pressure to modify the legislation under which the prosecution was taking place.

As long as Sharon remains prime minister of Israel, he benefits from immunity from arrest and prosecution under customary international law. In the Pinochet case, the House of Lords held that this immunity does not extend to former heads of state for certain types of crimes. But in a case arising out of the Belgian legislation (before the law was altered) the International Court of Justice held that current heads of state and ministers remain immune. Slobodan Milošević has no immunity before the Yugoslav tribunal because the UN Security Council removed that protection, while the statute of the International Criminal Court similarly states that immunities do not apply. The United States would veto any attempt to use the Security Council against Israel, and Israel will not ratify the statute of the ICC.

Under the principle of universal jurisdiction, any country may prosecute war crimes and crimes against humanity committed by anyone anywhere. For example, Adolf Eichmann, the architect of Hitler's 'final solution', was abducted from Argentina and tried and executed in Israel in 1962 for crimes he committed in Europe during the Second World War. Jurisdiction can also vest on the basis of the crime being committed on a country's territory or the perpetrator being a national of the prosecuting state. In some instances, jurisdiction will also exist if the victims are nationals of the prosecuting state or the crime poses a security threat to that state. Custody, immunity and jurisdiction do not pose impediments to the trial of Saddam Hussein by a national court in Baghdad.

When international courts and tribunals are created, stricter jurisdictional limits are usually imposed. The Yugoslav tribunal has jurisdiction over all war crimes and crimes against humanity committed in the former Yugoslavia since 1991. The jurisdiction of the Rwanda tribunal is limited to crimes committed in 1994. The International Criminal Court has jurisdiction over crimes committed after 1 July 2002, but only if they were committed on the territory, or by the nationals, of ratifying countries. The International Court of Justice – which like the Yugoslav tribunal and ICC sits in The Hague – is only able to hear disputes between nation-states that consent to its jurisdiction; it cannot prosecute individuals. However, when asked to do so by the UN General Assembly, the ICJ may issue an 'advisory opinion' – a non-binding answer to a specific question of law – even if the matter concerns the behaviour of a non-consenting country.

In July 2004, for example, the International Court of Justice advised that the so-called 'security fence' being constructed around and through the West Bank was incompatible with the Geneva Conventions and customary international law. Although the decision is a public relations blow to the Israeli government, the advisory opinion is a far cry from a criminal indictment of Sharon. Any prosecution of the Israeli prime minister will have to wait until he retires or is removed from office and travels to a country that is courageous and principled enough to place him under arrest.

The fact is that most alleged war criminals will never appear in the dock. The few that do are those who have lost political power and the protection of powerful friends, which gives rise to the accusation that international criminal law is simply 'victor's justice'. It is in this context that the International Criminal Court provides something dramatically new: a permanent court, largely immune to political interference, which can take over when countries are unable or unwilling to try alleged perpetrators, and to which the UN Security Council can assign jurisdiction over situations rather than having to create new tribunals each time from scratch. Although the ICC has yet to hear its first case, an investigation is under way, at the request of the Ugandan government, into atrocities committed by the Lord's Resistance Army in northern Uganda.

Close to half of the world's countries have ratified the ICC statute, including all the members of the European Union, Canada, Australia and over one quarter of African states. Only the United States has actively endeavoured to undermine the court. With troops in more than 140 countries, a propensity to intervene under dubious legal circumstances, and interpretations of the laws of war that sometimes differ from those of other states, the single superpower feels vulnerable to international mechanisms for enforcing international criminal law. Whereas the Clinton Administration sought to negotiate protections against the abuse of international procedures into the statutes of the tribunals it helped to create, the Bush Administration has adopted an entirely hostile stance. The US position could not consistently accommodate the use of an international tribunal to try Saddam and is uncomfortable with the Yugoslav and Rwanda tribunals.

Since coming to office, President Bush has 'un-signed' the ICC statute, pressured the UN Security Council into temporarily exempting US forces from the Court's jurisdiction, and obtained more than ninety bilateral treaties committing individual countries not to surrender US citizens to The Hague. Bush has even signed legislation that authorizes him to use military force to secure the release of any US service member detained by the ICC. The law is popularly known as 'The Hague Invasion Act'.

For the last six years, most international lawyers have insisted that the United States has nothing to fear from the ICC, because the Court cannot act if countries' own courts are willing and able to prosecute. But this assumes that alleged crimes will always be investigated diligently and prosecuted by US military lawyers, which might not occur if orders to commit the crimes (or policies encouraging them) originate at the highest levels. The torture at Abu Ghraib prison in Iraq – together with the subsequently leaked memorandum that sought to justify all but the most extreme methods of interrogation – certainly call the assumption of US prosecutorial diligence into question. Had Saddam ratified the ICC statute, the chief prosecutor would, quite properly, already be investigating the Abu Ghraib situation, with a view to possibly laying charges for command responsibility against the secretary of defense and president.

The United States, with British support, sought to protect itself against this kind of risk. UN Security Council Resolution 1422, adopted on 12 June 2002, provided immunity from ICC jurisdiction to the personnel of any non-party to the Court engaged in

UN-authorized action. Although initially intended to protect US soldiers active in UN peacekeeping, the resolution arguably also provided protection for US soldiers and their superiors in Iraq – if one accepts the controversial argument advanced by the US and Britain that the war was, in fact, implicitly authorized by the United Nations.

Although Resolution 1422 originally provided only twelve months of immunity, it was subsequently renewed. The resolution seemed destined to be renewed again in June 2004, until the Abu Ghraib prison scandal broke. Faced with an unexpected wave of opposition to any notion of US military immunity, the United States withdrew the draft resolution that would have provided another extension. The immunity lapsed. In practical legal terms, this may have little effect, given the more than ninety bilateral treaties that commit other countries not to surrender US nationals to the ICC. In political terms, the opposition to the extension of the US immunity was hugely significant because it showed that many countries had finally lost patience with the Bush Administration's contemptuous attitude toward international law. Saddam Hussein's show trial in Baghdad will only exacerbate the tension between a world that still wants a fair and sustainable international legal system and a single superpower that hardly seems to care.

Epilogue

War Law and the Single Superpower

In the early 1940s, German soldiers shaved off the beards of Orthodox Jews. In January 2002, US soldiers did the same to Islamic fundamentalists captured in Afghanistan, before flying them to a detention centre at the US naval base in Guantánamo Bay, Cuba. Given the religious significance that some devout Muslims attach to their beards, the action, which the Pentagon sought to justify on hygienic grounds, probably violated the detainees' right to human dignity under the Third Geneva Convention, several international human rights treaties and customary international law. At best, it was patently insensitive and unnecessary.

Other aspects of the United States' immediate response to the terrorist attacks of 11 September 2001 were similarly troubling. During the Afghan War, hundreds of civilians were killed or maimed as a result of careless targeting; thousands more were put at risk by unexploded cluster bomblets. At Mazar-i-Sharif, fifty detainees died with their hands tied behind their backs when air-to-surface missiles were used to suppress a prison revolt. The destruction of the Al-Jazeera television bureau in Kabul, plans for special military commissions with relaxed evidentiary standards, and the refusal to presume that detainees were prisoners of war all indicated at best a casual – and at worst a maniacal – disregard for international opinion and, more importantly, international humanitarian law. Most disturbing, however, were some of the threats uttered by President George W. Bush. The assertion that 'you're either with us or against us' obviated a central aspect of state sovereignty – the right not to be involved – and recast the

United States as the ultimate arbiter of right and wrong. The identification of an 'axis of evil' between Iran, Iraq and North Korea, and the concurrent claim to a greatly extended right of pre-emptive self-defence, challenged one of the twentieth century's greatest achievements: the prohibition of the threat or use of force in international affairs. Although it was possible at the time to think that the aberration was temporary, it is now clear – particularly after Bush's re-election in November 2004 – that something fundamental has changed.

The United States wields more power than any political entity since the Roman Empire. With twelve aircraft carriers and their accompanying task forces ranging the world's oceans, the only significant heavy airlift capacity and the only major stocks of precision-guided missiles and bombs, the US military can defeat any opponent with only minimal losses. And thanks to its massive defence budget, the United States is the only country that regularly makes major advances in military technology. Simultaneously, decisions reached in Washington and on Wall Street reverberate around the world. Corporate America, the regulatory infrastructure that supports it and the pension funds that propel it, are the dominant influences on economic policy in Latin America, Africa, Asia and even Europe, not to mention on the World Bank, the International Monetary Fund and the World Trade Organization. The 2001 collapse of Enron demonstrated the fragility of US corporate structures, but it also exposed the fevered mating that goes on between business and political elites. Until its demise, Enron was more influential than all but a handful of nation-states. A couple of years ago, I asked an Argentine diplomat what he thought about his country becoming part of the Free Trade Area of the Americas, then being negotiated at the initiative of a number of US-based corporations. He replied, with heavy regret: 'We have no choice.'

A country as powerful as the United States has many choices, even when struck by a blow as heavy as that delivered on 11 September 2001. George W. Bush notwithstanding, Dick Cheney,

Condoleezza Rice and Donald Rumsfeld were quick to spot the opportunities presented by the crisis. Doubters need only think of Jo Moore, adviser to Stephen Byers, the former British Transport Minister, who got into trouble for suggesting that the attack on the World Trade Center provided a perfect opportunity to bury bad news. The battle-hardened ideologues directing US foreign policy are no less cynical, and considerably more adept.

A 'coalition' was constructed to facilitate the freezing of terrorist assets and the gathering of intelligence overseas. But America's allies were fooling themselves to think that the events of 11 September had persuaded the Bush Administration of the value of multilateralism. On the contrary, the mistreatment of detainees at Guantánamo Bay and elsewhere, the renewed threatening of 'rogue states' and the 2003 invasion of Iraq have demonstrated renewed commitment to a unilateralist course.

During its first eight months in office, in 2001, the Bush Administration publicly rejected the Anti-Ballistic Missile Treaty, the Kyoto Protocol on global warming, the Rome Statute of the International Criminal Court, a convention on the sale and transfer of small arms and a protocol to the Biological Weapons Convention. Following 11 September, the United States rejected offers of a UN Security Council resolution to authorize the Afghan War, instead relying on an extended claim of self-defence against state sponsors of terrorism. The United States forged new alliances with illiberal regimes in Pakistan, Kyrgyzstan, Tajikistan and Uzbekistan, reversing years of efforts to promote human rights. And the US advanced a new, greatly extended conception of pre-emptive self-defence, setting in course the invasion of Iraq. In an age of increasing interdependence and cooperation, President Bush and his advisers were deliberately out of step with most of the Western world.

In many respects, Bush's team was a reincarnation of the second Reagan Administration, which was also stridently unilateralist; it, too, drew explicit distinctions between good and evil, claimed exceptional rights, promoted missile defence (and thus a new arms race extending into space) and relied on the threat of terrorism to justify it all. Following the terrorist bombing in 1986 of a Berlin discotheque frequented by US servicemen, then Secretary of State George Shultz said it was 'absurd to argue that international law prohibits us from capturing terrorists in international waters or airspace; from attacking them on the soil of other nations, even for the purpose of rescuing hostages; or from using force against states that support, train and harbour terrorists or guerrillas'. George W. Bush's speechwriter could not have put it better, but there were two important differences between the situations in 1986 and 2001. The end of the Cold War transformed the United States into an unrivalled superpower, making it more likely that claims to use force unilaterally would meet with acquiescence on the part of other countries. More important, the events of 11 September transformed a traditionally isolationist population into a nation that wanted its president to act decisively on the world stage. Despite obvious setbacks, much of the American populace retains this desire. It is likely to continue to do so, given that the 'war on terrorism' has been linked by Bush's advisers to three strands of thought that are central to the way Americans think about themselves.

The first is a narrow, reactionary conception of popular sovereignty. The US Constitution is regarded as the ultimate expression of the American people's consent to be governed; any exercise of authority not expressly vested in the Constitution is considered illegitimate. International law, which necessarily results from the joint law-making efforts of numerous countries, immediately attracts suspicion, particularly from the Republican Right. The suspicion is heightened by the possibility that international law might provide the means for the Federal Government of the United States – whose constitutional powers in the field of foreign relations are considerable – to override the careful delimitation between its powers and those of the fifty 'States of the Union'. Concern on the part of the Right about the aggrandizement of federal powers on the back of international law is most acute with regard to police and criminal justice matters, where the Constitution accords primary responsibility to the states.

This anxiety about popular sovereignty helps explain why, during the negotiation of the UN Charter in 1945, the United States insisted on a veto over Security Council resolutions. Anything less would have violated the US Constitution. In 2001, US negotiators sabotaged a treaty designed to regulate the international trade in light weapons, on the basis that it would violate the constitutional right to bear arms. At the same time, President Bush dismissed international concern over the execution of juvenile and mentally handicapped offenders in the United States as impermissible interference in domestic affairs. In terms of its adherence to a seventeenth-century, absolutist conception of sovereignty, the United States ranks with Burma, China, Iran and North Korea.

The second strand of thought influencing US foreign policy draws on Frederick Jackson Turner's 'frontier thesis', according to which the uniquely individualistic and entrepreneurial character of American society derives from the historical ability of its people to escape government control by moving to the frontier. Much of the history of US foreign policy could be explained as an ongoing attempt to acquire new frontiers. The United States spent much of its first century conquering or buying vast tracts of land from France, Russia, Mexico and the Indian tribes. The world outside North America was of little interest, except when it threatened the United States. The articulation of the Monroe Doctrine in 1823 suggested broader ambitions by signalling that the United States would not tolerate interventions in the Western hemisphere on the part of the Holy Alliance (a reactionary grouping of Austria, Prussia and Russia, agreed by their monarchs in 1815). By the end of the nineteenth century, the United States had turned its attention abroad. Its seizure of Cuba in 1898 contributed to the outbreak of the Spanish-American War, which gave the United States control of Hawaii, the Philippines and the Panama Canal Zone. The First World War brought a close alliance with Britain, which enabled the United States to join in that country's domination of international politics until the end of the Second World War. By then, America was alone at the top, with the Soviet Union emerging as the second great power. Forty years of nuclear rivalry and proxy wars fostered an imperialist vision, a powerful military-industrial complex and the extension of US influence around the globe.

The collapse of the Soviet Union marked the end of an epoch, but not the end of US involvement in the rest of the world. Other countries had become the 'new frontier' and the heads of US-based corporations the new frontiersmen. The focus of government policy shifted to making the world a more hospitable place for American business. The creation of the World Trade Organization – an institution grounded in the free-market assumptions of the 'Washington Consensus' (a collection of neo-liberal policies imposed by the World Bank and International Monetary Fund on developing countries after the Cold War) – was a notable achievement in this regard. The opening up of Iraq to Halliburton (Vice President Dick Cheney's former company) and other US-based multinationals may well have been another.

The frontier thesis lives on in everyday life too. The stereotypical middle-class American is a hardworking, gun-owning 'handyman', who lives in a large wooden house in a far-flung suburb and drives a four-ton SUV. After 11 September, President Bush's use of such expressions as 'dead or alive', 'let's roll', and 'smoking out of holes' resonated in the United States, helping him achieve dizzying heights in the polls; in November 2004, it helped him win re-election.

The third strand of thought concerns the faith that Americans have in technology. Technology is the ultimate panacea, whether for cancer, hyperactive children, climate change or terrorism. Even the almost invisible teleprompter that enables George W. Bush to deliver flawless speeches – looking straight through it at his audience – is celebrated as a technological achievement. In October 2004, most Americans were unconcerned by the possibility that the president was being coached through an earpiece during the election debates.

Technological superiority is a central theme of the one author we can be sure George W. Bush has read. In Tom Clancy's 2001 novel *The Bear and the Dragon*, technology enables the United States to follow the inner deliberations of the Chinese government, rout the Chinese army and ward off an intercontinental ballistic missile attack. Most of the Bush Administration's foreign policy up to 11 September was prefigured by Clancy, including missile defence, closer and closer links with Russia, reliance on the dutiful cooperation of Tony Blair, and a general lack of concern for the Chinese – referred to as 'Klingons' by Clancy's fictional Republican presidential hero. (Bush presumably also read Clancy's 1996 book, *Debt of Honor*, in which terrorists seize control of a jumbo jet and crash it into the Capitol Building, killing the president, Supreme Court and most of the Congress, though this story apparently had less impact on him.) Today, with their faith in technology reaffirmed by the apparent effectiveness of precision-guided missiles and bombs in the Afghan and Iraq Wars, many Americans are more than willing to see increased spending on high-tech weapons.

Powerful countries have always shaped the international system to their advantage. In the sixteenth century, Spain redefined basic concepts of justice and universality to justify the conquest of indigenous Americans. In the eighteenth century, France developed the modern concepts of borders and the 'balance of power' to suit its continental strengths. In the nineteenth century, Britain introduced new rules on piracy, neutrality and colonialism, again to suit its interests as the predominant power of the day.

George W. Bush's United States has been no different, except that, following 11 September 2001, hardly anyone was prepared to challenge its lead. The President's advisers took full advantage of the situation, applying pressure in pursuit of numerous goals that, under normal circumstances, could not have been achieved. Prominent among these goals has been greater flexibility to use force outside the UN Charter (through the extension of the right of self-defence to include action against state sponsors of terrorism and a much elongated right of pre-emptive action) as well as with regard to targeting and the treatment of detainees. To the degree that it succeeds in these law-changing initiatives – and it has not yet succeeded with the pre-emption, targeting and treatment claims – the United States contributes to marginalizing the United Nations in international peace and security, an area over which the Security Council was assigned 'primary responsibility' in 1945, and to diminishing fundamental human protections. By marginalizing the United Nations, it makes it more difficult for governments to draw upon this important source of legitimacy for the use of military force across borders. By undermining international humanitarian law, it squanders moral authority and the capacity to persuade and influence others. All this in turn diminishes the potential for cooperative, multilateral responses to threats and breaches of the peace, responses that would share the military and financial burdens of intervention among larger groups of countries and reduce the resentments that armed interventions so easily feed.

The actions of the United States have also made it more difficult to criticize violations of international law by other countries, most notably Israel. The use by the CIA of a Predator drone to kill six terrorist suspects in northern Yemen in November 2002 is difficult to distinguish from 'targeted killings', and the storm-trooper tactics of US soldiers in post-war Iraq are explicitly modelled on those of the Israeli Defence Force. The testimonies of Palestinians released from Israeli prisons – as well as those of six Britons released from Saudi Arabia in 2003 – bear more than a passing resemblance to the photographs taken at Abu Ghraib prison, and the stories told by detainees released from Bagram airbase and Guantánamo Bay.

Terrorism can cause great destruction and upheaval, but efforts to stamp it out can serve as a smokescreen for the pursuit of less worthy goals. America's friends and allies, while providing strong support for the American people, should offer their cooperation on specific issues only after careful consideration of their best interests, which prominently include the maintenance of a just, strong, equal and effective system of international law. Even if the United States has abdicated its leadership role in the struggle for a global system of justice and human rights, its partners in that effort must continue the fight.

There is regularly talk of a 'democratic deficit' with regard to supranational institutions such as the United Nations, World Trade Organization and European Union, whereby important decisions are made without there being much accountability to most of the people affected. Perhaps it is time to start speaking of a similar deficit with regard to the United States. Decisions made in Washington today eclipse the importance of decisions made in the United Nations – and not just for Americans. Citizens of other countries consequently find themselves in a position full of irony. Subject to the governance of a foreign power but deprived of any voice, the people of the world have become the victims of a twenty-first-century form of 'taxation without representation' – the very grievance that sparked the American Revolution of 1776.

Although imperfect, the international rules and institutions detested by neo-conservatives such as George W. Bush are more consistent with the founding principles of the United States than the imperialist principles to which they now subscribe. The Declaration of Independence affirms that the representatives of the United States will have a 'due regard for the opinions of other nations'. Many Americans maintain a strong desire to see their country return to the constructive, cooperative, law-abiding approach that led to the creation of the United Nations in 1945 at a conference in San Francisco. It's high time that America's friends supported them, by resolutely opposing the rule-twisting megalomaniacs who have dominated and corrupted US and global politics since 11 September 2001. The immense power of the United States carries with it an awesome responsibility: to improve the world – for everyone. Obeying the requirements of war law is a necessary first step.

Appendix

Charter of the United Nations, 1945

Preamble

We the Peoples of the United Nations Determined

to save succeeding generations from the scourge of war, which twice in our lifetime has brought untold sorrow to mankind, and

to reaffirm faith in fundamental human rights, in the dignity and worth of the human person, in the equal rights of men and women and of nations large and small, and

to establish conditions under which justice and respect for the obligations arising from treaties and other sources of international law can be maintained, and

to promote social progress and better standards of life in larger freedom,

And for these Ends

to practice tolerance and live together in peace with one another as good neighbors, and

to unite our strength to maintain international peace and security, and

to ensure by the acceptance of principles and the institution of methods, that armed force shall not be used, save in the common interest, and

to employ international machinery for the promotion of the economic and social advancement of all peoples,

Have Resolved to Combine our Efforts to Accomplish these Aims

Accordingly, our respective Governments, through representatives assembled in the city of San Francisco, who have exhibited their full powers found to be in good and due form, have agreed to the present Charter of the United Nations and do hereby establish an international organization to be known as the United Nations.

Chapter I
Purposes and Principles

Article 1

The Purposes of the United Nations are:

1. To maintain international peace and security, and to that end: to take effective collective measures for the prevention and removal of threats to the peace, and for the suppression of acts of aggression or other breaches of the peace, and to bring about by peaceful means, and in conformity with the principles of justice and international law, adjustment or settlement of international disputes or situations which might lead to a breach of the peace;

2. To develop friendly relations among nations based on respect for the principle of equal rights and self-determination of peoples, and to take other appropriate measures to strengthen universal peace;

3. To achieve international cooperation in solving international problems of an economic, social, cultural, or humanitarian character, and in promoting and encouraging respect for human rights and for fundamental freedoms for all without distinction as to race, sex, language, or religion; and

4. To be a center for harmonizing the actions of nations in the attainment of these common ends.

Article 2

The Organization and its Members, in pursuit of the Purposes stated in Article 1, shall act in accordance with the following Principles.

1. The Organization is based on the principle of the sovereign equality of all its Members.

2. All Members, in order to ensure to all of them the rights and benefits resulting from membership, shall fulfill in good faith the obligations assumed by them in accordance with the present Charter.

3. All Members shall settle their international disputes by peaceful means in such a manner that international peace and security, and justice, are not endangered.

4. All Members shall refrain in their international relations from the threat or use of force against the territorial integrity or political independence of any state, or in any other manner inconsistent with the Purposes of the United Nations.

5. All Members shall give the United Nations every assistance in any action it takes in accordance with the present Charter, and shall refrain

from giving assistance to any state against which the United Nations is taking preventive or enforcement action.

6. The Organization shall ensure that states which are not Members of the United Nations act in accordance with these Principles so far as may be necessary for the maintenance of international peace and security.

7. Nothing contained in the present Charter shall authorize the United Nations to intervene in matters which are essentially within the domestic jurisdiction of any state or shall require the Members to submit such matters to settlement under the present Charter; but this principle shall not prejudice the application of enforcement measures under Chapter VII.

Chapter II
Membership

Article 3

The original Members of the United Nations shall be the states which, having participated in the United Nations Conference on International Organization at San Francisco, or having previously signed the Declaration by United Nations of January 1, 1942, sign the present Charter and ratify it in accordance with Article 110.

Article 4

1. Membership in the United Nations is open to all other peace-loving states which accept the obligations contained in the present Charter and, in the judgment of the Organization, are able and willing to carry out these obligations.

2. The admission of any such state to membership in the United Nations will be effected by a decision of the General Assembly upon the recommendation of the Security Council.

Article 5

A member of the United Nations against which preventive or enforcement action has been taken by the Security Council may be suspended from the exercise of the rights and privileges of membership by the General Assembly upon the recommendation of the Security Council. The exercise of these rights and privileges may be restored by the Security Council.

Article 6

A Member of the United Nations which has persistently violated the Principles contained in the present Charter may be expelled from the

Organization by the General Assembly upon the recommendation of the Security Council.

Chapter III
Organs

Article 7

1. There are established as the principal organs of the United Nations: a General Assembly, a Security Council, an Economic and Social Council, a Trusteeship Council, an International Court of Justice, and a Secretariat.
2. Such subsidiary organs as may be found necessary may be established in accordance with the present Charter.

Article 8

The United Nations shall place no restrictions on the eligibility of men and women to participate in any capacity and under conditions of equality in its principal and subsidiary organs.

Chapter IV
The General Assembly
Composition

Article 9

1. The General Assembly shall consist of all the Members of the United Nations.
2. Each member shall have not more than five representatives in the General Assembly.

Functions and Powers

Article 10

The General Assembly may discuss any questions or any matters within the scope of the present Charter or relating to the powers and functions of any organs provided for in the present Charter, and, except as provided in Article 12, may make recommendations to the Members of the United Nations or to the Security Council or to both on any such questions or matters.

Article 11

1. The General Assembly may consider the general principles of cooperation in the maintenance of international peace and security, including the principles governing disarmament and the regulation of armaments, and may make recommendations with regard to such principles to the Members or to the Security Council or to both.

2. The General Assembly may discuss any questions relating to the maintenance of international peace and security brought before it by any Member of the United Nations, or by the Security Council, or by a state which is not a Member of the United Nations in accordance with Article 35, paragraph 2, and, except as provided in Article 12, may make recommendations with regard to any such questions to the state or states concerned or to the Security Council or to both. Any such question on which action is necessary shall be referred to the Security Council by the General Assembly either before or after discussion.

3. The General Assembly may call the attention of the Security Council to situations which are likely to endanger international peace and security.

4. The powers of the General Assembly set forth in this Article shall not limit the general scope of Article 10.

Article 12

1. While the Security Council is exercising in respect of any dispute or situation the functions assigned to it in the present Charter, the General Assembly shall not make any recommendation with regard to that dispute or situation unless the Security Council so requests.

2. The Secretary-General, with the consent of the Security Council, shall notify the General Assembly at each session of any matters relative to the maintenance of international peace and security which are being dealt with by the Security Council and shall similarly notify the General Assembly, or the Members of the United Nations if the General Assembly is not in session, immediately the Security Council ceases to deal with such matters.

Article 13

1. The General Assembly shall initiate studies and make recommendations for the purpose of:

a. promoting international cooperation in the political field and encouraging the progressive development of international law and its codification;

b. promoting international cooperation in the economic, social, cultural, educational, and health fields, and assisting in the realization of human rights and fundamental freedoms for all without distinction as to race, sex, language, or religion.

2. The further responsibilities, functions and powers of the General Assembly with respect to matters mentioned in paragraph 1(b) above are set forth in Chapters IX and X.

Article 14

Subject to the provisions of Article 12, the General Assembly may recommend measures for the peaceful adjustment of any situation, regardless of origin, which it deems likely to impair the general welfare or friendly relations among nations, including situations resulting from a violation of the provisions of the present Charter setting forth the Purposes and Principles of the United Nations.

Article 15

1. The General Assembly shall receive and consider annual and special reports from the Security Council; these reports shall include an account of the measures that the Security Council has decided upon or taken to maintain international peace and security.

2. The General Assembly shall receive and consider reports from the other organs of the United Nations.

Article 16

The General Assembly shall perform such functions with respect to the international trusteeship system as are assigned to it under Chapters XII and XIII, including the approval of the trusteeship agreements for areas not designated as strategic.

Article 17

1. The General Assembly shall consider and approve the budget of the Organization.

2. The expenses of the Organization shall be borne by the Members as apportioned by the General Assembly.

3. The General Assembly shall consider and approve any financial and budgetary arrangements with specialized agencies referred to in Article 57 and shall examine the administrative budgets of such specialized agencies with a view to making recommendations to the agencies concerned.

Voting

Article 18

1. Each member of the General Assembly shall have one vote.

2. Decisions of the General Assembly on important questions shall be made by a two-thirds majority of the members present and voting. These questions shall include: recommendations with respect to the maintenance of international peace and security, the election of the non-permanent members of the Security Council, the election of the members of the Economic and Social Council, the election of members of the Trusteeship Council in accordance with paragraph 1(c) of Article 86, the admission of new Members to the United Nations, the suspension of the rights and privileges of membership, the expulsion of Members, questions relating to the operation of the trusteeship system, and budgetary questions.

3. Decisions on other questions, Composition including the determination of additional categories of questions to be decided by a two-thirds majority, shall be made by a majority of the members present and voting.

Article 19

A Member of the United Nations which is in arrears in the payment of its financial contributions to the Organization shall have no vote in the General Assembly if the amount of its arrears equals or exceeds the amount of the contributions due from it for the preceding two full years. The General Assembly may, nevertheless, permit such a Member to vote if it is satisfied that the failure to pay is due to conditions beyond the control of the Member.

Procedure

Article 20

The General Assembly shall meet in regular annual sessions and in such special sessions as occasion may require. Special sessions shall be convoked by the Secretary-General at the request of the Security Council or of a majority of the Members of the United Nations.

Article 21

The General Assembly shall adopt its own rules of procedure. It shall elect its President for each session.

Article 22

The General Assembly may establish such subsidiary organs as it deems necessary for the performance of its functions.

Chapter V
The Security Council

Article 23

1. The Security Council shall consist of fifteen Members of the United Nations. The Republic of China, France, the Union of Soviet Socialist Republics, the United Kingdom of Great Britain and Northern Ireland, and the United States of America shall be permanent members of the Security Council. The General Assembly shall elect ten other Members of the United Nations to be non-permanent members of the Security Council, due regard being specially paid, in the first instance to the contribution of Members of the United Nations to the maintenance of international peace and security and to the other purposes of the Organization, and also to equitable geographical distribution.

2. The non-permanent members of the Security Council shall be elected for a term of two years. In the first election of the non-permanent members after the increase of the membership of the Security Council from eleven to fifteen, two of the four additional members shall be chosen for a term of one year. A retiring member shall not be eligible for immediate re-election.

3. Each member of the Security Council shall have one representative.

Functions and Powers

Article 24

1. In order to ensure prompt and effective action by the United Nations, its Members confer on the Security Council primary responsibility for the maintenance of international peace and security, and agree that in carrying out its duties under this responsibility the Security Council acts on their behalf.

2. In discharging these duties the Security Council shall act in accordance with the Purposes and Principles of the United Nations. The specific powers granted to the Security Council for the discharge of these duties are laid down in Chapters VI, VII, VIII, and XII.

3. The Security Council shall submit annual and, when necessary, special reports to the General Assembly for its consideration.

Article 25

The Members of the United Nations agree to accept and carry out the decisions of the Security Council in accordance with the present Charter.

Article 26

In order to promote the establishment and maintenance of international peace and security with the least diversion for armaments of the world's human and economic resources, the Security Council shall be responsible for formulating, with the assistance of the Military Staff Committee referred to in Article 47, plans to be submitted to the Members of the United Nations for the establishment of a system for the regulation of armaments.

Voting

Article 27

1. Each member of the Security Council shall have one vote.
2. Decisions of the Security Council on procedural matters shall be made by an affirmative vote of nine members.
3. Decisions of the Security Council on all other matters shall be made by an affirmative vote of nine members including the concurring votes of the permanent members; provided that, in decisions under Chapter VI, and under paragraph 3 of Article 52, a party to a dispute shall abstain from voting.

Procedure

Article 28

1. The Security Council shall be so organized as to be able to function continuously. Each member of the Security Council shall for this purpose be represented at all times at the seat of the Organization.
2. The Security Council shall hold periodic meetings at which each of its members may, if it so desires, be represented by a member of the government or by some other specially designated representative.
3. The Security Council may hold meetings at such places other than the seat of the Organization as in its judgment will best facilitate its work.

Article 29

The Security Council may establish such subsidiary organs as it deems necessary for the performance of its functions.

Article 30

The Security Council shall adopt its own rules of procedure, including the method of selecting its President.

Article 31

Any Member of the United Nations which is not a member of the Security Council may participate, without vote, in the discussion of any question brought before the Security Council whenever the latter considers that the interests of that Member are specially affected.

Article 32

Any Member of the United Nations which is not a member of the Security Council or any state which is not a Member of the United Nations, if it is a party to a dispute under consideration by the Security Council, shall be invited to participate, without vote, in the discussion relating to the dispute. The Security Council shall lay down such conditions as it deems just for the participation of a state which is not a Member of the United Nations.

Chapter VI
Pacific Settlement of Disputes

Article 33

1. The parties to any dispute, the continuance of which is likely to endanger the maintenance of international peace and security, shall, first of all, seek a solution by negotiation, enquiry, mediation, conciliation, arbitration, judicial settlement, resort to regional agencies or arrangements, or other peaceful means of their own choice.
2. The Security Council shall, when it deems necessary, call upon the parties to settle their dispute by such means.

Article 34

The Security Council may investigate any dispute, or any situation which might lead to international friction or give rise to a dispute, in order to determine whether the continuance of the dispute or situation is likely to endanger the maintenance of international peace and security.

Article 35

1. Any Member of the United Nations may bring any dispute, or any situation of the nature referred to in Article 34, to the attention of the Security Council or of the General Assembly.

2. A state which is not a Member of the United Nations may bring to the attention of the Security Council or of the General Assembly any dispute to which it is a party if it accepts in advance, for the purposes of the dispute, the obligations of pacific settlement provided in the present Charter.

3. The proceedings of the General Assembly in respect of matters brought to its attention under this Article will be subject to the provisions of Articles 11 and 12.

Article 36

1. The Security Council may, at any stage of a dispute of the nature referred to in Article 33 or of a situation of like nature, recommend appropriate procedures or methods of adjustment.

2. The Security Council should take into consideration any procedures for the settlement of the dispute which have already been adopted by the parties.

3. In making recommendations under this Article the Security Council should also take into consideration that legal disputes should as a general rule be referred by the parties to the International Court of Justice in accordance with the provisions of the Statute of the Court.

Article 37

1. Should the parties to a dispute of the nature referred to in Article 33 fail to settle it by the means indicated in that Article, they shall refer it to the Security Council.

2. If the Security Council deems that the continuance of the dispute is in fact likely to endanger the maintenance of international peace and security, it shall decide whether to take action under Article 36 or to recommend such terms of settlement as it may consider appropriate.

Article 38

Without prejudice to the provisions of Articles 33 to 37, the Security Council may, if all the parties to any dispute so request, make recommendations to the parties with a view to a pacific settlement of the dispute.

Chapter VII
Action with respect to Threats to the Peace, Breaches of the Peace, and Acts of Aggression

Article 39

The Security Council shall determine the existence of any threat to the peace, breach of the peace, or act of aggression and shall make recommendations, or decide what measures shall be taken in accordance with Articles 41 and 42, to maintain or restore international peace and security.

Article 40

In order to prevent an aggravation of the situation, the Security Council may, before making the recommendations or deciding upon the measures provided for in Article 39, call upon the parties concerned to comply with such provisional measures as it deems necessary or desirable. Such provisional measures shall be without prejudice to the rights, claims, or position of the parties concerned. The Security Council shall duly take account of failure to comply with such provisional measures.

Article 41

The Security Council may decide what measures not involving the use of armed force are to be employed to give effect to its decisions, and it may call upon the Members of the United Nations to apply such measures. These may include complete or partial interruption of economic relations and of rail, sea, air, postal, telegraphic, radio, and other means of communication, and the severance of diplomatic relations.

Article 42

Should the Security Council consider that measures provided for in Article 41 would be inadequate or have proved to be inadequate, it may take such action by air, sea, or land forces as may be necessary to maintain or restore international peace and security. Such action may include demonstrations, blockade, and other operations by air, sea, or land forces of Members of the United Nations.

Article 43

1. All Members of the United Nations, in order to contribute to the maintenance of international peace and security, undertake to make available to the Security Council, on its call and in accordance with a special

agreement or agreements, armed forces, assistance, and facilities, including rights of passage, necessary for the purpose of maintaining international peace and security.

2. Such agreement or agreements shall govern the numbers and types of forces, their degree of readiness and general location, and the nature of the facilities and assistance to be provided.

3. The agreement or agreements shall be negotiated as soon as possible on the initiative of the Security Council. They shall be concluded between the Security Council and Members or between the Security Council and groups of Members and shall be subject to ratification by the signatory states in accordance with their respective constitutional processes.

Article 44

When the Security Council has decided to use force it shall, before calling upon a Member not represented on it to provide armed forces in fulfillment of the obligations assumed under Article 43, invite that Member, if the Member so desires, to participate in the decisions of the Security Council concerning the employment of contingents of that Member's armed forces.

Article 45

In order to enable the United Nations to take urgent military measures Members shall hold immediately available national air-force contingents for combined international enforcement action. The strength and degree of readiness of these contingents and plans for their combined action shall be determined, within the limits laid down in the special agreement or agreements referred to in Article 43, by the Security Council with the assistance of the Military Staff Committee.

Article 46

Plans for the application of armed force shall be made by the Security Council with the assistance of the Military Staff Committee.

Article 47

1. There shall be established a Military Staff Committee to advise and assist the Security Council on all questions relating to the Security Council's military requirements for the maintenance of international peace and security, the employment and command of forces placed at its disposal, the regulation of armaments, and possible disarmament.

2. The Military Staff Committee shall consist of the Chiefs of Staff of the permanent members of the Security Council or their representatives. Any Member of the United Nations not permanently represented on the Committee shall be invited by the Committee to be associated with it when the efficient discharge of the Committee's responsibilities requires the participation of that Member in its work.

3. The Military Staff Committee shall be responsible under the Security Council for the strategic direction of any armed forces placed at the disposal of the Security Council. Questions relating to the command of such forces shall be worked out subsequently.

4. The Military Staff Committee, with the authorization of the Security Council and after consultation with appropriate regional agencies, may establish regional subcommittees.

Article 48

1. The action required to carry out the decisions of the Security Council for the maintenance of international peace and security shall be taken by all the Members of the United Nations or by some of them, as the Security Council may determine.

2. Such decisions shall be carried out by the Members of the United Nations directly and through their action in the appropriate international agencies of which they are members.

Article 49

The Members of the United Nations shall join in affording mutual assistance in carrying out the measures decided upon by the Security Council.

Article 50

If preventive or enforcement measures against any state are taken by the Security Council, any other state, whether a Member of the United Nations or not, which finds itself confronted with special economic problems arising from the carrying out of those measures shall have the right to consult the Security Council with regard to a solution of those problems.

Article 51

Nothing in the present Charter shall impair the inherent right of individual or collective self-defense if an armed attack occurs against a Member of the United Nations, until the Security Council has taken measures necessary to maintain international peace and security. Measures taken by

Members in the exercise of this right of self-defense shall be immediately reported to the Security Council and shall not in any way affect the authority and responsibility of the Security Council under the present Charter to take at any time such action as it deems necessary in order to maintain or restore international peace and security.

Chapter VIII
Regional Arrangements

Article 52

1. Nothing in the present Charter precludes the existence of regional arrangements or agencies for dealing with such matters relating to the maintenance of international peace and security as are appropriate for regional action, provided that such arrangements or agencies and their activities are consistent with the Purposes and Principles of the United Nations.

2. The Members of the United Nations entering into such arrangements or constituting such agencies shall make every effort to achieve pacific settlement of local disputes through such regional arrangements or by such regional agencies before referring them to the Security Council.

3. The Security Council shall encourage the development of pacific settlement of local disputes through such regional arrangements or by such regional agencies either on the initiative of the states concerned or by reference from the Security Council.

4. This Article in no way impairs the application of Articles 34 and 35.

Article 53

1. The Security Council shall, where appropriate, utilize such regional arrangements or agencies for enforcement action under its authority. But no enforcement action shall be taken under regional arrangements or by regional agencies without the authorization of the Security Council, with the exception of measures against any enemy state, as defined in paragraph 2 of this Article, provided for pursuant to Article 107 or in regional arrangements directed against renewal of aggressive policy on the part of any such state, until such time as the Organization may, on request of the Governments concerned, be charged with the responsibility for preventing further aggression by such a state.

2. The term enemy state as used in paragraph 1 of this Article applies to any state which during the Second World War has been an enemy of any signatory of the present Charter.

Article 54

The Security Council shall at all times be kept fully informed of activities undertaken or in contemplation under regional arrangements or by regional agencies for the maintenance of international peace and security.

Chapter IX
International Economic and Social Cooperation
Article 55

With a view to the creation of conditions of stability and well-being which are necessary for peaceful and friendly relations among nations based on respect for the principle of equal rights and self-determination of peoples, the United Nations shall promote:

a. higher standards of living, full employment, and conditions of economic and social progress and development;

b. solutions of international economic, social, health, and related problems; and international cultural and educational co-operation; and

c. universal respect for, and observance of, human rights and fundamental freedoms for all without distinction as to race, sex, language, or religion.

Article 56

All Members pledge themselves to take joint and separate action in cooperation with the Organization for the achievement of the purposes set forth in Article 55.

Article 57

1. The various specialized agencies, established by intergovernmental agreement and having wide international responsibilities, as defined in their basic instruments, in economic, social, cultural, educational, health, and related fields, shall be brought into relationship with the United Nations in accordance with the provisions of Article 63.
2. Such agencies thus brought into relationship with the United Nations are hereinafter referred to as specialized agencies.

Article 58

The Organization shall make recommendations for the coordination of the policies and activities of the specialized agencies.

Article 59

The Organization shall, where appropriate, initiate negotiations among the states concerned for the creation of any new specialized agencies required for the accomplishment of the purposes set forth in Article 55.

Article 60

Responsibility for the discharge of the functions of the Organization set forth in this Chapter shall be vested in the General Assembly and, under the authority of the General Assembly, in the Economic and Social Council, which shall have for this purpose the powers set forth in Chapter X.

Chapter X
The Economic and Social Council
Composition

Article 61

1. The Economic and Social Council shall consist of fifty-four Members of the United Nations elected by the General Assembly.
2. Subject to the provisions of paragraph 3, eighteen members of the Economic and Social Council shall be elected each year for a term of three years. A retiring member shall be eligible for immediate re-election.
3. At the first election after the increase in the membership of the Economic and Social Council from twenty-seven to fifty-four members, in addition to the members elected in place of the nine members whose term of office expires at the end of that year, twenty-seven additional members shall be elected. Of these twenty-seven additional members, the term of office of nine members so elected shall expire at the end of one year, and of nine other members at the end of two years, in accordance with arrangements made by the General Assembly.
4. Each member of the Economic and Social Council shall have one representative.

Functions and Powers

Article 62

1. The Economic and Social Council may make or initiate studies and reports with respect to international economic, social, cultural, educational, health, and related matters and may make recommendations with

respect to any such matters to the General Assembly, to the Members of the United Nations, and to the specialized agencies concerned.

2. It may make recommendations for the purpose of promoting respect for, and observance of, human rights and fundamental freedoms for all.

3. It may prepare draft conventions for submission to the General Assembly, with respect to matters falling within its competence.

4. It may call, in accordance with the rules prescribed by the United Nations, international conferences on matters falling within its competence.

Article 63

1. The Economic and Social Council may enter into agreements with any of the agencies referred to in Article 57, defining the terms on which the agency concerned shall be brought into relationship with the United Nations. Such agreements shall be subject to approval by the General Assembly.

2. It may coordinate the activities of the specialized agencies through consultation with and recommendations to such agencies and through recommendations to the General Assembly and to the Members of the United Nations.

Article 64

1. The Economic and Social Council may take appropriate steps to obtain regular reports from the specialized agencies. It may make arrangements with the Members of the United Nations and with the specialized agencies to obtain reports on the steps taken to give effect to its own recommendations and to recommendations on matters falling within its competence made by the General Assembly.

2. It may communicate its observations on these reports to the General Assembly.

Article 65

The Economic and Social Council may furnish information to the Security Council and shall assist the Security Council upon its request.

Article 66

1. The Economic and Social Council shall perform such functions as fall within its competence in connection with the carrying out of the recommendations of the General Assembly.

2. It may, with the approval of the General Assembly, perform services at the request of Members of the United Nations and at the request of specialized agencies.

3. It shall perform such other functions as are specified elsewhere in the present Charter or as may be assigned to it by the General Assembly.

Article 67

1. Each member of the Economic and Social Council shall have one vote.
2. Decisions of the Economic and Social Council shall be made by a majority of the members present and voting.

Procedure

Article 68

The Economic and Social Council shall set up commissions in economic and social fields and for the promotion of human rights, and such other commissions as may be required for the performance of its functions.

Article 69

The Economic and Social Council shall invite any Member of the United Nations to participate, without vote, in its deliberations on any matter of particular concern to that Member.

Article 70

The Economic and Social Council may make arrangements for representatives of the specialized agencies to participate, without vote, in its deliberations and in those of the commissions established by it, and for its representatives to participate in the deliberations of the specialized agencies.

Article 71

The Economic and Social Council may make suitable arrangements for consultation with non-governmental organizations which are concerned with matters within its competence. Such arrangements may be made with international organizations and, where appropriate, with national organizations after consultation with the Member of the United Nations concerned.

Article 72

1. The Economic and Social Council shall adopt its own rules of procedure, including the method of selecting its President.
2. The Economic and Social Council shall meet as required in accordance with its rules, which shall include provision for the convening of meetings on the request of a majority of its members.

Chapter XI
Declaration regarding Non-Self-Governing Territories
Article 73

Members of the United Nations which have or assume responsibilities for the administration of territories whose peoples have not yet attained a full measure of self-government recognize the principle that the interests of the inhabitants of these territories are paramount, and accept as a sacred trust the obligation to promote to the utmost, within the system of international peace and security established by the present Charter, the well-being of the inhabitants of these territories, and, to this end:

a. to ensure, with due respect for the culture of the peoples concerned, their political, economic, social, and educational advancement, their just treatment, and their protection against abuses;

b. to develop self-government, to take due account of the political aspirations of the peoples, and to assist them in the progressive development of their free political institutions, according to the particular circumstances of each territory and its peoples and their varying stages of advancement;

c. to further international peace and security;

d. to promote constructive measures of development, to encourage research, and to cooperate with one another and, when and where appropriate, with specialized international bodies with a view to the practical achievement of the social, economic, and scientific purposes set forth in this Article; and

e. to transmit regularly to the Secretary-General for information purposes, subject to such limitation as security and constitutional considerations may require, statistical and other information of a technical nature relating to economic, social, and educational conditions in the territories for which they are respectively responsible other than those territories to which Chapter XII and XIII apply.

Article 74

Members of the United Nations also agree that their policy in respect of the territories to which this Chapter applies, no less than in respect of their metropolitan areas, must be based on the general principle of good-neighborliness, due account being taken of the interests and well-being of the rest of the world, in social, economic, and commercial matters.

Chapter XII
International Trusteeship System

Article 75

The United Nations shall establish under its authority an international trusteeship system for the administration and supervision of such territories as may be placed thereunder by subsequent individual agreements. These territories are hereinafter referred to as trust territories.

Article 76

The basic objectives of the trusteeship system, in accordance with the Purposes of the United Nations laid down in Article 1 of the present Charter, shall be:

a. to further international peace and security;

b. to promote the political, economic, social, and educational advancement of the inhabitants of the trust territories, and their progressive development towards self-government or independence as may be appropriate to the particular circumstances of each territory and its peoples and the freely expressed wishes of the peoples concerned, and as may be provided by the terms of each trusteeship agreement;

c. to encourage respect for human rights and for fundamental freedoms for all without distinction as to race, sex, language, or religion, and to encourage recognition of the interdependence of the peoples of the world; and

d. to ensure equal treatment in social, economic, and commercial matters for all Members of the United Nations and their nationals and also equal treatment for the latter in the administration of justice without prejudice to the attainment of the foregoing objectives and subject to the provisions of Article 80.

Article 77

1. The trusteeship system shall apply to such territories in the following categories as may be placed thereunder by means of trusteeship agreements:

a. territories now held under mandate;

b. territories which may be detached from enemy states as a result of the Second World War, and

c. territories voluntarily placed under the system by states responsible for their administration.

2. It will be a matter for subsequent agreement as to which territories in the foregoing categories will be brought under the trusteeship system and upon what terms.

Article 78

The trusteeship system shall not apply to territories which have become Members of the United Nations, relationship among which shall be based on respect for the principle of sovereign equality.

Article 79

The terms of trusteeship for each territory to be placed under the trusteeship system, including any alteration or amendment, shall be agreed upon by the states directly concerned, including the mandatory power in the case of territories held under mandate by a Member of the United Nations, and shall be approved as provided for in Articles 83 and 85.

Article 80

1. Except as may be agreed upon in individual trusteeship agreements, made under Articles 77, 79, and 81, placing each territory under the trusteeship system, and until such agreements have been concluded, nothing in this Chapter shall be construed in or of itself to alter in any manner the rights whatsoever of any states or any peoples or the terms of existing international instruments to which Members of the United Nations may respectively be parties.

2. Paragraph 1 of this Article shall not be interpreted as giving grounds for delay or postponement of the negotiation and conclusion of agreements for placing mandated and other territories under the trusteeship system as provided for in Article 77.

Article 81

The trusteeship agreement shall in each case include the terms under which the trust territory will be administered and designate the authority which will exercise the administration of the trust territory. Such authority, hereinafter called the administering authority, may be one or more states or the Organization itself.

Article 82

There may be designated, in any trusteeship agreement, a strategic area or areas which may include part or all of the trust territory to which the agreement applies, without prejudice to any special agreement or agreements made under Article 43.

Article 83

1. All functions of the United Nations relating to strategic areas, including the approval of the terms of the trusteeship agreements and of their alteration or amendment, shall be exercised by the Security Council.
2. The basic objectives set forth in Article 76 shall be applicable to the people of each strategic area.
3. The Security Council shall, subject to the provisions of the trusteeship agreements and without prejudice to security considerations, avail itself of the assistance of the Trusteeship Council to perform those functions of the United Nations under the trusteeship system relating to political, economic, social, and educational matters in the strategic areas.

Article 84

It shall be the duty of the administering authority to ensure that the trust territory shall play its part in the maintenance of international peace and security. To this end the administering authority may make use of volunteer forces, facilities, and assistance from the trust territory in carrying out the obligations towards the Security Council undertaken in this regard by the administering authority, as well as for local defense and the maintenance of law and order within the trust territory.

Article 85

1. The functions of the United Nations with regard to trusteeship agreements for all areas not designated as strategic, including the approval of the terms of the trusteeship agreements and of their alteration or amendment, shall be exercised by the General Assembly.
2. The Trusteeship Council, operating under the authority of the General Assembly, shall assist the General Assembly in carrying out these functions.

Chapter XIII
The Trusteeship Council

Composition

Article 86

1. The Trusteeship Council shall consist of the following Members of the United Nations:

a. those Members administering trust territories;

b. such of those Members mentioned by name in Article 23 as are not administering trust territories; and

c. as many other Members elected for three-year terms by the General Assembly as may be necessary to ensure that the total number of members of the Trusteeship Council is equally divided between those Members of the United Nations which administer trust territories and those which do not.

2. Each member of the Trusteeship Council shall designate one specially qualified person to represent it therein.

Functions and Powers

Article 87

The General Assembly and, under its authority, the Trusteeship Council, in carrying out their functions, may:

a. consider reports submitted by the administering authority;

b. accept petitions and examine them in consultation with the administering authority;

c. provide for periodic visits to the respective trust territories at times agreed upon with the administering authority; and

d. take these and other actions in conformity with the terms of the trusteeship agreements.

Article 88

The Trusteeship Council shall formulate a questionnaire on the political, economic, social, and educational advancement of the inhabitants of each trust territory, and the administering authority for each trust territory within the competence of the General Assembly shall make an annual report to the General Assembly upon the basis of such questionnaire.

Voting

Article 89

1. Each member of the Trusteeship Council shall have one vote.
2. Decisions of the Trusteeship Council shall be made by a majority of the members present and voting.

Procedure

Article 90

1. The Trusteeship Council shall adopt its own rules of procedure, including the method of selecting its President.
2. The Trusteeship Council shall meet as required in accordance with its rules, which shall include provision for the convening of meetings on the request of a majority of its members.

Article 91

The Trusteeship Council shall, when appropriate, avail itself of the assistance of the Economic and Social Council and of the specialized agencies in regard to matters with which they are respectively concerned.

Chapter XIV
The International Court of Justice

Article 92

The International Court of Justice shall be the principal judicial organ of the United Nations. It shall function in accordance with the annexed Statute which is based upon the Statute of the Permanent Court of International Justice and forms an integral part of the present Charter.

Article 93

1. All Members of the United Nations are ipso facto parties to the Statute of the International Court of Justice.
2. A state which is not a Member of the United Nations may become a party to the Statute of the International Court of Justice on conditions to be determined in each case by the General Assembly upon the recommendation of the Security Council.

Article 94

1. Each Member of the United Nations undertakes to comply with the decision of the International Court of Justice in any case to which it is a party.

2. If any party to a case fails to perform the obligations incumbent upon it under a judgment rendered by the Court, the other party may have recourse to the Security Council, which may, if it deems necessary, make recommendations or decide upon measures to be taken to give effect to the judgment.

Article 95

Nothing in the present Charter shall prevent Members of the United Nations from entrusting the solution of their differences to other tribunals by virtue of agreements already in existence or which may be concluded in the future.

Article 96

1. The General Assembly or the Security Council may request the International Court of Justice to give an advisory opinion on any legal question.

2. Other organs of the United Nations and specialized agencies, which may at any time be so authorized by the General Assembly, may also request advisory opinions of the Court on legal questions arising within the scope of their activities.

Chapter XV
The Secretariat

Article 97

The Secretariat shall comprise a Secretary-General and such staff as the Organization may require. The Secretary-General shall be appointed by the General Assembly upon the recommendation of the Security Council. He shall be the chief administrative officer of the Organization.

Article 98

The Secretary-General shall act in that capacity in all meetings of the General Assembly, of the Security Council, of the Economic and Social Council, and of the Trusteeship Council, and shall perform such other functions as are entrusted to him by these organs. The Secretary-General shall make an annual report to the General Assembly on the work of the Organization.

Article 99

The Secretary-General may bring to the attention of the Security Council any matter which in his opinion may threaten the maintenance of international peace and security.

Article 100

1. In the performance of their duties the Secretary-General and the staff shall not seek or receive instructions from any government or from any other authority external to the Organization. They shall refrain from any action which might reflect on their position as international officials responsible only to the Organization.
2. Each Member of the United Nations undertakes to respect the exclusively international character of the responsibilities of the Secretary-General and the staff and not to seek to influence them in the discharge of their responsibilities.

Article 101

1. The staff shall be appointed by the Secretary-General under regulations established by the General Assembly.
2. Appropriate staffs shall be permanently assigned to the Economic and Social Council, the Trusteeship Council, and, as required, to other organs of the United Nations. These staffs shall form a part of the Secretariat.
3. The paramount consideration in the employment of the staff and in the determination of the conditions of service shall be the necessity of securing the highest standards of efficiency, competence, and integrity. Due regard shall be paid to the importance of recruiting the staff on as wide a geographical basis as possible.

Chapter XVI
Miscellaneous Provisions

Article 102

1. Every treaty and every international agreement entered into by any Member of the United Nations after the present Charter comes into force shall as soon as possible be registered with the Secretariat and published by it.
2. No party to any such treaty or international agreement which has not been registered in accordance with the provisions of paragraph I of this

Article may invoke that treaty or agreement before any organ of the United Nations.

Article 103

In the event of a conflict between the obligations of the Members of the United Nations under the present Charter and their obligations under any other international agreement, their obligations under the present Charter shall prevail.

Article 104

The Organization shall enjoy in the territory of each of its Members such legal capacity as may be necessary for the exercise of its functions and the fulfillment of its purposes.

Article 105

1. The Organization shall enjoy in the territory of each of its Members such privileges and immunities as are necessary for the fulfillment of its purposes.
2. Representatives of the Members of the United Nations and officials of the Organization shall similarly enjoy such privileges and immunities as are necessary for the independent exercise of their functions in connection with the Organization.
3. The General Assembly may make recommendations with a view to determining the details of the application of paragraphs 1 and 2 of this Article or may propose conventions to the Members of the United Nations for this purpose.

Chapter XVII
Transitional Security Arrangements

Article 106

Pending the coming into force of such special agreements referred to in Article 43 as in the opinion of the Security Council enable it to begin the exercise of its responsibilities under Article 42, the parties to the Four-Nation Declaration, signed at Moscow October 30, 1943, and France, shall, in accordance with the provisions of paragraph 5 of that Declaration, consult with one another and as occasion requires with other Members of the United Nations with a view to such joint action on behalf of the Organization as may be necessary for the purpose of maintaining international peace and security.

Article 107

Nothing in the present Charter shall invalidate or preclude action, in relation to any state which during the Second World War has been an enemy of any signatory to the present Charter, taken or authorized as a result of that war by the Governments having responsibility for such action.

Chapter XVIII
Amendments

Article 108

Amendments to the present Charter shall come into force for all Members of the United Nations when they have been adopted by a vote of two-thirds of the members of the General Assembly and ratified in accordance with their respective constitutional processes by two-thirds of the Members of the United Nations, including all the permanent members of the Security Council.

Article 109

1. A General Conference of the Members of the United Nations for the purpose of reviewing the present Charter may be held at a date and place to be fixed by a two-thirds vote of the members of the General Assembly and by a vote of any seven members of the Security Council. Each Member of the United Nations shall have one vote in the conference.
2. Any alteration of the present Charter recommended by a two-thirds vote of the conference shall take effect when ratified in accordance with their respective constitutional processes by two-thirds of the Members of the United Nations including all the permanent members of the Security Council.
3. If such a conference has not been held before the tenth annual session of the General Assembly following the coming into force of the present Charter, the proposal to call such a conference shall be placed on the agenda of that session of the General Assembly, and the conference shall be held if so decided by a majority vote of the members of the General Assembly and by a vote of any seven members of the Security Council.

Chapter XIX
Ratification and Signature

Article 110

1. The present Charter shall be ratified by the signatory states in accordance with their respective constitutional processes.

2. The ratifications shall be deposited with the Government of the United States of America, which shall notify all the signatory states of each deposit as well as the Secretary-General of the Organization when he has been appointed.

3. The present Charter shall come into force upon the deposit of ratifications by the Republic of China, France, the Union of Soviet Socialist Republics, the United Kingdom of Great Britain and Northern Ireland, and the United States of America, and by a majority of the other signatory states. A protocol of the ratifications deposited shall thereupon be drawn up by the Government of the United States of America which shall communicate copies thereof to all the signatory states.

4. The states signatory to the present Charter which ratify it after it has come into force will become original Members of the United Nations on the date of the deposit of their respective ratifications.

Article 111

The present Charter, of which the Chinese, French, Russian, English, and Spanish texts are equally authentic, shall remain deposited in the archives of the Government of the United States of America. Duly certified copies thereof shall be transmitted by that Government to the Governments of the other signatory states.

IN FAITH WHEREOF the representatives of the Governments of the United Nations have signed the present Charter.

DONE at the city of San Francisco the twenty-sixth day of June, one thousand nine hundred and forty-five.

Further Reading

Customary international law

Michael Akehurst, 'Custom as a Source of International Law', (1974–75), 47, *British Yearbook of International Law*, 1

Michael Byers, *Custom, Power and the Power of Rules: International Relations and Customary International Law* (Cambridge University Press, 1999)

Gennady Danilenko, *Law-Making in the International Community* (Martinus Nijhoff, 1993)

Law of treaties

Lord McNair, *The Law of Treaties* (Oxford University Press, 1961, reprinted 1986)

1969 Vienna Convention on the Law of Treaties, 1155 United Nations Treaty Series, also available at:

<http://www.un.org/law/ilc/texts/treatfra.htm>

Paul Reuter, *Introduction to the Law of Treaties* (2nd English edn), trans. José Mico and Peter Haggenmacher (Kegan Paul International, 1995)

Oscar Schachter, 'Entangled Treaty and Custom', in *International Law at a Time of Perplexity: Essays in Honour of Shabtai Rosenne*, ed. Yoram Dinstein (Martinus Nijhoff, Dordrecht, 1989), p. 717

International law on the use of force

Ian Brownlie, *International Law and the Use of Force by States* (Oxford University Press, 1963)

Yoram Dinstein, *War, Aggression and Self-Defence* (3rd edn, Cambridge University Press, 2001)

Thomas M. Franck, *Recourse to Force* (Cambridge University Press, 2003)

Christine Gray, *International Law and the Use of Force* (2nd edn, Oxford University Press, 2004)

International humanitarian law

Yoram Dinstein, *The Conduct of Hostilities under the Law of International Armed Conflict* (Cambridge University Press, 2004)

A. P. V. Rogers, *Law on the Battlefield* (2nd edn) (Manchester University Press, 2004)

War law and the United States

Michael Byers and Georg Nolte (eds), *United States Hegemony and the Foundations of International Law* (Cambridge University Press, 2003)

1: SECURITY COUNCIL AUTHORIZATION

United Nations and the use of force

Danesh Sarooshi, *The United Nations and the Development of Collective Security: The Delegation by the UN Security Council of its Chapter VII Powers* (Oxford University Press, 1999)

Bruno Simma (ed.), *The Charter of the United Nations: A Commentary* (2nd edn, Oxford University Press, 2002)

Korea

Country profile: North Korea <http://news.bbc.co.uk/1/hi/world/asia-pacific/country_profiles/1131421.stm>

Timeline: North Korea <http://news.bbc.co.uk/1/hi/world/asia-pacific/country_profiles/1132268.stm>

Country profile: South Korea <http://news.bbc.co.uk/1/hi/world/asia-pacific/country_profiles/1123668.stm>

Timeline: South Korea <http://news.bbc.co.uk/1/hi/world/asia-pacific/country_profiles/1132724.stm>

Edwin C. Hoyt, 'The United States Reaction to the Korean Attack: A Study of the Principles of the United Nations Charter as a Factor in American Policy-Making' (1961), 55, *American Journal of International Law*, 45

Southern Rhodesia

Country profile: Zimbabwe <http://news.bbc.co.uk/2/hi/world/africa/country_profiles/1064589.stm>

Timeline: Zimbabwe <http://news.bbc.co.uk/2/hi/world/africa/country_profiles/1831470.stm>

Vera Gowlland-Debbas, *Collective Responses to Illegal Acts in International Law: United Nations Action in the Question of Southern Rhodesia* (Martinus Nijhoff, 1990)

Myres McDougal and W. Michael Reisman, 'Rhodesia and the United Nations: The Lawfulness of International Concern' (1968), 62, *American Journal of International Law*, 1

Iraq (1990–91)

Country profile: Iraq <http://news.bbc.co.uk/1/hi/world/middle-east/country_profiles/791014.stm>

Timeline: Iraq <http://news.bbc.co.uk/1/hi/world/middle-east/country_profiles/737483.stm>

Oscar Schachter, 'United Nations Law in the Gulf Conflict' (1991), 85, *American Journal of International Law*, 452

Marc Weller (ed.), *Iraq and Kuwait: The Hostilities and their Aftermath* (Grotius, 1993)

Bosnia-Herzegovina

Country profile: Bosnia-Herzegovina <http://news.bbc.co.uk/1/hi/world/europe/country_profiles/1066886.stm>

Timeline: Bosnia-Herzegovina <http://news.bbc.co.uk/1/hi/world/europe/country_profiles/1066981.stm>

Simon Chesterman, *Just War or Just Peace? Humanitarian Intervention and International Law* (Oxford University Press, 2001)

2: EXPANDING REACH OF THE SECURITY COUNCIL

Somalia

Country profile: Somalia <http://news.bbc.co.uk/1/hi/world/africa/country_profiles/1072592.stm>

Timeline: Somalia <http://news.bbc.co.uk/1/hi/world/africa/country_profiles/1072611.stm>

Ruth Gordon, 'United Nations Intervention in Internal Conflicts: Iraq, Somalia, and Beyond' (1994), 15, *Michigan Journal of International Law*, 519

Rwanda

Country profile: Rwanda <http://news.bbc.co.uk/1/hi/world/africa/country_profiles/1070265.stm>

Timeline: Rwanda <http://news.bbc.co.uk/1/hi/world/africa/country_profiles/1070329.stm>

Roméo Dallaire, *Shake Hands with the Devil: The Failure of Humanity in Rwanda* (Random House, 2003)

Linda Melvern, *A People Betrayed: The Role of the West in Rwanda's Genocide* (Zed Books, 2000)

Haiti

Country profile: Haiti <http://news.bbc.co.uk/2/hi/world/americas/country_profiles/1202772.stm>

Timeline: Haiti <http://news.bbc.co.uk/2/hi/americas/1202857.stm>

Gregory H. Fox and Brad R. Roth (eds), *Democratic Governance and International Law* (Cambridge University Press, 2000)

David Malone, *Decision-Making in the UN Security Council: The Case of Haiti, 1990–1997* (Oxford University Press, 1998)

W. Michael Reisman, 'Haiti and the Validity of International Action' (1995), 89, *American Journal of International Law*, 82

East Timor

Country profile: East Timor <http://news.bbc.co.uk/1/hi/world/asia-pacific/country_profiles/1508119.stm>

Timeline: East Timor <http://news.bbc.co.uk/1/hi/world/asia-pacific/country_profiles/1508119.stm>

Mark Rothert, 'U.N. Intervention in East Timor' (2000), 39, *Columbia Journal of Transnational Law*, 257

Darfur, Sudan

Human Rights Watch, 'Empty Promises: Continuing Abuses in Darfur, Sudan', HRW Briefing Paper, 11 August 2004 <http://hrw.org/backgrounder/africa/sudan/2004/>

International Crisis Group, 'Darfur Deadline: A New International Action Plan', ICG Africa Report No. 83, 23 August 2004 <http://www.crisisweb.org/home/index.cfm>

Samantha Power, 'Dying in Darfur', *New Yorker*, 30 August 2004, pp. 56–73

3: IMPLIED AUTHORIZATION AND INTENTIONAL AMBIGUITY

No-fly zones in Iraq

Christine Gray, 'After the Ceasefire: Iraq, the Security Council and the Use of Force' (1994), 65, *British Yearbook of International Law*, 135

Jules Lobel and Michael Ratner, 'Bypassing the Security Council: Ambiguous Authorization to Use Force, Cease-Fires and the Iraqi Inspection Regime' (1999), 93, *American Journal of International Law*, 124

Kosovo (1999)

BBC News, 'Kosovo: An Uneasy Peace' <http://news.bbc.co.uk/hi/english/static/kosovo_fact_files/default.stm>

Simon Chesterman, *Just War or Just Peace? Humanitarian Intervention and International Law* (Oxford University Press, 2001)

Dino Kritsiotis, 'The Kosovo Crisis and NATO's application of armed force against the Federal Republic of Yugoslavia' (2000), 49, *International and Comparative Law Quarterly*, 330

Iraq (2003)

BBC News, 'Iraq in Transition' <http://news.bbc.co.uk/1/hi/in_depth/middle_east/2002/conflict_with_iraq/default.stm>

Dino Kritsiotis, 'Arguments of Mass Confusion' (2004), 15, *European Journal of International Law*, 233

Jane Stromseth, 'Law and Force After Iraq: A Transitional Moment' (2003), 97, *American Journal of International Law*, 628

Interpretation of Security Council resolutions

Jochen Abr. Frowein, 'Unilateral Interpretation of Security Council Resolutions – A Threat to Collective Security?' in Volkmar Götz (ed.), *Liber amicorum Günther Jaenicke – zum 85. Geburtstag* (Springer, 1998) p. 98

Michael Wood, 'The Interpretation of Security Council Resolutions' (1998), 2, *Max Planck United Nations Yearbook*, 73

4: 'INHERENT RIGHT' OF SELF-DEFENCE

The Caroline incident

R. Y. Jennings, 'The *Caroline* and McLeod Cases' (1938), 32, *American Journal of International Law*, 82

Protection of nationals

Michael Akehurst, 'The use of force to protect nationals abroad' (1977), 5, *International Relations*, 3

Derek Bowett, 'The Use of Force for the Protection of Nationals Abroad' in Antonio Cassese (ed.), *The Current Legal Regulation of the Use of Force* (Martinus Nijhoff, 1986), p. 39

Self-defence and reprisals

R. Barsotti, 'Armed Reprisals' in Antonio Cassese (ed.), *The Current Legal Regulation of the Use of Force* (Martinus Nijhoff, 1986), p. 79

Dino Kritsiotis, 'The Legality of the 1993 Missile Strike on Iraq and the Right of Self-Defence in International Law' (1996), 45, *International and Comparative Law Quarterly*, p. 163

5: SELF-DEFENCE AGAINST TERRORISM

Libya (1986)

Country profile: Libya <http://news.bbc.co.uk/1/hi/world/middle_east/country_profiles/819291.stm>

Timeline: Libya <http://news.bbc.co.uk/1/hi/world/middle_east/country_profiles/1398437.stm>

Abraham Sofaer, 'Terrorism and the Law' (1986), *Foreign Affairs*, 901

David Turndorf, 'The U.S. Raid on Libya: A Forceful Response' (1988), 14, *Brooklyn Journal of International Law*, 187

Afghanistan and Sudan (1998)

Country profile: Afghanistan <http://news.bbc.co.uk/1/hi/world/south_asia/country_profiles/1162668.stm>

Timeline: Afghanistan <http://news.bbc.co.uk/1/hi/world/south_asia/1162108.stm>

Country profile: Sudan <http://news.bbc.co.uk/1/hi/world/middle_east/country_profiles/820864.stm>

Timeline: Sudan <http://news.bbc.co.uk/1/hi/world/middle_east/country_profiles/827425.stm>

Jules Lobel, 'The Use of Force to Respond to Terrorist Attacks: The Bombing of Sudan and Afghanistan' (1999), 24, *Yale Journal of International Law*, 537

Ruth Wedgwood, 'Responding to Terrorism: The Strikes Against bin Laden' (1999), 24, *Yale Journal of International Law*, 559

Afghanistan (2001)

Michael Byers, 'Terrorism, the Use of Force and International Law after 11 September' (2002), 51, *International and Comparative Law Quarterly*, 401; reprinted in (2002) 16, *International Relations*, 155

Thomas Franck, 'Terrorism and the Right of Self-Defense' (2001), 95, *American Journal of International Law*, 839

Israel, Palestine and 'targeted killings'

Country profile: Israel and Palestinian Territories <http://news.bbc.co.uk/1/hi/world/middle_east/country_profiles/803257.stm>

Amnesty International, *Israel and the Occupied Territories: State Assassinations and Other Unlawful Killings* (AI Index No. MDE 15/005/2001, February 2001) <http://web.amnesty.org/library/index/engmde150052001>

Eyal Benvenisti, *The International Law of Occupation* (Princeton University Press, 1993; reprinted in 2004 with a new preface)

Adam Roberts, 'Prolonged Military Occupation: The Israeli-Occupied Territories Since 1967' (1990), 84, *American Journal of International Law*, 44

Michael Schmitt, 'State-Sponsored Assassination in International and Domestic Law' (1992), 17, *Yale Journal of International Law*, 609

6: PRE-EMPTIVE SELF-DEFENCE

The Caroline *Case and Article 51*

Derek Bowett, *Self-defence in International Law* (Manchester University Press, 1958)

Ian Brownlie, *International Law and the Use of Force by States* (Oxford University Press, 1963)

Osirak nuclear reactor (1981)

Timothy MacCormack, *Self-defense in international law: the Israeli raid on the Iraqi nuclear reactor* (St. Martin's Press, New York, 1986)

Bush Doctrine and National Security Strategy of the United States (2002)

Christopher Greenwood, 'International Law and Preemptive Use of Force: Afghanistan, Al-Qaida and Iraq' (2003), 4, *San Diego International Law Journal*, 7

National Security Strategy of the United States, September 2002 <http://www.whitehouse.gov/nsc/nss.pdf>

Report of the Secretary General's High Level Panel on Threats, Challenges and Change, *A more secure world: Our shared responsibility* (United Nations, 2004) <http://www.un.org/secureworld>

Ruth Wedgwood, 'The Fall of Saddam Hussein: Security Council Mandates and Preemptive Self-Defence' (2003), 97, *American Journal of International Law*, 576

7: PRO-DEMOCRATIC INTERVENTION

Pro-democratic intervention in general

James Crawford, 'Democracy and International Law' (1993), 44, *British Yearbook of International Law*, 113

Gregory Fox and Brad Roth (eds), *Democratic Governance and International Law* (Cambridge University Press, 2000)

Thomas Franck, *Fairness in International Law and Institutions* (Oxford University Press, 1995)

Brad Roth, *Government Illegitimacy in International Law* (Oxford University Press, 1999)

Oscar Schachter, 'The Legality of Pro-Democratic Invasion' (1984), 78, *American Journal of International Law*, 645

Grenada

Country profile: Grenada <http://news.bbc.co.uk/2/hi/americas/country_profiles/1209605.stm>

Timeline: Grenada <http://news.bbc.co.uk/2/hi/americas/country_profiles/1209649.stm>

Robert Beck, 'International Law and the Decision to Invade Grenada: A Ten-Year Retrospective' (1993), 33, *Virginia Journal of International Law*, 789

'Legal Adviser of the Department of State, Davis R. Robinson, letter dated February 10, 1984, addressed to Professor Edward Gordon, Chairman of the Committee on Grenada of the American Bar Association's Section on International Law and Practice' (1984), 78, *American Journal of International Law*, 661

Panama

Country profile: Panama <http://news.bbc.co.uk/2/hi/world/americas/country_profiles/1229332.stm>

Timeline: Panama <http://news.bbc.co.uk/2/hi/world/americas/1229333.stm>

Anthony D'Amato, 'The Invasion of Panama Was a Lawful Response to Tyranny' (1990), 84, *American Journal of International Law*, 516

Louis Henkin, 'The Invasion of Panama under International Law: A Gross Violation' (1991), 29, *Columbia Journal of Transnational Law*, 293

W. Michael Reisman, 'Sovereignty and Human Rights in Contemporary International Law' (1990), 84, *American Journal of International Law*, 866

8: UNILATERAL HUMANITARIAN INTERVENTION

Humanitarian intervention in general

Simon Chesterman, *Just War or Just Peace? Humanitarian Intervention and International Law* (Oxford University Press, 2001)

J. L. Holzgrefe and Robert O. Keohane, *Humanitarian Intervention: Ethical, Legal, and Political Dilemmas* (Cambridge University Press, 2003)

Sean Murphy, *Humanitarian Intervention: The United Nations in an Evolving World Order* (University of Pennsylvania Press, 1996)

Adam Roberts, 'The So-called "Right" of Humanitarian Intervention' (2000), 3, *Yearbook of International Humanitarian Law*, 3

Nicholas Wheeler, *Saving Strangers: Humanitarian Intervention in International Society* (Oxford University Press, 2000)

East Pakistan (1971)

Country profile: Bangladesh <http://news.bbc.co.uk/1/hi/world/south_asia/country_profiles/1160598.stm>

Timeline: Bangladesh <http://news.bbc.co.uk/1/hi/world/south_asia/country_profiles/1160896.stm>

Thomas Franck and Nigel Rodley, 'After Bangladesh: The Law of Humanitarian Intervention by Military Force' (1973), 67, *American Journal of International Law*, 275

Cambodia (1978)

Country profile: Cambodia <http://news.bbc.co.uk/1/hi/world/asia-pacific/country_profiles/1243892.stm>

Timeline: Cambodia <http://news.bbc.co.uk/1/hi/world/asia-pacific/country_profiles/1244006.stm>

Gary Klintworth, *Vietnam's Intervention in Cambodia in International Law* (Australian Government Publishing Service, 1989)

Uganda (1979)

Country profile: Uganda <http://news.bbc.co.uk/1/hi/world/africa/country_profiles/1069166.stm>

Timeline: Uganda <http://news.bbc.co.uk/1/hi/world/africa/country_profiles/1069181.stm>

U. O. Umozurike, 'Tanzania's Intervention in Uganda' (1982), 20, *Archiv des Völkerrecht*, 301

Kosovo (1999)

Kosovo: An Uneasy Peace <http://news.bbc.co.uk/hi/english/static/kosovo_fact_files/default.stm>

The Kosovo Report: Report of the Independent International Commission on Kosovo (Oxford University Press, 2000)

9: Responsibility to Protect

The Responsibility to Protect: Report of the International Commission on Intervention and State Sovereignty (Ottawa: International Development Research Centre, 2001)

The Kosovo Report: Report of the Independent International Commission on Kosovo (Oxford University Press, 2000)

Report of the Secretary General's High Level Panel on Threats, Challenges and Change, *A more secure world: Our shared responsibility* (United Nations, 2004) <http://www.un.org/secureworld>

Lloyd Axworthy, *Navigating a New World: Canada's Global Future* (Alfred A. Knopf, Canada, 2003)

Terry Nardin, 'The Moral Basis of Humanitarian Intervention' (2002), 16, *Ethics and International Affairs*, 57

W. Michael Reisman, 'Sovereignty and Human Rights in Contemporary International Law' (1990), 84, *American Journal of International Law*, 866

Fernando Tesón, *Humanitarian Intervention: An Inquiry into Law and Morality* (2nd edn, Transnational Publishers, 1997)

Nicholas Wheeler, *Saving Strangers: Humanitarian Intervention in International Society* (Oxford University Press, 2000)

10: PROTECTION OF CIVILIANS

Geoffrey Best, *War and Law since 1945* (Oxford University Press, 1997)

Crimes of War Project <http://www.crimesofwar.org/>

Yoram Dinstein, *The Conduct of Hostilities under the Law of International Armed Conflict* (Cambridge University Press, 2004)

Roy Gutman and David Rieff, *Crimes of War: What the Public Should Know* (W. W. Norton & Co., 1999)

International Committee of the Red Cross: <http://www.icrc.org/>

A. P. V. Rogers, *Law on the Battlefield* (2nd edn, Manchester University Press, 2004)

Marco Sassoli and Antoine Bouvier, *How Does Law Protect in War?* (International Committee of the Red Cross, 1999)

UK Ministry of Defence, *The Manual of the Law of Armed Conflict* (Oxford University Press, 2004)

11: PROTECTION OF COMBATANTS AND PRISONERS OF WAR

Geoffrey Best, *War and Law since 1945* (Oxford University Press, 1997)

Crimes of War Project <http://www.crimesofwar.org/>

Yoram Dinstein, *The Conduct of Hostilities under the Law of International Armed Conflict* (Cambridge University Press, 2004)

Roy Gutman and David Rieff, *Crimes of War: What the Public Should Know* (W. W. Norton & Co., 1999)

Seymour Hersh, *Chain of Command: The Road from 9/11 to Abu Ghraib* (HarperCollins, 2004)

International Committee of the Red Cross <http://www.icrc.org/>

A. P. V. Rogers, *Law on the Battlefield* (2nd edn, Manchester University Press, 2004)

Marco Sassoli and Antoine Bouvier, *How Does Law Protect in War?* (International Committee of the Red Cross, 1999)

UK Ministry of Defence, *The Manual of the Law of Armed Conflict* (Oxford University Press, 2004)

12: WAR CRIMES COURTS AND TRIBUNALS

Bruce Broomhall, *International Justice and the International Criminal Court: Between Sovereignty and the Rule of Law* (Oxford University Press, 2003)

Antonio Cassese, Paola Gaeta and John Jones, *The Rome Statute of the International Criminal Court: A Commentary* (Oxford University Press, 2002)

Steven R. Ratner and Jason S. Abrams, *Accountability for Human Rights Atrocities in International Law* (2nd edn, Oxford University Press, 2001)

Geoffrey Robertson QC, *Crimes Against Humanity: The Struggle for Global Justice* (2nd edn, Penguin, 2002)

William Schabas, *An Introduction to the International Criminal Court* (Cambridge University Press, 2001)

Chris Stephen, *Judgement Day: The Trial of Slobodan Milošević* (Atlantic Books, 2004)

EPILOGUE: WAR LAW AND THE SINGLE SUPERPOWER

Michael Byers and Georg Nolte (eds), *United States Hegemony and the Foundations of International Law* (Cambridge University Press, 2003)

Wilhelm G. Grewe, *The Epochs of International Law*, translated & revised by Michael Byers (Walter De Gruyter, 2000)

Christian Reus-Smit, *American Power and World Order* (Polity Press, 2004)

Selected Internet Sites

Academic Council of the United Nations System
<http://www.acuns.wlu.ca>

American Society of International Law <http://www.asil.org>

Amnesty International <http://amnesty.org>

British Institute of International and Comparative Law
<http://www.biicl.org>

Carnegie Council on Ethics and International Affairs
<http://www.carnegiecouncil.org>

Carnegie Endowment for International Peace <http://www.ceip.org/>

Chatham House <http://www.chathamhouse.org.uk>

Council on Foreign Relations <http://www.cfr.org/>

Crimes of War Project <http://www.crimesofwar.org>

Foreign and Commonwealth Office, London <http://www.fco.gov.uk>

Human Rights Watch <http://www.hrw.org>

International Committee of the Red Cross <http://www.icrc.org>

ICRC databases on international humanitarian law
<http://www.icrc.org/web/eng/siteengo.nsf/iwplList2/
Info_recources:IHL_databases>

1949 Geneva Conventions and 1977 Protocols
<http://www.icrc.org/Web/Eng/siteeng0.nsf/html/genevaconventions>

International Court of Justice <http://www.icj-cij.org>

International Criminal Court <http://www.icc-cpi.int>

International Criminal Tribunal for the Former Yugoslavia
<http://www.un.org/icty>

International Criminal Tribunal for Rwanda <http://www.ictr.org>

International Humanitarian Law Research Initiative
<http://www.ihlresearch.org/ihl>

International Institute for Strategic Studies <http://www.iiss.org>

International Law Association <http://www.ila-hq.org>

International Peace Academy <http://www.ipacademy.org/>

Iraqi Special Tribunal Statute
<http://www.cpa-iraq.org/human_rights/Statute.htm>

Lauterpacht Research Centre for International Law, Cambridge
<http://www.law.cam.ac.uk/rcil>

Max Planck Institute for Comparative Public Law and International Law
<http://www.virtual-institute.de/eindex.cfm>

North Atlantic Treaty Organization <http://www.nato.int/>

Special Court for Sierra Leone <http://www.sc-sl.org>

Stockholm International Peace Research Institute <http://www.sipri.se>

T. M. C. Asser Institute (The Hague) <http://www.asser.nl>

United Nations:

UN General Assembly <http://www.un.org/ga>

UN Security Council <http://www.un.org/Docs/sc>

UN Security Council Resolutions
<http://www.un.org/documents/scres.htm>

UN Secretary General
<http://www.un.org/News/ossg/sg/index.shtml>

United Nations Association of the United States of America:
<http://www.unausa.org>

United States Department of Defense <http://www.dod.gov>

United States Department of State <http://www.state.gov>

Index

The Obsession
of
Victoria Gracen

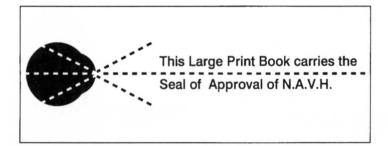

The Obsession
of
Victoria Gracen

Grace Livingston Hill

Thorndike Press • Thorndike, Maine

Published in 1998 by arrangement with Munce Publishing.

Thorndike Large Print ® Romance Series.

The tree indicium is a trademark of Thorndike Press.

The text of this Large Print edition is unabridged.
Other aspects of the book may vary from the original edition.

Set in 16 pt. Plantin by Rick Gundberg.

Printed in the United States on permanent paper.

Library of Congress Cataloging in Publication Data

Hill, Grace Livingston, 1865–1947.
    The obsession of Victoria Gracen / Grace Livingston Hill.
        p.   cm.
    ISBN 0-7862-1475-9 (lg. print : hc : alk. paper)
    1. Large type books.   I. Title.
[PS3515.I486O27   1998]
813′.52—dc21
                                                    98-3720

The Obsession
of
Victoria Gracen

1

The carriage turned the corner at a cheerful trot, and drew up before the door of a smart brick house in a row of new houses on a little new street. The occupants, one by one, alighted on the sidewalk with an air of relief and of duty well done.

Mr. Miller, tall and heavy, with a thick, red neck and a coarse, red face, got out first, followed by his sharp-faced aspiring wife in borrowed mourning — because of course one wouldn't want to wear mourning after the funeral for a mere sister-in-law who left nothing behind but a mortgage and a good-for-nothing son.

The three little Millers, Elsa, Carlotta, and Alexander, in black hair-ribbons and black hat-bands, who had gone along solely for the ride to the cemetery, spilled joyfully out, glad to be back home again; and finally the only mourner the carriage contained, Richard, the son of the dead woman, stepped awkwardly forth from his cramped position, and looked gloomily about him.

The setting sun was sending long, red rays across the pavement. It was good to the Millers to be back in every-day life again with thoughts to death put aside, and little, common, *alive* things going on everywhere — children calling to one another in the street, wagons and carts hurrying home after the day's work, the clang of the crowded trolley, the weak light of the street-lamps suddenly blinking ineffectually into the ruby light of the setting sun. It was good to see one's own house standing safe and homely in shining varnish and glowing painted brick, and to know that life could now go on in its regular pleasant monotony, which had been interrupted solemnly for four days by the sudden death of one who had been near without being particularly dear. The sister who had married above her station into a family who never received her or took any notice of her child; whose husband had the ill grace to die young and leave her to struggle on alone with their house only half paid for and a handsome, lazy boy whom she had allowed to grow up to have his own way, was not deeply mourned by any of them. They looked upon her son as almost irretrievably spoiled, but they intended to do their sensible best to make a man of him in their own way, though they felt that for his good his mother should have died ten years earlier.

They marshalled their forces on the sidewalk in front of the house, and looked closely at him now with a strange, new, possessive glance.

"Supper'll be ready t'woncet," said his aunt pointedly; "so don't you go to goin' off."

Richard regarded her defiantly, but said nothing. He was not hungry, but he had no relish for an argument with his aunt. He had always kept out of her way as much as possible. She knew he disliked her. He had once come upon her while she was in the midst of giving his mother some wholesome advice about his upbringing; and he had loomed darkly in the doorway and told her to go about her business, that his mother knew how to manage her own affairs. He had looked so big and fierce, with his fine, black brows drawn and his dark eyes blazing, that she had gone away, deferring her further advice until a more convenient season when he should not be by, but she knew that since then he had never liked her.

Richard looked furtively down the street; but his uncle's heavy hand was upon his shoulder, and there was that in his uncle's eye that made it apparent that the thing to do was to go into the house. The boy had no desire to make a scene. He wished to do all that was necessary to show respect to his mother, but his soul was raging at the necessity which made him a part of this group of unloved relatives. His uncle had once told a man in his presence that Richard resembled his father's family, with an adjective describing that family which was anything but complimentary, and that if he had his way with the boy he would be taken from school and made to work to get the foolishness out of him. He had said that it usually took two generations at least to get the "fine-gentleman" strain out of a family, but he'd take it out of Richard in one if he had half a chance. Since then Richard had hated his uncle.

Entering the house, they found supper all ready; a good roast of beef with vegetables and three kinds of pie in honor of the occasion. The family ate with zest; for they felt the hard part of the day to be over, and they might now enjoy the gala part, which consisted mainly in eating the things prepared as for a wedding-feast. This was a funeral-feast. Mrs. Miller had invited her two sisters to share it with them. It helped to pay a long-standing score of invitations, besides looking well to the neighbors that she went to so much trouble for just a sister-in-law.

The two sisters had brought their respective husbands and children, and arrived from the cemetery almost immediately, laughing and talking with discreetly crescendo voices. Altogether it was a jolly company that sat down to the table; and Richard, frowning, silent, was the only one out of accord. He ate little, and before the rest were half through, sat back with sullen gaze. His uncle talked much, with his mouth full of beef, to the two brothers-in-law, and laughed heartily. The funeral aspect was fast disappearing from the group. His uncle rallied the boy on his solemnity.

"It's no more than natural," said one of the aunt's sisters, peering at him not unkindly with curious, mild eyes. "Of course the boy feels it. But then it ain't as if he was all alone in the world. Richard, you'd really ought to be thankful you've got such a good home and such kind relatives to take care of you."

Richard's face flushed angrily. He was not in the least thankful, and he had no idea whatever of being taken care of by any of his kind relatives. He did not care for even the kindness in the eyes of this woman who was not a relative, for which latter fact he

11

was very thankful. He wanted to tell her to attend to her own affairs, but it did not seem a wise remark to make just then. He was one against many. He knew he could not knock them all down.

"Have another piece of pie, Richard," invited his aunt magnanimously, as if the second piece of pie were a panacea for all troubles. "His ma always let him have the second helping," she explained portentously to her sisters, as if it had been a habit of the dead woman much to be deplored. Richard declined the piece of pie curtly. The soul within him was at the boiling-point. He had never been outwardly a very loving son to his mother, but it frenzied him to hear her spoken of in his aunt's contemptuous tone.

"Richard goes to work at the slaughter-house tomorrow morning," stated his uncle to the brothers-in-law, as if it were something quite understood between the uncle and nephew. "Work'll take his mind off his loss. There's nothing like work to make a man of a fellow."

"That's so!" declared the other two men, heartily, "that's so! Right well do I remember when I first started out to work."

"So you're going to work in the slaughter-house, Richard," said the mild sister, again turning her curious eyes on him approvingly. "That's right. Your mother would 'a' been real pleased at that. She was always awful troubled about your idle ways, your not getting on in school, nor hunting a job —"

But Richard interrupted her further remarks.

"Not much I ain't going to work at the slaughterhouse," he blazed in a low angry tone that sounded like a rumble of thunder.

He shoved his chair back sharply, and rose to his feet. He would stand this thing no longer.

"You sure are going to work at the slaughter-house, Richard," declared his uncle; "and you're going to-morrow morning. I got a job for you just yesterday, and told 'em you'd be on hand. It's a good job with reasonable pay right at the start, and you'll be able to pay your board to your aunt like any young fellow that earns his own living. Of course you couldn't get board that low anywheres else; but it's a start, and when you get a raise we'll expect you to pay more. It's only reasonable. You'll have a chance to rise and learn the whole business, and some day you may have a business of your own."

"No, thanks!" said Richard curtly in the

tone that offended because it was so like his fine-gentleman father's manner.

"None of your airs, young man! I'm your guardian now. You'll do as I say, and I don't intend to have you loafing about the streets smoking cigarettes and learning to drink. You've got a *man* to deal with now. You're not mamma's pet any longer. You've got to go to work to-morrow morning, and you might just as well understand it right now."

Richard was too angry to speak. His throat seemed to close over the furious words that rushed to his lips. He stood facing his great, red-faced, beefy uncle, whose work had been in the slaughter-house since he was a mere boy, who had early learned to drink the hot blood of the creatures he killed, and who looked like one of his own great oxen ready for slaughter. There was contempt and scorn in the fine, young face of the boy, fine in spite of the lines of self-indulgence which his dead mother had helped him to grave upon it. He was white and cool with anger. It was a part of his aristocratic heritage that he could control his manner and voice when he was angry, and it always made his tempestuous uncle still more furious that he could not break this youthful contemptuous calm; therefore Richard had the advantage of him in an argument.

The boy looked his uncle defiantly in the eyes for a full minute, while the relatives watched in mingled surprise, interest, and disapproval, the audacity of the youth; then he turned on his heel, and without a word walked toward the door.

"Where you goin', Richard?" called out his cousin Elsa, disappointed that the interesting scene should be suddenly brought to a close by the disappearance of the hero. Elsa frequented moving-picture shows, and liked to have her tragedies well worked out.

Richard had never really disliked Elsa. She had but too lately emerged from babyhood to have been in the least annoying to him. Her question was merely the question of a child.

"I'm going home," he answered briefly, and his hand was on the door-knob; but his progress was stopped by the thundering voice of his uncle.

"Stop, you young jackanapes!" he roared. "Do you mean to defy me in my own house? Just come back to your seat at the table, and we'll have it out. Now is as good as any time. You've got to understand that I'm your master, if it is the day of your mother's funeral."

"And your mother scarcely cold in her

grave yet!" whimpered his aunt. "You're going to run around town and disgrace us all, you know you are."

"I am only going home, Aunt Sophia," said Richard with the calm dignity that was like a red rag to the fury of his irate uncle.

"Home!" thundered the uncle. "You have no home but this. Don't you know that the old house you called home was mortgaged to more than its worth, and that I hold the mortgage? Your mother was deep in debt to me when she died, and there wasn't even enough left to pay her funeral expenses. It's high time you understood how matters stand, young man. You *have* no home! You will have to come down off your high horse now, and get right down to business. A boy that can't even pay his mother's funeral expenses has no room to walk around like a fine gentleman and talk about going home."

Richard looked his uncle in the eyes again, a cold fury stealing over him, a desperate, lonely, heart-sinking horror taking possession of him. He felt that he could not and would not stay here another minute. He wanted to fly at his uncle and thrash him. He wanted to stop all their ugly, gloating voices, and show himself master of the situation; but he was only a lonely, homeless boy, penniless — so his uncle said — and without a friend in the world. But at least he would not stay here to give them the satisfaction of bullying him.

Suddenly he fumed with a quick movement, and bolted from the room and the house.

It was all done so quickly that they could not have stopped him. His uncle had not thought he would go after he heard the truth. His aunt began to cry over the disgrace she said he would bring upon the family, running around town the night of his mother's funeral, and perhaps getting drunk and getting his name in the paper. She reproached her husband tearfully for not having used more tact in his dealings with the boy this first night.

The two visiting brothers-in-law advised not worrying, and said the boy would be all right. He was just worked up over his loss. He would willingly come to terms next day when he was hungry and found he had no home. Just let him alone to-night. Elsa said she shouldn't think Richard would want to go to his home. She should think he'd be afraid. She said she'd stay by the window and watch for him, and thus she stole out of the uncomfortable family debate.

Richard, meanwhile, was breathlessly running block after block toward his old home.

It might be true or not that the house was mortgaged to his uncle. It probably was true, for he remembered his mother worrying about expenses when the boarders began to leave because the table was getting so poor they couldn't stand it, and she got sick, and the cook left; but, true or not, they could not take him away from the house to-night. It was his refuge from the world by all that was decent. He would go back to his home, crawl in at a window, and think out what he would do with himself. His uncle would not pursue him there to-night, he was sure; and, if he did, it would be easy to hide. His uncle would never think to look on the roof, which had been his refuge more than once in a childish scrape.

He stole in through the little side-alley entrance to the tiny kitchen-yard where his mother's ragged dish-cloth still fluttered disconsolately in the chill air of the evening. He was thankful it was too cold for the neighbors to be out on their front steps, and thus he had been able to slip in undetected.

It was quite dark now, and the distant flickering arc-light on the next street gave little assistance to climbing in at the window; but Richard had been in the same situation hundreds of times before, and found no difficulty in turning the latch of

18

the kitchen window and climbing in over the sink. Many times in the small hours of the morning after a jolly time with the fellows he had stolen in softly this way; while his anxious mother kept fitful vigil at the front window, weak tears stealing down her cheeks, to be mildly and pleasantly surprised an hour or so later on visiting his room at finding him innocently asleep.

Richard always assured her the next morning that it had not been very late when he came in, and joined in her wonder that she had not heard him; so she continued to have faith in him and to believe that she had been mistaken about thinking he was not in when she went upstairs from her nightly toil in the kitchen.

Oh, he had not been a model son by any means, but neither had she been a model mother. She was well-meaning and loving, but weak and inefficient; and the boy, loving her in his brusque way, while he half despised her weakness, had "guarded" her from a lot of what he considered "unnecessary worry" about himself. He was all right, he reasoned, and none of the dreadful things, like drowning, or getting drunk, or being arrested, that his mother feared, were going to happen to him. He would look out for that. He could take care of himself, but he was not going to be tied to her apron-string. There was something wild in him that called to be satisfied, and only by going out with the boys on their lawless good times could he satisfy it. There was nothing at home to satisfy. Women didn't understand boys; boys had to go, and to know a lot of things that women did not dream about. He did not intend to do any dreadful thing, of course, but there was no need for her to bother about him the way she did; so he kept her politely blinded, and went on his careless free-and-easy way, deceiving her, yet loving her more than he knew.

As for his gentleman father, the boy worshipped his dim memory, the more, perhaps, because his mother's family lost no occasion to cast scorn upon it.

But, as Richard climbed softly in over the sink, a kind of shame stole over him, and his cheeks grew hot in the darkness. He let down the window noiselessly, and fastened it. There was no need to be so quiet now, for no mother waited up-stairs at the front window for his coming. It was wholly unnecessary for him to remove his shoes before he went up the stairs; for the ear that had listened for his steps through the years of his boyhood was dull in death, and would listen no more for his coming.

But habit held him, and his heart beat with a new and painful remorse to think that he had ever deceived her. For the first time in his life his own actions seemed most reprehensible. Before this his deception had been to him only a sort of virtue, just a manly shielding of his mother from any unnecessary worry. It had never occurred to him that he might have denied himself some of the midnight revels.

They had been comparatively harmless revels, in a way. Temptations, of course, had beset him thickly, and to some he had yielded; but those of the baser sort had not appealed to him. The finer feelings of his nature had so far shielded him; a sense that his father would not have yielded to such things had held him. But he was young, and had not felt the fulness of temptations that were to come. His character was yet in the balance, and might turn one way or another, though most people would have said the probabilities were heavily in favor of the evil. He had taken a few steps in the downward course, and knew it, but was in no wise sure that he intended to keep on. He did not consider himself the bad boy that his mother's relatives branded him, though he was defiantly aware of the bad reputation he bore, and haughtily declined to do anything to prove that it was much exaggerated.

He crept stealthily through the silent rooms, now so strangely in order, the rooms that he never remembered to have seen quite in order before. The chairs stood stiff and straight around the walls, shoved back by alien hands after the funeral. He shuddered as he passed the doorway of the dingy little parlor. He knew his mother's casket was no longer there. He had stood by and seen them lower it into the grave; but somehow in his vision the still form, and white, strangely young, and miraculously pretty face of his dead mother seemed still to lie there. Quickly turning his head away from the doorway, he hurried up the stairs as though he might have been pursued.

He wondered about the youth and beauty that death had brought to his mother, of which he had never caught even a glimpse before. Now he understood how his father had picked her out from her uncomely family, and been willing to alienate his own people for her sake. He felt a passing thrill of pride in his father that he had stuck to her for the two years until his death, in spite of the many temptations of his wealthy relatives, though it meant complete alienation from all he had before held dear.

"Father was 'game' all right, if he *was*

used to different things," he said to himself softly as he opened the door of his own room, and avoided the creaking board in his floor, as was his wont. "Pretty punk family they must have been, though, to let him!"

He stood looking about his own room by the light of the street-lamp that shone dimly in at the window. It looked unfamiliar. Some one had evidently been up here clearing up also. The baseball pictures from magazines, and the pennants that came as prizes with a certain number of cigarette packages, which had clumsily decorated the ugly little place, had been ruthlessly disposed of. He suspected that this had been done by his aunt's orders; for she had once severely scored him for having such disreputable things about, and had told his mother that she was to blame if he went wrong, if she allowed things like that on his wall. He frowned now in the darkness, and wished he might find some way of getting even with his aunt. He resolved once more never to get within her power again — no, not if he had to run away before morning.

But his own room had an unfriendly look; his heart was sore, and his mind distressed. With a strange yearning that he could not understand he went out, closed the door

23

quietly after him, and stole softly down the hall to his mother's room.

This was cleared up, too; but still there were a number of things about that suggested her presence, and with a queer, choking feeling in his throat he suddenly turned the key in the lock of this door, flung himself full length upon his mother's bed, and buried his face in her pillow. There was something about the old, woollen patchwork quilt with which the bed was covered — it being the back room, and consequently not on exhibition, there had been no necessity for a white spread — that touched his heart and took him back to his babyhood; and here he found that what he wanted was his mother.

The mother that he had grieved so sorely, deceived, neglected, disappointed, and worried into her grave! But she was all he had had in the world. He knew that she had loved him; and it was the loss of that love that made him feel so terribly alone in the world now that she had been taken from him.

Tears! Unmanly though they were, they stung their way into his eyes, and sobs such as never had been allowed to take possession of him since babyhood now shook his strong young frame. For a time his desolation rolled over him like the darkness of the bottomless pit.

Then suddenly, when he grew quieter, a loud peal from the door-bell sounded through the empty house and echoed up to him.

2

Miss Victoria Gracen sat before the open fire in her pleasant library, under the light of a softly-shaded reading-lamp, with the latest magazine in her lap, ready for a luxurious evening alone.

Miss Gracen, always a pleasant picture to look upon, was especially lovely against the setting of this room. The walls were an indescribable color like atmosphere, with a dreamy border of soft oak-trees framing a distant, hazy sky and mountains. Against this background a few fine pictures stood out to catch the eye.

The floor was polished and strewn over with small moss-brown and green rugs, and the furniture was all green willow with soft green velvet cushions; even the luxurious couch with its pillows of bronze, old gold, and russet, and one scarlet one like a flaming berry in the woods. Every piece of furniture stood turning naturally toward the hearth as though that were the sun; the dancing flames of the bright wood fire played fitfully over the whole room, lighting up the long rows of inviting books behind the glass doors of the low, built-in bookcases.

Miss Gracen herself, in her soft lavender challis frock, with the glow of the lamplight on her abundant white hair, seemed like a violet on a mossy bank, a lovely, lovable human violet. Her face was beautiful as a girl's, in spite of her years; and the brown eyes under the fine dark brows were large, luminous, and interested.

People said she lived an ideal life, with her fine, old house full of rare mahogany furniture, priceless pictures, and china; her carriage and horses; three old family servants — of whom the kind is now almost extinct — to keep all in order and wait upon her; and plenty of money to do what she would. She had nothing in the world to trouble her, and everything for which to be thankful.

Yet, as she settled herself to the reading of the latest chapter of her favorite serial, she was conscious of a sense of restless dissatisfaction and of an almost unreasonable longing to have a companion to enjoy with her the story she was about to read.

She looked up with a welcoming smile for old Hiram, who tapped and entered with the evening mail. It was a relief to speak even to the old servant when she was in this mood. A fleeting whim that perhaps, after all, she would run in and see some neighbor instead of reading just now passed through her mind as she held out her hand for the mail; but when Hiram said it had begun to rain a little, she put the thought aside and settled down to open her letters and enjoy the evening beside her own bright fire.

There were bills for putting the furnace in order for the winter, and for mending the slates on the roof where the big tree fell during a summer storm. There was the winter's calendar for the Women's Club; a notice of the next Ladies' Aid meeting, with a reminder that Miss Gracen was chairman of the refreshment committee; a request from the president of the missionary society that Miss Gracen would read a paper on "The New China" at the next monthly meeting; a request for a donation from a noted charity in the near-by city; and a letter from an old college-mate whom she had invited to take a three months' trip abroad with her, saying that she could not possibly be spared from her family this winter.

There was also a single newspaper.

Miss Gracen went through them all hastily, keeping the letter from her friend till the last to enjoy; but she laid it down with a disappointed look. Somehow the letter was not what she had expected from her old chum. It expressed gratitude, of course, for the royal invitation; but it seemed by the answer that the possibility of accepting it had scarcely been considered; the mother's heart was so full of her children that she had not even *wanted* to go with her old friend for three short months. The rest, the delight of travel, and the reunion with her friend, were as nothing to her compared with losing three whole months of care and toil and love out of her home life. Well, it was natural, of course. It must be great to have folks of one's own; but then, they were also a care. One could not do as one pleased; still — and the wistful look lingered around Miss Gracen's mouth as she reached out her hand for the newspaper in a soiled wrapper, wondering idly what it could be. It was not the night for either of the weekly papers she took regularly, and the daily evening paper from the city came to her door-step by the hand of a small boy at five o'clock in the afternoon.

"Marked Copy" was scrawled in the corner of the wrapper. What could it be? Some notice of her last paper at the Club that had crept into a city paper and some one had sent to her? No, it was a Chicago paper. She had no intimate friends in Chicago. How strange! It must have got into her box by mistake.

She looked at the wrapper again, but her name was written quite plainly in a scrawling, cramped hand. There could be no mistake.

She hastily turned the crumpled pages to find a mark; and her heart gave one quick throb out of its natural course as she saw the black marking around a tiny notice in the column of deaths. Yet why should she be agitated? There could be no near friend in that locality. It was nearly fourteen years since the telegram had come telling of her brother Dick's death, and since then Chicago had held no vital interest for her.

Yet there it was, her own name, Gracen, with the ink-scrawls about it; and something tightened around her heart with a nameless fear she could not understand. Yet of course Dick's wife — that wife that her father had not been willing to recognize because the family was a common one, and beneath his son socially, educationally, intellectually, every way — she was there. If Miss Gracen had thought anything at all about her, it had been with relief that the tie that bound the unknown girl to them was broken by her brother's death. It would have been no more than natural for her to marry again, and the name of Gracen did not seem in any wise to belong to her.

There had been a child. After the death of her father and stricken mother, Victoria Gracen had written, offering to take the child and have him educated as befitted his father's son; but the offer had been ungraciously declined. The illiterate scrawl of the mother had reminded Miss Gracen of the low growl of a mother lion she had once heard in the Zoölogical Gardens when another lion came near the cub. She could remember yet the wave of mortification that had rolled crimsonly over her face as she read, and resented the name signed to that refusal. That woman had no right to that name, no right to her handsome young brother, whose face they had never seen after he went from them in anger the day his father refused to recognize his marriage with the foolish, pretty girl.

Yet there the name stood in clear print, with all the dignity of death about it. Death, the leveller of all ranks and stations:

Lilly Miller Gracen, widow of the late Richard Pierson Gracen. Relatives and friends are invited to attend the funeral on Thursday at 2:30 from her late residence, 3452 Bristol Street. Interment in Laurel Cemetery.

It was a simple enough statement, in the time-worn terms of such notices; but it strangely stirred the soul of the woman who read. The very name "Lilly" in connection with the family name of Gracen was an offence. It brought to remembrance the photograph of the silly, pretty girl-bride that Dick, her brother, had sent home to them when he had written to tell them he was to be married. The name "Lilly," with all its pretense and lack of dignity, seemed to express in a single word the sharpness of the sorrow of those bitter days.

Miss Gracen had come out from under the cloud of sorrow, and had made her own life sweet and calm again but she had never quite forgotten the beloved brother who had gone so suddenly out of it, nor had she ever forgiven the woman for whose sake that brother had left father and mother and sister.

And now the woman herself, it seemed, was gone! And what had become of the child, the child that was Dick's as well as hers?

As if to answer her question, she noticed a rude hand pointing to another column, where a brief paragraph was also marked:

Mrs. Lilly Miller Gracen, widow of the late Richard Pierson Gracen, died on Wednesday at her home on Bristol Street after a brief illness. Mrs. Gracen was a sister of Peter Miller, of 18 Maple Street, head foreman in the slaughter-house of Haste Brothers, and had since her husband's death kept a lodging house on Bristol Street. She leaves one son, Richard.

It was a strange item to creep into a great city paper when one considered it to be about an obscure lodging-house keeper, but it never occurred to Miss Gracen that it might have been put into the paper and paid for by the obnoxious family of the dead woman just that it might reach her eyes. If Peter Miller had been well acquainted with Miss Gracen, he could not have well planned a paragraph which would have been more mortifying to her family pride. A slaughter-house! A lodging-house! And in connection with the historic name of Gracen. The haughty pride wounded, the blood mounted in rich waves to the roots of Miss Gracen's white hair, and receded, leaving her pale and trembling, almost breathless.

For a few minutes she was filled with a strange weakness, as though she had been publicly brought to shame; for so bitter had her father been against the woman who had unwittingly come between him and his beloved son, that he had succeeded in making his whole family feel it more or less, although, as Miss Gracen in the silence of her thoughts had often owned, it was an utterly unfair prejudice; for she had never even seen the face of her sister-in-law, except in a photograph.

But now the woman was dead, and a strange sadness came into the heart of her patrician sister-in-law. False shame receded, and pity took its place. After all, the woman had been proud and had maintained a certain courageous attitude, not allowing them to give her money nor to take her child from her after the death of her husband. A boarding-house keeper! Miss Gracen in her sheltered home shuddered at the thought. It had surely been a hard life; and death had probably brought blessed relief.

And that child, a boy of sixteen now! What must he be? What was to become of him now? Would he go to live with that uncle who was foreman in a slaughter-house

— horrible, brutal creature — and sink back to the level of his mother's family — if, indeed, he had ever been above it? Yet he was Dick's child, Dick's only son, and bore Dick's name in full, the honored name of his ancestors for generations back — Richard Pierson Gracen. How dreadful to have Dick's son grow up to be manager or something in a slaughter-house! There were even worse depths, of course, than that, to which he might descend.

Well, what could she do? It was dreadful, of course; but they had not accepted her offer of help when he was a little child and she might have really done something toward bringing him up rightly. Now he was probably impossible from every point of view. She couldn't, of course, have him come to her now.

She looked around upon her pleasant room, the immaculate furniture, the spotless peace that reigned, and found it quite impossible to imagine a boy at home there. It seemed to be an invasion of her rights that she could not bring herself to endure.

And yet — her eye travelled back to the printed notice in the paper. "She leaves one son," it spoke to her in reproachful tones from the coarse ink of the paper. "One son!" Left! And suddenly the boy seemed to have taken on the form and feature of his father as he was, brightfaced and happy, bidding her good-bye so long ago; and tears filled her eyes. Dear Dick! How she had loved him, and how much he and she had always been to each other until that strange girl-wife had come between them! How Dick would feel to have his boy grow up with such surroundings! Ought she not for her dead brother's sake to try to do something for this orphaned boy of his?

But how? In that old, conservative town of her father how could she bring an alien grandson, who might, perhaps — very likely would — disgrace his memory and name? There were the servants, too, to consider; for they were getting old and had been faithful.

And there was her own life. She had a right to live it in peace, for had she not been faithful to her father and mother and given up bright hopes for their sakes? Now at least she had a right to enjoy herself as she chose. There was her trip to Europe. She would have to give that up, too, for of course she never could go off and leave a strange boy on the place with only the servants. No, that was entirely out of the question.

With a tightening of her sweet lips she folded the Chicago paper quite determinedly, put it on the under part of the table, and settled herself to her magazine serial.

She must have read fully half a column without letting her thoughts really stray from the story, when the pleading eyes of her brother Dick finally conquered, and made her look around the room again, as if she almost felt his presence there. She seemed to see a boy sitting across the table from her; and his eyes were the eyes of her brother, and somehow it suddenly seemed to be a very pleasant thing to have a boy there, and not nearly so incongruous as she at first had thought. With a warmer feeling at her heart she turned her mind back again to her story.

She had not finished the first page when she finally abandoned the magazine entirely, and closed her eyes for serious thinking.

The little clock on the mantel was striking eight when Miss Gracen got up with decision, and went over to her telephone to send a telegram, pausing on her way to reach under the table for the Chicago paper and search out the marked notice.

After a moment's thought she first called up her local banker, who was also a personal friend, and told him she wanted to send some money to a friend in Chicago; could he advise her where and how to place it?

He gave her the name of a Chicago banker who was his friend, and gave her all necessary directions for the sending. She thanked him, and hung up the receiver with interested face. The first step in her project was now perfectly plain before her.

The telegraph office in Roslyn was closed for the night, but she could telephone a message to the city twenty-five miles away and have it sent through at once. Her mind had worked swiftly, and she knew just what she meant to say. Her voice was calm, almost eager, as she gave the call and waited for the operator to take her dictation for two telegrams.

When she hung up the receiver after the messages were taken, her hand was trembling; but her eyes were shining, and her lips had a sweet line of pleasant decision that was most charming.

She started over toward her chair and magazine once more, but paused with a look of indecision. Somehow her chair and her magazine no longer fitted her present mood. She must do something to get used to her new arrangements. Her eyes travelled quickly about the room. How could she make that room look inviting to a boy? Suppose he came, and did not like it? It would be worse than if she had never brought him home at all. Was it possible for her now, at the age of forty-five, to take in a boy, any boy, even if he were a model, and assimilate him with her present life? And especially a boy against whom she was prejudiced; could she possibly be any kind of a guardian to him? Would it not have been better, after all, to have left him to his mother's relatives?

But no; she could not, would not, retract now. What she had done, she had done. She realized that it had been the hasty action of an impulse; but she would stand by it to the best of her ability, come what would. Perhaps, after all, the boy would elect not to come, and settle the matter for her. Then she could feel that at least she had done her duty. But with this thought came one of anxiety. Was it possible that she really desired to have Dick's boy come to her, invade her home, and fill her life with new cares and perplexities? A kind of pleasant wonder over herself began to dawn in her face.

With her eyes full of happy excitement she went quickly about the room, moving the chairs, drawing a big easy Morris-chair up to the light, throwing down a magazine open to a picture of a baseball field, as if a boy had left it for a moment; gathering the russet and green and crimson pillows out of their prim stiffness, and throwing them in pleasant confusion. But still she was not quite satisfied that it looked like a room where a young boy could live. She was trying to imagine how it would seem to him, and was wondering whether he would like it.

She was too restless to sit down again, and with a look of quiet enthusiasm she went out to the hall and upstairs, turning on the electric light in advance. Into each bed-room she went on her tour of inspection, looking at the house from a different viewpoint, the viewpoint of a boy of sixteen. The guest-rooms, with their fine old furniture and solemn air of rich gravity; he would never feel at home there. Her father's and mother's room. Not there! They had hated him. They would not have wanted him to come to their house, though of course they must feel differently now. There was but one other room on that floor besides the servants' rooms; and that was the room next to her own, the room that had belonged to her brother Dick.

It was just as he had left it; his fishing-rods, books, balls, and pictures were there. All the things that a boy of twenty years before had cared for, the bird's nest with three eggs that he had brought in when the old birds had been frightened away by the workmen when the house was repaired; the wasps' nest from the east gable! She could remember the day when Dick rigged up a pole, and cautiously detached it from the house while she stood in the yard below and watched and gave advice. She could not give the stranger boy that room, Dick's room! And yet he was Dick's boy, and that was just what Dick would have wanted, she knew.

With one of her swift looks of determination she gave a glance of surrender around the room, and, turning, went down-stairs. Just an instant she paused in the wide door-way of the great, stately parlor, swept her glance about and wondered whether that, too, would have to be sacrificed, then went on to her own library, and pulling the cord that was still connected with the old-fashioned bell of the servants' part of the house, she sat down with the magazine in her lap, but a sparkle of expectancy in her eyes.

In a moment old Hiram limped up to the door, and opened it.

"Hiram," she said with a pleasant smile, just as if she were going to ask him to put another stick on the fire, "I'm expecting my nephew to visit me. I wish you would tell Molly and Rebecca that I'd like my brother's room got ready for him to-morrow. He may be here very soon; I am not sure yet — in a day or so, I think."

There was nothing in Miss Gracen's voice to indicate that she was saying an unusual thing, save the suppressed excitement in her eyes; and the old servant bowed quietly enough, and turned to go, though one might have noticed that his hand trembled as it touched the door-knob. But just as he was about to close the door he opened it a trifle wider, and putting in his respectful gray head, said reverently, "Is it Mr. Dick's child you're expectin', Miss Vic?"

"Yes, Hiram," and Miss Gracen answered his look with a smile of indulgence. He and she had suffered together in the days of the elder Dick's banishment; but it was not a matter to be discussed, both knew.

"The Lord be praised, Miss Vic," said the old man again, reverently. "I knowed you'd do it sometime, Miss Vic; I knowed you'd do it."

Miss Gracen looked earnestly at her servant.

"His mother is dead now, Hiram. She would not give him up before. I have sent him word to come. I do not know yet what he will say, but we are going to get ready for him. Tell Molly and Rebecca."

42

The servant bowed, and went with shining eyes to tell his fellow-servants, while Miss Gracen lay back in her chair, and felt as if she had done a hard day's work. Would it pay, she wondered, or was it possible that she might be sorry for what she had done?

3

The peal of the bell startled Richard into attention. Could it be that his uncle had really followed him, and meant to carry out his threat of compelling him to work in that loathsome slaughter-house? His whole soul revolted in horror. Of course he must work somewhere now, he supposed, but not there!

He arose quickly, and stole through the hall to the front window where his mother had so often watched for his late home-coming. He must find out at once who was ringing that bell.

Softly pushing up the window and looking out, he saw a messenger boy in brass buttons, with a book and a pencil in his hand, impatiently looking up at him.

"What do you want down there?" he called out inhospitably.

"Telegram," answered the boy tersely.

"Guess you've made a mistake. There's no telegram coming here," answered Richard decidedly, preparing to shut the window.

"It's the number all right," said the boy with bold assurance.

"Well, it's a mistake. What's the name?"

"Richard Pierson Gracen," drawled the boy, getting close to the street-light to see.

Richard thumped the window down, and hurried wonderingly to the door. Could it be that his uncle had resorted to a telegram? Surely he would never spend a quarter unnecessarily. Or was this a ruse to get him out of the house, and was his uncle in hiding behind the corner ready to seize him?

He opened the door warily, kept his foot braced against it and his ears alert, while he signed his name with the stubby pencil against the door-frame, and drew a sigh of relief when the door closed on the impatient messenger boy.

He stole softly back up-stairs to his mother's room again with the telegram in his hand, wondering who in the world could have sent it. It very likely was something about a bill, and wouldn't be worth lighting the gas to see. However, no one from the street could see the light in that room, and perhaps it would be as well to read it.

He closed the door, drew the wooden shutters close, lighted the gas, and with a curious apathy sat down on the edge of the bed to tear open his first telegram.

45

Dear Dick, it read, *I wonder if you and I don't need each other. Suppose you come and make me a visit, and perhaps we can find out. Come as soon as you can, and telegraph me when you will arrive. I have only just heard of your loss, and am deeply sorry for you. Of course you will have expenses to meet, and I know it is not always easy to get money immediately at such a time; so I am placing five hundred dollars in your name in the Dearborn First Company Bank for you to use in whatever way you may need it. It will be there for your use by to-morrow morning. If you need more, just let me know. Buy a through ticket and a sleeper, and check your baggage to Roslyn. I hope you can come at once.*

Your aunt,
Victoria Gracen.

Richard felt his senses reeling as he read, so that at first he scarcely took in the sense of the word. He had to read it over again before he grasped the full meaning of this marvellous telegram, about which the most marvellous thing, after all, was its length and the fact that it had been prepaid. How could any one have the temerity to send a

46

telegram of that length when the prescribed number of words was ten?

"Gosh!" he ejaculated softly to himself.

The boy sat quite still, and stared blankly at the paper in his hand, while the dim gas-light from the worn-out burner flickered fitfully in the room, and the steady ticking of his mother's clock sounded loudly through the empty old house.

But the boy heard it not, for he was undergoing a change, and chief among his sensations was a desire to tell his mother what had happened.

True, his mother had always felt bitterly toward this aunt, who now invited him to visit her and hinted that perhaps they needed one another. True, his mother had always declined any help or suggestion from one who had scorned her as a sister-in-law, and he was proud of his mother for having done so. It was the one fine quality besides her love for him and for his father which linked her with aristocracy in his vague and unformed mind, this pride of hers that had caused her to work so hard to keep her child rather than to give him up, or to accept any help from those who had always despised her.

But she was gone now, and his situation was indeed desperate. His mother's family were not at all to his mind, nor the situation they were trying to force upon him. His mother had never seemed to want him to be with his uncle, even though he was her brother. He had an instinctive feeling that she would not want him to go with his uncle now. She had once sighed that she was unable to send him to college, as his father would surely have wished. He hadn't cared much about college himself; at least not for the sake of the education; but he remembered now that his mother had always wanted better things for him than just a mere place in the world to earn his living. Would his mother, now that she was gone, want him to hold out against his father's family? He thought not. Besides, it was a choice between going to work in the slaughter-house and running away if he did not accept this invitation of his aunt's.

Richard found himself longing inexpressibly for the sympathy, the thoughtfulness, the understanding, that seemed to breathe itself into the words of this telegram, though boylike he did not realize it.

"I wonder if you and I don't need each other."

When had anybody ever needed him before. Not even his poor, toil-worn, worried mother. The telegram implied that the writer was lonely, and his own lonely heart went out in quick response to the appeal.

Then there was another great thing. She had anticipated his penniless state, and had known how he would feel about paying expenses and things. She hadn't said a word about it, but had spoken just as if this money was his own, right from his father. She had conveyed that soothing impression to his queer, proud boy-heart. He wouldn't be accepting charity; it was *his*, placed in the bank without waiting to see whether he would do as she had asked, and plenty more if he needed it.

He could now pay the undertaker's bill; he could get a stone for his mother's grave, and could pay the long-standing grocery bill which had secretly mortified him beyond any of his childish troubles. He fairly hated the sneer on that grocer's face as he came and went by the store daily. The man had refused to let him have a chicken for broth for his mother the day before she died, and had said that he never expected to get a cent for all that she owed him. Richard hadn't blamed him so much for not giving him the chicken, but for the cold contempt in his face as he gave the denial he hated him. It gave him great comfort now to think that he could pay that bill. It was something more than a hundred dollars, but it should be paid, every cent of it.

His heart went out with gratitude toward his unknown aunt who had made it possible for him to hold up his head and pay his debts. There were other debts too, debts of "honor" he called them, for sodas and cigarettes and games that his mother did not know how to play, and his instinct taught him that his aunt would not approve; but she had said he was to use the money for what he needed, and he could not go away without making it right with the boys. It wasn't much. A few dollars would cover it, and he must treat them all handsomely to ice-cream and maybe a supper before he left. They had been loyal friends of his always, even when he hadn't a cent in his pocket and could not get a chance anywhere to earn anything. His mother had worried about his friendship with them, and his uncle had openly told him he was on the highway to destruction by associating with them; but they had been good friends to him through all sorts of scrapes, and they were all the friends he had left unless perhaps this unknown aunt was going to prove to be one.

A sudden wave of curiosity and gratitude made him read the telegram again, just to be sure it was all true. It sounded like what the fellows would call "pipe dreams." Yet there it was, all perfectly clear and plain. He knew where the big stone bank was, in the heart of the city and the next morning he could go and present his claim and put it to a test.

He liked the thoughtfulness of his aunt in suggesting a sleeper. A sleeper for a boy! His uncle would sneer at that, and call it extravagance. But he would take a sleeper. He would have the experience; it was what his whole soul had been hungering for all his life, experience. He would have experience, he would accept the invitation, and then if he didn't like it there he could go away. His aunt suggested that it was an experiment, and it suited him well to take it just as she put it. He thought her a rather jolly good fellow for having put it just that way. It laid no obligations upon either of them, and yet gave him a chance to like her if he chose. That she might not like him never occurred to him, so egotistical is youth; and, indeed, at that time it is doubtful whether he would have cared.

After a brief deliberation over the telegram Richard arose, accepting his new situation calmly, and went about making his plans.

He searched out a small trunk in the attic,

51

which some bankrupt boarder had left for his board; and into this he put the few articles that he cared for in the house. He found the hiding-place of his despised pictures and pennants, and put them in first; he examined his clothing and decided that he would need two new suits if he was to make a visit, and he would see about those in the morning if the money was on hand; he put in his mother's old Bible and a small, faded photograph of his father; and his packing was done.

He then lay down to sleep.

His first waking thoughts were dazed, and filled with the sudden remembrance of the shadow of death, and the sickening horror with which the realization of loss always comes after sleep. Gradually remembrance came to him. For a minute he felt sure that telegram had been a figment of his imagination, a dream of the night, but on turning over he felt the rattle of the paper; and, springing up quickly, he threw open the shutters, letting in the morning sun; and there were the words just as he remembered them. A strange glow of pleasure filled him at the thought that his aunt needed him, and his answering heart told him that he needed her — or some one — most mightily.

He dressed quickly, and hurried downstairs, hauling his trunk to the front door that it might be ready for the expressman when he came for it. With a glance of almost pathetic loneliness around him at the only home he had ever known he hurried out of the front door, and slammed it behind him, going straight down the street to the little corner grocery.

The grocer frowned as he looked up from weighing out sugar and saw him coming in, but Richard walked straight up to him with a new dignity in his face.

"Mr. Bitzer," he said in a clear voice, "I want to pay my bill here this morning. Can you have it itemized for me when I come back in about an hour?"

The insolent snarl on the man's face melted into a look of astonishment.

"*You* want to pay the bill?" he said incredulously. "You ain't got any money to pay any bill. Where'll you git the money?"

"I will be back to pay the bill in about an hour if you will have it ready for me," said Richard haughtily, and, turning on his heel, went out of the store. His heart was boiling with rage that a man had ever the chance to think of him with such contempt for lack of a little money. He felt again that

strange thrill of something — was it gratitude? love? — toward the woman who had
understood and who had made it possible
for him to hold up his head before this man
who had always despised his hard-working
mother because she was poor.

His first goal was the bank, and with no
thought of breakfast he spent his last nickel
to take a trolley downtown. It suddenly
seemed to him that he had a great deal to
do, and he was seized with a wild desire to
get it over with and be off before his uncle
tried to stop him.

Arriving at the bank, he found a lot of
other people ahead of him, and himself
obliged to stand in line. He felt himself
grow small as he saw business men cashing
large checks for hundreds of dollars, and
rolling the bills together as carelessly as
if they might have been ones instead of
fifties.

He was within two of the window when
a new difficulty presented itself to his mind.
The young man ahead of him was evidently
a foreigner who spoke little English, and was
having trouble to get what he wanted. "You
must be identified," the cashier was explain-
ing; and finally, after numerous shakings of
the head, the poor fellow had to turn away
with his check uncashed.

That was something Richard had not thought of, identification. What should he do? His uncle could, of course, identify him or get some one else to do so; but Richard did not want to ask this favor of him. He had a strong feeling that his uncle, if he knew of it, would find a way to get that five hundred dollars into his own possession under the plea that he would pay the bills himself and take care of the rest for his nephew.

Richard resolved that until he was safely out of the city his uncle should know nothing about that money. He set his lips more firmly, and decided to find some other way out of his difficulty. Would the telegram, he wondered, be sufficient identification?

With fear and trembling he put on a calm face, and took his turn in the line at the window, the open telegram in his shaking hand.

"Will I have to be identified?" he asked, quietly handing the telegram to the cashier. "I want to draw some of that money."

The cashier looked at him sharply and then at the telegram, and just at that moment another man walked breezily up to the window behind him, and in a pleasant voice said: "Why, good morning, Richard.

What are you doing way down-town this morning? Do you have a situation down here now?"

The cashier looked up quickly, and greeted the newcomer as if he were well known, as indeed he was, being a prominent business man as well as one of the stock-holders of the bank. His home was near to Richard's home, though in quite a different neighborhood.

Richard in his little-boy days had run errands occasionally for him, and had for a time delivered his morning paper. The charm of the man was that he never forgot the boy, and had always had a smile and a pleasant word for him, though it had been at least three years since Richard had done anything for him.

The boy felt a glow of pleasure now at the recognition, and he was just turning it over in his mind whether he dared ask the man to identify him, when the cashier saved him the trouble.

"You know this young man, Mr. Minturn?" he asked. "He's Richard P. Gracen, is he?"

"Sure!" said the big man heartily. "I've known him since he was a little chap so high. We're old friends. Anything I can do for you, Richard?"

"That's all right then, my boy," said the cashier nodding assurance to the lad. "We have some money deposited here for Richard P. Gracen, and we didn't know him; but of course, if you can identify him, it will be all right, Mr. Minturn."

"Yes, I can identify him," said Mr. Minturn heartily. "Got some money coming to you, have you, Richard? That's good news. Take care of it, and use it wisely. I guess you will, all right."

Then he turned to speak to another newcomer, leaving the boy with a glow of pleasure in his face and immense relief at his heart.

Five minutes later he walked out of the bank with more money in his possession than he had ever handled in his life before and a brand-new bank-book and checkbook in his pocket.

He had thought it all out before he went to sleep the night before, and decided to pay the big bills in checks. He enjoyed the thought that he had a bank-account and could pay in checks like any man.

He had drawn out only money enough to use for his immediate needs; but they included his ticket and berth, some new clothes, food for the day, and enough to pay his little outstanding debts to the boys; so the sum he carried made him feel exceedingly rich.

He went first to the station to buy his ticket and sleeper berth and send his telegram. Until those things were attended to he had no thought for breakfast. It was a wonderful experience to be buying a ticket for a long-distance journey for himself. He watched with awe the ticket-agent stamping the long strip of paper, and took it almost reverently into his own hands, proudly handing out the crisp new bank-bills in exchange.

He got the best berth in the first section of the through train, and with his tickets safely in his breast-pocket he went thoughtfully over to the telegraph office. The telegram he must send was the hardest part of his day's work. He had not been able to think what to say last night before he went to sleep. He felt a shyness coming over him at the thought of addressing the great personage who had so easily provided him with money and a way of escape from his uncle's espionage. No words seemed quite fitting, at least not the words that were familiar to him. But after getting a time-table and inquiring most minutely about arrivals and departures of trains he finally produced the following message with infinitely greater labor than any school composition had ever cost him:

Miss Victoria Gracen,
Roslyn, Penn.

Leave Chicago 10:30 to-night. Reach Roslyn 5:30 P.M., *Wednesday.*

Here he had paused with puckered brow, and deliberated. It seemed as though the occasion demanded some recognition of his aunt's friendly overtures after the years of coolness between the families. His boyish vocabulary was hard put to it for anything along this line; but at last with desperation he dashed off the rest, and sent his message before he would have opportunity for further hesitation.

Hope we will get along all right. Thanks for the cash.

Dick.

He reflected afterward that it would have sounded a great deal more friendly if he had said "dough" or "tin" instead of "cash," but perhaps an aunt might not understand. He had never signed his name Dick before nor been called that — the fellows had other and varied appellations for him — but he gladly accepted her attempt at intimacy by taking up the new name. He had a suspicion, which afterward proved to be correct, that she maybe used to call his father "Dick"; and in that case the boy welcomed it as a heritage hitherto unknown.

The telegram and ticket off his mind, he began to realize that he was hungry; and, as he was passing the station restaurant, the lure of coffee and the palm-guarded entrance summoned him with all the power that that elegant and mysterious realm had held for him from childhood. He decided that for once in his life he would eat in the station restaurant and have what he wanted from the bill of fare. He had money of his own in his pocket, enough and to spare; why should he not?

His wants were sensible, however. He ordered a beefsteak with fried potatoes, buckwheat cakes and maple-syrup, and a glass of cream. Cream was five cents more than milk, and he might have had coffee instead; but he had never had enough cream in his life; in fact, he had scarcely ever had any, and he wanted to see now what it would really be like to *drink* cream.

Refreshed in body and spirit, he went out

to pay his bills. He was just boarding an up-town car when he caught a vanishing glimpse of his uncle getting out of another car. He could not be sure whether or not his uncle had seen him, and he kept watching furtively from the back window, but saw no sign of pursuit.

It was queer for his uncle to be down-town so far from his place of business at that time of day. Could he have been tracking him? The fear made him feel that he must make all possible haste, for he did not wish to be interfered with until all his plans were carefully made. He must get that trunk out of the house immediately, or his uncle might put a stop to his taking it at all.

He stopped at the corner grocery to get the bill paid, and took much pleasure in the look of astonishment and disappointment on the countenance of Mr. Bitzer when he took out his new check-book and wrote a check for the amount of the bill.

"I don't like to bother with checks," said the man crossly. "I thought you'd pay the money. How do I know you've got money in that there bank?"

He took the check slowly, hesitatingly, and looked it over incredulously.

"Just call up the bank on the telephone," said Richard loftily. "Ask for the cashier. I'll wait till you get your answer."

Reluctantly the grocer went to the telephone, and in a few minutes came back with a sheepish look on his face and the check in his hand.

"It's all right," he admitted, and then, again reluctantly, "Thank you."

Richard nodded gravely and went out saying softly to himself, "Stung!" But even as his tongue finished the word there came a queer choking sensation in his throat, and he found himself wishing that he could tell his mother that the troublesome bill was paid at last. Did she know, he wondered, in that strange, far-off place to which she had taken her journey; or might it be that she didn't care any more about bills over there?

Well, he was glad to have it paid, anyway. It seemed like making good his mother's honor, for something in his uncle's taunt the night before had strangely stirred the dormant manliness of the boy.

The choking feeling was still in his throat when he unlocked the door of his home for the expressman to take out his trunk; and something like tears were near to his eyes as he gave a final glance back at the dingy, dismal rooms he had known so long, and would perhaps never see again. A great sense of loneliness swept over him as he slammed the door shut and jumped up beside the expressman to ride with him down to check his trunk.

There was one more disagreeable duty to be done before he could feel quite free. He must go to his uncle, get the undertaker's bill, and pay it. He wished that after that he need never see his uncle again.

As soon as the trunk was checked, he turned his face resolutely toward the office where he would be likely to find his uncle.

4

When Richard opened the door of the room his uncle called his "office," there were two men talking business with Mr. Miller.

That gentleman looked sharply toward the door, and frowned at his nephew.

"So you've concluded to come back have you, you young jackanapes?" he said when the two men turned away to discuss some matter together. "This is a pretty time of day to turn up. What do you think of yourself coming to work at two o'clock in the afternoon? It's a wonder your job isn't gone already. You sit down over there, and wait till I'm done here, and I'll tend to you."

"I didn't come to work," said Richard haughtily. "I came to get that undertaker's bill. Have you got it here? I want to see how much it is. I'm going to pay it."

"You're going to pay it!" roared his uncle derisively. "A lot you are! It'll be a long while before you save up enough money to pay that. I guess you don't know how much it costs to die. See there!"

He opened his wallet and took out the bill, flinging it at the boy triumphantly. His harsh, coarse voice made Richard shiver. It seemed as though it were trailing over his raw nerves.

The two men had come to some conclusion, and his uncle turned his attention to them once more. Richard, taking advantage of his uncle's turned back, pocketed the bill, and quietly slipped out of the door into the street. In a moment more he had boarded a down-town car and was safe from pursuit. When his uncle realized that he was gone, it would be too late to do anything about it.

Richard went straight to the undertaker's, made out a check for the amount of the bill, and asked for a duplicate receipt. He desired his uncle to know that the bill was paid, but he did not intend to let the receipt go out of his own possession. He did not realize that the check would be a sufficient receipt.

The undertaker took the precaution to call up the bank and ask whether the check was good, and then gave him the receipts as requested. Richard went straight to the waiting-room of a department store and wrote a letter.

It ran thus:

Uncle Miller:

I am sending you a duplicate copy of the receipted bill, to let you know I have paid it. I have the original. I had some money my aunt, Miss Gracen, gave me, and I have paid all bills I know anything about.

I leave Chicago to-night; so you needn't bother any more about me. My address will be Roslyn, Penn., in case you need to ask me anything about the house.

Yours truly,
R. P. Gracen.

It took him a long time to write the letter, because there were so many things he would have liked to say which he knew for his mother's sake he ought not to say and there were so many things he did not want to say that his uncle would naturally expect him to say, that it was pretty hard work. When it was written, he discovered that it was almost four o'clock, and he had had no dinner. He addressed the letter and put it into his pocket. His plan was to mail it in the station just as he took the train.

He decided that he would do the one other thing that he had always been longing to do and never had the money for — take a meal in the great tea-room up-stairs. It might be extravagant for a person whose entire fortune was well under five hundred dollars, but it couldn't do any harm just once, and, besides, this was a day of great things. He might perhaps never come this way again and then the experience would be impossible. He took the elevator to the tenth floor, and dined in state amid polished floors, hot-house flowers, and orchestral music but somehow he felt lonelier than he dreamed he could feel in that stateliness, and was glad when the meal was over.

It was when he was going down in the elevator that he remembered his plan to purchase some new clothes. He must hurry, or the store would be closing. But, boylike, he did not take long to make his selections. He chose a dark-blue suit and a rich leafy-brown with a Norfolk jacket, and decided to put the brown suit on for his journey; so his old clothes went into the suitcase, and a half-hour later, to all appearances, he came forth from the clothing department a new boy. It was because of the glimpse he caught of himself in the great mirror by the elevator that he decided on new tan shoes and a soft brown felt hat. Before he was through he had purchased socks, neckties, collars and cuffs, and a lot of other little necessities; and the suitcase was being taxed to its utmost to hold them all.

It was just as he was passing out of the store, and nearly closing-time, that the darkness of the sky sent him back to purchase a raincoat; and at the glove-counter he saw a young fellow about his own age buying a pair of kid gloves. He had never had a pair of gloves in his life that he remembered, and it suddenly occurred to him that he would like to have some; so they were added to his outfit. All together, when he came out of the store in the gathering twilight, he was a well-dressed fellow.

He took the suitcase over to the station and checked it, reserving the raincoat for a refuge in case the threatened storm came, and started out to find the "fellows." But again, as his startled eyes caught sight of his new self in the window of a great candy-store, in passing, he stopped astonished and looked himself over. He really was a nice-looking boy. Why hadn't he known it before? It would have been a great comfort to him, helping him through innumerable embarrassing places, if he had only known it was in him to look as well as that. How he wished his aunt and uncle and his little cousins could get a glimpse of him!

Wouldn't they be astonished? It would give his wounded pride a decided healing turn if he could only appear before them for a minute dressed in this way.

But he had too clear a remembrance of his uncle's face and the grip of his hand to risk any such meeting. His uncle hated the very thought of the Gracen family, hated him because he bore the name, and would never allow him to get away to any member of the family to be pampered and petted and made to hate his mother's family. There was no telling to what lengths his uncle might go if he knew what Richard was planning to do.

However, there would be no harm in letting Elsa see him. His uncle would hardly be at home yet; or, if he were, he would be in the house washing up for supper. He could easily whistle for Elsa. He had done it before when sent on errands by his mother. Elsa would keep his secret. She was the only one of the family he had ever tolerated. As he thought it over now, she was the only person in the whole city who would miss his going very much; and she was a giddy little thing, and would soon forget him. However, for the sake of the times when she had taken his part and helped to screen him from his uncle's wrath, he would go and say good-bye to her. She was very fond of chocolates; why shouldn't he take her some?

He stopped at a large candy-store, and purchased a two-pound box of chocolates, tied with a pink ribbon. As he did so he felt like a millionaire; this was truly the crowning-touch.

His uncle's house was not far out of the way he meant to take in his search for his friends; and, dropping off the trolley-car at the corner, he walked rapidly around the corner of the new street toward it. The sun was just setting, the lights appearing as they had appeared the night before when the carriages drove up to the door. The scene brought back his own desolation so strongly that he almost made up his mind to leave the candy on the side window-sill and slip away without being seen; but just at that moment Elsa came out of the front door with her red sweater over her shoulders, and ran toward the corner bakery.

She stared hard at Richard in his new clothes, but did not appear to recognize him until he spoke; and even to himself his voice sounded constrained and queer.

"Hello, Elsa!" he said embarrassedly.

Elsa paused, and stared hard.

"Why, Richard! Is that you all dolled up

so? Ain't you got the togs, though? Where'd you get 'em?" Her face expressed un-bounded admiration, and Richard's pride rose. He was pleased to have produced so favorable an impression.

"I bought 'em," said the boy with a proud lift of his chin.

A shade of anxiety came over the girl's stolid little face.

"Say, Richard, you ain't been stealing, have you? Mother has been awful worried lest you'll get into jail, and disgrace us all. She says if Aunt Lilly hadn't just died it wouldn't be so bad; but it's such a disgrace to have you acting this way just after the funeral, when everybody's noticing every-thing."

The boy's face hardened, and a steely glitter came into his eyes.

"No, I haven't been stealing, and I don't ever mean to do any such low-down thing in my life. Whatever put that into your mother's head, I'd like to know? She always thinks the worse she can of everybody. Did you think that about me, Elsa? Say, tell me honest; did you?"

He caught her by the arm, and glared at her in the softening twilight of the street till the child seemed almost frightened.

"No, course not; honest I didn't, Richard.

I told 'em I knew you'd come back all right. I knew you wouldn't steal."

The boy's face softened again.

"Well, I brought you something," he said in a less harsh tone; "but, if you were going to believe things like that about me, I would rather throw every bit of it in the gutter than give it to you."

The girl's eyes turned longingly toward the big, white box of bonbons.

"You know I never thought such a thing, Richard," she pleaded.

"Well, look here; I'm going to tell you something if you'll promise not to tell a word of it till to-morrow morning. Promise?"

"Mayn't I tell I saw you, and what you gave me?" she asked with gloating eyes on the box; "and mayn't I tell about your new clo'es? You look awful swell. I wish they all could see you."

"Yes; you can tell them you saw me and I don't care about the clothes or anything; but you mustn't tell where I got the money, nor where I'm going, until to-morrow morning. Do you promise?"

"Sure, I promise," said Elsa, jumping up and down delightedly and holding out her hands eagerly for the beautiful box.

"Well, I'm going to my aunt, Miss

Gracen. She's sent for me, and she gave me a lot of money to pay the bills; and I've paid everything, and bought these clothes. Now don't you forget, Elsa; you're not to tell a living soul till to-morrow morning."

"All right," said Elsa, already beginning to untie the gold cord that held the paper. "But why can't I tell till to-morrow morning?"

"Elsa! Elsa!" called her mother from the front door; and then, wrapping her apron around her head (for she had come straight from the hot kitchen), she stopped and stared. To whom could Elsa be talking? No one who lived in that neighborhood, and yet there was a very familiar look about him.

"Elsa, did you get that loaf of bread yet? Hurry in here with it."

"Oh my goodness!" said Elsa. "What'll ma say? I've got to hurry. Good-bye, I won't forget!" And she was off down to the bakery while her excited mother alternately called and stared at the strange boy with whom her child had been talking.

He was walking unconcernedly down the street and taking a trolley right before her face and eyes, and could it be? Yes no — it could not be; it *was* — Richard!

Alarmed, she rushed down the steps; but the trolley was under way now, and the motorman could not see her. Richard, smiling scornfully, stood on the lower step of the trolley, and actually had the impudence to tip his beautiful new brown hat to her as he vanished out of sight around the corner! Of all things! Her wrath boiled high; and she stood staring after the departing trolley and wondering what her husband would do now to that boy. The upstart! Dressed up like that and riding on trolleys like any dude; when his poor mother was just buried!

Elsa, hurrying back with her loaf of bread and trying to peer into her candy-box, almost ran into her mother, and was greeted with a volley of questions, which she answered by opening the wonderful box of bonbons in her astonished mother's presence and announcing that Richard had given them to her. All that evening she smiled serenely to herself over her chocolates, and answered not a word to their angry questioning. She would reserve her announcement till the morrow, and she felt it would lose none of its dramatic features by waiting. She was a keen child in many ways, and Richard had managed to impart to her somewhat of the spirit of the "gang" in being loyal to him. Moreover, she had an eye to other possible chocolates. That last was in the blood, and she could scarcely help it.

Richard, as they rounded the corner, caught sight of his uncle coming up the street, and quickly vanished inside the car, thankful that he had escaped, and very soon he changed cars, which made pursuit impossible.

He was not long in finding his gang, who duly admired his clothes, but were a little inclined to be jealous and sulky until he proceeded to hand them out the money he owed them, to the last penny, when everybody grew exceedingly happy; and the leader of the group proposed a supper in honor of the occasion. Richard declared that was just what he had come to invite them to; and, as most of them had not overeaten at their evening meal, they were ready to go with him immediately.

Richard himself was not hungry. Somehow, now that the time had almost come for him to leave his native haunts, he began to feel a strange shrinking and loneliness. The day had been filled with excitement and unusual occurrences; and when he came to sit down among the rest, he was mortally weary. So it was that his gay talk and laughter were missing as the jokes passed round the table, and their challenges brought no answering banter from his lips.

"Rich is all in to-night," whispered one

to another; "do you s'pose it's 'cause the old lady croaked?"

And the strange part of the remark was that, though the expression was most horribly irreverent and uncouth, it was said in sincerest sympathy and was received as it was meant.

"Sure!" said the other comrade heartily, with a sympathetic glance at Richard. "He'll be all right one o' these dry rains."

It was not till almost the last minute that he told them he was going away. It was characteristic of their code that they had not questioned him about his money and new clothes. They knew he would tell what he wanted them to know when he got ready, and not before. They would have done the same themselves. So now they listened as he told them briefly that he was going out to see his aunt, and might stay if he liked it; he didn't know.

Their faces were sober for a moment, but not with sorrow for his going. At that age they acknowledge no such thing as regret. They were each envious of his chance to see the world and wear those clothes and spend the money they heard jingling in his pocket.

They accepted his generosity, took chocolate and chewing-gum galore at his expense, and attended him pridefully to the train at last, bearing his new sole-leather suitcase noisily aloft on their shabby shoulders. They marched in to the sleeper to the annoyance of the contemptuous porter, who lifted his discerning nose of contempt and lowered in vain his discerning eyes to their shabby shoes. They were utterly unabashed, and felt that they had as good a right as he — better, perhaps — to stand there. Had not their comrade a ticket and a sleeper berth? They intended to make the most of it until the train departed. And they were not even college boys! The porter was *sure* of that.

They hung on until after the train had started, and ran noisily along, flinging in paper wads, cakes of chocolate, anything, shouting at the top of their lungs; as tough and uncouth as possible, and highly calculated to make the entire carful look with disapproval on the young traveller taking his first long journey.

And yet, when they were gone, Richard sat back alone, and felt that he was deserted of all who knew him, alone in the wide, wide world!

5

That was a busy day in the Gracen home following the evening announcement of Miss Victoria that her nephew was expected. The older servants worked with a will, for was not "Mr. Dick's" child coming home to them at last after the long years of family alienation? Both Hiram and Rebecca, his sister, had been in the family when "Mr. Dick" was born; and Molly, Hiram's wife, had been his nurse. It had been a sad day for the servants when the young man left his home forever. They had mourned as if he were their own, albeit their loyalty to his mother and sister had been so great that they had kept it to themselves for the most part, and humored the irascible old father, to whom they had also given deep devotion, while thinking him altogether in the wrong concerning his son.

Molly and Rebecca were up early, giving the house a thorough overhauling, and especially making the room next to "Miss

Vic's" sweet and inviting after its years of closed idleness.

Not a book that was not taken out and dusted carefully, not a fishing-pole or trinket of the elder Dick that was not tenderly handled and displayed to its best advantage. There were pictures of him everywhere about the room, taken with his school friends, his baseball-team, in his canoe on the creek; taken sliding down the great hill that started in the meadow back of the house; taken skating on the creek with his boy and girl friends. There was a large one with the dawn of seriousness in his handsome eyes taken just before he went away to accept that fine business offer in Chicago, and it hung surrounded by the pictures of his college life. Reverently the old servants touched the frames as they wiped off the dust, and more than one surreptitious tear was brushed away behind the closet door that day. They worked away with a will, and somehow contrived to give to the great room an air of expectancy, as if a boy might be coming home to it.

Old Hiram was doing duty with the carpets and rugs, and between times rubbing down the "colt," as the youngest one of the great black horses was still called, although it was several years since he had left coltdom. Hiram confided to the colt's ears that likely Mr. Dick would want to ride him, and he even went so far as to get down the elder Dick's saddle and rub it up, brightening the stirrups and buckles and bit, his face wearing a pleasant smile of reminiscence while he worked.

All this was well under way before they knew whether the boy was coming or not.

The Roslyn telegraph operator had gone to his lunch when Richard's telegram arrived; and so it was not until after one o'clock, while Miss Gracen was eating her belated lunch — late on account of the extra cleaning that had been going on that morning — that the telephone rang and the boy's message was repeated until every word was carefully copied down.

The three servants crowded near the library door, regardless for once of cooling tea and chops that ought to have been set in the oven until the lady returned, and boldly stood to listen.

"I think he's coming," said old Hiram, nodding his head happily; "I think Miss Vic's voice sounded that way."

Then, when she returned to the interrupted lunch, the copy of the telegram tucked inside the bosom of her morning dress and a smile of excitement and pleasure on her face, instead of rapidly dispersing to the kitchen they stood forth unabashed and eager.

"He'll be here to-morrow night at five-thirty," announced Miss Gracen. "Hiram, you may meet him at the station with the carriage and both horses. I think I will see him first at home. The boy may be embarrassed, and there might be people around watching. I don't want to have any talk. Molly, can you and Rebecca finish the cleaning this afternoon? Then you'll have plenty of time to do a little baking to-morrow."

So for the first time in their long service they forgot their relation of mistress and maid and grouped together around her, planning a welcome home for the boy to whom all their hearts went out with loving expectation.

Richard's first night in a sleeper proved to be anything but a restful one. The strange sounds and the stranger motion might have lulled his weary body to sleep sooner if the excitement of the day had not been keen upon him. He lay in the luxurious bed, wondering at everything that had happened to him, and tantalizing himself now with the thought that perhaps he had been disloyal to his mother by accepting this money and going to his aunt. But then came the thought of his father.

He knew that his father had anxiously desired a reconciliation, but would not accept it unless his wife were recognized equally with himself. But was not he the representative of them both, and had not his aunt invited him as such? If he found that she considered it otherwise he could go away from her at once.

Having settled so much, he fell into a doze, but was soon awakened by the slowing of the train and the calls of the trainmen. He simply could not lie down and compose himself, for were they not continually passing strange new places, some of the names of which he could even read when they went more slowly through the sleeping towns? They were places of which he had often heard, and his interest was awakened. It was so wonderful to pass the lighted streets, and see now and again people here and there.

More than half the night he lay propped up on one elbow, staring out the window and watching the wonders of the way, but more and more this journey gave him a sense of deep loneliness.

It was nearly morning when at last he

slept and awoke to the din of a great city station, having dreamed that the train had been going in a circle and was back in Chicago again, with his uncle and a long line of policemen waiting at the station to meet him.

He was greatly relieved to find the station a great, strange place, and that he was still on his independent way unhindered.

It was a new and embarrassing experience to get dressed in a sleeper berth, and he found that he was the last man in the car to rise. He made his way to the buffet-car, and enjoyed his breakfast in state alone, wondering what the fellows and his uncle's family would think of him if they could see him.

The window held new sights indeed now, for they were beginning to pass through the coal regions and over the mountains, and the boy was all eagerness to see everything. For a time this put his situation entirely out of his mind, and he forgot that ahead of him was a new and untried way, which he dreaded more than he had ever dreaded anything in his life.

However, as the afternoon waned, and he knew he was nearing his destination, his heart began to beat hard, and his hands and feet grew cold with apprehension. Just what he feared he could not put into words or scarcely into lucid thoughts, but he knew that if he had the chance now he would never have come. He would have run away — west, north, south, anywhere — rather than face a new and unknown relative, who might expect all sorts of disagreeable things of him.

As the train came nearer and nearer to Roslyn, he sat stiffly in his seat, his fingers clinched, his feet braced, his jaw set. He must go through it now, of course, but he would not stay if he did not like it. Well, the running was still good, and he could run away here, of course, as well as he could in Chicago.

This was his last thought as the train slowed down and came to a full stop at Roslyn, and he knew that his time had come.

"Best hurry out, young man," the porter adjured him. "We only stop here for passengers or on flagging. You ain't got no time to waste."

The porter caught up the suitcase from his cold, trembling hands; and Richard, with his new raincoat over his arm, followed confusedly, and, descending the steps, immediately found himself standing alone in a dazed condition upon the platform of a pretty little station, with his train hurrying wildly down the track as if angry at the moment's delay he had caused.

The sweetness and quietness of the place, even with the vanishing screech of the train yet in his ears, fell about him like a mantle of peace. He had never been in so quiet a place before.

The station seemed to have nestled down between softly-rising hills; the tracks gleamed away and vanished in a cut; and everywhere there was autumn foliage, glorious and beautiful in the low sunlight of evening. Off at the right, rose a sloping green campus, with academic buildings showing their classic lines between the trees; and to the left were pleasant homes all set in late greens, browns, crimsons, and gold, with close-clipped hedges or open lawns and pleasant streets stretching in every direction, all giving the atmosphere of plenty — plenty of time and rest and comfort for all who belonged there.

Richard instantly had the feeling that he did not belong there, and cast one more hopeless look after his unfriendly train now vanishing in the cut.

But this was his first instant's impression. In the next second he became aware of a carriage and a pair of shining black horses standing close to the platform, and an old man in dark-green livery approaching him. His first thought was that this was a cabman asking him to ride, and he began to wonder what he should do next. He instantly decided he would not take a cab; that would get him there too soon. He would inquire the way, and walk, and try to get his mind composed.

Then old Hiram spoke.

"This must be Mr. Dick, I'm sure," he quavered, respect and glee mingled in his old throat. "I knowed you the minute you stepped out, you look so like your father. We're right glad to have you, sir, right glad to have you home at last. We've been a-wearyin' to see ye these many years. Me an' Rebecca an' Molly an' Miss Vic have. Just step right over this way to the carriage. My! But you do look like Mr. Dick when he was your age. I'd 'a' knowed you anywheres. Just climb right into the back seat; an' gimme your checks, an' I'll see they bring your baggage right up. Just one trunk? All right! Here, Jim," motioning to the station hand, "take this check an' see that Mr. Gracen's trunk is sent up immediate."

The old man hurried up the platform to give the check to the baggage-man, talking as he went; and Richard, amazed and somehow comforted, sat waiting for him in the back seat of the carriage — his new suitcase beside him, marvelling over his reception.

Was this what it meant to get home? And who was this amiable old man? He had never heard of any living relative but an aunt before. But perhaps there were others. Whoever he was, the boy's heart warmed toward him.

He looked at the satiny backs of the fine horses, their long tails almost sweeping the ground, their noble heads curved proudly, their harness gleaming here and there with silver. He touched wonderingly the dark-green broadcloth of the cushions he sat upon, noted the shining immaculateness of everything, and realized with awe the lack of poverty. It was so new, so wonderful, to have aught to do with really fine, nice things, and have a right among them. For the first time he recognized that it satisfied something in him which had always seemed starved, some native longing, perhaps, that he had not understood. But he was only a boy, and did not think these things out in words; he simply felt them.

Hiram came back smiling, followed by a battery of eyes from the men hanging around the station. It was the first intimation that the town had had of a visitor coming to "The Beeches," as Miss Gracen's home was called. Hiram was enjoying the distinction of giving the loungers something to wonder about.

Who, indeed was Mr. Gracen? They didn't know of any other Gracen relatives. Why had he never appeared upon the scene before? He was exceedingly young, just a boy. Whose boy was he?

The question started, speculation was rife. Hiram went home serenely unconscious that he had untied the bag and given the cat a good chance to jump out.

"Well, well, well, ain't this just great, havin' you here at last?" exclaimed old Hiram, jumping in with agile movements scarcely expected of his years.

He slowly turned the blacks with their heads toward home, giving the bystanders a good chance to gaze at the handsome young face of the boy in the back seat; but he failed to hear the comment of an old resident as they drove slowly down the street.

"By gum! If that don't look jest like Dick Gracen did the year he went off to college!"

Richard was almost embarrassed by the attentions of Hiram as they drove down the street, but he was too confused to say much; and, indeed, Hiram did not require it. He was only too glad to get a chance to indulge in reminiscences about the boy's father.

Sunset again, and long, slanting, red rays lit up the crimson of the foliage as the carriage turned into The Beeches, and Richard saw lights appearing in the windows. The house stood far back from the street amid a grove of wonderful beeches, approached by an avenue of tree-arched beauty. There were soft shades of the lights, green and crimson, and a glow of firelight that Richard did not recognize, because he had never known a fireplace in his home. Everything indicated warmth, comfort, welcome; and yet the boy felt again a great trembling through his frame and a distinct desire to turn and run away. Not that he would have done so for worlds; but he realized that the coward in him was to the front, and he had much ado to hold him down from looking through the windows of his eyes and showing himself to the world.

The carriage stopped and the house door was flung wide open, letting out a flood of light to mingle with the evening shadows and long, slant rays of the sun.

Hiram threw open the carriage door, and lifted down the suitcase. Dick climbed out, and for one absurd moment recalled the look of the culprits who climbed down from the patrol-wagons in front of the city hall, looked wildly about for a hope of escape, and seeing none, fairly bolted into the open door if their prison that was to be. He felt as if he looked that way himself now.

There were three women standing in the hallway, one on each side of the door, two with long, white aprons and caps; and just a little back of them, in the very middle of the hall, under a great globe of light, with a gracious air of welcome, stood another, a beautiful woman with white hair and young eyes.

She stood with both hands held out to him, a smile on her face; and to his bewildered vision she seemed the most beautiful woman he had ever looked upon.

He stumbled in, and took her hand awkwardly, letting her lead him into the library, past dim visions of great rooms on either side of the hall, and knew she was saying kind, welcoming things, and must be his aunt, but knew not what words she was speaking.

He felt the beauty of everything about him without really seeing it.

The air was pervaded with the odor of good things to eat, and Molly and Rebecca appeared smiling in the doorway, giving a reminder of the supper that was ready. The aunt turned smilingly toward them.

"This is Rebecca," she said to the dazed boy. "She and Hiram were here when your father was born; and this is Molly, who was his nurse. They have been very eager for your coming."

Richard shook hands with both the women. He did it awkwardly. He wasn't used to shaking hands, and it came hard.

"I made some spice-cookies for you this morning," said Rebecca, smiling. "Your father used to like 'em. Do you like 'em, too?"

"Sure!" said Richard, turning rosy red, and smiling in spite of his embarrassment. Then they hurried him up-stairs to get ready for supper.

There was stewed chicken, with plenty of gravy, on tiny, little, puffy biscuits. There were more of the biscuits to eat with red raspberry jam and clear currant jelly. There was succotash such as the boy never had tasted before, made of corn sweet as a baby's breath, and queer red and purple calico beans. There were delectable pickles, and mashed potatoes without any of the dull, heavy lumps he supposed always went with that sort of vegetable; and there was a great glass of creamy milk foaming beside his plate. For dessert there was floating-island white as snow in a custard of delectable gold, and maple cake.

But the tragedy of it all was that he couldn't eat, because something in his throat kept closing down and almost choking him.

He had just to sit and stare at the vision of his beautiful, young, white-haired aunt, and wonder how he was to answer her remarks.

Hovering over it all, like two old beaming angels, came and went Rebecca and Molly; with a glimpse now and then, through the door of the butler's pantry, of Hiram handing out more eatables. It was all a wonderful dream, and Richard wondered sometimes whether he were not really asleep and whether this was not the reason that he could not do justice to the good things. He never had had a meal like it in his life, and he could not realize that all his meals were to be pretty much on this order after to-day. He just could not realize anything at all.

After supper his aunt took him back into the library, and he sat on the edge of the Morris-chair, and tried to act polite while she talked to him; but presently he forgot all about having to be polite, because she was talking to him about his father. She told him how he used to study and play, about his taking music-lessons, and being captain of a baseball-team, and doing great feats in college; how he looked the last time she saw him; and a great many other wonderful and interesting things, just fragments of them, for she did not go into much detail with anything, only sketched bits of scenes that made Richard eager to hear more.

And the boy never knew that she was talking against tears, trying to keep them from her eyes and from her voice because he brought back so vividly the face and form of her dear lost brother.

Then presently the little clock on the mantel chimed nine in a silvery tone, and his aunt stopped, smiling, and said she knew he must be tired and that he ought to go to bed right away.

She went up-stairs with him herself, and showed him where to switch on the electric light, and pointed out to him the white-tiled bathroom just across the hall, with its silver trappings and its wealth of splendid towels; showed him the pictures of his father on the walls of his room, just to make him feel at home; and then, with a half-wistful hesitation, she paused at the door and after a second said a sweet, cheery good-night, with a wish that he would sleep well in his new room.

She was gone, and he looked about in wonder; the daze began to wear off a little. He realized that he was terribly tired, and his eyelids smarted with the light. The choking sensation was growing in his throat, too, and he craved more than anything a chance to lie down in the dark, to be alone, and think.

He did not linger to look around, more than for a glance at that great picture of his father on the wall. He knew he looked like himself, though it seemed far handsomer than he could ever hope to be; but the look in those young, bright, kindly eyes was one that seemed to understand him; and, added to all that he had gone through, it was the one thing more that he could not bear. The choking in his throat was unbearable. Why had he missed having a splendid father like that?

Swiftly he undressed, and, turning off the light, crept into the great, lonely bed, burying his face in the pillow. He despised himself for it, but sobs shook his body and gasped in his throat; tears hot and fast blurred themselves into the pillow. He did not know what he was crying for; he only knew he was crying, shamelessly crying like a baby, and all because of a strange, unbearable something that yearned in his breast for a love he had never had. This, this home and kindliness that were offered him now, he did not seem to fit; it could never really belong to him. He had missed it all, and was alone, alone, alone!

He did not know how long or how short a time it was that this unforgivable emotion held him in its grasp before he heard soft steps coming down the hall to his door, and a gentle tap sounded through his muffling pillow. He only knew he held his breath to listen and wonder what he should do next.

6

It was his aunt's voice that broke the painful stillness of his dark room. "Dick, dear," she called softly, "are you asleep yet? May I come in a minute?"

He made a muffled sound in his pillow, not intending to answer her at all; but she waited for no more; she opened the door softly, and stepped inside, leaving the door ajar just a crack; and it sent a keen blade of light diagonally across the floor and wall, reflecting on her beautiful face and white hair.

He had raised his head partly from the pillow in consternation. To be caught crying by his aunt this first night of his arrival! This was too much! What would she think of him? A sissy-boy! That was the most awful reputation any boy could earn for himself. He would rather be thought *any-*thing than a sissy-boy!

He held himself rigid, motionless in the darkness, and tried to get control of his voice and act as if he didn't mind that she had come in. Perhaps she only wanted to find something she had left in the closet, and wouldn't look toward him.

But she came swiftly, softly, over to the bed in the darkness, and knelt beside him, throwing one arm across his shoulders as he fell back dismayed on his pillow and faced her in the dark. She leaned her head over his, and whispered softly:

"I couldn't go to sleep without kissing you goodnight, Dick. I always used to kiss my brother, Dick, good-night. It's been so many years now, and you are so like him! You won't mind if I do, dear boy, will you? I had to come and tell you how I love you. O Dickie, Dickie, dear, how I am going to love you!"

There was a sob in her voice, and as she bent down to kiss him the glint of light on the wall reflected on her sweet face, and showed it all shining and wet. Why, she was crying, too!

Then somehow Dick didn't mind any more. He put up his young, strong arms, flung them about her neck, and held her tightly in a fierce boy grip; and thus they mingled their tears together.

With her arms still about him, and her face close to his as she knelt, she whispered softly:

"O my heavenly Father, I thank Thee for sending me this dear boy. Bless him; and make him happy and good in this new home; and show me how to love and help him every day; and may we be a blessing to each other, for Jesus' sake. Amen."

Richard had never heard himself prayed for before. His mother had not prayed with him beyond teaching him "Now I lay me," which prayer he had long ago outgrown. But this prayer, coming as it did out of a loving heart, filled him with awe, wonder, and a strange new happiness.

When it was finished, she kissed him on the forehead again; and as she said, "Goodnight," he gripped her hand, and blundered out:

"Thanks, awfully! I'm glad I came. I — guess we'll — get on — all right."

It was a great deal for a boy like him to say. It was equivalent to a hundred loyal speeches and kisses thrown in, and it meant entire surrender. Perhaps her intuition taught her by the thrill the tone gave her soul as she slipped away and left him to sleep.

The boy lay back marvelling, and remembering. She hadn't said a word about finding him weeping! Yet she must have known. She was "game" all right. She hadn't let him know how she knew. Yet he knew she knew. She was the real stuff!

What was it that made him feel so different! Why, she had said she loved him! She loved *him!* Nobody had ever told him that before. Of course his mother had loved him; that was understood, but she wasn't the kind that talked of those things. But this aunt didn't have to love him, didn't have any reason to do anything but dislike him; and yet she had gone out of her way to tell him she loved him! That was great! And — *why, that made him belong! He belonged* there in that house, *because she loved him!*

Then he fell asleep. He dreamed that he went to heaven to tell his mother all about it; and she had smiled and was pleased, and pointed out his young, handsome father just like the picture on the wall.

When he awoke, it was morning, with the bright autumn sun shining broad across his bed into the pictured eyes of his father, regarding him kindly from the wall. He found himself filled with a kind of wondering ecstasy, as though he had been changed into a new being and all the old things were passed away. When he stopped to think why he felt this way, he knew it was because his aunt had kissed him and told him that she loved him.

The breakfast-table was a revelation. Set in a glow of autumn sunshine, the heavy linen, delicate china, sparkling silver, and cut glass made a deep impression upon his beauty-loving nature. Never had he sat down to a breakfast-table like this. People where he had come from sometimes fixed up the table for a company dinner or supper, but to take all that trouble just for breakfast started an entirely new world for him.

In the center of the table was a great bowl overflowing with late pears, peaches, plums and grapes. The oatmeal seemed to have no relation whatever to the sticky mess that had gone by that name in his mother's boarding-house, and the cream was rich and yellow. It made a delectable combination. There were tender beefsteak, fried potatoes, and golden-brown corncakes with thick maple-syrup. His mental comment as he surveyed the first plate of cakes that Molly brought in was: "Gee! but the eats in this house are great! I wish the fellows could have come!"

Richard had been almost afraid to come down-stairs, lest the recollection of last night should be embarrassing, but his aunt met him with a smiling "Good-morning," and no hint in her eyes even that there had been anything like tears or prayers or kisses between them. It put him entirely at his ease at once.

He looked with admiration at her in her pretty, pale-blue morning-gown with deep lace frills about her white wrists. The sunshine made her white hair into a lovely frame for her face, and he found himself wishing his mother could have seen her once. He was conscious of a growing pride that she belonged to him. He had never seen a woman of that age so beautiful before, and he had never connected loveliness in any form with growing old. His aunt fascinated him, and he found himself watching her every movement. He liked the fine lines about her eyes and the modelling of her delicate features.

Every line that the years had graven in her beautiful flesh was a pleasant line, as if she had always thought the best of every one. It filled the boy with admiring wonder. He had not known, he never even thought, that any woman could be like that.

He went with Hiram to the stable while his aunt was busy about her morning household duties, and took his first lesson in harnessing the horse. The city-bred boy eyed the horses with delight, and his face lit with joy when Hiram showed him the saddle and spoke of his riding. He made the acquaintance of the "colt," and took a brief lesson in saddling him, mounting him, and riding around the stable-yard. He finally drove the carriage up to the door of the house, his eyes aglow with happiness. He felt as if he had suddenly been snatched from the hard, gloomy realities of the world and set down in heaven, a better heaven than any he had ever imagined for himself; and something of his own unworthiness of it all looked out of his eyes as he smiled half shyly at his aunt when she stepped into the carriage clad in a lovely long, soft, gray cloak and a gray felt hat with white wings. He was both proud and embarrassed to be riding out with such a queenly woman.

He rode behind with his aunt, and Hiram drove in the front seat. Richard watched him eagerly, and wondered whether he would ever be allowed to drive those two shining horses by himself. His heart swelled with the very thought of it, and Miss Gracen, watching his bright, eager face, with keen intuition seemed to read his thoughts; for almost at once she said:

"You'll like to drive the horses to the store and post-office sometimes when Hiram is busy, won't you? Hiram, you'll have to show

Mr. Dick all about the horses. You know you taught his father to drive."

"Yes, indeedy, so I did, Miss Vic," said Hiram, his face lighting with the memory, "only he was a mighty leetle feller when he fust held the reins. I mind he used to sit atween my knees, an' holt the lines behind my hands, an' holler an' laugh, an' think he was drivin'; and his cheeks would be as pink as one of Rebecca's posies in the kitchen garden, an' his eyes as shiny as the stars.

"But I reckon this here Mr. Dick won't need much teachin'. He's almost growed up. Reckon he knows how to drive 'thout my teachin' him."

A wave of pleased consciousness rolled over the boy's face in a faint flush, while he modestly disclaimed any equestrian knowledge. Indeed, his knowledge of horses was confined to driving a grocery-wagon occasionally on a Saturday when there was a scarcity of hands; but he did not like to tell that to the dignified Hiram, who treated him as if he were a gentleman.

It was a new and pleasant experience to be treated as if he were wanted, and to be actually planned for as if he were a part of the things of consequence. He smiled back at Hiram with a pleased surprise, but said little. It was all too new and wonderful to last, he felt sure; and his native caution, which had been his constant safeguard all his life against the hard brunt of an unsympathetic world, warned him not to commit himself.

When these people found him out as he really was, saw what commonplace gifts were his, and knew about his past inclinations to wildness, they would probably not care to bother any further with him. It was the halo of his father's likeness, very likely, that made them care now; but they could not in the nature of things keep it up. Nobody had ever paid much attention to him, unless it was his mother, and she scarcely ever had time. Well, he would enjoy it while it lasted — and then?

But he had not opportunity to pursue his bitter thoughts, for his aunt kept directing his attention to things and people as they went along.

Up there on the hill was the college. That was the dome of the observatory showing through the trees; over there was the Carnegie Library, and next it the gymnasium and dormitories. A number of great men had been graduated from this college, and it ranked well with others of its size. Over there were the athletic grounds.

These last were a second thought. Miss

Gracen had never had much to do with college athletics. In her brother's college days athletics had been in their infancy, and regarded with doubt and suspicion by many thoughtful people as being a menace to high scholarship. Her circle of friends had scarcely been one to change this impression, though of course she had felt the general trend of thought of the day in regard to such matters, and was a broad-minded woman.

But now she saw like a flash the lighting of the boy's eyes as she spoke of athletics, and went on to tell of games that had been won from other large colleges, growing quite enthusiastic in her telling. So Hiram was told to drive up around the athletic grounds, and the boy feasted his eyes upon the wide stretches of velvety, green turf and the generous grand-stands.

Were there any games soon now? Football and basketball must be at their height, he said; and his aunt shook her head.

"I'm sure I don't know, Dick; we'll have to find out. I suppose, if that's the thing to be doing this time of year, our college is at it," she said; "but I know very little about such things. However, we'll take means to discover at once. Here comes our minister, and his son. Boys all know about the games,

I suppose. We'll ask."

She leaned from the carriage, and greeted the pleasant-faced gentleman in a gray suit who was coming toward them; but Richard's eyes were on the boy who accompanied him. He was almost as tall as his father, well knit, with a homely, freckled face lit up by the handsomest pair of wine-brown eyes that Richard had ever seen. His hair, when he took off his rough tweed cap to speak to Miss Gracen, showed a deep, rich red; and there was a reckless grace in his movements and a mischievous twinkle in his brown eyes that made the other boy's heart warm toward him at once. The newcomer eyed the stranger curiously, as boys will, narrowly, sizing him up at a glance.

"Mr. Atterbury, this is my nephew, Dick Gracen," said Richard's aunt, leaning out to shake hands with the minister; "and this is Tom Atterbury, Dick," she said informally; and the two boys awkwardly and gravely acknowledged the introduction, each determined to be cautious in going a step further with the acquaintance until he was at least sure of its desirability.

"Dick was asking me about the games, and I couldn't tell him," said Miss Gracen with a pleasant laugh. "I wonder if you can enlighten us."

She looked straight at Tom Atterbury, and wondered why she had never noticed before what handsome eyes he had. She had always regarded him with a slight disfavor. He had a name for being in all the mischief in town, and she had always felt sorry for his father; but Tom's eyes softened her heart toward him greatly, and she had a passing wonder whether possessing a boy of her own would give her an interest in all boys.

"Sure!" said Tom Atterbury in a slow, drawling voice and with a smile that lit his freckles into a pleasant, merry face. "There's a game this afternoon, a big one. Our men play against Carnegie Tech. Would you like to go? I'll take you if you say so"; and Tom lifted a mischievous triumphant eye of inquiry toward his strong-faced, kindly father.

Now it happened that Tom carried under his arm a stack of school-books, and had just been undergoing a kind, but firm lecture on the subject of staying away from foot-ball-games and studying up some of the things in which his reports had been showing him to be sadly deficient during the past month.

Tom had no deep interest in taking Dick Gracen to the game; but he did have a consuming desire to go to it himself, and he knew that he was striking his father in a weak spot when he touched him on the side of parish work. His father would want him to be kind to Miss Gracen's guest of course, and he would be willing to have him go to the game under those circumstances, he was sure; and the kindly response in his father's eyes showed Tom that he had judged correctly.

In a moment more the arrangements were made, and Tom Atterbury went on his way to his belated schoolday with a smiling countenance, to become the torment of his teachers and the despair of the principal for the day, in honor of the victory he had won over his father and the game he was soon to see.

Miss Gracen, however, sat back in her seat as the horses started on again through the college campus, and found her mind suddenly troubled. Here she had let that scamp of a Tom Atterbury make an arrangement to take her boy to a football-game! How had she so blundered? How had she been so blind?

She had planned in the watches of the night how she would introduce him to the boys who would be likely to be the greatest help to him in every way, and perhaps steer him clear of all the wickedness of the town, and keep him from knowing the wild ones at all.

She had completely forgotten the minister's son. Of course he had to be introduced, being the minister's son, but he was the wildest of the wild, if all the stories she heard of him were to be credited; and now she had put her Dick right into his clutches the first one.

If Dick began to go with Tom Atterbury, then none of the other nicer boys would have anything to do with him. There was George Barry, who lived with his mother and waited upon her so beautifully whenever they went anywhere; and there was James Clovis, who had won the scholarship in the preparatory school and had been chosen twice on the debating-team; and there were the Jarvis brothers, who worked every summer in the bank to save money for their winter's schooling so that their mother would not have to work so hard. They were all fine fellows. There was Brice Parker, the son of the burgess of the town, whose manners were perfect and whose character was both strong and charming. These were the companions she coveted for her boy. They all went to church and Sunday-school, and attended the Christian Endeavor Society regularly. They dressed well, and studied well, and behaved well everywhere, and never had a thing said against their reputations.

Tom Atterbury went to church and the Christian Endeavor Society, too; but he went because his father expected it of him, and he sat in the back seat if he could, and made mysterious noises that convulsed the little boys, who cheerfully bore the reprimands for the sake of watching his antics. There were notable pranks in the annals of the village years set down to the credit, or rather the discredit, of Tom Atterbury, the penalties of which had been borne by the younger fry, but which every one knew had been instigated and encouraged by the minister's son; and rumor said that he grow no better as he grew older.

Miss Gracen's soul was troubled more with every step her horses carried her away from the minister and his scapegrace son. How could she have been so thoughtless as to introduce Dick to him the very first one? She might have avoided it as well as not by telling Hiram to drive on quickly and by merely greeting the minister with a smile and a bow.

She had made a grievous mistake at the start. What should she do to rectify it? She tried to think as they drove to other places of interest; to the preparatory school, the high school, the church, the bank, the post-office, and the largest stores.

At last, after she had made some purchases and was back in the carriage again, she suggested that perhaps Dick would be too tired after his long journey to go to the game that afternoon, and that, if he would like to have her do so, she could telephone to Tom Atterbury and excuse him from the engagement; but Richard, beaming on her brightly, declared he was not in the least tired and would be delighted to go to the game. He added that Tom seemed like a good sort of fellow. He thought he should like him.

"He has a good father," said Miss Gracen cautiously, with a sigh of anxiety. "I'm not sure that Tom is always a comfort to him."

Richard said nothing. He did not know much about fathers or being a comfort to them. Her words made him wince over the fact that he had never been a comfort to his mother.

But he decided that Tom Atterbury was all right and that they would get on famously. There were hallmarks upon him that made him seem akin to the fellows he had left in Chicago, and it made him feel less alone here to find a boy he could understand. There had been the right kind of gleam in the eye of the minister's son when he spoke of the game. Other things didn't matter so much.

Miss Gracen, with many compunctions, watched her boy go off that afternoon, in company with the minister's son, and it seemed to her at the moment when they walked down the front path together that a great weight of responsibility settled down upon her.

The minister's son wore a rough brown Norfolk-jacket suit that just matched his hair and his wine-brown eyes, and there had been something altogether pleasing and engaging about him as he tipped his rough brown wool hat when he bade her good-bye and turned away smilingly to go with Dick.

Something in her — was it her misgivings? — had turned over in her heart as he looked at her, and suggested to her that perhaps Tom Atterbury was not quite so bad as people said; but still, when they disappeared behind the tall hedge and she knew that Dick was to be under his influence for two or three long hours, she turned away with the troubled feeling that a hen with one chicken wears on her brow, and sat down in deep thought to try to plan how to put Dick under good influences.

She decided that really no great harm could be done in one short afternoon, and she must expect to meet outside influences and cope with them; nevertheless, she was by no means at rest, and spent an hour in alternately seating herself in deep thought and walking to the window to look out, though she knew it was a long time before she could expect to see her boy coming back.

One thing was very sure; she must have a good talk with Dick that evening, and they must both know just where they stood. Then her mind would be more at rest and she would know how to plan.

On her fifth trip to the window she saw a figure turn in at the gate and hurry up the walk with a quick, nervous gait. She recognized it at once as belonging to Miss Lydia Bypath, and turned with an impatient sigh. Ordinarily she was good nature itself to this most unwelcome of callers, for she knew and warmly loved the good side of Miss Bypath; but this afternoon, with anxiety on her mind, and her talk with her new nephew to plan for, she dreaded the bright, prying eyes, the cattish flings, and the curious questions that she knew she would have to meet.

Miss Bypath had of course heard of Dick's

coming, and had come to inform herself concerning the stranger in her friend's home. There would not be a bit of tender heart history or family pride that would not be turned over and thoroughly aired before she was through with her subject. Miss Gracen dreaded the encounter.

Hitherto she had been able to keep on the right side of the village gossip and critic by never doing anything that Lydia Bypath disapproved and by being always ready to listen sympathetically to all the poor, little, narrow soul's grievances. But by all tokens she knew, as she turned away from the window and prepared to meet her guest with her most ceremonious smile, that her own turn had now come, and that she must meet it bravely.

Doubtless, too, the very thing that worried her most would be burned into her soul with scorching sentences, for in all probability Miss Bypath's sharp eyes had seen Dick go by to the football-field with the minister's scapegrace son. Miss Gracen girded up her strength, and went forth to meet her unwelcome guest.

7

Miss Lydia Bypath had thin lips, eyes that bored like gimlets, though they were blue as the sea and had been pretty in their time, and a nose that was always ready to sniff at anything she doubted. She doubted almost everything that was told her, but told it as truth to the next person she met. She was slender and small, with an alert movement like a sharp blackbird, and she always wore dull black clothes with dazzling white lines near together. They seemed to reverse in color the fine lines of dissatisfaction in her thin, pursed lips, and up and down on her narrow forehead, vanishing under her gray, frizzy hair.

She came from a very fine old family, and had a patrician tilt to her chin, and most delicate little hands; but poverty and disappointment had so long been allowed to eat into her soul that nearly all the sweetness and beauty were gone. In their place had come only a most unworthy curiosity about her neighbors for the still more unworthy object of finding out whether they had been better treated by the world than she had been.

She had a poor opinion of all men in general, especially of husbands, a strong jealousy for all women, except perhaps Miss Gracen, whom she strongly admired, and a dislike for all young people and children. It was hard to find anybody that Miss Bypath quite approved, and harder to say anything with which she agreed.

So far no one but Miss Gracen, not even the minister, had been able to keep in her continual good graces; and now Miss Gracen was about to pass her first test by the sting of this most accomplished village gadfly. Her solitary condition, her pride and poverty, the fragments of her lost beauty, all appealed deeply to the sympathy of Miss Gracen, and had so far helped her to be patient with Miss Bypath's besetting sin.

The visitor perched herself on the edge of the Morris-chair, as if to lean back were to capitulate to a weakness of which she could not be guilty, and having removed her cape, gloves and "fascinator," pursed her lips into a disagreeable smile, and began:

"Well, Victoria," fixing her sharp gimlet blue eyes upon her victim, "I've come straight to you for information. I've always said, you know, that 'twas the only way to find out the real truth — to go straight to the fountainhead; and so I've come. I wasn't going to let anybody tell me things about my very best friend and not know how to deny them. I must say that I think you might have confided in me, an old friend, but, of course, there may have been some excuse for your not doing it. You know best about that. However, I've come to find out before I said a blessed thing about it to any one."

"Dear me, Lydia, is somebody saying something about me now?" said her hostess with a forced smile. "It was good of you to come straight to me, of course; but really, don't you think it's just as well not to pay any attention to gossip? It dies down soon enough when people find out there isn't any foundation for it."

She arose and placed a lovely bronze cushion behind her guest's back, rang for a cup of tea to be brought, lowered the shades, then settled down to what she now saw was inevitable.

"Yes, but Victoria, isn't there any foundation? *Isn't* there?"

The blue eyes pierced her very soul as if they would extract the information against the will of the other. The two had gone to school together, had lived as neighbors for many years, and Victoria Gracen knew what she had to encounter.

"How am I to tell you, Lydia, when I don't know what they're saying?" she laughed lightly, toying with a carved paper-knife that lay on the table, and remembering with a curious pleasure that Dick had been studying it just before lunch. She marvelled at the hold the boy had upon her thoughts already.

"They say," said Lydia, and her voice took on a terribly sepulchral whisper that held both imprecation and implication, "they say that you have turned against your dead mother's wishes and have brought home the child of your brother, the disinherited grandson. They say, too, that if you keep him you will surely bring a curse down upon your home and yourself."

Miss Gracen sat up very straight, a bright spot of color in her cheeks and her dark eyes shining with battle, an almost haughty smile on her sweet lips.

"Really!" she said, and then again, "Really!" Then she laughed.

But little Miss Bypath sat still, held her thin hands primly in her lap, and drew in her thin lips until they almost vanished in a line of stern disapproval. She did not laugh. She conveyed the impression that she was most deeply hurt by Miss Gracen's laughter and that she considered it no subject for merriment.

Then Miss Gracen suddenly grew sober and dignified.

"Really, Lydia, I should scarcely think that was worth noticing," she said pleasantly. "It isn't any one's affair but my own, you know; and they can't bring any curses by their absurd remarks.

"If you really feel it incumbent upon you to say anything about the matter, you may just tell them the plain fact that my nephew, Dick, has, indeed, come to stay with me for a time, how long or how short a time will depend upon whether or not he likes to stay.

"I would have had him long ago if his mother could have spared him, but she could not see her way clear to do that. Since her death he has been lonely and accepted my invitation to come to me. I hope we are going to be very, very happy together."

There was something in the sweet dignity of the hostess that prevented the sharp queries the guest would have liked to make. Miss Gracen's tone said as plainly as words could have said that the subject was closed so far as she was concerned.

Lydia Bypath suddenly found an unaccountable lack of words wherewith to push her inquiries, though she was an adept in prying out and exhibiting to the world other people's private affairs. Now she could only shake her head ominously and murmur:

"Well, I'm sure I hope you will! I'm sure I hope you will! But the prospect looks anything but likely to *me*." What was there about Miss Gracen's direct and simple way of telling a few facts frankly that seemed to leave nothing further to ask, although the eager questioner would fain have known a thousand other details, but had not the effrontery to go further?

"Here is the tea," announced the hostess cheerily, as Rebecca entered with the tempting tray, on which were the delicious rolled sandwiches of brown and white bread for which Miss Gracen's receptions were famous, and Lydia Bypath dearly loved, as well as the delicate almond cakes and fragrant tea, with the choice of lemon or cream. It pleased Miss Bypath that the choice was always given her, although she invariably answered severely: "Cream, of course. I'd as soon put a pickle in my tea as lemon." Nevertheless, if the lemon had not been on the tray, she would have felt that Victoria Gracen thought her old-fashioned, and hadn't considered it worth her while to observe all the formality that she always gave to Mrs. Elihu Brown and to Mrs. Norman Constable.

Miss Bypath waited in grim silence, save for the usual lemon-and-cream dialogue, until she had had her tea and sandwiches and Rebecca had withdrawn. Then her voice took on its sepulchral whisper again.

"You've taken an awful contract on your hands, Victoria; and you'll be sorry, or I'll surely miss my guess," looking straight at her hostess. "Boys are terrible creatures to manage, and they will always disappoint you. I'm sorry to have to tell you right at the start this way, but I consider it my duty to put you on your guard before it is too late. Why, your young scapegrace nephew is in bad company already. He went by my house not half an hour ago arm in arm with that good-for-nothing Tom Atterbury, and you certainly know what he is! They were headed toward the football-field, and I said to myself, 'Well that's the end of him' " — as if football were synonymous with evil; " 'Victoria Gracen had just better send him right back to where he came from as fast as he can go, or there'll be another disgraceful member of the family to worry her into the grave.' I knew him by his close resemblance to his father. He has that same reckless, daredevil black eye —"

Miss Bypath here extinguished further speech in a delectable bite of rolled brown bread and lettuce, but it is doubtful whether she would have continued further in her remarks; for Miss Gracen had risen with an air of finality, her deep eyes showing flashes of fire that Lydia Bypath had presumed never to see directed toward herself. She saw them now with dismay, and shrank visibly before the look.

Miss Gracen stood thus looking at her guest scarcely a second before she spoke; yet it seemed an aeon to the presumptuous soul before her.

Then she merely said:

"Yes, I asked Tom to take Dick to the game. I want him to feel at home as soon as possible, and there is nothing like athletics to bring young people together. But, if you please, Lydia, we will not discuss my family any longer. Won't you let me give you a little more tea? I'm afraid the cream has cooled it.

"By the way, did you know that we are to be favored with Professor Hammond's lecture on Shakespeare at the next Club meeting? Won't it be great to have him lecture for us? I hadn't dared even to hope for anything of the sort, because they said he had come here only to rest; but he told

Mrs. Constable he should be delighted to help us in any way we desired."

Miss Bypath, for once meek, readily caught on to the thread of the new topic of conversation, yet she realized none the less that she had indeed been on the very verge of dismissal, not only from the house, but from her friend's regard forever. She had dared many things and she had outraged many people, but never before had she been made so thoroughly to see and realize the fulness of her offence; and yet no verbal rebuke had been uttered. The remainder of her visit — and she stayed until the shades of evening were beginning to fall — she spent eagerly trying to placate her dignified hostess.

Perhaps it was as well that Miss Gracen had no leisure to worry that afternoon, for surely she would have worried about the very thing Miss Bypath had suggested; but now her soul was roused in indignation against the meanness of the village gossip, and she began to find in her heart excuses for the son of the minister. His wistful brown eyes haunted her, and when, glancing out of the window as the dusky shadows of the early twilight drew on, she saw the two boys coming down the street together, laughing and talking, a glad smile broke out upon her face. Her boy was coming back to her sane and sound. Nothing very bad could have happened to him in one short afternoon, although Lydia Bypath had said that he was going to a football-game in the same tone in which she might have told how fast he was going to destruction.

Miss Gracen felt a sudden unaccountable sympathy with the son of the minister, who had acquired a doubtful reputation, and wondered again within herself whether all that people said about him were really true, after all. Perhaps he was not so bad as he was thought to be, and anyhow his father was a good man.

When, a moment later, Richard, not knowing that his aunt was entertaining a guest in the library, entered with his new friend, Miss Gracen greeted him with an outstretched hand and a sweet smile of welcome. A sudden desire to show Miss Bypath how wrong had been her attitude toward Tom came over her.

"I'm glad you came back with Dick," she said. "I was wanting to ask whether you wouldn't stay to supper. I'm sure Dick would like it."

Dick's eyes lit happily.

"Sure," echoed the boy. He hadn't been in the habit of having friends home to supper. It was a new and delightful experience.

"Why, I just came in to see some photographs Dick was telling me he brought with him," drawled Tom in his soft, hesitant, appealing voice; "but I'd like awfully to stay; only dad said if I didn't come straight home and study I couldn't go to another game this semester. But it would be just jolly to stay. I'd like it awfully, Miss Vic."

Tom's brown eyes touched again the chord of sympathy in Miss Gracen's already awakened heart. She determined to have Tom stay, the more as she turned and saw Miss Bypath's cat-like eyes of disapproval fixed upon her, and suddenly realized her duties as a hostess.

"Excuse me, Miss Bypath," she said, turning toward her; "let me introduce my nephew, Richard Gracen of Chicago; and Tom Atterbury of course you know."

There was that in her tone that made Richard feel as though she had introduced the son of a millionaire, and his face flushed with pleasure. He liked his aunt for the deference she paid to him, a mere nobody of a boy.

He shook hands with Miss Bypath with an easy grace that astonished his aunt, and Miss Bypath was quite overwhelmed for the moment, though she could not forbear a jab of advice as she submitted her reluctant hand in greeting.

"I'm sure I hope you'll turn out to be a comfort to your aunt in her old age, and not bring trouble the way some boys do."

With the keen instinct of youth the two boys knew immediately that Miss Bypath had been talking about them to Miss Gracen, and Richard seemed to fret, for the first time since he had entered his aunt's house, the reproach of what his father had done, while Tom's face took on the sullen, dogged expression of the hunted one of whom no one ever thought any good.

An angry wave of color rolled over Richard's face, and he felt something throbbing and choking painfully in his throat. His fingers involuntarily clinched themselves, and he lifted his chin proudly in a way that his father used to have when he was hurt, which went straight to the heart of his aunt.

Instantly Miss Gracen stepped to Richard's side, and slipped her hand lovingly, confidingly within his arm, putting the other soft white hand gently over his fierce clinched fingers.

"Dick is a great comfort to me already," she said confidently; "and I am sure we are going to have delightful times together."

She felt his fingers relax at once under

her touch, and saw with relief his wondering eyes turn to her with a pleased look. She smiled, and his face lit up with something beautiful to see, that the boy himself scarcely understood. It was a strange experience to have any one take his part, or show any outward sign of caring. His mother had been too meek and tired to answer back when his aunt and uncle blamed him for anything. He knew she cared, of course; but she never said so. He was surprised to find how sweet it was to have some one care.

Tom, meanwhile, was looking on surprised, his own expression changing back to wistfulness as he saw Miss Gracen's smile of understanding. He was glad for the other boy, glad that any one understood a boy as she seemed to do. Miss Gracen looked up, and caught his glance, and reached out her hand to him also.

"Now, Tom," she said with one of her bright, happy smiles, as if the other matter were entirely settled and forgotten, "would it do any good, I wonder, if I were to telephone your father and ask him to let you stay for supper? You could go straight home and study afterward, couldn't you? And you wouldn't be able to do much between now and supper-time, you know."

Tom's freckles melted into smiles. The

sinking sun shot out a parting ray through the long west windows, and laid a touch of gold upon his deep-red hair, making the boy really attractive. Miss Gracen's heart went out to him in earnest now. If this boy was wrong in some ways might he not be helped to be right? At least, she would get acquainted, and find out. If he was to be guarded against, she must know what she had to guard against.

Tom laid a rough red hand confidingly, wonderingly, on her white one, as he would have laid it on the head of his favorite collie, that loved him. It was his way of responding to Miss Gracen's kindness. He was pleased beyond measure at what she had done, and especially in the presence of this crabbed, sharp-eyed woman who had always seemed to have an especial spite against him.

"Oh, I'd like it just awfully, Miss Vic," he said gratefully, "and I'm most sure father wouldn't refuse you. That would be just fine if he only would let me stay. Yes, sure, I could go right home afterwards and study. I'd study *hard*, too."

"Then I'll telephone at once," smiled the hostess.

But Miss Bypath made herself felt at that instant with her most effective sniff, as if to say that this was no company for a respectable woman like herself; and to the relief of all she made a stiff adieu, and took her way home, declining coldly the offer of company, though Miss Gracen suggested sending Hiram with her.

When she was gone, Miss Gracen went to the telephone and talked with Tom's father, who reluctantly consented to allow him to stay to supper; and the two boys went noisily and happily up to Richard's room to make ready for the evening meal.

"Gee! but that woman Bypath makes me tired," said Tom as he followed Richard up-stairs. "Father says she makes him more trouble in the church than any five other members put together. I'm glad your aunt didn't ask her to stay to supper. She never did like me, and she'd put one over on me whenever she could.

"Say, your aunt is all right, isn't she? I always did like her, though I never knew her very well. Father thinks she's just great."

Richard's face had darkened at mention of Miss Bypath, but it lighted with a tender smile when his friend spoke of Miss Gracen.

"Yes, she's pretty fine, all right," said Richard, half bashfully.

"She sure is! She's a peach!" proclaimed Tom, as they entered Richard's room and closed the door.

The echo of their voices had come down to Victoria Gracen as she stood still beside the telephone, wondering whether, after all, she had done the right thing; for she feared lest she had let herself be carried away by her indignation with Lydia Bypath, and had perhaps fostered an intimacy with this wild boy, who would do her boy no good. But, when she heard the unqualified approbation in the young voices, and realized that it was herself who was being discussed in these strange boy-terms, her heart beat with a wild thrill of happiness. She was not very familiar with modern slang, but she had discernment enough to know that when Tom Atterbury said in that tone that she was a "peach" he could give her no compliment higher, according to his way of thinking, and she resolved to hold and keep his admiration if possible. Like a flash her common sense showed her that, while she might have made a mistake in introducing her nephew to this boy in the first place, he would have had to meet him sometime, and it was better for them to meet in Richard's home and under her companionship than out and away from her knowledge.

It was not likely that the boy who had come to her had been brought up in pink cotton so far. He might indeed, for aught she knew, be even a more dangerous companion than the much-talked-of Tom. At all events, she would keep Tom's friendliness now that she had it, and see whether there was any way in which she could help him back to the confidence of the neighborhood.

It was with this in view that she sat down to her well-spread table and prepared to be as fascinating as she knew how for the sake of these two boys.

The supper table was very pretty in its usual whiteness of fine linen, its glitter of silver and its shimmer of cut glass, and the effect of it all was just as strange and just as wonderful to the boy from the parsonage as it was to the boy from a forlorn little Chicago boarding house. There was a great bowl of roses in the center of the table, and touches of old rose showed here and there on the beautiful soft gray gown that Miss Gracen wore.

Tom suddenly became aware of the largeness and redness of his hands as they protruded from his last year's sleeves, that were too short. However, he was not much used to worrying about his appearance; and Miss Gracen and Richard were so hearty in their expressions of pleasure at his being there that he soon forgot his hands, and made himself so agreeable that Miss Gracen in her turn was surprised and pleased.

She decided that people had judged Tom without knowing him. He certainly had charming ways, and a wistful fashion of looking at one that appealed tremendously to the heart.

The roast beef was of a quality that seldom came the way of the parsonage, where the meagre salary was always in the process of stretching itself to cover the multitude of needs of a family of seven. There was custard pie, plenty of it, with a crust like flakes of snow, a golden luscious center, and browned to a perfect cinnamon tinge on the top. Also, Miss Gracen not only offered, but urged, two pieces on the hungry boys; and Tom, whose methods of obtaining the second piece at home were not always the best, was overwhelmed at such open bounty.

The conversation finally fell on football; and the hostess, who had never been to a football game in all her life, and had indeed shared the feeling of more than half the village that it was a terribly useless and dangerous waste of time, began to see an entirely different side to the question. She saw the eagerness with which both boys entered into the merits of the game they had witnessed that afternoon, describing the different plays, denouncing or praising this or that player, rejoicing that the home college team had won. She asked questions, and the boys proceeded eagerly to instruct her, using the salt and pepper bottles to illustrate the different plays and an olive for a ball.

Even Rebecca lingered in her waiting, watching the little green ball move from one pepper bottle to another as Tom gave a demonstration of the game that afternoon; and Hiram was seen to apply one eye to the crack of the door of the butler's pantry, both servants beaming over the good cheer that had so suddenly come to the home after the long years of silence.

Miss Gracen's eyes were bright and her lips smiling with interest as she began to understand the game, and she laughingly agreed to go with the two boys to watch the next big game that was played in town, wondering furtively what Lydia Bypath would think of her now, to be contaminated with football at her age.

But then probably the boys would forget all about it before time for the game to be played; and it pleased her that they had asked her.

"I haven't had so pleasant a tea-party as this since my dear brother went away," she said happily, as they rose from the table.

"Indeed, you must come and see Dick again, Tom." And with a sudden loving thought she reached over, selected two of the most beautiful buds from among the roses, and pinned them to the boys' coats before they left the dining-room.

As he made his adieu, Tom Atterbury came impulsively over to his charming hostess; and, putting both big, rough hands confidingly on her sleeve, he said in his most winning drawl:

"Miss Vic, I want to thank you for that dinner. It certainly was simply great. I'm awfully obliged to you for inviting me to stay."

With that look in his brown eyes Miss Gracen's heart was entirely won over to champion the cause of the minister's wild young son.

"I'm glad," she said brightly. "Then you'll come often again. And now you must study hard all the evening, as you promised, so your father will be willing for you to come the next time."

"All right, I will, I surely will. You'll see, Miss Vic. I'll bring my report-card down to prove it to you next week, when we go to that game."

He bade them a laughing good-night, and Miss Gracen turned away from the door with a qualm of conscience. What had she done? Committed herself to a standing friendship between her nephew and this youth, who had hitherto been considered dangerous? Nay, she had done more. She had even encouraged it.

But a glance at the look of deep admiration in the eyes of Richard as she closed the door made her forget all in a rush of joy that she had this boy. Her home was no more lonely; she had some one to love; and something in his eyes told her that he was not averse to loving her. She slipped her hand within his arm, and so they walked back to the cheerful light of the library fire.

8

"Nice fellow he is," said Dick with a shade of embarrassment in his voice. He didn't know how to talk to a lady very well. His aunt was so delicate in her make-up and so dainty and refined in her dress that she filled him with a sort of awe.

"He does seem nice, doesn't he?" said Miss Gracen, watching him thoughtfully. "He has the name of being rather wild, but I couldn't help liking him to-night. Perhaps he has been misjudged."

"Hardly anybody's as bad as folks think they are," vouchsafed the youthful Richard with a frown, remembering his own case and how he had been, as he felt, misjudged. "I'm not any angel myself," he added belligerently. "I don't s'pose you'd have asked me here and done all you have for me if you'd known all about me."

He turned and looked at her half defiantly, as if he would give her opportunity even now to withdraw her kindness and send him back to his own place.

It had come — the opportunity she had been longing for and dreading — the opening to have a personal talk with the boy for whom she had become responsible. She knew she must not let it slip, and that it must be talked out to the finish, faithfully, patiently, and with infinite wisdom. She put up a breath of prayer for help, while her heart began to beat wildly. Never in all her quiet, well-ordered life had she met with a task more difficult and more unequal to her experience.

Pressing her fingers gently on the boy's arm, she said, after a moment's searching, tender look into his eyes:

"That wouldn't have made any difference, Dick. And it doesn't make any now. You are my dear brother's child, and as such I wanted you. Now that you are here I love you. Whatever you are, I shall have to bear with. If you choose to do wrong, I shall have to suffer."

The boy's eyes grew cloudy with moisture. He had never heard anything like that speech in his life. It touched him, comforted him, and made a baby of him all in one.

"I don't want to make you suffer," he growled in a choked voice, lowering his eyes and half turning away.

A sudden great joy sprang into Victoria Gracen's eyes.

"Oh, Dick, dear, thank you! I don't believe you're going to. Sit down and tell me all about it, won't you? I think we have made a good beginning."

They had come into the library, and were standing in front of the fire; but Richard drew away from her, and brushed his hand hastily and angrily across his eyes as though the lights hurt them; then he leaned his elbow on the mantel, and rested his forehead on his hand so that his face was shaded from her view. He made no move to sit down, and his very back was eloquent of deep disturbance.

"I'd better go away," he growled out at last. "I don't belong here. I'm not fit to be in a home like this. Don't you suppose I know it? I knew it when I came, I guess. I could tell from your telegram you were different. Mother was a good woman, and did the best she could; but she wasn't like you. And I've knocked around a lot and done a lot as I pleased. You wouldn't like what I've been, I know, and I ought to go away right off. I'd better go at once before it's any harder."

A choke in his voice ended the speech; the boy dropped his head on the mantel, and his shoulders drooped piteously. The heart of the woman went out in great motherliness, and she felt the tears filling her own eyes. She got up from the chair in which she had been sitting, and came and stood beside him, putting her hand, shyly, unaccustomedly on his thick brown hair.

"Dick, dear, didn't I tell you that I love you? Didn't I tell you that doesn't make any difference? I'm going to keep right on loving you in spite of everything you may say you have been. Can't you understand that? This is just as good a time as any for us to understand each other. Come, sit down, dear."

With ready tact she drew a chair opposite her own low one in front of the fire, and turned out the lights in the room; for the fire was burning brightly, and soft, flickering leaps of light and shadow played about the walls and floor and on their faces. She had seen that the boy was stirred to the depths of his nature, and readily guessed that the talk would be less embarrassing for him if his own face were not subjected to the glare of the bright electric lights.

He dropped into the chair she had drawn, and watched her furtively, his brows attentive, his eyes full of a growing admiration. She made a charming picture there in the firelight, the play of shadow over her soft, gray dress, and the light glowing in the touch of rose color and illuminating her white hair and sweet face. Richard, as he looked, thought he had never seen any one so lovely, not even a young girl. And this beautiful, motherly, understanding woman loved him, and wanted him!

His soul was filled with a deep comfort such as he had never known before, and he found himself wishing his mother knew about it.

Miss Gracen began by telling a little story of her brother Dick and some escapade of his which had put him into disgrace. She pictured herself and her brother sitting in this very room talking it over, and told the younger Dick how she had loved her brother in his trouble, and wanted to protect him, because she felt that he was truly sorry, though his elders did not seem to be thoroughly convinced of it.

Perhaps what she said might not have been considered wise by trained educators and psychological experts; but she followed the promptings of her heart, and was perfectly frank with the boy. She felt that what they needed first was perfect confidence in each other, and then they could go ahead.

"Now, Dick, dear," she said as she turned

from the incident of his father, "I'm getting to be an old woman; at least, I'm on the way there; and I don't suppose I'm very wise. I'll not be able to do all for you that your father would have done in helping you to be a splendid man; but I thought if we could just begin by being good friends, and always perfectly frank and true with each other, it might make things easier. I'd like it very much if you could feel you would never hide things from me, even if they were things you knew I didn't like. I'd promise always to be ready to talk them over fairly and try to see your point of view as well as my own. Do you think you would be willing to do that?"

Richard's eyes were upon her earnestly, and they took on a glint of appreciation. His look spoke volumes, but his lips only said in a low, reserved growl:

"Sure!"

It wasn't much of an answer, and yet his aunt felt that he had given her full assurance. Something in his eyes and in the loyalty of his tone filled her with joy inexpressible. She had not thought it would be like this to have a boy of her own. She had hoped she would like him enough so that his presence would not be a burden, but that her life should suddenly be filled with a great glory and beauty because of his coming she had not dreamed.

"Dick, tell me," she said, looking at him earnestly, and speaking low and tenderly, "are you — do you think you are going to like to stay here? Do you think you can learn to love me a little?"

The boy tried to take his eyes away from her face, but before he succeeded he gave her a look of so deep reverence and affection in answer that she felt she never would forget it; and then his voice, hoarse and gruff, and sounding strange to his own ears, growled out again:

"Sure. I like it better than anything that ever happened to me before, and — I like you already." He couldn't make his lips say "love"; but he thought it in his heart, and the aunt felt that was what he meant.

They were silent for a moment, looking into each other's eyes in the firelight; then the boy looked down embarrassedly, and said quickly, sharply:

"But I know I'm not fit to be here in this beautiful home, and with you. I know well enough I don't belong here, and I ought to go back and work in the slaughter-house where my uncle wanted to put me. I hate it, but that's all I'm fit for in this world, and I've got sense enough to see it. You'd better send me right back."

He drew his hand across his eyes hastily, and his throat moved convulsively. Miss Gracen was on her knees beside his chair in a second, with her arm about the strong, young shoulders, and her white hair close to his dark head.

"Dick, my dear, dear boy," she said tenderly, "don't ever say that again. You do belong right here in your dear father's house, and you are fit for it, I know, or, if there is any way in which you are not fit, we will make you fit. You shall never go away unless you do not like to stay. Do you understand?"

For answer Richard's fingers closed tightly about his aunt's hand that had crept into his.

"Thank you; you're awfully good to me," he managed to murmur hoarsely after a minute. "I'll try hard to deserve it all."

"I hope you will, dear," said his aunt gently; "but remember that, after all, it isn't a matter of deserving. It's your inheritance. It is your right as your father's son. You must try to live up to what your father would expect of you. Will you try to do that?"

"Sure," said Richard tersely, though evidently deeply affected.

"And now, Dick," said his aunt after a minute, feeling that the strain must be relieved, "suppose you tell me all about yourself. Remember I don't know anything about your past, nor what you've been used to; and I think perhaps we'd get along a little better if we understood each other's ways. I'll tell you in turn anything you want to know. Shall we do that?"

Richard assented almost inaudibly, and his aunt arose and stood beside him for a moment, passing her hand lovingly over the dark bowed head; then, drawing her chair quite near to his, she sat down.

"Now, will you begin?" she asked pleasantly.

"What do you want to know?" asked the boy. "How bad I've been?"

The woman smiled tenderly.

"Why, yes, if you care to tell me," she said, "and how good you've been, too. I'd like to understand all about you; then perhaps I wouldn't make so many mistakes at the beginning."

"There hasn't been much good to tell, I guess," muttered the boy, "at least, not what you would call good, I suppose. I haven't been so awfully bad, either, though I guess some things you wouldn't like. But a boy has to have a good time somehow, you

144

know, and there weren't many good times coming my way unless I went out and made them for myself."

Miss Gracen's hand stole out sympathetically, and touched the hand that lay on the arm of his chair. The boy seemed to gather courage from the gentle touch for what he had to say.

He talked slowly, in broken sentences that seemed somehow to have little relation to one another, and there were long pauses between them; but, when he was through and turned with an apologetic laugh to say, "That's all, I guess," there were tears in his listener's eyes, and she found she had a very clear picture of the life her brother's boy must have led. It made her heart ache. She wanted to say so much to him, and felt herself so unequal to the task she had before her. How was she to get wisdom to guide this fervid, passionate, lonely young soul into the right way? It seemed as if he had so far been struggling through life practically alone. She probed for just the right word to say first.

Before she had spoken, however, Richard broke the silence again.

"You think I'm only fit to go back and work in the slaughter-house, now don't you?" There was a curiously hard, fierce tone in his voice that almost broke his aunt's heart.

"Oh, Dick!" she cried out, hardly able to keep the tears back, "don't say such a thing —"

But the boy, mistaking her meaning, brushed her hand away roughly, and sprang to his feet with an unpleasant laugh.

"I know that's what you think; only you don't want to say so; and I'll go the first thing in the morning. I won't stay around here and disgrace you —"

Cut to the heart at the desperate look in the boy's face, his aunt went to him, and drew him down on the couch beside her.

"Dick," she said, "dear Dick, my own dear boy, how can you say such things? It is awful to me to think of your going back to work in the slaughter-house, and nothing you have said has made me feel you do not belong here. What more can I say to make you feel at home than just to tell you once more that I love and always shall love you? You belong right here, and here you are going to stay as long as you are willing to stay. Do you believe me?"

There was a long pause during which the boy's head was turned entirely away from her, and she could see only the strong, attractive outline of fine head and well-knit shoulders. The boy was thinking hard, and trying to gain command of his voice.

"Do you believe me, dear?" she said softly again; and at last the boy replied hoarsely:

"Yes, if you really mean it."

"I do."

"Then I want to stay," he said, fiercely gripping her hand in his eagerness. "And I'll try every way I can to do what you want me to do. I'll try to live up to your standard as much as I know how."

"Dear boy, that's all I could possibly ask," said his aunt, deeply moved; "and I'll try to help you and to make it as easy as possible for you. There are certain things which this community will expect of your father's son. I am sure you will want to come up to their expectations and bring no dishonor on your father's name. Am I right?"

"Sure," came the muffled voice, with nevertheless a deep, true ring.

"They'll expect you to be law-abiding and courteous, honest and true, not to drink intoxicating liquor, nor smoke, nor swear, nor loaf around in idle ways, but to take your place in the community in a pleasant, useful way; to go to church on the Sabbath, and to stand well in your classes at school. That is also what your father would have expected of you, and what I want. Does that sound too hard?"

The boy looked up startled.

"School?" he asked.

"Why, yes, didn't you expect to go to school? You didn't think you had finished your education yet, did you, Dick?"

"I don't see how I could go to school. I'm way behind, and it's a long time since I stopped."

"Why did you stop?"

"I had trouble with the teachers. I guess it was my fault," he added shamefacedly.

"Never mind, Dick. Perhaps they didn't understand. And anyhow you are older now. You will know better how to conquer those things. I should be greatly disappointed if you didn't go on with your education."

"I'll go if you want me to," said the boy, as if that settled it; "but I don't see how I'll ever catch up."

"You won't have much trouble if you're anything like your father. Besides, I can help you some. I used to help him. I enjoy that, and you'll soon be up to the boys of your age, ahead of them, perhaps. You'll like to go to college, sha'n't you?"

"Mother always talked about it. She wanted me to. She'd have liked it."

"And so would your father," added his

aunt softly. "What grade were you in when you left school?"

They turned up the lights, and sat down to a thorough canvass of the school question. Miss Gracen sent upstairs for some of the elder Dick's school-books, and telephoned to the principal of the high school for information; and before Dick knew it he was poring over books, and remembering things that he had in some way imbibed from the atmosphere of the school-room during the days when he fooled away his time and opportunities in nonsense.

For the first time in his life he realized just how serious a matter it had been, and more than once he threw down the books and told his aunt that there was no use at all in his trying, he was too far behind; but always she opened the books again, and went on encouraging him, asking him quiet questions, until his desire to conquer began to grow.

When ten o'clock finally came, Richard was surprised, and laid aside the books and plans almost reluctantly.

"We'll go over to the high school Monday morning," said his aunt, smiling. "I've made an appointment with Professor Holloway to meet you, and he will tell us just what we ought to know. Then you and I will get to work next week and brush up a few things before you go, so that you will not feel uncomfortable.

"Now, to-morrow is Saturday. How should you like to take a long walk down the meadow and out through the ravine where your father used to go? There is a beautiful creek there, and a swimming-hole, and I know all the spots where your father used to fish and go canoeing and camping. I haven't been on a tramp in a good many years; but if you think I'd do for a companion, we'll go."

Richard was delighted. He had never been in the country in his life, save on Sunday-school picnics. For him, born and bred in the city, nature held a certain charm that was entirely new.

He came over to his aunt, great embarrassment in his face, but determination in his manner.

"You're awfully good to me," he said shyly. "Good-night."

9

Rebecca and Molly were making sandwiches the next morning, and Miss Gracen was arraying herself in a short walking-dress and stout walking-boots, her eyes as excited and happy as a girl's in view of the picnic she and Richard had planned, when, happening to glance out of the window, she saw to her dismay two boys entering the front gate. One of them she felt sure by his walk was Tom Atterbury, and who was the other boy? Instinctively she knew that they had come after Richard, and both alarm and disappointment arose within her.

In the still watches of the night, thinking over her boy's prospects, in spite of her anxiety, she had been very, very happy; and she had decided that even a friendship with Tom Atterbury might not be so bad if it were tempered judiciously with other friendships.

She had resolved to see whether she couldn't do something for Tom, invite him to the house often, and try to make it pleasant for him. If Richard saw him at home, perhaps there wouldn't be so much danger of his wanting to go off with him.

But now here he was the first thing in the morning, coming just when they were going off together; and Richard would, of course, prefer going with the boys. What should she do? And who was the other boy?

She came closer to the window, and her heart was suddenly filled with trouble when she saw that it was Harold Constable.

Now, Harold Constable was as much worse than Tom Atterbury in the estimation of the entire village as Tom Atterbury was worse than some of the more exemplary boys. Mrs. Constable was a society woman, spending much of her time in the near-by city, always entertaining and being entertained. She was also an active Clubwoman in a very superficial sort of way, and these two vocations gave her little time to look after the welfare of her family. Harold was always well dressed, had plenty of spending money, and an automobile of his own, although he was still slightly under the lawful age to run it. This fact, however, did not in the least hinder him from running it to exceed the speed limit whenever he thought he could do so without being caught. He loafed and smoked continually, had been a pupil in nearly every school in the locality and in several at a distance, and he was now enjoying a season of idling at home.

His reputation had grown more and more unsavory during the increasing years of his life, though nothing more definite had ever been said than could be expressed in a phrase "wild," conveyed in more or less eloquent terms, according as the speaker could use a shrug of the shoulders and a meaning glance of the eyes.

Harold was handsome, daring and reckless. He had gained the ill-will of almost everybody in town, but went on his way as serene as a summer morning, doing whatever he pleased and only daring the more because people looked coldly at him.

And Harold Constable was coming to see her Richard! She felt appalled. For a moment she had the attitude of a mother hen who sees a hawk about to swoop down upon her chicken. Then her eyes flashed. How dared he come there? How dared Tom Atterbury bring him? She would have to hurry down and make Tom understand that this was the end of all relations if he was going to bring boys like this to her house.

In feverish haste she put on her hat and coat, and went down; but Richard was already talking to the two visitors. She caught his voice with a wistful tone, saying:

"I'm awful sorry, but I guess it can't be helped. Aunt Vic planned something else for this morning, and I mustn't disappoint her."

Her heart warmed in sudden gratitude to her own dear boy. He wasn't going to ask to run away and leave her, after all. He was loyally going to stick by their plan, although she could plainly see that, whatever the invitation was, he was longing to accept it.

Then she turned to look at the other boys, and saw both their faces fall in blank disappointment. They had really wanted Richard to go with them, and it was going to spoil all their fun; yet she could not, *could* not trust her boy in such company as that. How thankful she was that he had refused of his own accord!

Tom Atterbury spied her coming down the stairs, and raised his red-brown eyes to greet her.

"Oh, Miss Vic, good morning," he said in his pleasant drawl. "Say, Miss Vic, couldn't you just change your plans a little, and spare Richard? We want to take a hike, and we want him to go with us. You know Harold; don't you, Miss Vic?"

Now it happened that Miss Gracen, although she had known the boy by sight for several years, had never spoken to Harold Constable, nor he to her; and, as she turned, half vexed, to acknowledge the introduction, he flashed his fine white teeth at her in a confiding smile, and opened at her his big, gray, handsome eyes, shaded by long golden lashes; and a remarkable thing happened to Miss Gracen.

Had she suddenly become daft, she wondered, because she had one boy all of her own, that she should now find a most unprecedented interest in her heart for all boys? What was the matter with her that she could not look at Harold Constable in cold disapproval, as she had fully intended to do, thereby conveying both to him and to Tom Atterbury, who had presumed to bring him there, the knowledge that he was not at all welcome? But indeed she could not. She could only smile and give him her hand in friendly greeting.

Harold took it with a grace and ease that showed the one thing his elegant mother had taught him, and in his winning way he proceeded to speak.

"I don't believe we know each other, but I wish we did," he said gracefully. "I've always admired you, and Tom here tells me you are great. He says you're as good as one of the fellows, and that you're going to a football game with him next week. I wish you'd let me go along."

"Why, of course," said Miss Gracen in utter rout and confusion; for who could resist the disarming look of innocence in those gray eyes, the fine possibilities expressed in the half-formed lines of the face, the sunny smile, the daring waves of light-brown hair tossed carelessly back from a fine forehead, the whole spoiled only by the look of recklessness half graven over it?

She looked the boy over, smiled back at him pleasantly, and felt that she liked him, yet was still fearful of herself, because she *knew* this boy was not all that he ought to be, and she had her own boy to think of now. Yet she was conscious of a passing wish to do something also for this child of luxury, this boy who was so evidently being neglected by his own mother.

She smiled at Tom Atterbury, and began to say how sorry she was that she must be in the way of any pleasure, but, as she and Richard had planned to do something special this morning —

At least, that was what she intended to say; but, as she looked from the red-brown eyes of one boy to the wide gray ones of the other, and then into the great, dark ones of her own boy, she suddenly did the unexpected, *most* unexpected even to herself.

Instead of sending those boys on their way disappointed she said:

"Why, Tom, why shouldn't you and Harold come with us? You'd like that, wouldn't you, Richard? We're going on a hike ourselves. At least, I guess you'd call it that, and we'd be pleased to have your company. Maybe you won't care to have an old woman along, though. I suppose I can't walk so fast nor as far as you can."

"Oh, Miss Vic! That will be great!" shouted Tom joyfully. "Of course we want you along. We'd have a great deal nicer time, and we don't care how far or how fast we go. We just want to get out and have a jolly good time together."

Richard's face was all alight with joy, and he looked adoringly at his aunt as though she were some angel who could divine and always give him just what he most wanted. Well pleased, his aunt turned to the third boy half hoping the affair would be too slow for him, and he would courteously decline to go, and withdraw from the scene; but, when she saw his expression, her heart went out to him with a sudden sympathy; for the gray eyes were alight with a real pleasure, and the whole face had softened with a look she could not quite understand.

"I'd love to go, Miss Gracen," he said earnestly. "Are you sure I wouldn't be intruding? I don't want to butt in where I don't belong."

His gray eyes searched her face longingly, and she suddenly realized, to her surprise, that she no longer hoped that he would not go.

"You're not intruding one bit," she said graciously; "we want you very much. It will make the day a great deal pleasanter for Dick. Come in and sit down while I tell Rebecca to put a few more cookies and sandwiches into the lunch-basket."

"Cookies! Ohh! Ummmm!" drawled Tom, drawing his breath in a suggestive sound. "Say, Harold, we've dropped right into a good, soft place to-day. Some hike! Real cookies!"

Miss Gracen flashed a look of pleased sympathy at them, and vanished into the dining-room, where she gave directions for more sandwiches to be made in a hurry, and then herself slipped up to her bookcase to find a book that might perhaps interest the boys in case they sat down to rest for a few minutes.

She didn't want to give any chance to those other boys to harm her boy, but she meant in her heart to make them all have the best time she could.

She felt almost guilty going off this way with two of the worst boys in the town, and her own dear boy unwarned and unguarded; but somehow she could not help feeling very happy about it. If indeed she was doing wrong, at least she would be on the alert; she would discover it at once, and perhaps never do it again; but she meant to find out just exactly for herself whether these were bad boys or not. Her boy was to be of their world now; she could not hope to keep him utterly apart from them, even should she wish it. It would be well for her to know exactly what they were. One day together ought to tell her something.

Of course, she supposed, they all would far rather have gone without her, but she must do so much for Dick to guard him; and so, whether they liked it or not, this once she would go along.

The lunch was packed in two boxes, so that it could be easily carried and the boxes thrown away when empty. Tom and Richard took possession of the boxes, slinging them knapsack-fashion on heavy cords from their shoulders. Miss Gracen was deeply touched and greatly relieved when, as they started out the door, Harold Constable walked beside her and lightly helped her down the steps, saying:

"Miss Gracen, may I walk with you?"

It suited her plans exactly to walk with Harold, for then she could find out about him, and then also she might prevent her own boy from being in doubtful company.

Down through the brown meadow, windswept and dry; out under tall oaks, whose rustling leaves were falling in great golden heaps; down the steep, winding way to the little creek they treaded their steps; and Harold Constable, as carefully and thoughtfully as a man would have done it, helped Miss Gracen over every root, rock and rough place in the way; and, as they walked, he talked.

"I'm awfully glad you came along with us to-day, Miss Gracen," he said earnestly, when they had reached the bank of the creek and were walking slowly along the mossy path among the rocks. "I'm lonesome, I guess. You see, my mother sailed from New York yesterday for a three months' stay in Italy; and somehow home seems kind of empty, just dad and myself, and dad off on trips most of the time. I didn't realize it till mother went; but they have shrouded everything in our house in denim and netting, and it looks like ghosts everywhere. Dad and I could hear our voices echo back to us last night when we were eating dinner, and I guess dad'll stay at his club in town after this for dinner mostly. I could have gone to boarding-school, but I didn't want to. I'll just bum around, I suppose; but you can't think how I appreciate your inviting me this morning. It looks like a regular peach of a time to me. Look out for that branch, Miss Gracen; it's too low for safety. Here, I'll cut it off. It might have got in your eyes. Watch that rock there; it's slippery, and inclines right over the swimming-hole. Ever go swimming, Miss Gracen?"

As if she had been a girl again, an intuition seemed to come to her now to talk to this attractive, lonely boy; and her whole heart went out to shelter him from all the dangers that she knew must surround a boy left as he was, without his mother or his home or much of a father. Her indignation boiled inwardly that a mother should so neglect a splendid fellow like this one, and allow him to get the reputation that he had gained in the community.

Then with a glance at her own boy in front she breathed a quick prayer that she might not make such mistakes; that she might not be blind to the dangers that Richard must pass through, or neglect any opportunity for strengthening him on every hand.

She discussed swimming with Harold Constable, and talked of canoeing. He said that his canoe was still down by the water-side, just about a mile up the creek, and suggested joyfully that they walk to it and then paddle up to the head of the stream.

Now, Miss Gracen had always been informed that canoeing was the most dangerous form of navigation, and she was secretly very much afraid of the water; but with three eager pairs of eyes upon her, and three eager voices telling her that a canoe was the safest thing in the world, she could not spoil the sport.

She would be "game," as they called it, and even get into a canoe if they so desired. For one day, at least, she would do as they asked her; and then perhaps she would be in a position to ask favors of them some-time.

Into the canoe she submitted to being put, with plenty of cushions pulled from the locker under a tree, and stuffed around her, and a great steamer-rug from the same receptacle tucked about her. She sat for a few seconds in some trepidation, expecting every instant to be tipped into the water; but there was, after all, a serene consciousness that the day was not cold; and, if she did fall in, there were three strong swimmers to rescue her.

The boys clambered in, and the little craft was shoved silently into the stream. Then there came to Miss Gracen a sense of surprised delight and delicious restfulness such as she had not known before. She perceived suddenly what a joy all its own there was in canoeing, and rested back among her cushions as cosily as she would have done in her own rocking-chair at home, and watched the ripples as they glided up the stream.

Wonderful and beautiful colors came into view, and were pointed out familiarly by the amazing Harold, who developed a poetry of thought and a keen appreciation of nature that was most unexpected in the boy the whole town had always supposed him to be.

"Look up there, Miss Gracen," he called from his seat behind her. "Now watch as we round this bend. You'll see some mighty pretty coloring. There! See that crimson maple against the background of the other golden leaves. And did you ever see anything slicker than that red vine climbing up that gray old stone, and the dark spruce-trees leaning over to watch? It always makes me think of a real old man smiling at a lot of gay little kids playing in the sunshine. I come up here early every fall just to look for that vine to turn red, and it keeps pretty till all the others have dropped off. Do you see that bit of squawberry vine netted among the roots of the spruce? It has a lot of red berries already. Say, would you like it to take home? Wait, we'll go over that way and get it."

In a moment more the canoe was steered close to the bank, and the red-berried squawberry vine was reposing at Miss Gracen's feet.

They went on up the stream as far as it was navigable; then, fastening their bark to a tree on the bank, they climbed the hill over crackling brown and yellow chestnut leaves, and went hunting chestnuts, the boys filling their blouses and sleeves in lieu of any other receptacle, and keeping a great handkerchief-full of choice ones for Miss Gracen.

They found a flat rock, and spread out the lunchboxes. They were all famously hungry, and Rebecca's chicken sandwiches, stuffed eggs, potato salad, baked beans, peach turnovers, and sugar cookies disappeared like dew before the morning sun, to say nothing of the cup-custards in tiny blue jars. The jars were taken to the spring and washed and brought back full of sparkling cold water. There was gingerbread, too, and spongecake, and olives tucked in between things here and there, some delicious cheese and crispy crackers; and one end of the box was filled with black and white grapes.

The boy from the parsonage, where eating was plain and scarce, the boy from the handsome house on the hill in the distance, where eating was abundant and appetites pampered by skilled servants, and the boy who had spent his life in a poor little Chicago boarding-house, alike ate with keen appetites; and every one voted it the greatest lunch a picnic ever had.

"Big eats! Big eats!" said Tom Atterbury solemnly, as he emptied the last custard-cup into the stream, and prepared to fill it at the spring.

"Yes, big eats, son," said Harold soberly. "Hand me over that last cooky. If nobody wants it, I can't see it left alone. We never have cookies like that at our house. Miss Gracen, I wish you'd invite me along again when you're going on a hike."

There was a wistfulness in his tone that went straight to that good lady's heart, and she straightway did what earlier in the day she would have been filled with horror at the very suggestion of doing; she invited Harold Constable to come to her house as early and as often as he chose.

Perhaps in sober thought alone at home she might regret what she had done; might wish that she had kept some reservations until further revelation made her way clearer; but at present she had decided that this boy, too, was well worth helping, and that the whole town must be mistaken in their estimate of him, for certainly no boy could have been pleasanter, kinder, and more courteous than he had been all through the day.

He had made her his especial care, and the others had vied with him in trying to give her a good time. They went ahead and cut down branches; they gathered sprays of scarlet leaves because she admired them. They pointed out the easiest foot-paths, and praised her endurance every step of the way, so that, had she been worn out, she would never have been willing to confess it. But she was not weary. The air and the un-wonted brightness of the young company about her filled her with a new exhilaration. She almost felt like a girl again, and her cheery laugh rang out clear in the fine autumn air.

Coming back to the canoe, they established her among her cushions, and started slowly down the stream. There were little drifted huddles of curled brown beach leaves lying here and there upon the water, like tiny boats moored together for protection. When the canoe slid through them, they gave forth a soft, rustling music like the gentle touching of violin strings by a master hand.

It was Miss Gracen who noticed it first and cried out with pleasure, telling the boys that it was the music of the stream and of the day. They all looked at her wonderingly, and then, gravely listening, they turned their attention to the little singing leaves. When they came to another patch of the fallen leaves, Harold gave one mighty, silent sweep with his paddle, and then held it up from the water; and so with bated breath they drifted through, playing the mimic harp as they went.

A little way down the stream Harold steered the small craft between two great bowed branches of a spruce-tree that had broken away from the parent tree, and were now dipping into the water like two mammoth plumes; and there, with a beautiful arch of green over them, feathering down about their shoulders in delicious fragrance, they held the little boat. Miss Gracen exclaimed rapturously over the loveliness of the spot.

"It only needs one thing to make it perfect," declared Tom; "and that's a book and somebody to read to us. Miss Vic, why didn't you bring a book along?"

"Why, I did," said that good lady with a sudden remembrance of how much she had enjoyed the afternoon. "I did bring a book, but I'm afraid it won't be just what you would like."

It suddenly seemed the most uninteresting book she could have found, and she wished heartily she had made a better selection.

"Spill it out, and give us a try," said Tom, and then sat up quickly in his place with his cheeks as red as his hair and a most contrite look in his red-brown eyes.

"Indeed, indeed, Miss Vic, truly I didn't mean to say that," he drawled anxiously. "I do surely hope you'll forgive me. I never thought for a minute who it was I was talking to. You see, Miss Vic, you don't seem the least bit like a — a — lady —"

But his speech was drowned in shouts of laughter that echoed back and forth from rock to hillside.

"Better button up yours lips, At," called Harold between the shouts of laughter; "you're just making things worse all the time. What do you mean by telling Miss Gracen she isn't ladylike?"

"Why — I — I didn't say that," cried the distressed Tom, his face growing redder and redder. "I meant just that she seemed like one of us," he finished desperately.

"That's the very worst thing you could tell her, old man," laughed Harold. "Now you better subside, or I'll give you a ducking, talking to our guest like that."

"Now, Miss Vic, don't you understand?" said the horrified Tom. "You'll forgive me, won't you?"

"Of course I will," said Miss Gracen, laughing heartily with the rest. "Don't you suppose I know you've given me the finest compliment you know how to give? I don't suppose a lady would have been much fun to have along to-day; but, if I've managed to make you think for a little while that I'm one of you, why, then I can hope that I haven't been a bore nor completely spoiled your little expedition. Thank you very much, Tom."

"Great woman!" cried Harold; "she knows how to be a boy with us. She shall be our queen, and be crowned. Here's for our white queen"; and he reached out and secured a delicate crimson trailer of woodbine from a dead tree-trunk at the water's edge, placing it carefully like a fillet about the white coil of her hair, for she had long ago discarded her hat and laid it in the bottom of the boat.

Miss Gracen lifted her merry eyes to see her own nephew looking at her with a face filled with deep admiration and love. She knew by his expression that he was proud of her, and it gave her a thrill of joy.

At that instant as if by contrast she seemed to see what Lydia Bypath's expression would be if she could stand up above them on the bank, and hear and see all that was going on. Lydia Bypath would be thinking that not only the nephew, but the aunt as well, was on the rapid road to destruction. Miss Gracen could only hope she would never know, and continued to rejoice in the good time she was having and giving.

10

"And now, if you have got quite done making fun of your only old guest, I will read a little," said Miss Gracen merrily, pulling a tiny volume out of her pocket and opening it slowly.

"I think it must have been in some such spot as this that this beautiful story opens. At any rate, there were water and trees and rocks, and a steep bank like that over there; I am sure there must have been. Listen, boys." And she began to read:

> "*The stag at eve had drunk his fill,*
> *Where danced the moon on Monan's*
>   *rill,*
> *And deep his midnight lair had made*
> *In lone Glenartney's hazel shade;*
> *But when the sun his beacon red*
> *Had kindled on Benvoirlich's head,*
> *The deep-mouthed bloodhound's heavy*
>   *bay*
> *Resounded up the rocky way,*
> *And faint, from farther distance borne,*

Were heard the clanging hoof and horn —"

Tom Atterbury started upright in his place with a smothered exclamation; and Miss Gracen looked up, already sure that the book would not attract her audience; but the light of interest in Tom's eyes surprised her.

"Say, Miss Vic, that's 'The Lady of the Lake,' isn't it? Say, do read that, please. I'm mighty glad you brought it along; for I have an exam on it the first thing Monday morning, and I promised dad I wouldn't flunk this time. It's been worrying me all this day, because I knew I ought to be home studying it, for I just can't get that poetry stuff into my head."

"Why, surely, we'll read it; won't we, boys?" she said, looking around on the rest of her audience for approval. "I was afraid you wouldn't care for this at all; but, if Tom needs it —"

"Sure! Go ahead!" assented Harold with interest. "Guess we can take a little dose of poetry if it's going to help you on your exam any. We don't want to make you flunk, At."

A light suddenly came into Miss Gracen's eyes, the fire of a great resolve. What if she could really conquer the interest of these

172

boys? If she could make them actually *like* that reading? Her own boy needed it, too. True, she saw no enthusiasm in his face, and she felt he would probably care as little as the others if he were made to tell what he really was thinking. But he, too, would probably have to take an examination on the book some day if he went to school. Why could she not make the story so fully his this afternoon that he never would forget it?

With one swift look across toward the shore she made her plans.

"Then suppose we get to work and teach this lesson to Tom," she said; "and then I'll invite you all home to dinner, and we'll see whether we can make up for the hard work by a little extra fun."

Her proposition was greeted with a shout and cheer, and Richard's eyes shone. Life seemed to be going to be one continued fête hereafter, with an aunt like that, who understood.

"Very well; then suppose you paddle over to that green mossy bank, and let's have a map of the place. We'll understand it better that way, you know. There's a map in this book, and we'll copy it in moss and stones and earth. Harold, you take the map and locate all the places; and Dick, you and

Tom cut this card into small sign-boards while I read. First, we will locate Glenartney, where the stag was taking his evening drink, and then Benvoirlich and Uam-Var. You know these places are all real, and Walter Scott must have known them well."

Then, while she hastily removed the map from the book, giving it to Harold, and hunted out some calling-cards from her jacket-pocket, she told briefly of the great man who wrote the poem, until with her few words he had become a living being to the boys, and she saw their attention was held. While Glenartney was being modelled from moss and ferns and its name eloquently printed with Tom's fountain pen, she plunged into the poem again, and found no wandering audience this time. They were all attention in the hunt and in laying out the land and getting it just like the map. Child's play, perhaps; but Tom's examination was its excuse, and they all three were but little out of childhood, though they never would have owned it.

It was in the dipping shade of a great spruce-tree that they tied the canoe; and the moss rose green on the bank beside them, peopled presently with the characters of the story. Miss Gracen read on rapidly, stopping only when there was a decided difference of opinion about the size or exact location of some mountain, glen, or lake.

Then the sun dipped low, and the story went on until the dusk gave sudden warning. Reluctantly they left their mimic Scotland, and the paddles silently bore them back to the landing-place.

"That certainly was great, Miss Gracen," drawled Tom. "I never'll forget it now. I can see every one of those places, and I'm afraid I'll scare the 'prof.' He'll think I had the book open. I'm sure I can pass now. Won't dad be surprised when he sees my mark? Say, couldn't you finish it for us after supper? Is there so very much more, or are you too tired?"

"Not a bit tired," said the triumphant lady, her eyes gleaming with pleasure in the darkness; "but maybe the other boys have had enough."

"No, it's interesting," said Richard, who had not spoken about it before. "I'd like to see how it came out myself. We started reading it in school; but I left before we finished it, and anyhow I didn't care much for the teacher. I didn't get on to the story at all then."

"Here too," called Harold, as he skillfully brought the canoe to the landing.

They climbed the little hill through the

dusk. Miss Gracen, with her pretty hair all tumbled and fluffy and the red garland wreathed gracefully about its white masses, her hat swinging in her hand, and Harold helping her up the steep places, was laughing like a girl at the funny things the boys were saying.

"Don't hurry, Miss Gracen; you'll be all out of breath at the top," declared Harold.

"Yes, Miss Vic, I'm afraid you're expeeding the seed limit," drawled Tom comically. "There's plenty of time, I'm sure, though I left my watch up-stairs when I came away this morning."

"Let it run down," quickly finished Dick; and then they burst into a torrent of puns, plays upon words, and comical phrases such as their cultured, quiet companion had never heard before.

What delightfully merry, bright boys these were! The things they said were really witty, though they were couched in the vernacular of modern slang; and she perceived, too, with a great pride, that her own boy could hold his own with the rest.

By this time Miss Gracen had actually so far forgotten herself as not to be shocked at the excessive amount of slang to which she had been listening all the afternoon. She was laughing in happy abandonment as

Harold let down the meadow bars and helped her into her own yard; and Hiram heard the echo of it, and called Molly and Rebecca to the window of the butler's pantry to see and listen. With awe they looked at one another, a great light spreading over their faithful faces.

"Now hear the pretty voice of her!" exclaimed Rebecca. "Ain't it fer all the world like she was a little girl again, and coming home from school afore her brother went off and made all the trouble? Oh, I wish her poor mother could hear her!"

"It's all that young Master Dick," averred Hiram. "He's goin' to make the house that cheerful again, with plenty of young folks. I can feel it in my bones. Got plenty to eat to-night, Rebecca? She might want 'em all in to stay for supper."

"Ain't there always plenty to eat?" tossed back Rebecca, holding her gray head high and hurrying back to give the mashed potatoes another good beating before they were to be taken up.

The three boys went noisily up to Richard's room, and Miss Gracen could hear his proud young voice pointing out the pictures on the wall. "That's my father when he was captain of the baseball nine."

Her heart swelled with pride and joy, and

the tears started unbidden to her eyes, as she went to smooth her hair in her own room.

Harold Constable's clear voice rang out:

"Say, your father's all right. Gee! but you must be proud of him, Gracey."

They had nicknamed him Gracey that afternoon, and she had perceived that it was their way of christening him as one of their own.

"He's got an awfully fine face. Say, Gracey, turn around to the light. Say, I believe you look like your father. Sure you do. Can you play ball? At, you must get him on our team right away."

Something in the tone and the tribute to her dead brother made Miss Gracen pause in the act of removing the gaudy garland from her hair and smile at herself in the glass. No, she would not take it off; she would leave it just as the boy had placed it for the evening. It would please him, and wouldn't hurt her. The servants might think it silly; but the boys would be pleased, and, after all, what harm could it do? She smoothed the hair about it as best she could, and slipped on a soft pearl-tinted gown that seemed a fitting background for the crimson wreath in her hair; so she went down to meet her noisy, eager guests.

There was roasted veal with stuffing and plenty of gravy for dinner. The dessert was a beautiful brown baked Indian pudding heavy with raisins and currants and smothered in whipped cream.

"We never have anything like this at our home," said Harold wistfully, handing back, with a polite show of reluctance, his dish for a second helping of pudding. "Gee, but it's good! I wish mother knew about it."

Some one called Miss Gracen to the telephone just as they rose from dinner, something about the next topic for the missionary meeting and who was to look after the mite-boxes. While she was talking, the boys drifted into the big parlor. It was perhaps Harold who led the way.

Harold was used to great, stately rooms and was accustomed to ceremony. It was perfectly natural for him to drift into the wide doorway, and the formality of the place held no restrictions for him, as it did for both Tom and Richard. In fact, that big, formal, serious room had not as yet been appropriated by Richard as a part of his new home. It seemed to him to be a place only for strangers, written with a large "S" and represented by Lydia Bypath.

But Harold walked in quite naturally, as though that was what would be expected of him; and quite as naturally seated himself at the piano, touching soft chords at first, and then striking the piano with a perfect crash of jolly, happy-go-lucky sounds chasing one another up and down and rippling hilariously over the keys with all the wild abandonment of the pianos in the "movies."

Richard drew near in open-eyed amazement, wondering that a boy of his own age could bring forth such effects. They seemed marvellous to him. Of real music he knew almost nothing.

Harold, never embarrassed by his surroundings, broke forth into the raggiest sort of a rag-time song. He had a clear, high tenor, a trifle strained and rasping from continuous rag-time and "rooting" at football games, but entirely capable of better things; and he had a way of bringing out the words with distinctness and dramatic effect which made them extremely funny.

"Will that young man go home to-night,
Or eat his breakfast here.
Out on the old front porch?"

he chanted, and Richard and Tom were convulsed with delight. In the chorus of the second verse they chimed in with various growls, for they were both quite familiar with the monotonous melody, though neither of them could have carried it alone.

When Miss Gracen came back from the telephone and paused in the doorway, wondering, to listen, Harold had just struck into the choice selection of "The Noodle Soup Rag" and the other two voices dropped obediently into the really pretty harmonies of the opening lines:

"O, the old folks seem to like it;
They would sit all night and listen."

Suddenly Harold spied Miss Gracen standing against the soft gray-green of the portières, smiling; and he sprang from the piano-stool in mock dismay, breaking off at the very instant of the entrance of the soup upon the scene.

"Oh, Miss Gracen, I didn't know you were there. Maybe you don't like rag-time played on your piano."

Now Miss Gracen had never even heard of "The Noodle Soup Rag" — though in theory of course she deplored the presence of rag-time music in the world, being somewhat of a delightful musician herself — and she had no idea what the words of this new song might be, that sounded like the beginning of "Old Kentucky Home" or some sweet old ballad; so she stood smiling happy approval.

"Is that rag-time?" she asked innocently. "It really sounds quite pretty to me. Won't you sing the rest of it for me? You all have wonderfully good voices. I like to hear you sing. Do go on."

Thus encouraged, Harold turned to the piano, and rattled into the "Noodle" again, while his hostess settled herself to enjoy. It must be confessed, however, that, as the song progressed and it became plain what the old folks enjoyed sitting around to listen to, she drew in a quick breath of surprise, much as if a sudden dash of cold water had met her face.

The boys, however, were intent upon the rhythm of the jig and the fun of the words. It was just funny to them, that ending of the sweet, pathetic strain with "When father eats his soup."

Watching them with a half-shudder as they rollicked out the careless disrespectfulness, she suddenly realized that they were not quite to blame for liking such things. It was just a part of the recklessness and the daring of the age in which they lived. It held a certain rough challenge to their fun-loving natures and gave them a license to say under the protection of the song things that were forbidden otherwise. Then there was an irresistible "swing" and a rollicking "go" to the music that caught and held them fascinated. They did not mean any coarseness or any disrespect either to age or station. It was simply unmitigatedly funny to them; and fun was the one thing they liked best of all in life, no matter what it was about.

As she meditated, the rag-time clattered on. It struck her as being the most noisy, monotonous music she had ever heard; perhaps that was why they liked it. Would it perhaps be possible to interest them in another kind, and make them dislike this because they grew to like the other better? Perhaps they enjoyed this because it was easy and they could do it themselves. Better music was beyond their powers, and they didn't understand it.

> *"I should worry like a tree*
> *And have somebody trimming me,"*

shouted the clear young tenor, and "Who put the rove in Rover?" he asked in a minute more; and then the sharp chorus of confused whistles blended with the song, and she watched the faces of the trio, happy, carefree, having a good time with all their might.

It came to her to wonder what Lydia

Bypath would think now if she could suddenly enter the room, and see her, the heretofore respectable Victoria Gracen, sitting by and smiling while the two most condemned boys of the neighborhood sang ragtime with her nephew.

She wondered whether the minister, even, would approve of her course; and a swift vision of the horror in the faces of the women of the music section of her club caused her to draw a quick breath.

But at that moment from her position near the open doorway she caught a glimpse of the smiling face of Hiram peering interestedly from the half-open pantry door, and Molly and Rebecca smiling and stretching their necks behind him; and she smiled a quick sympathy with them. They were glad to hear the silent old house ring with laughter and song, rag-time or no rag-time; and in her own heart she knew she was glad, too.

Suddenly Harold wheeled toward her on his stool, and demanded:

"Have we driven you half wild, Miss Gracen? We're going to stop now, for I know you don't really like this rag-time."

"Why," hesitated that truthful lady, "why — I really never heard it much before. Some of it sounds rather — lively and pretty.

Don't you think the songs are a good deal alike? There isn't much real melody to many of them, is there? But they are all right for a change, I dare say." Her smile was even more of an admission than her words; and she thought again of her mentor, and was glad she had not asked Lydia Bypath to run over this evening, as she sometimes had done on Saturday nights to make it less lonely for her.

"Harold, I'd like to hear your voice in something else. Won't you sing for me?"

"Oh, I don't know anything else, Miss Gracen; really, I can't sing. I've got a voice like a fishman," protested Harold, rising in dismay from the piano.

"Try this," she suggested, coming forward to a pile of music, and selecting some songs. "Here is 'Love's Old Sweet Song'; I'm sure you've heard that," and she sat down at the piano and touched soft chords.

Harold was interested at once, and bent over the piano to study the words. Yes, he had heard it before, he didn't know whether he could sing it or not, and he began to hum the notes as she played the accompaniment.

The other two boys stood with their arms across his shoulders, and so for almost an hour they sang, going over the old ballads and the well-known songs, sometimes singing solos and sometimes in chorus, until they were all hoarse and had to stop.

"Play us something, Miss Gracen," pleaded Harold, dropping into a chair as the last note of "The Rosary" faded softly into silence. And without comment she played a part of "Elsa's Dream."

They knew nothing about Wagner, any of them, nor had they heard much real music; but they listened intently, respectfully, with a new kind of absorption in their eyes, though she could not tell whether the real message of the music had reached their souls.

"That's surely got tune enough," commented Tom. "I like it immensely. It seems sort of like going to sleep. It's mighty pretty."

"Yes," said Harold, "I'd like to hear it again sometime soon. It's the kind of a thing that gets into your mind and goes over and over. If I come to see you soon again, will you play it for me, Miss Gracen? I like music. Mother hardly ever plays."

Miss Gracen turned a radiant smile upon the boy, and, searching his face, saw that he really wanted it; so she readily promised.

But Tom turned their attention back to literature at this juncture.

"Say, Miss Vic, you're too tired to read us the rest of 'The Lady of the Lake' to-night, aren't you? Maybe you'd let us come a little while to-morrow afternoon, and finish it. I never know what to do with Sunday afternoons. It would be awfully nice if you'd read to us awhile."

There was a wistfulness in his slow speech that quite touched her.

She looked at him, startled, and suddenly saw into the emptiness of a Sunday afternoon for a boy who had no religious interests.

"Why, Tom," she smiled indulgently. "I'd be glad to read to you awhile on Sunday afternoon if you would enjoy it; but we don't want to read lessons on Sunday, do we? That would be a good deal like work, and I think we might find something that would be more in keeping with the day, don't you? But we want to finish that poem to-night, for you need it Monday, don't you? Dick, get the book, will you, please? I left it on the library table — or wait! Suppose we go in there. There are more easychairs, and it's cosier. Dick, light the fire in the grate. I think we can finish by ten o'clock. Your fathers won't expect you home before ten, will they, boys?"

"Father won't expect me at all. I come

and go as I please," said Harold, with a shrug of his handsome shoulders. "Like as not father won't be home till the midnight train himself, if he comes then."

Miss Gracen's eyes lingered sorrowfully, pitifully on the hard, handsome young face; and her smile warmed his heart as he looked up surprised.

"Ten o'clock's all right for me," drawled Tom, settling down in front of the fire lazily. "If you're sure you're not too tired to read, Miss Vic."

It was five minutes to ten when she finished and the boys got up from their comfortable positions reluctantly, and prepared to leave.

"It's been awfully nice, Miss Vic, all day," said Tom in his confiding tone of gratitude. "We just can't thank you enough —"

"It certainly has," said Harold gracefully; and then, with a wistful glance into her face, "It seems presuming to ask you, after the peach of a day you've given us, but would you really mind if we came a little while to-morrow afternoon? Sundays are awful. You didn't want to study lessons on Sunday, but I guess you'd think what I did was worse. I go fishing or canoeing, or play tennis, or go out in my car; but the day is miles long. Father often stays in town over

Sunday. It's all right when I can get some fellows to go off and have a good time, but sometimes it rains. It would be just awfully good to come and see you. Maybe you'd play for us again, too."

And thus she promised, wondering meanwhile what her respectable and horrified neighbors would think of her allowing boys — and *such* boys — to come to her house on Sundays. And would even the minister understand it? Still, how could she refuse such a request from a boy who was, for the time being at least, worse than orphaned?

"I'll tell you, boys," she said with sudden inspiration, "I'll read to you to-morrow if you'll promise to go to church with me to-morrow evening."

Tom made a wry face, but Harold responded quickly and willingly.

"Sure! Miss Gracen, we'll go anywhere you want us to; won't we, Tom?" and Tom bowed a willing assent.

"Then come at four o'clock," she said, and bade them good-night.

As they turned from shutting the front door, Richard threw on his aunt a look of adoration.

"I say, Aunt Vic," he said, "you're just great! The fellows think so, and I'm mighty glad you sent for me." He reached out, gave her hand a squeeze, then bolted up the stairs, and left her standing in a tumult of wonder and joy in the hall.

This, then, was what it meant to have with her in her home a boy of her own!

11

Miss Gracen, in her soft gray robes and gray hat wreathed in gray plumes, that looked like the clouds at sunset when a touch of pink is shining through, walked down the church aisle the next morning, attended by her handsome young nephew in his new dark-blue suit, the observed of the whole congregation.

Lydia Bypath watched them jealously as they passed her seat, and sniffed. It had been made known to her by some occult method all her own that Miss Gracen had wasted a whole day going off on a tramp with this boy and two others of the village's worst. To a late hour the evening before sounds had proceeded from the hitherto respectable mansion of Gracen which had not gone to the furthering of the honorable name of Gracen. Miss Bypath classed these sounds with the rioting of the college students on the street at night, and knowing little of rag-time, called them "revelry," thinking possibly of Belgium's capital and the disaster that her school reader had portrayed so touchingly.

She watched her old friend go softly to her seat in the church, and sniffed again as Miss Gracen sat down with bowed and reverent head. Victoria Gracen needn't think she could carry on like that on Saturday, and then cover it all up by a reverent attitude in church. She, Lydia Bypath, could see through it all. Victoria had taken a white elephant on her hands, and was trying to make it appear that she approved of what she could not control. Any one could see at a glance that the black eyes of that nephew by her side had deviltry in them, and of course it would come out. His father's had. Very likely Victoria hadn't been able to keep the boy away from those other two, and so had gone with them to give the expedition countenance. Well, Victoria Gracen would find herself in a kettle of hot water if she tried to keep up that sort of thing.

The jealous eyes of the woman fastened themselves like claws of a vampire on the backs of the two innocent worshippers, and seemed to seek to draw from the smooth, thick black hair of the boy and the soft pinky-grayness of the feathers of the aunt some idea of the sinful thoughts hidden beneath their quiet attitudes. She fancied before the sermon was over that she could see the worry in the puckers around Miss Gracen's eyes, and in the set of the boy's handsome shoulders and stolid determination to have his own way. But she was quite mistaken.

Miss Gracen was sitting happily by her boy's side, conscious of the joy of again having some one who belonged, to sit at the head of her pew and be her protector. It had been a great joy to have her boy help her over the curbstones and open the doors for her this morning with all the ease and grace of Harold Constable. Had he learned it from Harold yesterday, or was it just innate, the heritage of his blood? She glanced sideways at him, and was filled with pride over his handsome bearing. He was a boy to be proud of; and, to add to her thrill of joy, as if he understood, the boy turned at that moment and glanced at her, with a look of deep admiration and perfect content. It was just a mere flicker of a smile that passed between them, but a flash of perfect understanding and love had been in it that made them both feel the hour and place sacred. Miss Bypath saw it pass, and said sourly to herself:

"Victoria Gracen is going to make a perfect idiot of herself over that wild boy, and she'll rue it, she certainly will." She said it as though she would be glad of such a result.

Dick could not remember ever to have enjoyed church so much in his life as he did that morning. He used to go with his mother sometimes when he was a little fellow; but the seats were hard, the air was bad, and he could not understand anything. After he began to grow up he never went if he could help it, unless some of the fellows took a notion on a rainy night to sit in the back seat and make each other laugh. He had gone once or twice to please some interested Sunday-school teacher, but he had not been regular at Sunday-school; so that had not occurred often.

But now he sat proudly beside his beautiful aunt, found the place in the hymn-book for her, joining his voice in the hymns, and even mumbling a little in the responsive readings. It was dear and pleasant to be near her, to belong and to know that she cared.

He didn't analyze his feeling; he only knew he was happy and liked to be there. He "liked" his aunt; that was the way he put it to himself, this strange new delight in belonging to a lovely, loving woman who wanted him and tried to make him happy. He couldn't get over the joy it gave him to have her look at him in that understanding way, almost as if she herself were another boy, and knew just how he felt about everything.

Tom, sitting in the pastor's pew, turned furtive glances in his direction, and Dick smiled back as if they had been old chums.

Dick wondered what the fellows in Chicago would think of Tom. He wondered what they would think of him. He wished they could be there, some of them, and have some of the good times. They never had had such good times as yesterday — none of them. There was Jim who had never had half a chance. Would Aunt Vic perhaps sometime allow him to have one of them on for a visit, just so he could tell the rest? But no, of course that wouldn't do; they weren't her kind — and yet — there was no telling but sometime she might let him do it.

He smiled another recognition of Tom's greeting, and this time Miss Bypath sniffed so she could be heard half-way up the aisle. Such actions in church! The minister's son, too! And there sat Victoria Gracen under her gray plumes, quite unaware. It was plain she was going to be entirely blind to her protégé's faults. Next thing the boys would be snapping rubber bands back and forth over the heads of the congregation. Tom Atterbury was quite capable of it. She had seen him do it once when his father was conversing with an elder, and on Communion Sunday, too. It showed how utterly brazen he was that he would smile right during the sermon, when his own father was preaching. The curse of the Lord was on children who did not honor their parents, and Miss Bypath felt it would fall with full justice upon luckless Tom. She had disliked him heartily all through the years, and now she fairly hated him. It seemed that he had had something to do with her first quarrel with her only friend and she could not forgive him.

She shut her thin lips tight; and, while she sat and hated the ruddy glow of Tom's hair under the sunshine that fell through the yellow glass of the Constable memorial window, and inspected the many finely-matching freckles on his kindly, wistful face, she planned what she would say to Mrs. Cora Craig, who sat in the next pew, about Miss Gracen's indiscretion in adopting a nephew of so uncertain character and lineage at this late date in her career, and its probable disastrous outcome. She could see by the set of Cora Craig's shoulders, and the turn of her head as she looked at her husband when Victoria came up the aisle, that Cora Craig would fully understand her and agree with her. Mrs. Craig had once been overheard to remark that she didn't see why Victoria Gracen should be chairman of all the committees and vice-president of all the societies merely because she had more money than some other people who were just as good. Mrs. Craig had a boy of her own, a sly creature with white eyebrows and a skulking look, whom she never could make go to church. Mrs. Craig had not been a success in bringing him up; but that would not matter; she would understand all the better why boys were degenerate and that unmarried women without experience should never try to bring them up.

As they passed down the aisle after service, the minister laid a detaining hand on Miss Gracen's arm, while Tom took possession of Dick and walked on to the door.

"Tom tells me that you asked him to come over for a time this afternoon," said the minister in troubled hesitation. "Miss Gracen, you have been most kind to my boy, but I don't wish him to trouble you — and Sunday, of all days —"

"Why, I've promised to read to the boys a little while this afternoon," said Miss Gracen, suddenly wondering whether the minister would approve. "They said they didn't know what to do Sunday afternoon, and I want to make the day a happy one for my own boy. If you are willing, I shall be glad to have Tom join us."

"Thank you," said the minister, his brow still troubled. "I have never quite believed in Sunday visits; but you are most kind, and I can see how the right kind of reading might be most profitable. To tell you the truth, I have never been able to get Tom interested in keeping the Sabbath in the way we have brought him up. We have provided religious literature, but he does not seem to take to it. In fact, I do not think he cares much for reading to himself, at least, not as I did when I was his age. I am very much troubled about him sometimes. I don't seem to understand him."

His tired brown eyes reminded her of Tom's, and she longed to comfort him. People had criticized him for having been so indulgent a father; and many of them had said he was blind, or didn't care; but the eyes told their story of anxiety, and she could see that it had been merely that he hadn't understood the boy.

"Well," she said brightly, "I guess I've got a lot to learn about bringing up boys; but I'll have to learn it for my boy's sake; and, if there is anything I can do for yours at the same time, I'll gladly do it. He is a dear boy. I fell quite in love with him yesterday. We are very good friends already. I'm sorry I haven't known him all these years. You see, I've got to know boys now because I have one."

The minister's face relaxed. It was the first time since Tom was a baby in a perambulator that any one had said anything loving and kind about him. People had always found fault with him since the day of his christening, when he had dipped his fist into the christening-bowl and splashed the water full in the face of the senior elder who held it, and then with his tiny kid shoe had kicked the bowl out of the outraged elder's hand and splashed water down the front of his mother's new gown. The gown had been a silk one, the kind that spotted, a present from the Ladies' Aid, and worn for the first time that day. There had not been enough to make over the front breadth, and it couldn't be matched; so his mother had shamefully worn the spotted silk, a symbol of her son's lawless nature, and tried her best to cover it with her hands in her lap or some furtive arrangement of girdle-ends or mantle-ties; but the spot had been patent to the whole church for years as a sign of the blight on her boy's character, and nothing would ever make them forget it.

"You are very good, Miss Gracen," he said. "I thank you. No one seems to like my boy very much. I'm afraid it's his father's fault. I wasn't sure when he told me about this afternoon. I have tried to restrain him from going out on the Sabbath; but if you say you wish him to come —"

"I have a good religious story to read aloud that I think the boys will enjoy," said Miss Gracen eagerly, for she had begun to look forward with some interest to her afternoon, "and I thought perhaps they would also like to sing hymns for a little while afterward. I hope it will be a good, quiet way to keep the Sabbath afternoon, and yet make it pleasant for them."

She spoke shyly, half doubtfully. She had been brought up most strictly as regards the Sabbath, and yet she had felt the need in the wistful tones of the boys as they complained of the usual dulness of the day.

"I am sure it will be all right, Miss Gracen," said the minister with relieved brow. "To tell you the truth, I was half afraid Tom might be deceiving me and that he was inventing some way to get out away from the home restraint for a little while. I shall be very glad to have him come over this afternoon, but you must promise me not to let the boy intrude upon you too much. He is very much in love with you already, and would live at your house continually if allowed. You must be frank and send him home when he is not wanted."

Miss Gracen promised, and went on down the aisle to find her boy, her heart aglow at the thought that Tom was fond of her. Perhaps, after all, she might be able to help the dear boy a little. She would try. A fleeting memory of the time some years before when she had been asked to take a class of boys in Sunday-school, and, being appalled at the very idea, had refused, assailed her now. Might it be possible that she would have enjoyed it, and been able to do some good? Had she perhaps missed a great opportunity? She had not known that one could get joy from association with rough, unformed boys; for, theorize as she would, the astonishing fact remained that she looked forward to her afternoon with her companions of the day before with not a little feeling of pleased anticipation.

She had spent a couple of hours the night before in carefully selecting the book that she would read; and Rebecca, unbeknown to her mistress, had worried not a little and got up three times after retiring, to look from her window in the servants' wing of the house and wonder why Miss Vic kept her light burning so late.

Miss Gracen had carefully gone over several books of thrilling interest to herself, but laid them aside as not fitted for the immediate purpose, and had finally decided upon a story of Western life with all its wild adventure and thrilling situations, with one man single-handed struggling in the name of Christ against the vice and evil influences that had dwelt in the place since its beginning. She knew the boys would like the setting of the story, and she felt sure the climax in which death and hell struggled for the souls of some of the characters would stir their hearts and make them thoughtful. She hoped the ending would give them a vision of the Christ that would at least make the Sabbath a profitable one, if it did no more.

The story was a religious one, not in any milk-and-water sense of the word, but treating religion as one of the great facts of life. It was a tale to make a reckless, care-free, adventure-loving boy think, without making him feel that he was being preached to. Miss Gracen had found herself all during church service that morning praying quietly that

God would use her reading that afternoon to help the three boys who were coming to her that she might brighten what seemed to them a dull day without meaning.

Perhaps it was her intense desire for the success of her afternoon that made her eyes so bright and her cheeks flush so prettily pink as she walked down the church steps by the side of her boy. Passing Lydia Bypath she smiled happily into her spiteful eyes.

"She'll smile on the other side of her month when that pretty nephew of hers brings her into disgrace," snapped that soured soul to Mrs. Craig.

But Victoria Gracen passed happily on with her boy, and was saved from a knowledge of the poor lady's ill-will. She was rejoicing in the ease with which her boy lifted his hat as she bowed to her friends, and she took pride and pleasure in stopping to introduce him to her intimate acquaintances. Somehow she had never realized before how lonely it had been always to go and come everywhere alone.

They walked down the wind-swept autumn street, and Miss Gracen was unspeakably happy. She thanked God that he had sent this boy to her, and she prayed in her heart that she might be shown how to lead him in the best and wisest way.

12

It was in the cosy library that she awaited them, a big easy chair apiece in readiness, and plenty of cushions piled luxuriously on the couch. The fire on the hearth was blazing cheerfully, and a great platter of molasses candy in delicious golden squares that Molly had made the night before stood alluringly in the broad windowseat. Miss Gracen's own little reading-chair was placed at just the right angle where the light from the bay window would come over her left shoulder, and she could see the occupants of the three big chairs. The book lay innocently under a pile of religious papers, and even Dick did not suspect its presence as yet.

Dick's pleasant whistle could be heard up-stairs in his room. He was beginning to feel quite at home in that big new home of his. He had been out among the horses with Hiram after dinner, and wandered about the place a little; and now he was up-stairs exploring some of his father's books and pictures.

His aunt fancied that already his face seemed to have lost some of its hard, defensive look, and his eyes were glad when he looked at her and smiled.

On the piano in the parlor Miss Gracen had collected all the hymn-books in the house. She would get the boys to sing a little while, she thought, as she hovered about the rooms, putting a touch here and there as though she were expecting grand company. Somehow she was as eager as a child over a party. She wanted the place to look pleasant and attractive to them all, not only for her boy's sake, but for the sakes of them all; and how strange it was that a few days ago she had no interest whatever in any of them! Was it because they had each given her a bit of a glimpse into their hearts, and she had seen the restlessness and longing, and really wistful looking out to life for something more than it had as yet given them?

It wasn't in nature that they should notice the big bronze bowls of red and gold chrysanthemums that stood on mantel and table; yet she touched their bright masses happily, and looked about on the pleasant rooms with a hope that it might seem good to the boys. What would Lydia Bypath think now, if she could see how interested she really was in those terrible boys?

She walked the length of the great parlor, and drew aside the costly curtains of frostlike lace to look out. The sun was shining, and the world held that autumn-gold look in the atmosphere. It was almost too pleasant to expect the boys to care to come indoors. Perhaps, after all, they would not come. She wondered a little at the twinge of disappointment this thought presented to her mind. Yet even as it passed, and while she yet stood looking out the window, she saw them coming down the street; and there were *three of them!*

At that moment the silver chime of the library clock tolled half-past three, and she had not told them to come until four; yet they were even now turning in at the gate, and who was that with them? She did not know him. Perhaps they had company, and did not care to come, but were stopping at the house to excuse themselves. Very likely they were going to take a walk, and wanted her Dick to go with them. That would be another problem for her to face; Sunday walks and all sorts of companions.

A feeling of blankness and disappointment grew upon her, after all her pleasant preparations. She shrank within the screening lace to think what she should do. Of course it had been foolish to think that she, an elderly woman, could hope to hold a lot of big boys against the attractions of the great, free world. How silly she had been!

Then a sudden panic, lest they leave a message and depart without her seeing them or having a chance to find out what was the matter, seized her; and before they could ring the bell she had hurried through the hall and opened the door herself, not waiting for the servant.

There they stood waiting, eager, their hats off, with not a thought of going walking, all ready and anxious to come in. She saw it in their manner at once, and she was glad. But her eyes were held by the face of the third boy, who stood slightly back of the others, respectful, waiting, keenly observant, almost hesitating, she thought. She smiled at the rest with a warm greeting, putting out her hand to each; but at the stranger she gazed earnestly, meeting his eyes and his questioning look with one as questioning and intent; and his face interested her at once, even though she did not know him. He had a dark, unhappy look, and deep lines about his mouth and eyes for one so young. His brows were dark and distinctly pencilled. He drew them down over his deep-set, almost lowering, eyes in a strange way for a boy. He looked as if he had suffered much and doubted nearly everybody and everything; yet had left, hidden deep somewhere, wonderful, beautiful possibilities in his nature, and an unsuspected sweetness of temperament if only the cloud could be lifted from him. His face was finely cut, and showed strong character, yet all was masked by that haughty withdrawing and the defiance in his manner.

"We've brought Wayne Forrest with us, Miss Gracen," said Harold Constable lightly. "He hadn't any plans for this afternoon, and we thought you wouldn't mind. He's my friend."

Harold cast an arm about his friend's shoulders as he spoke, and drew the other tall fellow forward. Miss Gracen noticed the loyalty and deep admiration of his tone as he said, "He's my *friend*," that meant something more than just a schoolboy attachment. They made a marked contrast, too, as they stood thus together, the one boy handsome, airy, care-free, sure of himself, light in his manner, smilingly at ease, and dressed in the costly attire of a rich man's son; the other, fine and strong, but almost severe in his manner, frowningly defiant, holding back from all advances, and dressed in much-worn garments that would have been shabby if they had not been worn with the air of a conqueror who needed no accessories to give him preeminence among men. He stood, resisting his friend's drawing, refusing to say a word or break the darkness of his countenance by even a smile, awaiting her word.

She felt that he was searching her face for any sign of disapproval of him, and that, if she should hesitate by so much as an instant to second his coming to her house, he would break away from his friend's arm and flee from the place forever. There were not only keenness and defiance in his glance; there was a heart-breaking hunger in it that went straight to the depths of her soul; and with a clear, sweet look of welcome from her kind and understanding eyes she held out her hand, and a smile broke over her face.

"I'm so glad you brought him!" she said in that rich, musical voice of hers. "I like him right at first sight, and I know he's going to be a great addition to our little company. Besides, if he's your friend, of course we want him."

The boy's face, which had been almost like a thundercloud in its intensity, broke suddenly into astonished light. The hard lines relaxed; the forehead cleared; the dark brows went up from lowering into startled, amused attention; the fine eyes showed their beauty, and almost danced with a merry appreciation of her greeting; and the strong yet sensitive mouth curved into a reluctant smile. He held back for just an instant more to study her and make sure it was really true that she wanted him; and then he put a shy hand forward to take the white one she held out. Standing so with that warm hand-clasp, and her eyes looking steadily into his for a full, long gaze, she began to know the spirit of the boy, who more than all the others, perhaps, needed her, and by association in her home was uplifted and helped to be what God meant him to be.

Wayne Forrest accepted the challenge in her eyes, and showed her in that long, clear look the answering challenge in his own. She knew from that time forth that whatever the meaning of the hard, reckless lines she had seen at first, he had not wholly gone away from the right, and that he still had a decent, loving, hungering soul behind his hard exterior. Then suddenly his face broke into a smile, and she knew that he felt she was a friend.

"I'm sure I thank you very much," he said as they turned finally to go in; and the maturity and dignity of his voice startled her. It sounded like a voice that had suffered and grown old while it still should have been young in experience.

"Forrest, Forrest, where have I heard that name?" she questioned herself as she led her little company into the library and seated them. And why did she not know the boy? His face was not familiar. Perhaps he was some one from the city down to visit Harold over Sunday. But, Forrest — ah! Was that the name of the man who had been imprisoned for forgery five years ago? The wife was an invalid, and they were in poor circumstances. They lived at the other end of the village, quite out of the section where Miss Gracen's carriage was seen.

It was said that Mrs. Forrest would not go out to see visitors since her husband's disgrace. Miss Gracen herself had called twice, but received no response to her knock. They had come to the town shortly before their trouble, and had remained utter strangers by their own choice. Could this boy be the son? A sudden wave of pity swept her face as she turned and looked into the boy's eyes again, reading in the hard lines written there his story of bitter shame and disgrace. Her heart went out to him suddenly. If this were really his story, how he needed some one, something, to help him!

Then suddenly she remembered Lydia

Bypath, who represented what the town would say; and she thought of her own boy. What was she doing? Gathering from the offscouring of the town to form a coterie for her boy's companionship? Was she doing right? Probably everybody would tell her she was not, and yet — it seemed as though she had not sought this herself; it had come to her. Could, *ought,* she to have turned these boys away who seemed to want her — even to need her — and seek only those who were perfectly refined and entirely good and reputable for her boy to know?

Well, it was a question for her to think of at leisure, and prayerfully. The boys were here now; and, having invited them, she could not turn them away. It remained for her to do what she could for them in this present, and it certainly would take all her thought and energies.

Her troubled eyes met the merry ones of Tom as he turned from a friendly scuffle with Harold for the corner of the couch that had the most cushions, and at once her anxiety and dismay fled.

A week ago she might have stood cold and disapproving if these boys had entered her house and made free in this way. She might even have called them rude, bad boys and have turned them severely away; but a wonderful change had come over her way of looking at things. Yesterday's experience in the canoe had given her a new viewpoint, and she was conscious of a distinct feeling of pleasure that they felt enough at home with her to act just as their natural selves. What did a pillow and a couch matter, even if they were roughly handled? It was not the act that was rude; it was the boy that felt at home and happy, and was expressing his good will by acting as if she were another boy. The true values of couches and cushions and other people's houses had nothing whatever to do with the matter. They were having a good time, and she was a part of it. They were not afraid of her.

She found herself still hampered by that thought of Lydia Bypath, and was glad she was not present to see, for she would never understand. Blessed little Miss Gracen, that she did understand!

Wayne Forrest stood by, smiling, half uncertainly at the pleasant contention, and watching her furtively to see how she would take their being so free in her house. It did not occur to her that the two might be showing off a little before this third one, to let him know how much at home they already were with her. But she saw the question in his eyes, the half-deprecating smile of apology as he turned toward her, and she met his look with a bright smile.

"While they are having it out with the couch, suppose you and I look after ourselves. You take this big chair by the fire. It really is more comfortable than the couch, I think," she said.

She was surprised at the ready grace with which he drew it forward and urged her to take it herself. His manner was as easy as Harold Constable's, although his ways were quieter and graver. Where had he got his ease and refinement, living in the shabby little house on the out-of-the-way road? Surely she must be mistaken. His ways were those of one accustomed to culture and refinement, although she saw there was an outer crust of hardness about him, perhaps something that would almost be called in common slang "toughness." Yet every time she looked at him she liked his face better. It was as if the hardness had been forced upon him, but was not native to his soul.

She decided that he must have come from the city to visit Harold as she had at first surmised. But before she could put any questions Dick came down, and it appeared at once that Dick had met him before. They had been together at the football game the day after Dick's arrival, and there was something about the new boy's face as he stood greeting her boy toward which her heart warmed. She could see at once that they had taken to each other; and somehow, though her heart misgave her with secret fears, she couldn't help being glad.

"Shall we go into the parlor and have a little singing before we read?" she asked as the noisy greetings of Dick subsided. Now that they were here, she began suddenly to doubt whether she had selected the right book to read to them, and to wish to put off the reading for a little till she could think more about it.

"Sure!" chorused Harold and Tom, rushing headlong from the seat for which they had contended, and then rushing back to escort her to the piano. Perhaps they were hoping for more rag-time; there seemed no Sabbath hush upon their eager spirits; but the hymn-book was open at a hymn Miss Gracen thought they would like. She handed the pile of books to Dick to pass around, and began at once to play, Tom catching up the melody and following it in a clear whistle.

The new boy accepted his book with a curious manner, as though he did not quite belong to the group, and was uncertain about partaking in the exercises; but he turned to the place, and followed the music. Miss Gracen watched him furtively as she played.

He did not sing at first, yet watched the book interestedly; but at the second verse he began, softly at first, then louder, in a clear, high baritone as mature as a man's. It rose and swelled above the other voices, and sent a thrill of delight through the music-loving heart of the hostess. What a voice was this, all in the rough! Did he know how wonderful, how marvellous it was for a boy of his age to have a voice like that? She studied him as he sang; but he seemed not to know that he was bringing forth unusual sounds, and he sang on, gaining confidence, and wholly absorbed in the pleasure of the music.

"You have a beautiful voice," she said to him in a low tone, bending toward his chair and laying her hand on his arm to attract his attention. They had stopped for a moment to search the index for a special hymn Tom wanted, and the others were not noticing. The boy looked up quickly, keen suspicion in his eyes; but when he saw the sincerity in Miss Gracen's face, his look quickly changed to one of pleased surprise.

"It's not much," he said embarrassedly.

"I don't know anything about singing, but I like it."

"You must take good care of your voice," she went on. "It has a remarkably sympathetic quality. It should be worth a good deal to you some day after you have had it cultivated."

He laughed.

"Not much chance of my ever getting my voice cultivated," he said in a bitter tone.

"Oh, but you *must*, you know. Such voices are gifts that must be counted precious. There will be a way some day. You must make it."

He stared at her with eyes that seemed to say she knew very little about it, and his whole face took on the hard, resentful look; but he did not answer. Just then Tom announced the number of the hymn; and she noticed that Wayne joined in with zest.

When they had sung one verse, she paused.

"Suppose we ask Wayne to sing the next verse," she suggested, looking at him pleasantly; "and we'll come in on the chorus."

It was a venture following a sudden impulse; and, when the words were spoken, she was sorry, because if he should refuse she would have lost a point in her acquaintance with him; but, to her surprise, after an embarrassed hesitation of a second or two he stood up and began to sing, and his voice sounded even better than it had promised.

He did not seem to be shy about it, and was evidently doing his best. There was a clear resonance about it that held the other boys silent, wondering, somewhat awed. She could see his singing pleased them, and they were proud, not jealous, of him; nor was he by his expression in any wise set up about what she had said of his voice. He was simply, earnestly trying to do his best. Her heart thrilled at the sweet sounds that her words had evoked.

"That was beautiful, beautiful," she said when the song was over. "It is great for a boy to have a voice like that." The boy sat down, suddenly abashed, and looked at her piercingly from under his dark brows, as though he would be quite sure she was sincere; and there was something in his face which seemed to say: "Yes, but you don't know who I am, do you? When you do, you won't say such things to me."

He seemed to have withdrawn from them all in spirit, and Miss Gracen perceived that some subtle change had come over him. By this token she knew that the singing was over for the present.

She led them into the other room, seated them comfortably, told Dick to pass the platter of candy; and, sitting down opened her book and began to read.

Miss Gracen was a good reader, with a sweet voice and a natural way of making her story live before her hearers. At the Club meetings she was often asked to read some poem that was being studied, or some rare bit of prose sketch, because she could read so well, but she had never read to so inspiring an audience before.

Harold, from his corner of the sofa, sat bolt upright, his eyes upon her face every instant, attention held from the first words, his speaking face changing with the story; ready to laugh and bring out a bright comment now and then; his eyes clouding with sympathy during the more pathetic parts, or lighting with triumph or delight as the story progressed.

Tom, lolling luxuriously in a nest of pillows at the other end of the couch, was inclined to fool and laugh a little at first; but his interest was soon caught and held, his brown eyes lost their mischief, and were filled with earnestness. It seemed as though he had dropped his mask of impishness for the time and let the true soul of the boy look out from them with all its longings, failings, disappointing repressions, and occasional attempts at goodness.

Dick sat in one great leather chair on the right side of the fire, and Wayne in its mate on the left side. Dick's eyes were watching the flames as they flickered and leaped, and his face wore a look of content and pleasure that was good to see. He was enjoying life as he had never enjoyed it before, and there were whole vistas of such enjoyments in the possibilities of the future. What would his uncle and aunt say if they could see and know? How glad he was they were not here to try to spoil it, for spoil it they would, he was sure, if they got anywhere near him.

Then the story got its hold upon him, too, and the firelight took on the form of the scenes through which its characters were passing. He, too, became absorbed in listening, and forgot everything else. No one had ever tried to interest him or make him happy before, or to cultivate the latent forces of his mind and soul; and this first experience was a wonderful one to him.

From the big chair on the left of the fire the boy Wayne, his head slightly bowed upon his hand, raised a pair of intense eyes under his defense of dark brows, and watched her unflinchingly. Whenever she raised her eyes, she felt his eyes upon her, questioning, analyzing, weighing every word that dropped from her lips. She had a strange feeling that a man's mature mind dwelt behind those eyes, and that the story meant more to him than to any of the others. Perhaps it was with an intuitive divining of some hidden need of his that she put her own soul into what she was reading, and brought out the fine shades of helpfulness in the well-balanced story, making a truth live before her hearers that was scarcely even expressed in words on the printed page. She knew how to read such things into the words, just with the varying of her tones, and it was thus that she always swayed her listeners.

The autumn twilight deepened; and Dick, with a little proud thrill of being at home and having duties as host to perform, slipped silently up, and switched on the electric light in the reading-lamp on the table, leaving the other lights off, so that the corners of the room were still in shadow. The boys' earnest faces glowed out of the dusky places in the room; and Miss Gracen, her voice quiet and sweet, read on, knowing that she held her audience as she had never held an audience before.

They had reached the spot in the story where death and the devil contended with the man of God for a soul and where simple purity and sincere faith made good under terrible stress. Harold Constable's alert, watching eyes suddenly closed, and he rubbed them as if there was something in them. Wayne Forrest's gaze was down now, with the kind of look that often accompanies anguish-wrung tears, though one could see that the boy would suffer anything rather than let a tear appear in his fierce young eyes. The reader was aware of all this, and prayed in her heart, as she read, that the story might touch some hidden spring of longing that should lead to better things for these young souls.

Softly Dick reached for more wood from the big wicker hamper near the fireplace, and put it on the fire. The flames leaped up lighting the young faces, and Miss Gracen knew that for the time being each one of her hearers was alone in the room with the story and with God.

13

The candy-platter, which had gone its silent rounds during the afternoon, was now standing empty on the floor by Dick's chair, and the story had reached its first climax when Hiram opened the door and brought in a tray.

The boys suddenly drew up alertly, and realized for the first time that they had been listening. The consciousness that they had been off their guard was embarrassing to them; and they sought at once, boylike, to cover this with a degree of hilarity out of all proportion to what they felt. Only the boy Wayne did not join in. He sat silent, thoughtful, with a softened, yet deeply sad, look on his face, gazing into the fire. Miss Gracen, as she looked at him, longed to ask him to tell her what was the matter. There must be something terribly wrong when a young face could wear a look of anguish such as that.

On the tray were delicate sandwiches of brown and white bread with delectable filling, and a pot of hot chocolate with a bowl of whipped cream; Rebecca stepped softly behind Hiram, bearing a plate of little frosted sponge-cakes.

Wayne Forrest looked at the tray startled, and arose as though he had inadvertently committed a terrible breach of etiquette.

"It's time we beat it," he said in an undertone to Harold, whose end of the couch was near his chair. "I didn't know it was supper-time, did you?"

But Tom Atterbury sprang up to help pass the plates, and cried out:

"Gee! Isn't this great? I say, Miss Gracen, you're the right stuff!"

It required Miss Gracen's gentle, persuasive hand on Wayne's arm, and her earnest insistence, to make him sit down again and partake of the good things. He seemed all too conscious of his shabby suit, his sleeves, which were too short, and his hands, which reached too far out from them; but his hostess noticed that he ate what was given him like a gentleman.

She took her own plate, and drew her chair over beside that of the boy.

"I'm very glad you came," she said in a low tone that the others could not hear. "I hope you'll come again and let us get real well acquainted. It will give me great pleasure to hear that beautiful voice often."

"I should think you'd had enough of us staying all this afternoon," he said pleasantly; and she noticed that his speaking voice was deep and musical.

"Indeed, I've enjoyed it," she insisted. "Will you come again?"

His eyes went keenly to search her face again with that wordless questioning, "Do you mean it? Do you know who I am?" in them; but she met his look with a steady smile, and after a moment he answered:

"If you really want me, I'll come all right."

"Thank you," she said, smiling; "I really want you." And the boy's eyes showed her he was pleased and almost happy.

When the tray was nearly empty and the brief clamor of serving had subsided, Miss Gracen spoke.

"Boys, there's one thing I should like to do before you break up and go into the parlor to sing a little more if you don't mind."

She hesitated and looked around.

"Anything you say goes, Miss Vic," declared Tom joyously. "What is it?"

"Well, boys, I'd like to read just a short story to you from the Bible; that would give a true touch of the Sabbath to our gathering."

She looked about on them appealingly with her sweet eyes, and a dead hush filled the room. Dick felt a queer, cold chill creeping down his back, and a hot anger rising at any possible opposition to his aunt's proposition. He didn't care much about the Bible himself, but he didn't want these fellows to be rude to his aunt.

For once Tom's vivacity was hushed, and his mischievous eyes dropped. Wayne's eyes swept the face of every one in the room, and waited with his tense expression to see what would come.

It was Harold who rose to the occasion.

"Sure, Miss Gracen, we'll be glad to hear *any*thing *you* care to read to us."

"We'd *rather* hear some more of the book," drawled Tom wistfully, the mischief appearing in his eyes.

"We'll have the book again next Sunday," said Miss Gracen, and wondered if she had given herself another uncomfortable time to regret the promise, yet knew in her heart that she was glad she had said it; for at once a subdued cheer arose.

"Oh, that's good! Fellows, say!" called Tom. "No more stupid Sundays. Miss Vic, you're a peach!"

"Cut it out, Tom," said Harold, placing a sofa-pillow firmly over the mouth of the minister's son. "Miss Gracen only said 'next Sunday.' Don't go to taking it for granted that means forever."

"Say, Miss Vic, you won't stop at next Sunday, will you?" pleaded Tom.

"We'll see," said Miss Gracen, smiling. "That depends. You know your side of the contract is that you are to go to church —"

"Sure," said Tom, "I have to do that anyway; so it doesn't faze me."

"Of course we'll go," said Harold quickly; "that's a dead cinch."

But Wayne started, and looked around darkly. Had he been caught in a trap? His eyes sought the open doorway for a second, like some wild creature seeking to flee. But he sat quite still, and listened intently while Miss Gracen read the story of the arrest of Jesus in the garden and of His trial and crucifixion, from the eighteenth and nineteenth chapters of John.

She made no comments upon it; but, when the reading was finished, the whole story was pictured vividly for them; the dark garden, the questioning, troubled disciples, the rough, cruel soldiers, the smug, deceitful Judas, impulsive Peter, the firelight, the condemning maiden — all stood out like a living drama upon the stage before them. "Peter's 'turned yellow,'" muttered Tom, as she read of the denial; and the reader understood, and went on with an appreciative nod. Their faces grew grave with awe as the story of the cross unfolded itself before them, and she noticed that Wayne especially looked deeply thoughtful and startled as if the story were almost new to him.

They were all quite still as she closed the Bible and arose, laying a hand on Wayne's shoulder.

"Come, I want to hear you sing again," she said, and smiled down at him. He looked up sharply.

"Oh, I couldn't," he refused. "I really must go. I oughtn't to have stayed so long."

"But you are to go to church with me to-night. You knew that was the agreement. I was to read if they would all go to church."

"I didn't know," he said, flinging his head back almost defiantly, as if he would even then escape from the room. "I really couldn't go. I'm not fit," and he looked down at his shabby clothes, and then held his head proudly like a young king.

"You're perfectly all right," said Miss Gracen, "just as you are. We don't wear full dress to church; and, besides, I want you." She smiled a winning plea into his frowning eyes, and a strange thing happened. He looked down at her with refusal in his eyes, but after a second his brow cleared and a tender look broke over his face.

"Well, it's up to you," he said, "if you're sure you're not ashamed of me."

"Not in the least, my dear," said his hostess lightly. "Thank you. Now, come on and sing. There's a song in the other room that I'm sure will fit your voice. Suppose you try it."

And Wayne, surprised into happiness, went smiling by her side, and was soon singing his best for her.

They started early to church, but Lydia Bypath was there ahead of them, whispering in sepulchral tones to her neighbor in the next seat; and when Miss Gracen, attended by her four stalwart escorts, came down the aisle, she settled back and fixed each one with her piercing glance as they passed by, her thin, sharp face growing more and more filled with disapproval as the identity of each boy became known to her — the son of a forger, the son of a disinherited brother, the prodigal son of an indulgent minister, and the handsome, dare-devil son of an unmitigated society woman, than whom, Miss Bypath felt, there could be no worse on the face of the earth. Poor, little, narrow, old

Pharisee! What a lot she'll have to learn in heaven! If Miss Gracen was chilly in church, it surely must have been due to those cold eyes piercing her back all during the service.

By some strange happening Wayne had followed Miss Gracen next in order; and, when they reached the pew door, she motioned him in first and sat next to him, the minister's son coming after, with Harold and Dick at the end. The minister, as he took his seat in the pulpit a few minutes later looked down upon his congregation, and saw with relief his oldest son sitting next to one of the best women in his church; the son who went to church always on protest, and who often was missing at the hour of evening service, in spite of his father's most urgent efforts and commands. It is true the other boys in the company were no guarantee of virtue, but to see his son sitting beside Miss Gracen and hunting for the place in the hymn-book for her made his weary heart warm and kindle.

How wonderful to have those boys there, anyway! Oh for a touch on his lips from the altar of God, that his words might have power to reach those young hearts!

Does anything just happen in this God's world of ours? Was it happening that made the minister select that nineteenth chapter of John for his sermon that evening? And his text was "Behold, the man!" As he began to read, there was a flash of wonder and interest in the faces of the four boys, and especially in Wayne Forrest's face. He bent his head as though to look down, but fixed his eyes on the minister's face from start to finish, with that odd upward look under his dark brows that made him so noticeable a listener; and the minister, whose apathetic congregation often filled him with heart-sickness and discouragement, saw him, and took courage. If just one soul wanted to listen, he had a message worth the telling; and in his heart he prayed for the blessing of the Spirit.

Watch as she might, even during prayer-time, Lydia Bypath could not find anything in the conduct of the son of the forger to criticize; for a more quiet, earnest, thought-ful face was never set upon young shoulders; and he sang the hymns with his beautiful voice, looking over the same book with Miss Gracen, whose gray feathers came only to his tall shoulder, and looked down upon her almost reverently when she glanced up at him.

Dick grinned once when Tom snapped a rubber band and slyly hit the toe of an elder across the aisle, who crossed his feet twice and uncrossed them, and never knew why he did it. Several times Tom and Harold exchanged rattling confidences in the form of small articles from their respective pockets. Miss Bypath saw it all with her eagle eye, and set it all down against them, adding to the curse of sorrow that she saw with her mind's eye rapidly approaching the house of Gracen; but she was uncomfortably conscious of the fact that she could not see anything wrong in the conduct of "that disreputable young Forrest fellow with the hardened countenance." She supposed it was because Miss Gracen had him cornered off by himself in the seat that way. She didn't know his father well enough to trace a resemblance, but she spent much holy time tracing out signs of an evil inheritance in the strong, fine, young face, and she joined with fervor in the closing hymn,

> *"When, free from envy, scorn, and pride,*
> *Our wishes all above,*
> *Each can his brother's failings hide,*
> *And show a brother's love,"*

and knew not what a travesty it was upon her soul.

It was the first time that Wayne Forrest had been inside any church in Roslyn, and the first time that any minister in town had taken him by the hand; so Mr. Atterbury's warm clasp, and hearty "Glad to see you, Forrest. Wish you'd come every Sunday," did a good deal toward helping him to bear the curious scorn of some other people who stared at him and whispered openly about him. He walked home in the starlight, listening to Miss Gracen's pleasant talk, and bade her good-night at her door with real gratitude in his voice as he said:

"I want to thank you for the nicest Sunday afternoon I can remember."

And Miss Gracen wholly commited herself to the future as she replied:

"I hope you will let me give you many more of them. I shall look for you next Sunday, early. Remember!"

Home through the starlight he walked after parting from the boys, out past the village, into the lonely road of the country, and opened the door of the unattractive little house he called home fully two hours earlier than usual. His sister looked up sharply from the book she was reading, and called out half anxious, wholly pleased:

"What's eating you, Wayne, to come home so early?" She was a pretty girl with a fine mind and rather old manners upon her young shoulders. "Where've you been?" she persisted.

"Been to church," said Wayne gravely, as if that were his habit every Sunday of his life.

"Church!" his sister exclaimed. "Church! What do you mean, Wayne?"

"Mean what I say. I've been to church." He sat down without smiling, greatly enjoying her bewilderment.

"Yes, a lot you've been to church. Mother," raising her voice to reach the invalid in the next room, "listen to Wayne. He says he's been to church."

"I only wish he had," sighed the feeble voice of the mother. "I always went to church twice on Sunday. I never meant my children to come up this way."

But the sister, with a keen look into her brother's face, slipped from her seat, and came and stood beside his chair, touching his hair lightly with her fingers, and brushing it back from his forehead.

"What's the matter, Wayne dear?" she said, and her sweet voice had grown gentler. "Has somebody been being mean to you?"

"No," growled the boy, half-laughing. "I tell you I've been to church. I'm not kidding you. I've really been to church."

His sister sat down suddenly as though

she were too much astonished to stand.

"What made you do it?" she asked, watching him intently.

"Oh, some of the fellows were going; so I just thought I'd go too."

"Where did you go? Which church?"

"Presbyterian."

It happened that the Presbyterian was the church of the wealthy and scholarly in Roslyn, and this made the surprise all the greater.

"You went to the Presbyterian church, and in those clothes, Wayne!"

"Hadn't any others with me, had I?"

"But suppose you had happened to sit with some of those rich swells. How would you have felt?"

"I did," said Wayne. "The fact is, I went with one of them, sis."

"Who?"

"Miss Victoria Gracen."

"Wayne, I wish you'd stop joking and talk sensibly. Where have you been to-night, anyway? You don't suppose I'm going to believe all that nonsense. Wait! I'll get you some supper. There's some hot johnny-cake put away in the oven for you, and I saved a little of mother's cream. You'll like that with it, won't you?"

"No, sit down, Rhoda; I'm not hungry

to-night. Eat the cream yourself. I know you went without your supper to save it for me. Now go and get it, and let me see you eat it. No, you're not going to save it for my breakfast, either. I want to see you eat it. I tell you honestly I'm not hungry. I had a grand supper."

"Where?"

She faced him curiously.

"Why, I took supper with Miss Gracen."

He sat watching her with keen enjoyment as she dropped into her chair again and stared at him.

"You took supper with Miss Gracen?"

"I did."

"I don't believe you. It's one of your miserable jokes; and by and by you'll tell me what you mean, I suppose. Well, if you had supper at Miss Gracen's, what did you have? Come, you can't tell."

"Sure I can. I had sandwiches, little, thin, rolled ones, lots and heaps of them, with chicken and nuts and all sorts of nice stuffings in them. Had so many I put one in my pocket to show you. Thought you'd like to use it for a pattern the next time you gave a pink tea to your college friends —"

Rhoda gave a quick glance about the bare room, and tears came into her eyes. It was an old joke between them, this about her college friends and her round of society duties. It was their way of making light of the long days of hard toil, the lack of books and opportunities to study, and the absolute lack of any friends whatever. But to-night her nerves seemed to have stood more strain than usual for some reason, and the threadbare joke fell keenly on her tired heart. The little mother had seemed frailer than usual, and there had been less in the house to eat than last Sunday. It was still two weeks till Wayne's next pay-day, and how were they to make things go much longer?

"Oh, Wayne, I wish you wouldn't tease to-night," she whispered. "You're just making a miserable joke, and I know there is some trouble or other behind it all."

"Nothing of the sort," said the boy in gruff tenderness; "everything I said is true. Put your hand in my pocket, and get that sandwich. There's some cake there too. She kept passing the plate, and passing it; and I ate all I could swallow, and thought it wouldn't be any harm just to let you see a sample. Chuck your hand in."

He held out his sagging pocket, and Rhoda put in a disbelieving hand, and pulled out the piece of cake somewhat crushed as to frosting, but still intact, and the delicate rolled sandwich, all thoughtfully wrapped in a crumpled railroad time-table. She gazed at them a minute, took one small testing bite of the sandwich, and then put her head down on the table, and cried.

Her brother looked on in amazed perplexity.

"Well, what's eating *you?* I'm sure, if I'd known it was going to affect you that way, I would have eaten them myself, if it choked me."

Rhoda lifted a sparkling face.

"Don't mind me, Wayne; I just lost my nerve for a minute. I thought perhaps you'd been to that saloon down at the corners where they give away fried oysters with every drink. I saw the sign in the window the day I walked to Mrs. Cranford's with her mending. You never tell us where you are at night, and I got to worrying lest you boys went there sometimes, perhaps —"

Wayne turned away with reproach and disgust in his face.

"What do you take me for?" he asked roughly. "Did you think I was that kind of a guy?"

"Well, no; only everything was so horrid, and it wouldn't be strange if you did as the others do; you never have any good times like other boys."

"Well, Rhoda, I had one to-day all right,"

he said emphatically; "and I rather guess I'm in for another one next Sunday, too."

"Did she ask you to come again?" Rhoda was now almost breathless.

"Yes, she did," said Wayne, his tone only half concealing his own feeling that it was nothing short of a miracle that she had. Then he gave her a detailed account of the afternoon, her eyes sparkling with astonishment and pleasure as he went on telling the nice things Miss Gracen had said to him. But, when he had finished, they were both silent for a few minutes; then Rhoda leaned forward, a trouble evidently rankling in her mind.

"Wayne," she said in a low tone that could not reach the invalid in the next room, "Wayne, are you *sure* she knows who you are?"

The boy's face clouded; and a dark, forbidding look enveloped and transformed him into another being. He did not answer at once; and, when he did, the wretchedness and despair in his voice made it like an old man's.

"I don't know," he said hopelessly, then added after a minute: "I don't suppose she did, but I guess she'll find out before another Sunday. She don't look as if she went around with her eyes shut. Oh, I don't suppose she'll want me again. I guess I sha'n't go unless she sends me word somehow, and I don't suppose she'll do that. I don't suppose I'll ever have another afternoon like that again; it was great! Simply great! And, if she turns me down," he added blackly, "if she turns me down when she finds out, I *have got that!*"

His sister reached out her rough, little, toil-worn hand, slipping it into his big strong one, and together they sat for an unusual moment of silent understanding. Then Wayne arose, and prepared to go to his room for the night. It was the way with most of the good things that flashed across his way; they never came again, and those he had turned bitter with his own thoughts afterward. It was hard, hard to be turned down everywhere and for no fault of his own. And what was even harder was to have Rhoda, his beautiful, gifted sister, hidden away with the responsibility of a woman upon her young shoulders, and not even so much chance as he himself had to get out and away from it.

He seldom voiced these bitter feelings even to himself but they swelled and rankled in the anguish of his young soul till sometimes he lost all faith in everything and wished that his life were over.

14

Wayne was right; Miss Gracen was not one to go about with her eyes shut; and the thing she had upon her heart the next morning was to find out about the strange, silent boy whose face had attracted her at the first glance. Yet she already had too much loyalty to the boy himself to go about her discovery in any public way. She meant to keep her eyes open and discover for herself. She felt in a sense allied to him, and did not wish to break the unspoken contract of friendship between them by trying behind his back to find out about him. Neither did she care to have any one know that she had invited a guest to her home of whom she knew nothing.

However, her opportunity presented itself at the breakfast-table the next morning, and it was Dick who began the conversation.

"I'm awful glad you were so prime to that Forrest fellow, Aunt Vic," he said as he ate his luscious grapes and reflected on the comforts of a home like this. "He's up against it hard, the boys say. I guess you know more about him than I do, but it must be tough to have your father do a thing like that. It must be worse than having him dead. You can be proud of him if he's dead, but not when he's committed a crime. The boys say he's awfully proud, and won't go anywhere. At asked me if I thought you'd mind about his bringing him here. He asked me after church yesterday morning. I meant to tell you on the way home; but those folks walked with us, and I forgot it. You ought to see Forrest play football. He has more nerve than any two others put together, and he's always everywhere that he's most needed. He played at that game up at the college. Some fellow got hurt and they got him to take his place. It was great to see him. If he ever plays again here, I hope you can go. But it was dandy of you to make him feel at home that way. At says he thinks you're great. He says he had all kinds of a time getting him to come. He thought you'd think he was butting in; and, if he'd seen the least little sign that you didn't like it, he would never come again. The fellows were awfully pleased that you were so prime to him."

His aunt smiled. She had her information and without the asking.

"I liked him," she said warmly, "and I'm glad if he enjoyed himself. We must try to give him some happy times. He has a wonderful voice. I wish I knew his mother. I called there twice, but never got in. I must try again sometime when I know him better," and she fell to planning how, without hurting his pride, she might find out more about the boy's home and his needs.

Later in the day, after the momentous visit with Dick to the high school, she sat down at her desk, and wrote this little note:

Dear Wayne:

I've found a song that I have a fancy to hear you sing. I would like you to sing it for us next Sunday afternoon; so, if you can find time to run over to my home on Thursday evening for a few minutes, we can try it over together. Hoping you will be able to come,

Sincerely your friend,
Victoria Gracen.

Wayne, coming home from his poorly paid officework, dropped into the post-office more from habit than from any hope of finding mail. He took the letter, and read the address in great surprise. The envelope was of a soft pearl color, exhaling a delightful fragrance of violets; and somehow his own familiar name, written in that clear, strong, fine hand, took on a kind of dignity and beauty of which he had never suspected it before. He carried the note home in triumph to his sister; and together they took it to the poor little invalid mother, who listened, smiled feebly, and when they were gone out turned her sad countenance to the pillow, weeping for the boy whose birthright had been taken from him, and who was forced to depend upon the paltry whim of a stranger for all the pleasant things of life. She was glad that this joy had come to him, but wept that she had never been able to give him any good times.

Meantime Dick had found that he knew more than he had given himself credit for. In spite of the careless, studyless habits of his school-days he had managed to imbibe from the school atmosphere a large amount of knowledge concerning a number of studies. He had remembered many things from hearing others recite, though he had never studied them himself; and he possessed a native talent for mathematics which made him quick at figures. The school principal, being a man of discernment, decided that

Dick could easily enter the second year of the high school, and might possibly be able in two or three months, if he studied, to skip into Tom Atterbury's grade. Whereupon Dick made up his mind to study. He had a feeling that he could do better than Tom if he had Tom's chances, and he meant to prove it. It was due to his father's memory that he should.

So Dick did not return to the house with his aunt that first Monday to be coached by her until he was able to enter school, but he delved straight into school-life with all his might. If anybody had told him three days before that he would have done this, he would have stolen a ride back to Chicago on the freight-cars, and would gladly have worked in the slaughter-house rather than go to that school for the first time; but somehow that talk with the principal and his newly-formed acquaintance with Tom had made a wonderful difference, and he went bravely through the eventful first morning, and came home at lunch-time with eager, shining eyes. His talk was all of the football team. They wanted him for left guard if he could make it; but you had to stand just so in your marks in class, or you couldn't play. He would have to make his first week's marks come up to the required measure, or there wouldn't be any chance at all for him.

It was all so breathless and happy, and for his aunt so like having a real boy of her own, to have him look to her to be interested in these things. It was so nice to feel that he was going to hold his own, and pleasant to urge him to take more soup and take time for another helping of rice pudding, and to promise to look up all the subjects that he had to study for the next day, so that she would be able to help him at night.

That first evening together around the light, puzzling over the next day's problems and hunting out Latin verbs and finding their derivations, was a delight far beyond any study she had ever done to write essays for the Woman's Club. She felt as if she were a young girl again going to school herself on the morrow; and her heart kept growing lighter all the time.

Tom dropped in for a half-hour about nine o'clock. He said his father had given him permission to come over to see whether there was anything Dick wanted to know about his work for the next day; and he sat on a low hassock at Miss Gracen's feet, and played with the ribbons of her gown while she showed him how to read a paragraph in his English which he confessed didn't make any sense to him. When he had gone home, it suddenly came to her that Tom had in these short three days become to her a being entirely different from the disagreeable, red-haired, bad boy she had heretofore thought him. She had begun to see the real boy in him, and to love it. He, too, had been grateful for her treatment of Wayne Forrest.

"Miss Vic, you were just prime to Forrie," he said, twirling the rose and gray tassels on her ribbon-ends. "He enjoyed it here immensely. He said he'd go to church seven days in the week for you."

And Miss Gracen found her hitherto well-conducted heart dancing gayly with delight.

From that time forth life to Miss Gracen began to take on an entirely new aspect. The boy, and after him the boys, became the center of her existence.

The regular Club meeting, usually a brilliant social affair with some speaker from town, and charming refreshments, where every one wore her prettiest frock, and the finest musical talent of Roslyn did its best to make the occasion a notable event, happened that week to fall upon the very day of the game to which she had promised to accompany the boys. It had not occurred to her when she had promised; and on the morning in question Dick reminded her of the game with bright, shining eyes, telling her that the boys were "way-up pleased" that she was going with them. They were planning to keep the very best seats to be had on the stand for their party, and to take cushions and rugs and a hot brick for her feet if it seemed to be cold.

Like any girl her eyes sparkled with anticipation, and she promised to be ready for them the minute school was out. No thought of the sacred Club meeting entered her head — she had never been absent from the regular meeting since the Club was formed, unless she was out of town — until a neighbor called her up and asked whether she could take her place on the serving committee, as the neighbor had a dressmaker and couldn't get away.

"Oh, I'm so sorry," exclaimed Miss Gracen into the receiver in dismay; "but it's going to be absolutely impossible for me to get there this afternoon. I — have — another engagement," and she laughed, half-ashamed to think what the engagement was. "I really had forgotten it was the Club day when I made it."

"For pity's sake, Victoria Gracen, what possible engagement can you have in this town on a Friday afternoon? Nobody has anything then. You surely can't be going to run away to town to attend the symphony concert, are you?"

"Why, no," said Miss Gracen, feeling more young and foolish than ever before in her life, and half vexed with her friend for being so inquisitive, "I'm only going with my boy and his friends to a game at the athletic grounds. I didn't know it was Club day when they asked me, but they will be disappointed if I back out. I'm sorry not to oblige you, but you surely won't have trouble in finding plenty of people to serve in your place. Clementine Holmes will be delighted, I know."

"A game! You go to a game this cold day! Victoria, you'll get pneumonia as sure as you live. Tell those boys you can't possibly go. Don't be a silly at your time of life. Take my place, and pour tea, do. Besides, I want somebody who will be responsible for the whole committee. Clementine would forget to pass the sugar and cream. I can't trust it with anybody but you. Do take my place, Victoria."

But Miss Gracen, with dismay in her face, gathered her forces, and answered decidedly:

"Indeed, Caroline, I couldn't think of

breaking my promise to the boys!" And Caroline with a vexed "Well, of all things!" hung up the receiver with a click that told her state of mind.

Miss Gracen, flushing like a guilty school-girl, sat in her chair happily, and reflected that she had brought the gossip of the town upon her head now, hot and heavy, and must be prepared to meet it. Well, what of it? She had a right to stay away from the Club and go to a ball-game if she chose, and she did choose, most decidedly. She wouldn't disappoint those boys, and her boy most of all, with his shining, trustful eyes, and his brow so like his dear father's, not for all the clubs in Christendom.

She went to the game in Harold's automobile, attended by the three boys and smothered in fur rugs and foot-stoves. She could not have been more comfortable in her own parlor. They explained each point of the game to her carefully, and she entered into their enthusiasm as if she had played all her life.

Then, when it was over, they whizzed by the Club house just as the meeting was out, and the ladies in their best attire were pouring out into the street. It wasn't exactly the way to Miss Gracen's home, but Harold was bent on meeting Wayne's train and giving him a glimpse of the good time they had had. The ladies, as they walked leisurely down the street in the gathering twilight, or stood in groups about the steps and on the sidewalk, looked up in surprise, stared and bowed, and stared again.

"Why, isn't that Victoria Gracen in the Constable car? Why, she wasn't at the Club meeting, was she? How very strange!"

Caroline came down the walk in time to hear the remark. She had puckered herself together and left her dressmaker to her own confusion, while she herself did her stern duty by the Club.

"No, she wasn't," she snapped. "She went to a ball-game instead. What do you think of that? Victoria Gracen at a ball-game! I tell you that woman is just obsessed by boys!"

"Obsessed" was one of the new words that the Club had taught Caroline. She enjoyed an appropriate occasion on which to use it.

"H'm!" said Mrs. Hiram Rushmore meaningly, as she gazed after the flying car. "Well, that's the way with some unmarried women when they get hold of a man creature; they just go crazy. But I thought Victoria Gracen had too much sense."

But Victoria Gracen, happily unconscious

of the gathering storm of disapproval, rode away to the station.

"Now I'll tell you what we'll do," she said, as Wayne, his eyes shining with the attention shown him, leaped in and took the vacant seat beside her. "You'll all go home with us to supper. I told Rebecca to cook plenty of chicken and make pies enough for a regiment. I think there's pumpkin pie, if I'm not much mistaken."

A shout of joy from Tom and Harold hailed this announcement, but Wayne looked down at himself in dismay. The grime of the office was upon him, and he felt an unspeakable shrinking from going out to dinner, much as he would like it.

"Oh, thank you, but I'll have to get home," he declared with one of his dark looks. "They expect me. I really couldn't go, you know."

"Of course they expect you," said Miss Gracen. "It wouldn't do at all to let them worry. Couldn't we telephone them?"

The moment she had said it she knew what a mistake she had made, and Wayne's face darkened, but she caught up her own words with:

"But maybe you aren't bothered with a 'phone. Harold, suppose we drive out there; it wouldn't take long would it? You see, I'm determined to have you, and you can't possibly get out of it."

Wayne looked down with tender awe at the small gray glove on his rough coat-sleeve, and actually smiled although his whole being was in a tremor of expectation.

The door of the shabby little shingled cottage burst open suddenly as the car stopped noisily before the gate and a young girl with her sleeves rolled above her elbows and her brown hair tumbled back from her face came distractedly out, exclaiming in a frightened tone:

"Oh, Wayne, what is it? Has anything happened? You haven't had an accident have you?"

And Wayne sprang out deftly over the car door without opening it, and shouted hilariously: "Not on your life. I'm going out to dinner. Step out of the way till I get a clean collar."

The last words were spoken just as he dashed into the door, but they were distinctly audible to the four people in the car.

Miss Gracen leaned forward, and raised her voice.

"My dear, we're carrying Wayne home with us to dinner. I hope his mother can spare him for the evening. We really couldn't get along without him."

Rhoda, her fears relieved, gave a gasping "Oh!" pulled down her sleeves, and fluffed her pretty, rumpled hair all in one movement, and came slowly, shyly a few steps down the path.

"You're awfully kind, I'm sure," said the girl with a touch of her brother's haughty dignity, yet a hidden pleasure showing in her gray eyes. "He appreciates so much being at your house, I know. He just can't talk of anything else any more."

"I hope I may soon have the pleasure of knowing his sister," said Miss Gracen with her pleasantest voice and sweetest smile; and the girl grew rosy with pleasure in the rapidly growing dusk.

"Oh, thank you," she said, withdrawing at once into her shell again, "but I couldn't leave mother."

"Well, then, may I come to see you — and mother, too, I hope, if it won't tire her too much — some day soon?"

Rhoda was spared further conversation by the reappearance of her brother, his face shining from a rapid toilet. He sprang into the car, and called boyishly to Harold:

"Let her go-oo!" And Harold waited not on ceremony; but, as the car swept away from the door, Miss Gracen waved her hand in good-bye, and called out, "Don't forget! I'm coming soon."

Miss Gracen went giddily up the stone walk of her own house, and entered into her hall attended by four of the noisiest boys that ever entered a respectable home; but she never even noticed that they were noisy until she threw open the door of her own library for them to enter, and saw, sitting stiffly in the straightest chair, with retribution in her eye and relentlessness in her thin face little, sharp, vindictive Lydia Bypath!

15

Dismay fell upon the joyous group as they stood in the bright room and stared blankly at the formidable occupant.

"Gee!" said Tom under his breath.

"Gee!" echoed Dick in the same instant, and:

"Gee!" whistled Harold softly.

But Wayne only stood like a wild thing at bay, and frowned darkly.

It must be admitted that Miss Gracen herself felt slightly as though she had met with a dash of cold water in her face as she went graciously forward to welcome her most unwelcome visitor.

"Well! You're come at last, have you?" was the severe greeting, like a teacher to a naughty child. "I've been waiting here since the Club meeting let out —"

"Oh, I'm sorry you were detained so long," said the hostess sweetly. "Won't you sit down and lay aside your wraps? The room is warm."

"No, I wish to speak with you in private.

I'll just wait here until you are done with these —"

She waved her hand, and looked severely at the group of boys, as if they were a set of criminals who had obtruded themselves into her friend's house and must be attended to first. She did not need to add a noun to give a full and finished idea of what she thought they were. One felt that she would have liked some expression like "generation of vipers" to express her sentiments entirely.

Wayne's brow grew darker, and he half turned toward the door. Harold's chin went up in the air haughtily; Dick's eyes flashed fire from their dark depths; but Tom's kindled with mischief. He had been the butt of this mistaken woman's wrath for many a year, and had found it harmless. He rather enjoyed her remarks; they added zest to the occasion, especially when they were attended by the unusual circumstance of his not being in the wrong or to blame in any way.

But Miss Gracen was equal to the situation, and with her gentle face raised just the least bit in dignity she smiled toward the boys reassuringly, and answered:

"Oh, these are my friends, and they are going to stay to supper with me to-night. Won't you stay also? Then after supper we can take a little time together —"

Three of the boys were appalled at the prospect of a spoiled frolic, but Tom's sense of fun was uppermost.

"Yes, do stay, Miss Bypath," he drawled in his most dulcet tones. "Miss Vic said there was to be chicken, and we'll give you the wish-bone."

There was a joke of some kind, old in the village, connected with a number of wish-bones that had once been tacked to Miss Bypath's front door. Tom had not been the boy who put them there; but he knew all about it, and could not resist the temptation to remind her of it. He felt that she deserved it for the way she talked to his hostess.

Miss Bypath withered him with her glance, and, turning to Miss Gracen, angrily said:

"Oh, if you have company, I won't intrude. I see my errand is quite useless after all my trouble. I'll go at once," and she swept indignantly from the room, with a furious glance toward the defiant boys, who, if she had been a man, would gladly have thrashed her.

Miss Gracen followed her into the hall, but purposely left the door of the library open. She had no mind to be browbeaten by Lydia Bypath, and kept her sweet dignity as she said gently:

"I am sorry you have taken trouble. Was it anything I could do for you?"

"No, it was something I could have done for you, if you are not too far gone. 'Obsessed' was the word they used about you at the Club, a word that may be new and fashionable, but it never seemed quite respectable to me. They said you were obsessed by boys, and I came to warn you of it; but I see it is true."

Her eloquent speech was interrupted most unexpectedly by a ringing laugh from Miss Gracen.

"Is that all?" she asked merrily. "I thought you must be ill or in trouble. So that is what they are saying about me! Well, it cannot hurt them or me. Just tell them I said it was perfectly true." And she broke into another silvery laugh.

Two steel points were Miss Bypath's pale blue eyes; flat and straight was her indignant back. She stood and looked at Miss Gracen in speechless wrath for the space of a full second, and then turned and marched from the house without another word; and the boys, the naughty, triumphant boys, joined in an ill-suppressed cheer as the door closed upon her.

"Miss Vic," called the irrepressible Tom, "your name is not Miss Gracen any more, for now you are Dis-Gracen."

Miss Gracen was really more annoyed at the passage at arms than she cared to show. It was the most unwise thing that could have happened in the hearing of the boys; but it had happened, and she could not help it. It had been in no wise their fault, and she must not let them feel any discomfort from it.

"You see, boys, what kind of a scrape you have got me into by inveigling me off to a wicked football game when I should have been serving tea and pink cakes at the Club; so now you will have to make up for it by having the very best time you know how this evening. Run up-stairs, and wash your hands if any of you want to, while I see that there are plates enough on the table."

She hurried into the dining-room, but the echo of their voices came distinctly to her.

"Say, she's the real stuff!" came Wayne's clear baritone, and her heart told her that she had a new friend among the boys.

"Isn't she, though?" answered Harold. "She's surely a peach."

"You bet your life she is," said Tom, noisily, "a regular pippin!"

And then Dick's endearing growl: "Who

is that old tartar, anyway? What business has she got coming round here trying to tend to *my aunt?*" There was ownership in his voice, and "my aunt" could scarcely restrain herself from rushing up-stairs and embracing him. She felt rich in his love.

Nothing was said at the supper-table about the unpleasant occurrence; for Miss Gracen kept the conversation humming on all sorts of interesting topics appealing to boys. They knew her well enough by this time to talk freely in her presence and to express their hearty approval of the bountiful supper which the wise Rebecca had prepared.

It was Wayne, the thoughtful, who later in the evening broached the question in a roundabout way.

"Miss Gracen, aren't we taking too much of your time from other things? It's awfully kind of you, but we mustn't presume."

Miss Gracen laid her small, white hand on the boy's arm, and smiled up at him.

"I've not had anything in years so interesting as you boys to take up my time, and I want you to take just as much of it as is pleasant to you. My boy is going to be the main object of my life from now on, I hope" — she smiled lovingly across at Dick, who answered with a soft light of understanding and gratitude in his eyes — "and I guess I shall have to take in and love all his friends as well. If you don't get tired of me, I shall not get tired of you."

"Not much danger of our getting tired," said Wayne huskily; and she could see that he was deeply affected by her kindness.

She was quick to seize her opportunity.

"I want to know your beautiful sister. She is your sister, isn't she? The one who came to the door to meet you? And your mother. Will she let me call?"

The boy looked down embarrassed, half-pleased, half troubled.

"Mother isn't well," he said in a low tone, "she doesn't see people."

"I know," said Miss Gracen, her own tone so low now that the other boys who were talking could not hear, "she has suffered. I am so sorry. But I do wish she would make an exception of me and let me get to know her, because I love her boy."

The slow color stole into the boy's face and up into his soft, dark hair, and the hard lines softened into gentleness. He lifted his intense eyes, and looked into the gentle, true ones that were lifted to his; his own kindled into trust and answering affection. Then she knew who he was — and she still cared to

262

have him come! It was wonderful, but it was true!

He put out his strong, young hand, taking her fine, small elderly one in an earnest grasp that sealed a compact of love and trust between them; but all he said was:

"Thank you! I'll tell her what you said."

That night, when she was alone and thought the evening over, Miss Gracen found little space in her mind for the incident of Lydia Bypath. If Lydia wished to be foolish, and interfere in her affairs as she had done in other people's, it was time to make her understand that it could not be done. She dismissed her disagreeable incident, and went singing back over the signs of progress in her boys, the little indications that they thought and cared for higher, better things than merely having a good time. She had begun to see great possibilities in every one of them, and she knew that her readiness to take in the other boys had only endeared her the more to her own nephew.

But the next morning there came an indignant letter from Lydia Bypath, insisting that she had been insulted within her former friend's door by the minister's son and demanding retribution upon him for his impudence. She also made it quite plain to her correspondent that unless Victoria

263

Gracen should immediately change her way of doing she would be the town talk. She gave valuable and untrue information concerning the ill deeds of every one of the boys, and declared that she felt it her duty in the face of all insults to make it plain to Miss Gracen that she was doing wrong to bring her young and innocent nephew into dangerous companionship with boys who were marked for the prison cell and the electric chair. She finished with a scathing picture of the elderly female who made a fool of herself with boys just out of leading-strings, broadly hinting that because Miss Gracen had never been married she had lost her head and was infatuated with these boys, a thing which she, Lydia Bypath, could never be guilty of, for she knew too much about the wickedness of the male creation. They never came near a woman but to bring her trouble, as Victoria Gracen would soon find to her sorrow.

She had scarcely read this letter, and laughed over it, before the telephone rang, and another friend called her up with fifteen minutes of good advice to the effect that she had chosen the wrong kind of companions for her nephew, and she ought to have asked her about boys. She was the mother of two sons who were models (only in their mother's eyes), she could have told her what boys to invite to her home, and she named a few eligibles, her own among the number; but she informed Miss Gracen that she must get rid of the others at once. Harold Constable, of course, was respectable, though he didn't seem to amount to much; still, he had manners at least; but the others were an actual disgrace to the community. Everybody knew how worthless Tom Atterbury was, of course, and that Wayne Forrest! Why, his father was serving a term in the State prison for forgery. Of course Victoria hadn't known that, or she wouldn't have had him about —

Miss Gracen here interrupted to say in most decided tones that she knew all about Wayne Forrest and liked him very much; that he had been at her home a number of times, and she felt the boy had been sadly misunderstood. She went into a few details of facts which caused a cessation in the volubility at the other end of the line, as the informer dissolved into "Ohs!" and "Ahs!" and, "Why, you don't meant it! Has a voice? How interesting! I suppose we ought to be kind, of course, but —" and, when Miss Gracen finally hung up her receiver, she was boiling with wrath.

This, then, had been the matter with these

boys; they had been tagged bad boys because of mischievous things they had done, and the village was determined to keep them bad boys. No one was to be allowed to help lift them up to anything better. Well, she would see whether she was to be prevented. God had sent her these boys unexpectedly, without effort on her part; and she would do her best for them. If the town disapproved, let it disapprove. When had ever a Gracen bowed to public opinion enough to give up a righteous deed when the need was for it?

So the days went by, and the three boys became regular, almost daily, visitors at the house. Sometimes they only ran in for a minute to see Dick, sometimes to borrow a book or try over a song, sometimes to bring a great branch of red leaves still found clinging to some sheltered tree; and once Harold came breathlessly to the door, on his way to meet his father at the train, to leave a clump of squawberry vine dotted with bright red berries, which he had found and carefully dug up for her.

It grew to be a regular thing that they took long tramps on Saturdays when Wayne had an afternoon off; and sometimes they inveigled Miss Gracen into a moonlight walk, just to see how the light shone on the little falls below the creek, with the branches of the tall, bare trees stencilled clear against the night-blue sky.

But the Sunday-afternoon meetings were not long confined to the four, for every now and then a new boy would be brought along, and would somehow steal a place in the heart of the hostess and be asked again.

Willing hands prepared on Saturday night the delicate sandwiches and cakes, the little tarts or crisp cookies; or set away dainty dishes of salad and bowls of delicious broths that needed only a few minutes over the gas-stove to make them ready for serving with the accompanying toasted wafers. Rebecca and Molly and Hiram rejoiced over this opportunity of helping on "Miss Vic's good work," as they called it; for in their good old souls they felt that a wrong had been done the father Dick, and it must be righted for his son, and that through him these other boys were being uplifted and helped as all boys had a right to be.

Expensive? Yes, the good things to eat cost a little; but it was a mere trifle to Miss Gracen, who might have spent it otherwise on going to the city to the opera, or giving bridge-parties, or taking trips to Europe; and she enjoyed it as no society woman ever enjoys her follies.

Just how the story of her doings got out is uncertain. The boys did not tell it; that is, they never intended to do so. They may have let it out sometimes more by what they did not say than by what they did; but it got out somehow, in distorted form, all about Miss Victoria's ridiculous and disgraceful goings-on. It may have been the time when Miss Earwig from the next door ran in late Saturday afternoon to borrow some soda for her gingerbread, and found Molly making rolled brownbread sandwiches with minced chicken filling. Or it may have been Mrs. Harold Constable's letter from southern France to her most intimate friend, Mrs. Cornelius Cornell, secretary of the Club, wherein she made some jocose remark about Harold's having written that he took supper with Miss Gracen every Sunday night, and she wondered whether Miss Gracen was losing her Puritan ideas about keeping Sunday so strictly, and getting like other people at last. However the story came, it was out, with all the embellishing that much telling can give.

"Feeding them! Actually pampering their stomachs, and making them think they're just the greatest things on earth! Those *bad boys!*" almost screamed Mrs. Dr. Toosun when the story was told to her at a Club meeting. "Why, it's the worst thing she could do for them. They'll all end in jail, and she'll be to blame for it!"

"Yes, feeding them, and on Sunday, too! I think it's wicked," said fat Mrs. Thorndike, gulping her last drop of strong coffee. And all those who sat in condemnation, as they finished their delicate ices and cakes, sat back and agreed that it was a dreadful thing to do on the Sabbath, and never remembered how they resembled the Pharisees who found some such fault with Jesus on the Sabbath day.

But Victoria Gracen, independent of nature, and happy in the new work that God had given her, went serenely on her way, hearing little of the scandal about herself, because now Lydia Bypath, whose letter of vituperation had been answered by a brief, calm note of dignity, came no more to tell, and to warn, and to cast the eye of scorn.

The Sunday meetings had become quite an established fact, and were no longer confined to four boys, but had a regular attendance of from ten to twelve; and among these were numbered both high and low; for somehow a few of the really "respectable" boys, whose parents disapproved of the whole performance, crept stealthily in now and then until their presence became a regular thing; and, on the other hand, four or five fellows of the lowly walks of life were brought by the original boys, who felt that these needed it. A word of low explanation from one of them to Miss Gracen was enough to bring out her smile of welcome, and thus her house became the resort of some of the outcasts among the boys of Roslyn.

These were not all of them so intimate as the original four, nor did all go on the pleasant little tramps and expeditions, and occasional evening trips to the city to hear some fine singer or great orchestra; but they all were welcome to share the reading and the luncheons on Sunday afternoon, and all of them afterwards tramped their unabashed way into church with Miss Gracen Sunday night to pay for it. The minister eyed the growing company with interest and hopefulness. His own boy was becoming more thoughtful, more obedient, more attentive to his lessons and duties. Surely, this strange experiment Miss Gracen was trying in the goodness of her heart was not wholly a bad thing, even if she did give them things to eat on Sunday.

Also, they all shared in a good time about once a month, which Miss Gracen got up for them at her home, in which games, music, readings, mirth, and food were judiciously mingled. At such times the noises that arose from the staid and dignified Gracen mansion were such as to cause the elderly and respectable passers-by to look in horror and in wonder to see who was being murdered, and rag-time frequently vied with shrieks of laughter so loud that it reached clear down the street to Lydia Bypath's windows, which, in spite of the bitter cold that winter, she kept open a trifle on the evenings when Victoria Gracen's "wild mob," as she called them were to meet for "another hullabaloo."

Lydia Bypath was biding her time, but she had not given up her one-time friend utterly to the error of her way. She meant to rescue her yet when the right time came, and until then she meant to keep well informed. Oh, if old Mr. and Mrs. Gracen could only look down from above and see the disgraceful actions that were going on in their dear old home, and how their daughter had become utterly foolish and reckless in her "obsession" — yes, Lydia Bypath acknowledged in the secret of her soul that it was an obsession — they surely could not be happy in heaven. It was not in Lydia Bypath's nature to enjoy having anybody happy even in heaven, when she was so wretched on earth.

But the climax came one day late in December when a beautiful blanket of snow had covered field, hill, and valley, and the boys, Tom, Dick, Harold, and Wayne — for it was Saturday afternoon — had coaxed their comrade, "Miss Vic," to go coasting with them.

They brought up their double-decker just at lunchtime; and about two o'clock they all started off to the hill at the back of the house; the long, gracious hill that lent itself to the snow in curves and bends and downward glides such as were not to be found anywhere else in that part of the country.

And Victoria Gracen enjoyed it as she had not enjoyed an afternoon since she was a girl. She wore an old gray serge dress, a white sweater, and a knitted woollen cap; her eyes were like stars and her cheeks like roses. She was having the time of her life. Her hair was all in a lovely tumble of misty white about her face; the little cap was set jauntily back on her head; and her face seemed to have grown ten years younger with the laughing and exercise.

At three o'clock sharp, Miss Bypath, having taken long counsel of herself in the night-watches and for many days, locked the door of her modest and respectable dwelling, and walked down the snowy path in her large, neat arctics, shuddering as the frosty air caught her thin nose and nipped it spitefully, for all the world in the same fashion as her words sometimes nipped other people.

16

It was not far to Victoria Gracen's house, and Lydia Bypath stalked up the steps — if so little a creature can be said to stalk — like a Nemesis come at last.

She was rather balked when Hiram told her that Miss Gracen was out and might not be back for some time. Hiram did not like Miss Bypath. It dated back to a time when his Molly was a little girl, and Miss Bypath had looked down upon her as a servant. He was secretly glad that his mistress was not in.

But Lydia Bypath was not easily balked. She demanded to know where her victim might be, and Hiram discreetly told her that she had gone out with her nephew, and hadn't intended coming back till supper-time.

Now, Miss Bypath was sharp; Miss Bypath was keen; moreover, from her little back-kitchen window she could easily see the small, black, bobbing specks of boys as they coasted down the Gracen hill. She knew the town and its habits. She knew that coasting was the order of the day among boys, and that the hill had been covered all the morning with many shouting, gesticulating, ridiculous, little black figures, "fooling their time away like apes," as she put it.

Moreover, her unusually sharp eyes had discerned the marks of a double-decker in the snow tramped about with many footsteps, going around the side of the house toward the pasture fence that led to the top of the coasting-hill; and at Hiram's second attempt to mislead her she looked down at those same footprints in the snow. Then she turned to the startled, easily abashed servant, and fixed him with her eyes, saying:

"Hiram, you don't mean to tell me that Miss Victoria Gracen has — *gone* — *coasting!*"

Hiram's sheepish face left no doubt in the matter though he did not open his lips.

"Gone coasting with the boys at her time of life!" she fairly screamed.

Hiram stood mute.

"Hiram, conduct me to the spot. I have important immediate business with her. I say, conduct me to the spot at once."

But Hiram was rheumatic, and the thought of all the overshoes and mufflers he would be obliged to put on if Rebecca found out what he was going to do, as well as the impossibility of the idea of presenting himself to Miss Gracen with the disgrace upon him of having given away her secret to the enemy, was more than he could bear.

"Indeed, miss, you'll have to excuse me, miss; I've something very important to do in the house just now, miss. I can't say just which way Miss Gracen has gone, miss; but, if you follow the tracks through the meadow, I've no doubt you'll find her if she's there, miss."

And so with his most studied manner he managed to close the door upon her and not actually seem to have insulted her.

"Well, upon my word!" ejaculated the worthy woman. "I never thought it would come to this in the house of my friend!"

She studied the landscape for a little season, and then with an appealing glance at her trusty arctics she plunged into the snowy footprints, and wallowed bravely forth to the battle.

It was a long, hard struggle for the weak little respectable legs. The arctics were heavy and her breath came painfully; but she managed it at last with only two or three actual falls, in which her inadequate cotton gloves dived helplessly into billows of cold feathers, and arose struggling with the snow that had gone up her sleeves. Each time she gathered herself from a fall she gathered more fury to her wrath; and her face was distorted with ugliness when she appeared at the top of the hill down which Miss Gracen, in all the glory of her wild dishevelment, in the seat of honor on the double-decker, with four tall gallants to guide and protect her, had sailed joyously away. Victoria Gracen should pay for this; Oh, *she should!*

And so in lonesome wrath she stood and awaited the return of her victim as she came, laughingly assisted by first one boy and then another, joyfully climbing back for another coast down the long hill.

They were almost two-thirds up the hill before Dick, looking up, discovered her, and gave a dismayed whistle of warning.

"Good-night!" he exclaimed, and then they all looked up quickly.

"Say, fellows," whispered Tom, nothing daunted, "let's put her on the sled, and give her a ride down the hill. That'll take the pep out of her all right. Come on, what do you say, boys?"

The three, Tom, Dick, and Harold, were off up the hill in a trice. Wayne happened to be conducting Miss Gracen, and until the boys rushed ahead with that peculiar air of having sudden urgent business neither of the two had seen the new arrival.

But, as Harold tore by Wayne, he murmured roughly under his breath:

"Get on to the skeleton at the feast?" and Wayne, looking up, saw Miss Bypath. His face overspread with the dark look that Miss Gracen had come to watch for that she might discover the cause; and she knew instantly that something was the matter, even before he exclaimed:

"Say, isn't she the limit?"

Looking up, she saw with dismay the small, gaunt figure in black, and realized her own tumbled hair and undignified employment.

Then almost instantly both she and Wayne knew what the boys intended to do, for they were shouting now at the top of their lungs:

"Come on, Miss Bypath; you're just in time. We'll take you down the next trip. The hill's fine and you'll have the time of your life. Just stand right still, and we'll put you on —"

"Oh, Wayne, don't let them!" exclaimed Miss Gracen. "They mustn't. They would frighten her to death. Go. Stop them!"

She took her hand from his strong arm,

and pushed him forward; and Wayne, with a back glance of assurance at her, took long strides upward, shouting at the very top of his strong lungs:

"Cut that out, boys! Cut it out!" Though of course in the clamor his words were not heard.

Miss Bypath stood her ground in snow nearly a foot deep, and frowned ominously at the oncoming boys. At first she did not understand them; and then her ire rose with increased force at the indignity put upon her, a respectable woman. She did not think it worth while to answer them. She would crush them by ignoring them. But, when they made toward her with that fragile sled, and declared their intention of putting her on it and sending her down that fearful declivity, with its bumps and curves, and glistening, winding, ribbony track, panic seized upon her.

"Don't you dare to lay a finger upon me, you — you —," she screamed, and stamped her foot in its squashy arctic ineffectually in the deep, powdery snow.

Then to her excited imagination it seemed that Victoria Gracen was laughing at her, and that she had sent another boy to help them on in their disgraceful attempt to put her on the sled and ride her down that hill, probably just so that Victoria might have company in her own disgrace.

If those four boys had been four fiends rushing on to drag her down to the bottomless pit, Lydia Bypath could not have picked up her respectable skirts with more expedition, nor made her thin ankles fly faster through the impeding snow. On she went, faster and faster, her breath growing shorter, her eyes blinded with the flopping veil which descended over her face, her arctics getting heavier and heavier, until, just as she was almost to the pasture fence where the bars were let down, she caught her foot against a boulder that lay hidden under the blanket of snow, and went down full length, with her nose in the cold, cold snow: with snow up her nose, and snow in her eyes, and snow in her ears, and even, when she gave an involuntary cry, snow in her respectable, back-biting mouth. It was a terrible fall for both her pride and her body; and she lay there for a whole second, dazed and floundering, until the snow up her sleeves made itself felt, and she was impelled to rise.

The boys stood bent double, laughing at the grotesque figure as it fled across the snowy pasture; and even Miss Gracen had to smile at the precipitate flight of their guest when offered the entertainment of the occasion, albeit her smile had a shade of trouble in its wavering.

She arrived at the top just before Miss Bypath's downfall and just in time to hear Tom's disrespectfully expressed wish that he could wash her little, mean face for her in the snow.

"Oh, Tom," she said sorrowfully, "Oh, Tom, that isn't right. You must not speak so about her."

"Aw, Miss Vic," said Tom, his face as red as his hair because he had been overheard, "I didn't know you were there; but indeed, Miss Vic, I can't bear that woman. You don't know all she's done to me all my life. Why, one time I was with some boys that stole her apples. I hadn't touched one. I was too little; I was just a real small kid; and she caught 'em at it, and chased 'em, and they got away; and so she grabbed me. I told her I hadn't touched her old apples, but she wouldn't believe me. She said I'd told a lie and she was going to punish me for it; so she took me into her kitchen, and got some soft soap and hot water, and washed my mouth out, for a lie she knew I hadn't told. I hadn't an apple, nor hadn't had, and *she knew it*. She's the meanest old thing alive."

"But she's a woman, Tom; and, oh, see,

she's fallen down! I'm afraid she's badly hurt."

It was Wayne who went with long, swift strides through the snow to her assistance, and went before there had been time to ask him to do it.

Lydia Bypath lifted her head fearfully from her cold, feathery plunge, and gazed about her, gasping, brushing the snow from her eyes; and there close at hand was one of those terrible boys coming rapidly on.

Floundering and almost hysterical, she scuttled to her feet, and turning to face him, her frightened eyes flashing blue sparks, her shaking voice calling out:

"Don't you come another step toward me! Don't you dare to lay a finger on me! You bad, *bad* boy!"

"I was only coming to help you up," said Wayne haughtily, stopping at once. "Are you hurt?"

"Help me up? Yes, help me up! I understand what kind of help you would give me. I know who you are. Your father is in prison for committing a crime, and you'll be there some day yourself. You are a wicked boy. Don't you dare come another step!"

Wayne stood, tall, broad-shouldered, fine and handsome, facing her as she hurled the hideous words at him; and his face grew white with wrath. He clinched his fists hard inside his sweater pockets. If she had been a man, it would have gone hard with her that day; but she was only a foolish, cranky woman, and he was a gentleman; so he stood, and answered her not a word, with his hands held hard in his pockets, his chin held haughtily like a young king, his fine eyes looking steadily, blackly into hers. Something in their look warned her that she had said enough, for she turned shakily, and began to wobble and wallow her way out through the pasture to the road.

Wayne stood and watched her until she crept through the fence and made her way to a cleared path; then he turned, with darkness in his face and a tumult in his shadowed heart, and came back to the waiting group.

"She's a mutt!" he said, frowning, and that was all he said; but Miss Gracen knew that something very great had troubled the soul of her boy, and she set about thinking how she might heal the hurt.

They went on coasting, but Wayne laughed aloud in free enjoyment no more. He took his place solemnly, went silently down with the rest; was kinder and more thoughtful to Miss Gracen than ever, seeming to anticipate every little need and prepare for it; but he said nothing, and at last Tom blurted out:

"What's the matter, Forrie? Where'd you get the grouch? Lost your heart to Lydia Bypath?"

But Wayne only frowned, and did not answer.

Meantime, Nemesis, trembling, but still determined, made her slow and tortuous way to the street and to her own home. She was much shaken by her fright and falls, and she was still trembling with anger; but she meant now to let nothing stand in the way of her vengeance. Those boys should meet with the punishment they deserved, and Victoria Gracen would have to take her disgrace along with them. She would hide Victoria's degrading "goings-on" no longer. They should come to light and have the judgment of public opinion upon them. Only public opinion could now save Victoria Gracen from utter wreck and ruin.

She stole to her home, set the key in her lock, and went in to put on some dry gloves and remove the extra snow from her wrists and ankles. It took half an hour to dry the inside of her arctics by the kitchen fire and get on a set of dry sleeves throughout; then, fortified by a cup of strong tea, the little vixen girded herself up once more, and set out on her self-appointed mission down the street to the parsonage gate.

Now it happened that the minister had just returned, cold and weary, from a far funeral in the country. He had driven in the teeth of the wind twenty miles, over roads that were still unbroken, and where sometimes the only way to get on was to follow the tops of the fences and get out and help the horse wallow through the drifts. The harrowing scenes through which he had passed at the house of mourning, and the long, hard drive back, had taken his strength. His wife had just brought him a cup of tea and a plate of delicious buttered toast made by her own hands, with a soft-boiled egg invitingly dropped on the toast, when the door-bell rang and Lydia Bypath entered.

The minister's slippered feet were slowly thawing in front of the study fire, and he had taken but one bite of the toast and one life-giving swallow of that tea; but the blundering maid, a farmer's daughter who was cheap and self-sufficient, ushered Miss Bypath into the sacred precincts of the study because the wily visitor had asked whether she might go right in where the minister was, as she had some very private business with him.

The minister was taken at a disadvantage. He saw in his visitor's eye keen disapproval of a mid-afternoon meal for a man who had a large parish and should have been at work. At a single glance she took in the dressing-gown and the slippered feet, the bright fire, and easy chair, and with a tone of implication said:

"Oh, I didn't know that you were ill, Mr. Atterbury."

"Not ill, Miss Bypath," said the minister with as good a grace as he could command, getting to his feet with the plate and cup in his hands. "I'm getting a bite after a long, dinnerless day. I've just returned from a funeral over at West Forks."

"Oh," perked Miss Bypath, ready for a bit of gossip before she opened up her budget, and quite prepared to study the contents of the minister's plate and report to the congregation how his wife fed him.

But the minister had no mind to eat his lunch under inspection, and with a courteous "You will excuse me for just a moment, Miss Bypath," he carried his comfortable lunch into the cold dining-room, gulped his cup of tea, took one bite of the delicately browned toast, and with a lingering, wistful glance at the rest went back to his caller. There had been that in Lydia Bypath's manner and eyes that indicated an unpleasant interview ahead, and he wanted to get it over as soon as possible.

He had, however, made nothing by carrying his plate away from her gaze, for she always doubled her animosity when people tried to escape her vigilance. Moreover, he had given her time to gather her shaken forces and prepare her initial remarks. She opened up fire even before the minister sat down, and her tone caused him to choose a stiff, hard chair by his desk rather than the comfortable seat in front of the fire. He would have need of his utmost dignity, he knew; for he had experienced calls like this from her before.

"Mr. Atterbury, the time has come for something to be done, and done quickly," she announced with righteous vehemence; "and, as your own eldest-born is involved in the disgraceful case, I thought it best to come straight to you with the matter."

This was the way she had begun on several former occasions when Tom had been supposed to have been stealing apples, smashing street-lights, or breaking windows with his ever-blameful ball.

The minister started, and sighed. He had been a little more comfortable about Tom lately, for no one had complained of him for six whole months. He had hoped the boy was beginning to grow up and leave behind some of his youthful sins and follies.

"I am very sorry to hear that my son has been getting into trouble again," said the minister gravely. "What is the charge you have to bring against him?"

"It is a most painful matter," wept Lydia Bypath, getting out her handkerchief and allowing the copious drops to trickle down her thin cheeks; "but I always do my duty by my friends, and I felt you must know at once —"

"Yes?" said the minister, preparing himself for the worst. He knew one could not hurry Miss Bypath in her preamble.

There was silence in the study, broken only by dramatic sniffs for a minute; then the caller raised her vindictive little eyes and in a half whisper that reminded the minister of a serpent's hiss, she told him.

17

"I have been grossly insulted and ill-treated, Mr. Atterbury, this very afternoon, and by your son, in company with a lot of other good-for-nothing ruffians — ruffians — it is the only word I can use to fully express what they are, one of them the son of a common thief. I have only escaped as by a miracle from an actual assault, and I am so much shaken that I can scarcely tell the story calmly."

"You cannot mean that my son insulted you, Miss Bypath. I am sure there must be some mistake. Tom has been rather a mischievous boy, but I am sure he has always shown respect to ladies."

Miss Bypath lifted her tear-stained face impressively.

"Did you ever know me to tell a falsehood, Mr. Atterbury? You know that I am speaking the truth, and I am not mistaken. It was your son who started the whole thing, and who put the other — ruffians — up to giving me chase. I will tell you just how it happened, that you may understand the case; but you won't mind my breaking down, for I have been through a great deal, and am scarcely able to sit up." She eyed the big chair by the fire; but the minister sat up very straight, and took no hints. He wanted to hear the story to its finish now, and she was forced to go on.

"I have been very much troubled for weeks about my *dear* friend Victoria Gracen, and the disgraceful way in which she is going on. Of course, it is an infatuation, and at her time of life it is all the more pitiable. Mr. Atterbury, you have no idea to what lengths she goes. Why, the sounds that proceed from her house at all hours of the day and night whenever those wild, ungoverned creatures are let loose there are unbelievable! And Sundays! *Sun*days! Just think of it. They have regular feasts I am told. Think of the old Gracen mansion harboring an orgy of wild, disreputable, *bad* boys on the Sabbath! And the respectable servants are obliged, I am told, to work harder on the Sabbath than on any other day to provide feasts for all this mob. I wonder they don't leave, I certainly do. Poor Victoria has no more idea than a babe in arms what she has brought upon herself, for the whole town is talking about her. They are using very severe expressions indeed; in fact, they are using words about her that are not at all nice." She lowered her voice to the hissing whisper again. "Obsession," she hissed "that was the word they used. They said she was *obsessed* with boys. I wouldn't mention it if it weren't important that you should know, being a minister of the gospel and of course you'll understand. I know, of course, that some of the modern women are using it in their club papers just to be fashionable; but I don't think it is at all a pleasant word to use, and it breaks my heart to have it used about my d-e-a-r — o-l-d — f-r-r-i-e-n-d."

Here she sobbed tenderly.

"But," raising her head and going at her duty again, she went on, "you'll quite understand how I hated to tell her; and I put it off, and put it off, hearing as I do from my near vicinity the awful sounds almost every night of the week, *not excepting the Sabbath.* They tell me it is the kind of music used in saloons called 'the rag.' I'm sure I can't understand how Victoria, being a musician, ever brought herself to endure it. It drives me into a sick-headache three doors away. Well, as I was saying, I made up my mind to go and tell her all this very afternoon; and I took my life in my hand, and went through this light snow, and me with the lumbago and neuralgia. But, when I got to her house, I found her out. And *where* do you think she was? Why, Mr. Atterbury, I couldn't have believed it. Even her faithful, old, man-servant was embarrassed, and wouldn't tell me till I guessed and made him own up. *She was out behind the house with a whole mob of boys sliding down hill!* At her age, *sliding down hill!* Her hair was all mussed up; and she had on a cap and mittens, just like a giddy girl; and those boys were *helping her up the hill as fine as you please,* just exactly as if she were one of them; and she didn't seem to mind a bit! I tell you this that you may see that she really needs somebody to talk to her and make her understand. She's — I beg your pardon — she's *obsessed;* that's what she really is."

She paused for appropriate shock to appear in the minister's face; but instead a kind of sympathetic gleam came into his eyes, and his face wore an inscrutable expression, an unbiased watcher might even have thought it a look of satisfaction. But the story went on before he had opportunity to say anything.

"I saw her go sliding down that awful abyss." Miss Bypath had learned many hymns as a child, and occasionally utilized some of their vocabulary in her conversation. "I saw her with my own eyes, though I could scarcely believe my senses; and then, when she came back up the hill, those awful boys came ahead of her; and your son was ahead of them all. When he saw me, I grieve to say, he gave a shout of wicked glee, and ran at me with all his might, calling to me in the most insolent way, that now he was going to give me a ride, and threatening if I refused he would put me on his sled in spite of myself. Think of the outrage of even suggesting such a thing to a respectable woman like myself." Here the tears flowed freely. "And the worst of it was," she said, sobbing now with an "et-tu-Brute" manner "that — my — dear — old — friend, who used to sit in the same seat in school with me, and give me apples and cake out of her lunch-basket, not only didn't stop them, but actually sent another boy, that son — of — a — forger, to chase me; and I'm sure she was laughing at my dis-dis-dis-comfiture."

Here her feelings completely got the better of her, and she sobbed outright.

The minister, who was having all he could do to control his facial muscles, attempted to interrupt with an "Oh, no, Miss Bypath, you're mistaken. Miss Gracen would never do that."

But she put in fiercely once more:

"No, you wouldn't think she would; but I tell you she's utterly changed. Utterly! Why, the other night I was there, and asked to see her alone; and she as good as told me that whatever I had to say I must say before that whole mob of *boys!* And your son, I regret to say, was present on that occasion also, and got off a very insulting remark about wish-bones to me. I have put up with a great deal from that boy through the years, but I felt that the time had come to make all known to his father —"

"But Miss Bypath," began the minister.

"Kindly let me finish my story," she went on with dignity, "and then I will leave the matter in your hands. They insulted me, as I was saying; and, when they found I resented their insolent language, they came at me to put me bodily on that awful sled of theirs! But for a miracle I might even now be lying, a ghastly spectacle, scattered in the valley by the creek."

It was not from his gentle mother's side of the family that Tom Atterbury had inherited his keen sense of the ridiculous, and there suddenly came over the minister such a strong desire to throw his head back and laugh that for an instant he felt it impossible to control it. The vision of severe, little Miss Bypath flying down the long Gracen hill and lying scattered over the snowy valley in many fragments seemed a possibility so grotesque that he was about to beat a hasty retreat from the room until he could bring his face into order again; but just then Miss Bypath terminated her effective pause, and began again.

"Now, it is not for myself that I have come to you; it is for the salvation of your son. When I remember Eli's sons, and the bears that ate the forty and four thousand children, I feel that I should be unpardonable if I did not bring this to your knowledge; and I know you will be grateful. It seems to me that the first thing you should do would be to stop your son's going to Miss Gracen's, and forbid his having anything more to do with those evil companions of his. A Sabbath-breaking crowd is no fit place for a minister's son, and I have been surprised at you for allowing him to go out on the Sabbath, though, of course, I suppose you did not know what he was doing."

It was not the first time since Mr. Atterbury had been pastor in Roslyn that Miss Lydia Bypath had attempted to teach him how to bring up his children. He had the meek and quiet spirit which knew how to take the thing sweetly and go on doing as he thought best in spite of it, but the warning she gave this time touched an uneasy spot in the minister's mind. He had never been satisfied about those companions of Tom's, nor quite happy about his going out every Sunday evening for supper. Several times he had questioned Tom, but always to have his worst fears allayed, and a shadow of hope for his boy's future raised in its place. Now, however, the vague uneasiness returned.

"Miss Bypath," he said kindly, when he saw she had quite finished, "I am sorry, indeed, that my boy has distressed and frightened you in any way. I shall talk with him about it as soon as he returns home, and I feel convinced that he will be able to explain his side of the matter so that the affair will be proved to be nothing worse than a mistaken attempt at fun. Tom has no unkindly feeling toward you. He is a kindhearted boy —"

"We do not always see into the hearts of those with whom we live the closest; the human heart is deceitful and desperately wicked," quoted the visitor righteously.

"And as for Miss Gracen's Sabbath afternoons," went on the minister ignoring her implication, "I have been given to understand that they are most orderly affairs. Miss Gracen reads to the boys, and they sing hymns; the feasts, I am told, are simple — sandwiches and cookies and the like. I have really felt that Miss Gracen was most kind to try to help the boys in this way."

"You have been given to understand," repeated Miss Bypath ominously. "May I ask *who* gave you to understand?" She faced the minister unflinchingly with her keen, little eyes, and read her answer in his guilty brown ones so like his son's.

"Your son gave you to understand, didn't he? Of course. Where else could you find out? And I am grieved to tell you that he has probably told you his own version of what goes on. Naturally he wants to keep up his Sabbath-breaking, and he knows he can't if you find it out. But let alone the question of whether you want your son to be a Sabbath-breaker or not, Mr. Atterbury; you surely don't want the whole town talking about you because you let your son take part in disorderly gatherings on Sunday. Mr. Atterbury, if those afternoons of Miss Gracen's are all right, why doesn't she invite you to come and speak to the boys? What right has she to set up a meeting in her house as if she were an opposition church? I should think you as her pastor would think it your duty to investigate, and I have come here this afternoon to demand as a member

of your flock that you exercise your official duty over my friend Victoria Gracen, and go and find out what she is doing on Sunday afternoon."

"I have no doubt Miss Gracen would be quite glad to have me come in on one of her meetings if she were asked," risked the minister, trying to be evasive, but his caller caught him up quickly enough.

"Don't ask her for pity's sake," put in Lydia, the ferret; "just drop down upon her, and catch her in the midst of her folly. Then you will be able to speak to her from what you have seen. If you tell her beforehand, like as not there won't be a boy there, and everything will be as staid as the meeting-house. Just go in there to-morrow afternoon after they all get there, and see for yourself. Come over to my house, and you can watch till they all go by, and you can hear them sing the first song; and then you can be sure they're well started."

Miss Bypath's eyes gleamed with the excitement of the chase, as the old Pharisees' eyes must have twinkled when they were pursuing the Christians. She honestly thought she was doing God service by exposing Victoria Gracen's follies to the minister, who had a right to upbraid her and show her the error of her ways.

The minister sat calmly facing her, wondering how best and most quickly to send her on her way. At last he said gravely, quietly,

"Very well, Miss Bypath; I will do as you have suggested to-morrow afternoon, on one condition, and that is that you do not open your mouth on this subject to a living soul until I give you permission." He looked at her kindly but firmly, and she drew her breath in a quick gasp of disappointment.

She opened her mouth to speak, and shut it with a snap. Then she opened it again.

"But —"

The minister raised his hand.

"Miss Bypath, you have put this matter in my hands for investigation; and, if I am to deal with it, I want it absolutely left with me. I cannot consent to do anything about it unless you will be absolutely silent about the matter to every one."

"Do you mean that I mustn't mention the indignities that were put upon me by those evil boys, either?"

"I do."

"But isn't it right that people should know how bad they are?"

"I don't see what is to be gained by it."

"Don't you believe in punishing sinners?"

"Yes, but not necessarily in publishing their faults."

"But I tell you I had a bad fall, and got all wet with snow; and I expect I shall be very sick. I feel as though it were coming on now. I shall have to call in the doctor. I suppose you've no objection to my telling him."

"I must insist that you mention the matter to no one."

"What will the doctor think? I'll have to tell him something."

"Tell him you had a bad fall in the snow, and were frightened. He doesn't need to know anything else."

"But isn't that deception?" asked the little woman sharply.

"Not to tell him a lot of details that are not his business? No."

"You talk very heartlessly," sniffed Lydia; "but I suppose I don't understand the heart of a parent."

"Probably not, Miss Bypath. However, on this occasion I am not thinking so much of my son's reputation as of Miss Gracen's and I must insist on having this kept absolutely between us for the present."

With much dissatisfaction Miss Bypath arose to take her leave. She had not started the tremendous rumpus that she had expected, and it was quite flat to go home and keep still until to-morrow afternoon. Her heart burned hotly against her one-time friend and against those horrid boys who dared to ridicule her. To see them set up in high places where she would fain have been herself was more than she could bear. And yet, if she would have her way and let the minister investigate, she must do as he had bidden.

In silent but submissive wrath she went her grim way home. Her thin limbs trembled more than when she came, and her whole being was utterly used up. She wanted nothing so much as to lie down and rest. The tears weakly trickled down her faded cheeks, and yet they were mad tears. She was outraged to the depths of her respectable, embittered nature; and her hurt pride demanded redress. She wanted with all her heart to have Victoria Gracen suffer for it, suffer for the mortification she herself had passed through when she fled through the snow and lay in a heap at the mercy of the village boys, the echo of their ridiculing laughter ringing all about her.

So she crept to her home and her bed; and, as there was no satisfaction in sending for a doctor who couldn't be told the cause of her disaffection, she made some herb tea and drank it, rubbed herself well with arnica, and went to bed. Albeit the next morning, stiff and sore though she was, she could not refrain from gathering herself together and going to church just to see whether Victoria Gracen would be there, and hear whether the sermon would contain some covert hit at her goings-on.

The minister did not need to put his son through an inquisitorial process to get his side of the story that evening; he gave it freely and with many amusing variations at the supper-table.

"We offered her a ride, father," he said, his eyes twinkling with the memory; "and you just ought to have seen her beat it. I don't guess she'll chase Miss Vic out to the meadow again in a hurry."

Plainly Tom had nothing to hide, and had apparently told the whole story. The minister hesitated on the edge of a reproof, and scarcely knew what to say, there were so many subtle shades of difference between Tom's story and Miss Bypath's.

Moreover, he did not at present wish to let the boy know that Miss Bypath had been complaining to him.

"Were you entirely respectful to Miss Bypath, my son?" queried the minister with a troubled look.

"Why, yes, dad," responded Tom heartily. "We were real cordial, and offered her a ride the minute she appeared on the scene."

"Wasn't it rather impertinent in you to do that, son, when you knew she would not care for that sort of thing? Would she not take it as a sort of insult, an attempt to hold her up to ridicule?"

Tom's innocent brown eyes looked roundly into those of his father.

"Why, dad, there wasn't any reason for her to take it that way. We'd have taken her down in great shape if she'd let us. I even offered to put her on the sled comfortably. Of course, she's no old sport like Miss Vic, but she might have been polite. We meant to show her a good time for once; we really did. Say, dad, wouldn't it have been great to see Miss Bypath sailing down the long hill? I bet it would have got into her blood after she once tried it, and you'd have seen her out on the sly, moonlight nights, sliding by herself. Miss Vic enjoyed every minute of the afternoon, and didn't mind a tumble any more than us fellows, though, of course, we didn't let her tumble much."

The minister suddenly asked a question which appeared to his son entirely irrelevant.

"What kind of a boy is Wayne Forrest?"

"He's all right, father. You'd like him, you really would," said Tom eagerly. "Miss Vic thinks he's great. She raves over his voice, and I certainly do like to hear him sing. He's polite and all that. You and mother would think he was *some*. He *thinks* to do all the little things you are always talking about, taking off hats and helping people. Why, he even ran ahead to try and pick up Miss Bypath when she fell over in the snow after she had been so impolite as to run away from us and call us names. Forrie was as mad as anybody at the way she acted, but he went and tried to pick her up; and then she wouldn't let him. She just reared up when he came near her, like a fishing-worm, and began to rave at him till he got his chin up in the air, and stood back and let her get up herself. She told him not to dare to touch her, and she called him the son of a thief. He didn't know I heard her, and he never said a word about it when he came back; but we all heard enough to know she was reminding him of his father's disgrace. I tell you it was pretty tough on Forrie, but he came back and never said a word about it, just looked dark and had a grouch on the rest of the afternoon. Even Miss Vic couldn't bring him out of it, and he wouldn't hear to staying to supper, though she asked us. He went home and so we all did. He's an all-right fellow, dad. He seems to like to come to church now, too."

The minister walked his study that night for a long time, trying to make up his mind what to say to his son about apologizing to Miss Bypath, and finally decided to wait until the next day. He did not want to re-prove him for nothing, neither did he want to do any half-way business if the boy really was to blame. He decided to investigate a little further, and perhaps have a conference with Miss Gracen before moving in the matter. It was his ability to look on the other side of a question which made some of his flock feel that he hadn't any backbone when certain pet hobbies of theirs were at stake. However, late that night, when he heard Tom starting upstairs to bed after an evening of really hard study, he called to him.

"Tom, I feel troubled about your conduct toward Miss Bypath. I would like you to go to her sometime to-morrow and explain that you meant no discourtesy in offering her a ride on your sled."

Tom's face grew blank. "Oh, dad!" he protested. "She'll just flare up some more."

"Never mind; you will have done your duty. I shall feel concerned about the matter until you have made it right. Will you attend to it to-morrow?"

"Sure," said Tom, his ready cheerfulness coming uppermost. After all, he bore Miss Bypath no ill-will, and she had given them a good laugh. Why should he not explain if it pleased his father? He supposed it was pretty tough on her, getting all that snow up her sleeves and falling down, though she had no business to speak to Wayne Forrest that way; and his heart burned hot with wrath as he mounted the stairs to his room, pondering in his boy-way whether he could not work in a little reproof to her along with his own apology and explanation, and kill two birds with one stone. If his father could have known his thoughts, he might not have sat down to his belated sermon with quite so easy a mind. However, Tom was not all bad, and he really meant to make it right with Lydia Bypath, even if he did intend to give her a few facts concerning her own conduct which he felt she ought to know.

The household slept. The minister finished his sermon, and knelt to pray for a blessing on his work of the morrow, and to plead that the task of investigating the matter of Miss Gracen's boys might not be so difficult as it seemed at present; then he went up-stairs to his well-earned rest.

Two miles out on a lonely, country road in the little, cold attic chamber a strong boy tossed on his bed, and his heart burned hot within him over the words of shame that had been flung at him by a woman's lips that afternoon. In the darkness hot, scorching tears burned their way into his eyes. His father! Oh, his father! Why had he sinned and left such a heritage of shame for his son and daughter when he went to pay his penalty by a living death? Was there a God, as Miss Gracen had almost made him believe? And, if there was, why did He let such things happen to people who were not in the least to blame?

18

Miss Gracen was in her place in church that morning, with the boy Richard by her side; and a few minutes later, just as the first hymn was being announced, Harold Constable came hurriedly up the aisle as if he were being waited for, and, slipping past Dick and Miss Gracen, sat down on the other side of her. It was the first time he had been to church in the morning, and Miss Gracen gave him a radiant smile in welcome. Lydia Bypath took that smile as a personal insult. Next to the minister's son and the forger's son she hated this child of a wealthy and snobbish mother who never recognized her on the street, nor asked her to any of her teas, though they had been members of the same club for five years or more.

The minister from his seat in the pulpit noted the look of devotion on the boy's face, and knew without being told that he had come to church to please Miss Gracen. Involuntarily Mr. Atterbury glanced toward

Miss Bypath to see whether she had noticed; and he caught the gleam of hatred in her face, and sighed as his Lord might have done over the Pharisees, who paid their tithe of mint, anise, and cumin.

When service was out, he took special pains to shake hands with Harold Constable. Something in the hearty grasp of the lad's hand as he said in his easy way, "Good-morning, Mr. Atterbury; thank you; I enjoyed being here," gave him a thrill of new hope for his ministry. What if such young fellows as this would give their lives to Christ and come into the church and serve the Kingdom? How wonderful it would be! What if his own Tom would some day love and serve the Lord?

He smiled understandingly at Miss Gracen as she murmured her pleasant "Good-morning," and knew that the joy in her eyes was because the Constable boy had been in the morning service.

"I'm glad you preached just that sermon this special morning," she murmured in a low voice as she passed him; and her eyes sought significantly the handsome, curly head just in front of them.

The minister had asked for light about the investigation he was to make that afternoon, and it would seem as if the heavenly

Father were answering his prayer in a very special way that day. As he walked slowly and thoughtfully from the church study, where he had been detained by one of his elders in a few minutes' conversation, he came up with Mr. Constable, who in high silk hat and Prince Albert coat, with a long cigar, a white bulldog, and a quaintly gnarled cane for company, was taking a Sunday stroll. Indeed, it seemed that Mr. Constable actually halted, and turned to wait for the minister, instead of hurrying by and ignoring him, as was his custom. Mr. Constable had little use for churches and ministers in his life.

"Good-morning, Mr. Atterbury, good-morning," he greeted him. "Fine morning for the middle of winter, isn't it? Too bright to stay indoors. Had a big congregation this morning, didn't you? I think I saw my son coming out. Well, it can't hurt him. Pretty good place to pass away the time for a boy of that age. Since his mother's away I guess the boy does about as he pleases. But I'm glad to see he's taking an interest in church. I used to when I was a boy, myself; had to go, in fact, every Sunday, and got enough of it to last the rest of my life, ha, ha!" He laughed as if the joke were a good one. "But it's different when a boy goes of his own free will. I'm glad to see Harold taking an interest. That young Gracen's a nice sort; seems like his father before him. I remember what a good ball-player he was. Miss Gracen's got a lot of sense about boys. My boy's quite stuck on her. She makes her home very attractive for them. Harold thinks there's nobody like her. By the way, I want to make a contribution to the church if my son is to share in its benefits."

He put his hand into his pocket and drew out a long wallet, selecting two bills of large denomination and handing them to the bewildered Mr. Atterbury.

"Just take those, and use them where they're most needed, won't you? And when you've any special call for more, just let me know. I'll be glad to contribute regularly. Good-morning. I'm glad my boy Harold is taking an interest in the church. I wish I'd done so myself when I was young."

And the portly gentleman touched his hat and turned down the avenue before the minister could recover from his surprise sufficiently to thank him.

It happened that the home-mission collection for that month had been very small indeed, and the minister had been troubled in his own heart about how he could afford to swell it to less mean proportions out of

311

his own slender "tenth," which often stretched and stretched until it became more like a fifth than a tenth.

While he was eating dinner, there came a call for the minister to come at once to an old man who was dying just on the outskirts of the village; and whom should he meet as he came out of the house after his call was made but Wayne Forrest.

Wayne's brow was still dark and his eyes were burning unhappily. He had almost made up his mind — not quite — to stay away from Miss Gracen's house that afternoon, just from the memory of those awful words of Miss Bypath's. If he had known the minister was to open that door and come out to the road at the moment he was passing, he would have gone miles out of his way to avoid the meeting. He frowned now, and tried to hasten his steps, hoping the minister would not know him; but Mr. Atterbury held out his hand with a smile of greeting. Here was another answer to his prayer, another opportunity to find out about Miss Gracen's work among her boys.

"Well, Forrest, glad to see you," he said, grasping the reluctant hand the boy held out. "I've been hearing good things about you from my son. He is telling me what a fine voice you have. Going down to the village? That's good; then I shall have company."

Wayne's brows lowered. He did not want to walk with the minister, but there seemed no choice; yet, strange to say, they had not been walking together five minutes before he forgot his gloom, and was laughing. The minister had a way with him that reminded him of Tom, and Wayne was surprised out of himself.

When Mr. Atterbury referred to his singing again, the boy answered half shyly:

"Oh, my voice isn't much; it's only that Miss Gracen likes it, I guess. I just sing a little to please her. I never sing for any one else."

"She's a great little woman, isn't she?" said the minister leadingly; and before he knew it Wayne was telling some of the things she had done for him. She was helping him to keep up with the school studies, so that if opportunity offered he could go to college some day.

"Of course I can't ever go to college," added the boy as if it were a joke; "but it's rather interesting to get ready. I want to know all the things, anyway, and what's college, after all, if you know as much?"

"That's a sensible way to look at it," said the minister; "still, college is college, and there are ways to go, you know. Keep on getting ready. Maybe one will come your way."

"No chance of that ever for me," said the boy gruffly kicking a block of frozen snow out of his way. "My life's cut out all the way ahead."

The minister, studying the fine, strong, sad face of the boy, was stirred as Miss Gracen had been, and decided that Tom had been right. He did like Wayne Forrest. His heart burned within him that Lydia Bypath had dared to hurt him by a reference to his father.

Mr. Atterbury linked his arm in the boy's as he might have done with his own son, and so walked into town with him; he might have preached at him, but he didn't. All he said was: "Maybe not, maybe not. We can't always see ahead"; and then he led him to talk of other things and of Miss Gracen's Sabbath afternoons until they reached the parsonage, and the boy's eyes lighted with pleasure in saying good-bye as the minister told him how glad he had been to see him in church, and how he should enjoy him all the better as a listener now that he knew him as a friend.

He had rather planned to stop at Miss Gracen's on the way home from his call, but it seemed unwise to do so in Wayne Forrest's company; moreover, Wayne had made no move to go into the Gracen gate himself. It was probably too early for the meeting to have begun. So Mr. Atterbury sat by his study window, watching behind the curtain until he saw Wayne Forrest return with Harold Constable and two other boys and whistle softly for Tom, who presently joined them. They went down the street together. Even then he paused, and waited a half-hour, kneeling by his old study-chair for guidance in this most delicate matter that he was about to undertake.

Out in the street again he perceived a large gray-haired man across the road, who took especial pains to bow to him, and finally, after hesitating, crossed over at the next corner and walked with him. He was a contractor, and anything but a religious man. He had never had much use for Mr. Atterbury before, and had always gruffly declined the various invitations to church the minister had given him; but now his ruddy countenance was beaming.

"Pleasant afternoon," he said, and adjusted his gait to the minister's.

Mr. Atterbury, much surprised, answered him affably, and wondered inwardly at the changed manner of his companion.

"Say, you got one member of your church that's an A No. 1 Christian all right," was his next remark.

"Is that so?" laughed the minister. "Which one is that?"

"Well, there ain't but one like her," said the man, "and from all I hear tell she's doin' fer your son same's she is fer mine; so I've no need to mention her name. I think you know who I mean."

The man's heart was so evidently over-flowing with pride that his son should even be counted in the same category with the minister's that it was impossible to resent the implication of the words; besides, Mr. Atterbury knew that Tom's life had not been exemplary in all ways; so he responded most heartily:

"Oh, is your son one of those who goes to Miss Gracen's house? She seems to be giving them delightful times there. Does he enjoy it?"

"Enjoy it! I should ruther guess he does," said the man heartily; "why, he can't talk of nothin' else from mornin' to night when he's home. It's 'Ma, don't fergit to have me a clean shirt fer to-night, 'cause I hev to go to Miss Gracen's,' er, 'Ma, you'd jus' oughter make some cake oncet like Miss Gracen's Rebeccer made last week.' He's took to singin', too. I guess he ain't got much voice, but it sounds real cheerful round the house; and he reads a lot. I don't think myself he keers much about books, but he'll do any old thing fer her. Why, he's even took to goin' to church nights. I guess you've noticed."

The minister remembered that this man's stolid, young son had been of the group that Miss Gracen marshalled into service last week.

"You see," he went on volubly, "he ain't much fer church, bein' as he never cared for settin' still much; but he says it's only right he should do it when she asks. She don't just say they sha'n't come to Sunday meetin' else they do, but he says as how that's the only way they know they can sorter pay her back fer all she does fer 'em — that an' bringin' the other fellers. They seem to set a big store by that there Sunday meetin'. My son's just went. Well, so-long. Guess I turn off here."

The minister walked on more slowly toward the Gracen house.

When he opened the gate, a burst of song greeted him clear and strong from rich, deep, boy voices,

"O Love that wilt not let me go,

I rest my weary soul in Thee;
I give Thee back the life I owe,
That in Thine ocean depths its flow
May richer, fuller be."

He paused half-way up the walk, and caught his breath. There was something in the song that touched his soul — an appeal, a wonder, and a prayer. How they could sing! Surely no one could object to music like this on the Sabbath.

He looked cautiously up at the front windows, but saw no sign of any heads or eyes looking out. They were all engaged in singing. He stepped shyly up on the porch, and for the first time it struck him that his presence there at that hour might almost be regarded as an intrusion. His son would be likely to regard it as such, he was sure, and perhaps resent it.

This thought struck him as he placed his finger on the electric bell, and caused him to half withdraw it even as he heard the ringing of the bell in the distance. If he had not rung already, perhaps he would have turned and gone softly down the steps and out of the gate again without entering; but now he must at least wait until some one came, or he might be caught stealing away from the door.

The second verse of the song rolled on more distinctly now; for he was nearer, and he noticed that a window in the front was part way open.

He forgot to think what he should say when he got inside, for his mind was filled with the words of the song uttered with so much feeling from these unaccustomed voices. It made his heart thrill to think of such boys singing such words, and his son among the rest. He wished Miss Bypath could hear this singing. What could she have meant by her strange account? But then, of course, she was too far away to distinguish what songs they were singing. He glanced down the street at the old brick house, shabby and staid with its stiff, box-bordered path and its two silver poplar-trees rustling dismally in the clear winter air, and frowned at the thought that he had been obliged to come on this most unpleasant errand because of its owner's whim. He began to feel himself in an awkward position.

Then the front door opened silently. Hiram stood with question in his eyes, and the minister felt still more out of place.

"Is Miss Gracen in?" he asked, purely out of habit, for he had not thought what he would do.

"She's in, sir, yes, sir," murmured Hiram

almost in a whisper, "but she's havin' her boys. I could call her?" He put the suggestion as though it were a precedent scarcely to be thought of.

"Don't call her, Hiram," said the minister, catching at the chance; "I won't disturb her now. I'll come in another time. It was just a little matter I wanted to speak to her about. I'll stand here a minute, and hear them sing and then I'll go on —"

"Step inside, sir," said Hiram with pride. "You can sit in the dark of the alcove in the hall, sir, and never be seen. That singer fellow'll likely be having a solo in a minute or so. I'll put a chair in the shadow, and you can set as long as you like, and slip out when you get tired, without their ever knowing you're here."

Hiram set the chair with absolute silence, and the minister like a culprit in a crime slipped into it and kept silence, listening to song after song that rang full and strong from the chorus. They were grouped around the piano, he could see from his sheltered alcove; and his own son stood in their midst, with an arm over Dick's shoulder on the right and another over Harold's on the left. Then Wayne Forrest, standing close to the piano, sang alone; and the minister's heart stood still for a moment with the wonderful thrill of the voice in its plaintive appeal from the depths of a soul that had suffered. Where had the boy gained the sympathetic tone and clearness of expression that sent every word he sang home to the heart of the hearer?

"O Jesus, Thou art standing,
Outside the fast-closed door
In lowly patience waiting
To pass the threshold o'er."

There was that in the song that held the little company perfectly quiet as they sank into the chairs around the room, and a hush settled over them. When the song was finished, to the minister's surprise, there followed a prayer.

"Dear Father, be in our midst this afternoon, and show us how to find Thee. Let the songs we sing be acceptable praise, and open our hearts to hear whatever message Thy word shall bring us. May we none of us be left out in the blessing Thou hast for us. In Jesus' name we ask it. Amen."

It startled him to hear Miss Gracen's voice. She had always begged to be excused from taking part in public meetings, though he knew she sometimes led in prayer at the women's missionary meetings; but here in her home, among these strange boys, whom no one else seemed able to reach, and whom no one cared to try to, she spoke to God as a man speaketh to his friend, face to face. He glanced across the hall and into the room where the light of the afternoon flooded the scene and showed the bowed heads and closed eyes. Not a boy was staring about. All was quiet and reverent.

They sang again, lustily, and then there came the Bible reading. Tom had never divulged the fact that the word of God was a part of their afternoon reading. The minister sat astonished, and listened while the leader read the story of Elisha at Dothan with his frightened servant who reported the surrounding of the city by the Syrian host, and of the opening of his eyes to see the hosts of God with their chariots and horses of fire in a multitude upon the mountain, ready to deliver them. A few illuminating explanations were given as she went on with the reading, but most of the explanation and vividness of the story was due to the remarkable reading it received. The reader then turned to the story of the blind man healed, as told by John, and read it as though it had been a drama, until the Pharisees, the neighbors, the father, the mother, and the blind man lived and moved and spoke before the audience. There was a tense stillness in the room when the Pharisees had cast the man out and Jesus came and found him.

Miss Gracen closed her book, and said just a few words about three kinds of blindness in the chapter they had read — a blind follower of God who couldn't see God's help all about, ready to sustain him; a blind soul who had never known the light and could not understand what he was missing; blind Pharisees who had every reason to see aright, yet chose to be blind. There was no preaching about her words, but the minister felt that each boy listening knew he was included somewhere in that list of blind people who might receive sight.

It was a strange study to watch those boys through the wide-open doorway, as they sat about the room absolutely quiet, either watching their leader intently, or gazing off thoughtfully through the window, or sitting with closed eyes. The boy Wayne was exactly opposite the door, and his keen eyes were fixed upon the reader as though he might miss a word if he took them off; and all the sorrow, anguish and disappointment of his life, with all the hopeless longing, seemed to come and sit in his face unre-buked as he listened. It was as if he had caught a glimpse of the light somewhere, and had forgotten himself.

As the afternoon waned, the hall grew darker; and the minister in his quiet corner dared watch the interesting group. Harold silently arose to turn on the electric light, while Dick touched a match to the fire laid in the fireplace; and firelight and electricity made visible all the little audience to the interested watcher in the hall.

There was a stir in the other room as Miss Gracen closed her book and went to the piano. They were going to sing again. But Tom Atterbury's voice broke in, and hushed them to stillness.

"Miss Gracen, you said the other day when you were reading about Saul that everybody sometime in his life got a vision of Christ, or a call to serve Him. I'd like to ask you if you think they have to wait for that, and how do you think it comes? Does everybody know it? Is it always something big and startling like lightning, or is it some-times just a kind of conviction?"

Something strange and queer gripped the minister by the throat. He didn't sense the answer that was given, except to know af-terwards that it had been all that it should have been. He only felt the voice of his dear, mischievous, hard-to-manage eldest son, whose life was entwined about his heart-strings in a more than common love. His boy, his bad boy, was asking a question like that, and asking it as if he really cared about the answer! Oh, had his boy heard any slightest call, seen any glimpse whatever of the light that shines in the face of Jesus Christ?

He did not know it; but he sat all during the hymn that followed with tears streaming down his face, sat in the dark alcove weeping and praying for his boy, and for these other boys; and for this woman who was so quietly and wonderfully ministering to them all.

After the song they all settled down in their chairs again, and Miss Gracen read several chapters in Elizabeth Stuart Phelps Ward's remarkable story, "A Singular Life." It appeared that they had all heard the beginning and were deeply interested in the story, and it also appeared that the reader had selected her chapters, and was sketching what came in between with remarkable skill, omitting some parts that might have been merely worldly, or touching lightly upon them, but gathering up the thread of the story in such a way that the one central figure of the man, the "Christman," of the story stood out before them.

It occurred to the minister that he ought to get away before he was discovered; but this was no time to make his escape, for the room was so quiet that any sound from the hall would attract attention. He must wait until they sang again, and were all standing around the piano with their backs to the door. So he heard the story too, and saw the tray approaching at last, with Hiram carrying it as though it were a sacrament; although he did not know that the old servant had sat just within the back-hall door with it open a crack, and enjoyed the whole service as much as any of the boys.

He made his escape out into the clear winter dusk with the tears still wet upon his cheeks, and a song of thanksgiving within his heart which rivalled the song, "It is well with my soul," that rang out from the lighted parlor as the meeting came to its close. A moment he lingered outside the window, and watching, saw his son among the rest; saw him courteously handing a cup of something steaming hot to his hostess and smiling adoringly down upon her in her cushioned chair by the window. Then he turned and hurried home to tell the boy's mother what he had seen and heard.

And Lydia Bypath, watching, ferret-like

at her front window, after her long afternoon's vigil, saw with mortification that he
was not coming in to report to her!

19

The minister entered the pulpit that evening with a glorified expression on his worn face that made him almost look young again. He glanced down at the double row of boys surrounding Miss Gracen and saw their faces in the light of the afternoon's revelation. Heretofore he had looked upon most of them as so many hindrances in the way of his son's living a right life; now he saw them as immortal souls awakening to the call of the Christ, and his heart was filled with a great desire to say some word, leave some thought, which would help them to make the great decision.

Wayne Forrest looked up, and caught his eye, with a gleam of recognition; and the minister smiled slightly, with just a suggestion of a nod. Lydia Bypath, stiff and sore, sitting erect in her pew, saw it all, and fairly glared. If the boys had seen her, they would have said, "She certainly has it in for the minister." But fortunately the boys did not see her. They sat quietly, reverently, joining in the hymns with a vigor that made the dear old senior elder turn and look at them approvingly more than once; and the only disturbance that arose in their company was the silent scuffle that went on over every hymn, each boy trying to be the first to give Miss Gracen the book with the place found. This explained the few quick smiles and nudges and winks that Lydia Bypath rolled as a sweet morsel under her tongue as she sat by, looking on. Oh, she certainly "had it in" for that minister!

The sermon that evening was short and plain, with two or three brief illustrations that had come to the minister during his two hours' reflection in Victoria Gracen's hall alcove — striking stories in themselves and leading up to the great thought of self-surrender. They caught and held the boys' attention, and deepened the impression made by the afternoon meeting. When service was over, the boys went down the aisle more slowly than usual, and gathered affably about the minister at the door, perhaps because Wayne stood talking easily to him as if he had been an old friend. There was a new look of friendliness about the minister that the boys were quick to appreciate and expand under.

But behind them, grim, forbidding, with

pursed lips and snapping eyes, stood Lydia
Bypath awaiting her turn; and every word
the minister spoke to every boy was an of-
fense in her eyes, because she knew he saw
her standing there waiting, and he ought to
have sent them off instead of smiling at them
in that ridiculous way, "encouraging them
in their conceit," she called it.

But at last Miss Gracen and her escort
moved out of the church door; and Mrs.
Atterbury, turning from her kindly inquiry
about the janitor's baby, saw Miss Bypath
approaching her husband, and knew they
were in for another half-hour at least.

"You have something to tell me, Mr. Atterbury," she challenged, as the minister
closed the outer door and turned back to
his study to get his coat and hat.

"Oh, why, good evening, Miss Bypath,"
said the minister cordially, yet fencing for
time. "Let me see, you wanted to know
about the boys' meetings, didn't you? Yes,
well, suppose you come into the study,
where it is a little warmer. It makes this
room cool off quite suddenly to have both
those doors wide open on such a sharp
night, doesn't it?"

The minister led the way up the aisle to
the study back of the pulpit, and motioned
to his wife to come with him.

Miss Bypath followed perforce, remarking that some people kept the door open unnecessarily long, it seemed, on Sunday night. They might do their visiting and laughing on another evening, to her way of thinking. It dispelled the solemn influence of the service to allow a lot of gossip after it was over. For her part —

But the minister broke in upon her reflections with a cordial "Sit down, Miss Bypath. Here's Mrs. Atterbury. She's interested, too. I've just been telling her before service what a wonderful time I have had this afternoon. I really can't thank you enough for leading me to make this investigation."

For an instant Miss Bypath's firm jaw relaxed in pleased surprise, and she straightened herself proudly, and flashed an "I-told-you-so" gleam into her eyes; but the minister hastened on quickly.

"I must tell you that you have been entirely mistaken regarding the gatherings held at Miss Gracen's. There is nothing whatever objectionable about them; and on the contrary, the work that Miss Gracen is so quietly doing is led, I believe, by the Holy Spirit, and is being greatly blessed. I am glad to be able to tell you that there is a most reverent attitude among the boys and that some of them are really in earnest in trying to live better lives."

"Who told you this?" burst forth Miss Bypath with flashing eyes.

"No one told me; I heard and saw for myself, and the sight was one I shall never forget. I do not feel at liberty to tell more about it, Miss Bypath, save to say that you, as a member of this church, have reason to kneel and thank our heavenly Father that He has put it into the heart of Victoria Gracen to give her time and thought to work for these boys. I believe our church and our town will be the better in the years to come for what she is doing; and, if more people could devote their time to cultivating the young human souls all about them, the world would be a better place in which to live. I think it would be well, Miss Bypath, for you to say nothing further to any one about this matter."

"Indeed," said Miss Bypath, rising with offended dignity. "I shall do my duty, whatever anybody else does. I suppose that because your son goes there he has been able to pull the wool over your eyes and make you think black is white; but, Mr. Atterbury, there are people who know; and this is a serious matter. I do not intend to be insulted by your son or any other boy, and keep perfectly quiet. If you will not do something about it, I will, and as for Victoria Gracen, she is making herself simply ridiculous, and I do not feel that it is my duty to shield her any longer. It is time such doings were shown up. If your eyes are blinded, too, it is all the more necessary that some one speaks."

Then up spoke little, quiet Mrs. Atterbury.

"Miss Bypath, our son Thomas had no idea that he was insulting you yesterday. He asked you to ride in genuine earnest, because he says he wished to be polite to you and give you as pleasant a time as the boys were giving to Miss Gracen."

It is possible that even Tom himself would have opened his wide brown eyes in surprise over his mild, credulous little mother's faith in him; but there would have been a tender gleam in them for her for taking his part, and there is this to be said: Tom's mother always believed the very best of him, and she honestly thought that what she was saying about her son was true. His father saw through many of his pranks and pretenses, but his mother never did. Perhaps this was one reason why Tom had found it so exceedingly easy to tread the downward path of mischief and madness, because his mother believed in him, whatever he did, and never saw any harm in him.

But Lydia Bypath was not one to allow any illusions to remain if she could help it. She turned upon the small, meek woman, like the little fighter that she was, and fairly spluttered in her rage:

"Polite! Trying to be polite! Now, Mrs. Atterbury, don't you know any better than that?" she screamed. "That boy wouldn't be polite to anybody in the world, and he just hates me because he knows that I won't stand his nonsense. There's none so blind as those that will not see. As for you, Mr. Atterbury" — she turned to the minister with a withering glance — "as for you, I'm compelled to believe that you are bad as Victoria Gracen yourself. I think you have become *obsessed*."

Miss Bypath drew her small figure to its greatest height, and sailed out of the minister's study. The minister turned troubled eyes to his wife, who was quietly weeping into her handkerchief.

"Never mind, dear," he said gently, putting his hand tenderly on her shoulder. "It really doesn't matter what she says. Let us be glad over the change that is coming to our boy. Come; we will go home, and I will tell you all about that wonderful meeting. Do you think I ought to confess to Miss

Gracen how I sat in her hall and looked and listened this afternoon?"

And so he comforted his timid wife, and soon had her smiling again.

Mrs. Atterbury went up-stairs to see whether the younger children were tucked safely into bed; and the minister went to his study window, and stood looking out on the moonlit snow and thinking of the earnest boy faces he had seen that afternoon. A great longing for his own boy filled his heart.

And just then he saw them come up the street, Tom, Harold and Wayne, whistling in soft, clear harmonies the song they had sung that afternoon for closing, "It is well with my soul."

Tom turned in to his own home, and the other two went on, calling, "Good-night" in joyous, care-free tones. Was it imagination, or did the minister catch a note in their voices of better intent than had sounded there at other times when he had heard them thus?

Tom came into the house still whistling softly, and, glancing into the study, saw his father by the window.

"Hello, dad!" he called, and there was a ring of genuine pleasure in his voice.

"Hello, son," said the father, turning toward him quickly and smiling.

"Say, dad, that was a real good spiel you had tonight. The fellows liked it."

"Thank you, son," said the minister, almost choking with sudden emotion, and throwing his arm across the boy's shoulders lovingly.

The boy stood thus for a moment, half shyly, as if there was something he would like to say, but could not. At last he drew his father up to the window again, and they stood together looking out. It touched the minister beyond anything the boy had ever done before since he was a little fellow. For of late Tom had rather avoided his father's company, having always some escapade to hide or some delinquency to cover. But tonight he seemed to like just to stand there quietly with the man's arm around his shoulders.

"Dad," said Tom almost inaudibly, "when's the next communion?"

The father almost started with the joy and the hope in his heart.

"Six weeks from this morning," he answered, and tried not to show his agitation. "Why?"

"Oh, I don't know," said the boy evasively, "I was just thinking." He paused, and the silence was deep between them as they gazed out into the moonlight. Then the boy's voice in slow, hesitating drawl took up the sentence again. "I was just thinking — Miss Gracen's been reading us a lot of things — I was just wondering — if maybe I wouldn't like to join church sometime —"

The father's arm tightened about his shoulders.

"Son, you know what it would mean?"

"I think — I — do," came the slow answer.

"You know it would mean making your life fit your profession."

"Yes, sir; that's where the rub comes in. I'm not sure I could do it."

"You'd not have to do it alone."

"I know," said the boy seriously, and then after a pause, "I know," and breathed it reverently.

"Oh, my dear son," said the father deeply, tenderly; and then they stood a long time together silently. At last the boy turned to go up-stairs.

"I don't know, dad," said the boy shyly; "I haven't got it all doped out yet. But I'm thinking about it. I thought I'd better tell you."

"My son, you know this has been my wish, my prayer for years, your mother's and mine."

"Yes, I know, dad. Good-night."

The boy caught his father's hand, and pressed it hard; then, flinging it from him, hurried up the stairs, whistling again and breaking softly into the words,

> *"My sin — oh, the bliss of this glorious thought —*
> *My sin, not in part, but the whole,*
> *Is nailed to the cross, and I bear it no more,*
> *Praise the Lord, praise the Lord, O my soul!"*

The father could hear him moving around in his room above and singing the chorus.

> *"It is well, it is well with my soul."*

And this was the boy that Lydia Bypath thought was past all redemption!

Yet, when Tom Atterbury first sang that song at Miss Gracen's house, he used to sing it with a twinkle in his eyes, and come out loud and clear in the chorus with his deep rumble of bass; and the words that he sung were these:

> *"It is* swell, *it is* swell *with my soul."*

The change in the chorus had come to

express the change in the whole attitude of the boy.

By and by it was very quiet up in Tom's room. His father was still standing by the study window, looking out on the white moonlit world. He was thinking about his son. Then again he heard the stir and moving about up-stairs, and the soft echo of that chorus,

"It is well, it is well with my soul."

as the boy threw up his window and jumped noisily into bed. A startling thought came to his father. Had the boy been praying during that silence overhead? Something thrilled through his soul like unto no joy that had ever come to him yet in his ministry. His own son praying, trying in his awkward, boyish way to "dope" out the matters of eternity, and to adjust his own shy, fun-loving soul to God and the great plan of salvation. Could it be?

The father stole softly up-stairs, and listened a moment by his son's door. Then, as he heard no sound, he softly opened the door and slipped in, tip-toeing over to the bed. The boy was asleep already, his happy, healthy body yielding quickly to the pillow and the darkness. And there in the quiet room, with the moonlight in a long pathway across the carpet at his feet, the minister knelt beside his eldest-born, with his hand upon the boy's head, and prayed as he had never prayed before for his son.

It was just a little more than three weeks from that time that Lydia Bypath broke her leg.

"Gee! Wasn't it lucky she didn't break it the day she did that sprinting stunt down in the meadow?" exclaimed Harold Constable when he heard of it. "We'd have been in wrong forever after, sure, if that had happened. Gee! I'm glad she waited three weeks. She'd have tried to blame us with it if it had happened the same week."

"I should worry," answered the others in chorus with that peculiar shrug that expresses so forcibly the self-centered life.

Only Wayne Forrest had stood still, frowning, and said nothing. For it all happened in this way.

Tom Atterbury on his way to attend the Friday-evening frolic at Miss Gracen's was called back by his mother to take a bundle of clothing for the missionary box which was being packed by Miss Bypath, who was in charge of the box work in the missionary society. The bundle contained a dozen pairs of new stockings for the missionary and his wife, sent by an absent church-member to the minister's wife to put into the box. Mrs. Atterbury was anxious to have it get to Miss Bypath that night before the box was nailed up, and so called Tom back, and gave him directions.

When Tom again reached the snowy street, he heard a peculiar whistle that caused him to halt and wait until a dark figure in the distance caught up with him. It was Wayne Forrest.

"Say, At, did you remember to call up Brownie and give him Miss Gracen's message about that lantern she wants to borrow for the pictures to-morrow night?" he asked as he came up.

"Great Scott! No, I didn't," said Tom. "Say, Forrie, you just run back and phone from the drug-store for me, won't you? I've got to do an errand for mother before I can go to Miss Vic's."

"Not on your tintype, At," said the other boy darkly. "I'm in wrong with Brownie; it wouldn't do a bit of good for me to ask him. Better go yourself. What's your errand? Can't I do that for you?"

"Why, yes, I guess you can," said Tom, thrusting the bundle into his hands. "Just take this to Miss Bypath's, and tell her it's from old Mrs. Corson for the missionary box. She'll understand."

Wayne looked down at the bundle in dismay.

"Good-night! At, I can't go *there!*" he exclaimed.

"Oh, yes, you can," shouted Tom, who was already off toward "Brownie's." "You needn't go in; just hand her the package, and tell her it's for the missionary box. She won't know you from a bunch of beets."

By this time Tom was almost a block away and making good time toward his errand, for they both desired to be at Miss Gracen's early.

Wayne turned, frowning in the darkness. He had half a notion to put the bundle on the parsonage porch and tell Tom he could do his own errand, but a sense of honor made him finally turn and reluctantly walk toward Miss Bypath's house. After all, distasteful as it was for him to go near her again, he could probably get the errand over with a single sentence and hurry away before she had had time to recognize him.

He marched up to the front door, sent the bell pealing viciously through the house, and waited impatiently for the door to be opened. He even wondered whether it would do to leave the bundle on the steps and retreat but decided that wouldn't be quite the square thing. She might think it was a joke or a personal donation, and make all kinds of trouble for Tom's mother or the missionary box, though why he should care he didn't know.

But no one came to the door, and he rang again. Still no answer when even a third ring clanged through the empty hall. He stepped back and down the path to survey the dwelling. Surely he had seen a light. Ah! yes, there it was at the back. She was out in the kitchen, likely; but why hadn't she heard the bell? She didn't seem to be deaf the last time he saw her. He had never heard that she was. Well, he wouldn't have done his duty, and he couldn't get rid of that package, until he tried everything; so he took his way around to the back door.

20

Ten minutes before, Lydia Bypath had stepped out of her back door wrathfully to search for the broom. She had given it to the plumber to brush the snow from his feet, when he came to fix a leak in the water pipes, and of course he had not put it back in its place. The broom was just outside the door, leaning against the wall in the darkness; and the light that streamed across the back porch wickedly left the broom in the deepest shadow at one side.

Miss Bypath stepped out on the brick pavement to see whether he had thrown the broom down in the snow, and her foot slipped on an icy brick. She put out her hand to catch hold of the porch pillar, but missed it and fell, her feet twisted under her, and her head striking the edge of the porch. It was a most humiliating position, as well as uncomfortable, and her wrath at the plumber and the lost broom increased. Both bare hands were reaching vainly for something to catch hold of; and she felt a strange, sickening pain in her leg just above the knee. The wind was sharply cold, too; and she had come out now without even her little shoulder-shawl, a carelessness of which she was seldom guilty.

She tried to rise quickly, but that strange, sick pain caught her, and held her fast when she even attempted to move; and once the sickness overcame her, and the starry sky overhead seemed to darken and lift far away into eternity. Something was the matter with her leg. What could it be? That was ridiculous. She must get into the house. She made another frantic attempt to rise, and succeeded in getting to a sitting posture only to fall back with a groan, this time her head and shoulders in the snow.

It was the cold that finally brought her out of her faintness, and that made her call aloud for help, little realizing how short a distance her little thin, inadequate voice would carry.

When she had called until she was weak, and the cold had seemed to chill her through and through, she lay and wondered how long she would stay there before some one found her and helped her in.

What could be the matter with her leg, anyway? Was it broken? Horrible thought. Perhaps she would lie there all night, and freeze to death; or, if not that, at least she would suffer terribly, and perhaps lose a chance of having the fracture set, if it was a fracture.

Thus in sad plight she lay and began to think the day of judgment had arrived for her at last, when suddenly she heard steps in the distance, crunching cheerfully down the street, and a clear, sweet whistle. Ragtime, and she hated it! It was some wicked boy, of course. How terrible if they should see her here and gather around to point a finger of scorn! Her brain was already hazy with pain and anxiety, and in imagination she could see a set of village boys dancing about her and loudly rejoicing over her downfall. It seemed to her upset mind that she must keep very still until this boy had passed.

But the steps came nearer, and she heard her own door-bell. Instinctively she roused herself to one more effort to get up and answer her bell. It seemed that her house was undefended against an enemy; but she could not rise, and only a low moan escaped her white lips.

It was thus that Wayne came upon her in the broad belt of light that streamed from the kitchen door and lay across the fallen victim in the snowy path. With an exclamation of surprise he stopped and looked down upon her. Lydia Bypath, her old nature still vivid within her, opened her eyes and saw the boy upon whom she had uttered an anathema a short few days before.

"What business have you here in my back yard?" she snapped, and then closed her eyes because of the pain a sudden movement had brought.

Wayne's face darkened, and he would have turned away but that he saw by her attitude and expression she was in pain.

"I've brought a package from the parsonage for the missionary box," he said; "but I won't trouble you if you feel that way about it."

Then, as he turned, something of Miss Gracen's recent talk about the good Samaritan flashed into his mind, and he swung back again.

"Is there anything I can do for you? Shall I help you up?" he asked.

"Well, you can help me up, I suppose," she said ungraciously. "I seem to have twisted my leg."

Like a flash it went through his mind that here was a good opportunity for revenge, but with the thought came flocking the word-pictures Miss Gracen had made the Sabbath before of the soul in the sight of

God when harboring hate. A wistful tenderness that hovered around her mouth and eyes as she had talked about loving people, even loving enemies, seemed to appeal to him now and his hatred melted within him.

He stopped, gathered her in his strong, young arms, and tried to lift her upon her feet; but a cry burst from her white lips, and she fell back unconscious. Then more swiftly he gathered her up again, and carried her into the house; through the kitchen, on into her sitting-room, where he laid her down upon the couch, and stood back, wondering what to do next.

His mother's long invalidism had made him gentle and helpful. He stooped over her and arranged under her head a hard little pillow embroidered with stiff lilies. He went out to the kitchen, brought some water, and bathed her head and face with a towel that he had found hanging by the sink.

Presently he saw a quiver in her face, and her eyes opened; but she began at once to groan with the pain, and he thought by her ashen look that she would faint again. He saw she was in no condition to be questioned, and he looked about frantically for a telephone, but, discovering none, concluded perhaps she couldn't afford one. Then he made a dart out of the back door and around the house to the front. Putting his fingers to his lips, he sent a long, shrill, double whistle into the crisp night air, waited a moment, and repeated it; then faintly from the distance came an answering echo.

Tom had heard. He whistled a bird-call signal that only the favored few of the boys understood, and received an immediate answer; sent a "Hurry up" after it; and this time the answer was near at hand, and he could hear Tom's flying footsteps.

"Get a doctor, At," he called as soon as he felt his words could be heard. "And go get your mother or somebody quick! Miss Bypath's fallen down and got badly hurt. Beat it! I'll stay here till you come back. I think you'd better get the doctor first."

Tom turned without a word. These boys were accustomed to obeying orders from each other when given in that tone of voice, and asking questions afterward; it was a part of their code, a bit of the loyalty to one another that kept them all such fast friends.

Tom simply flew to the doctor's office, and caught him just before his office-hours were over. But it was not his mother he went after, for she was almost sick in bed with grippe; but he hurried down the street to tell Miss Gracen. She would know just what ought to be done.

Ten minutes later Miss Gracen entered Lydia Bypath's sitting-room in time to see Wayne bending over his patient and trying to adjust the pillow and cover her with a thick, plaid shawl according to her querulous directions, given in a strained, shrill tone between groans.

A second later the doctor came in and set them all to work at once; but it was that first glimpse of Wayne, with his face all gentle and pitying, trying to do his awkward best at nursing the cross, suffering creature who cried out upon him at every move he made, that filled Miss Gracen's heart with a great joy.

She had seen the dark look on his face when this same woman had turned upon him and had sent to his soul those deadly words about his father, and she knew from some hesitating questions he had asked that forgiving was not an easy thing for this boy. She had half suspected that this was one thing that held him away from God. Yet here he was, gentle as if the cross old woman upon the couch had been dear to him.

Tom, with Dick and Harold, who had been at the Gracen home when the summons came for Miss Gracen, entered the house a second later, and, standing in the open kitchen door, looked on with a kind of admiring dismay at their comrade.

"Gee!" said Tom, looking at Harold.

"*Good*-night!" responded Harold under his breath.

"Some situation for Forrie," appreciated Dick, turning away to hide the emotion that suddenly threatened to show itself in his eyes.

Then they proceeded quietly and swiftly to obey the order given by the doctor.

A broken leg was the verdict of the doctor, and the patient must be got to bed at once.

Tom was sent for a nurse; Harold, to the doctor's office for a certain roll of bandages which had been forgotten in the hurry; and Dick and Wayne were ordered to prepare the way to carry the patient to her bed in the adjoining room. But just the second before they left on their various errands, while they stood in a huddled group by the kitchen door attentive to the doctor's directions, Lydia Bypath opened her ferret eyes, and for the first time in her pain seemed to recognize her enemies.

"What on earth are those wicked boys doing out there in my nice, clean kitchen? Won't somebody put them out? The idea of their taking advantage of my helplessness in this way! You see, Victoria Gracen, just what they are —" and her weak voice trailed off into silence, for she had fainted again.

"The poor stew!" said Harold as he started out with Tom. "Hasn't she any sense at all? If Forrie hadn't found her out there in the snow, very probably she'd have been lying there yet."

"She doesn't deserve anything," answered Tom indignantly; "but we've got to do it for Miss Vic's sake." He paused, and a sudden thought came to them both. They each knew that Miss Gracen would say, "Do it for Christ's sake"; and in the silence the two boys looked up to the stars shyly, without a word, while each in his heart offered his service in a queer, half-questioning, boy way; and wondered whether, with all the childhood years of boyish dislike back of it, it would be accepted or not; each wistfully hoping it would, but neither daring to tell the other. Perhaps each understood how it was with his fellow, and respected the silence. It was a part of their code again.

The evening was over at last. They got poor Lydia Bypath into her bed, and quiet under an opiate while the bone was set; they established a good nurse by her side and a strong woman in the kitchen to look after the house; and then, after having worn themselves out to make her as comfortable as they could, they all went home.

"It's too late now for our programme," said Harold wistfully.

"But you'll all come in and have the refreshments," said Miss Gracen smiling. "You've worked hard, and deserve a bite to eat; and the things are all ready. Rebecca will be disappointed if they are not eaten. Then you can have one song before you go home."

"Sure! We're in for the eats every time," responded Tom heartily; and into the house they all trooped, Wayne as usual, lingering gallantly to help Miss Gracen up the steps.

"My dear boy," she said in a low tone, her hand on his arm as they stopped a second by the door, "I want to tell you how deeply touched I am by all that you have done to-night."

"It was nothing," said Wayne embarrassedly.

"Yes, it was something. It was a great deal," breathed Miss Gracen softly. "Do you think I don't know how you feel toward that woman? Do you think that I didn't hear what she said to you the other day when she fell in the snow and you went to pick her up, my dear, great-hearted, splendid boy?"

The rich waves of red rolled over Wayne's fine face, and a flood of gladness came into his handsome eyes. There was a mingling of rage and love in his face; rage toward the woman who had spoken those awful words about his father; love for this woman who could appreciate how he had felt.

"I did it for your sake," he said, looking his gratitude into her eyes in one quick flash, and then dropping his gaze to the floor.

Her eyes flashed back their love and appreciation, and she took his hand in a warm, quick grasp.

"Thank you, my dear boy," she said earnestly, "and — you did it for Christ's sake, too, didn't you? Am I right, Wayne?"

He returned her hand-clasp, and looking down upon her tenderly, said, in tones that were half ashamed for their admission:

"Mebbe," and smiling, turned away. It was a great deal for him to admit, but she knew it meant far more than he had said.

She went smiling and happy in to meet the rest of the boys, who had awaited her return in the big parlor, which had gradually changed its stately aspect and became their regular meeting-place.

The frail furniture of delicate workmanship had retired to a small reception-room on the other side of the hall; and had been replaced by plenty of big, easy chairs of heavier build and comfortable aspect, and a big table of dimensions suitable for evenings of study or almost any kind of a game. The piano and the rich Oriental rugs alone remained, and seemed to blend and harmonize entirely with the new surroundings. There were still some fine old paintings on the walls, but even some of those had been replaced with modern pictures, etchings and photogravures of notable men and places about which the boys had been studying.

The whole aspect of the room had changed so entirely that Mrs. Elihu Brown, calling one afternoon to adjure Miss Gracen concerning some Club duty, and letting herself by habit into the big room on the right instead of the small room on the left, where Hiram was timidly endeavoring to escort her, paused in utter dismay on the threshold. She put up her lorgnette, surveying the place as though it had been the ruin of some treasure-city lying waste and desolate, then turned and fled to the shelter of the confines of refinement within the smaller room that Hiram, with his silver card-receiver, was indicating. Here, poised upon the edge of a Chippendale chair, she identified one by one the Gracen articles of vertu, recalled others missing, which had been relegated to the attic on account of lack of room, and marvelled at the extremity of Miss Gracen's obsession. To give up her drawing-room! That seemed to a Club woman the height of all possible fanaticism. To give up her great, beautiful drawing-room to a pack of ill-mannered boys! Where now could she hold receptions? No place for bridge-whist parties! What a calamity!

"And you don't mean to tell me that you really serve refreshments to those young boors in your exquisite priceless china?" asked the caller a few minutes later, when in response to her voluble questions Miss Gracen took her eagerly about the reconstructed parlor, and showed her all the devices for giving a good time to the boys, pointing to the little tea table with its delicate cups and silver fittings as ready as when the room had been for her lady friends. "And you let them use your silver spoons! Do you think it's quite right to put temptation in their way like that? They tell me one of the boys who comes here has a father in jail for stealing. Did you know it?"

"Wayne Forrest is my dear and trusted friend," responded the hostess with quiet dignity. "There is no more conscientious boy in town, and he would protect me and all that belongs to me with his life."

"H'm!" The caller turned her lorgnette upon her hostess curiously with the air that in a boy would have meant, "Well, you have got it bad"; but she only replied:

"Well, you always were good. I hope you won't be disappointed in your paragons, but I must say it's more than I would do. I can't see, myself, why ironstone china wouldn't do for them to eat from. It's likely all the most of them have at home, and the boys could hardly appreciate Dresden china and antique silver."

Then she turned back to the more congenial atmosphere of the small reception-room and her Club business.

Miss Gracen thought of it now as she stood in the doorway and watched her boys handle the delicate cups and plates and deftly pass the spoons. They knew her silver spoons now almost as well as she did herself, and often helped pick them up and count them at the close of an evening, when all hands pitched in and helped to save the servants from extra work. She smiled to remember that not a single cup or fragile plate had been broken yet in all the handling back and forth that had been done that winter; and she believed in her heart that her boys did know the difference between them and the ironstone china, and that her dishes were a part of the refining influence that they needed in their lives.

Not that these things were, of course, essentials. If she had had nothing but iron-stone china in which to serve her simple refreshments, she would not have been greatly troubled about it; but, as she had these, why should they not be consecrated, and set to work their charm of beauty, and give the uplift that all rare and lovely things can give?

Now and then she had given a word, a hint, a story, that helped them to be interested in rare things. Did they know how cloisonné was made? Naturally they studied it with new wonder and interest as she showed them the delicate metal tracery, and spoke of the wonderful effects achieved by the patient workmanship and rare colorings. Those two cups were two hundred years old! They looked at them with awe, and handled them with infinite pains, speaking of their cups out of which they drank as individuals. They grew to respect the fine, old, costly cups even more than the modern handpainted ones, beautiful as they might be; and so the spoons, some of them, came to have stories connected with them, for Miss Gracen had told about her funny experiences at the Chicago Fair and her ride in the first Ferris wheel, as she showed the tiny spoon, half gold and half silver, with Columbus on the handle and the city of Chicago on the bowl. They knew the story of the spoons that came from Paris, and were fond of holding up the little gold ones to look through the Russian enamel set in the filigreed handles.

In fact, each beautiful adornment or elegant furnishing of her house had come to mean to these boys a part of their education; for she had told them wonderful stories of other lands, and hung them for memory on the pegs of pictures, vases and books.

It was when the changes were being made in parlor and reception-room that they learned to tell Chippendale furniture, and Sheraton, and began to take an interest in Oriental rugs, to hear how many hand-tied knots each had to the square inch, and to know that there was a lore connected with them, and an infinite variety of story and patient wonder in their weaving as well as in their strange, fantastic names. And it was so, without any word being said about carefulness or manners, that they grew to have respect for things in her house, while incidentally adding to their own stores of knowledge.

She stood looking at her boys as they ate,

joked and laughed. Especially did her eyes linger on her own boy and Wayne; for of late they had been growing into close friendship, and she found herself glad. Wayne was developing in many ways, and not the least of all signs of his fine character was the way he had waited on the crabbed woman whom he had just cause to dislike. If he could forgive like that, she felt he was near to the Kingdom; for she knew by this time his hot, fiery temper and his keen sensitiveness.

Before they broke up for the night Miss Gracen stepped into their midst, and, raising her hands for silence, spoke to them in a tender, gracious tone.

"I'm as sorry as I can be, boys, that your evening was spoiled; but do you know I'm glad in a way, too, because it has given me a glimpse of the true kindliness and gentlemanliness you have in hiding in your hearts. I want to thank you for the way you have taken your disappointment, and for the beautiful way in which some of you have helped to-night, and shown real love in spite of your dislikes; and" — she paused and looked around on the group hesitatingly; then her face broke into one of its beautiful young smiles that they loved — "it is my Dick's birthday next Friday — I wonder how you would like to go as my guests to the city, take dinner there, and attend the Symphony concert? There's a wonderful singer, John McCormack, as the soloist, and I thought you would like to hear him."

There was dead silence for a second, and then there arose a shout of joy from the group, which gathered strength and threatened to raise the roof before it was finished.

It is true that more than half the boys had only a vague idea what a "Symphony" concert might be and would have been far more attracted by a lively vaudeville or a good, stirring "movie," but whatever Miss Gracen wanted was the thing, and a jolly time together on the train, with dinner at some swell hotel, was good enough for anybody. They could stand a little dry music in between, if that was her whim. They never suspected that she had been studying the prospectus of the winter's amusements ahead for weeks with a view to selecting just the evening's programme that would elevate and awaken the latent tastes in their various natures. She thought she had detected a love of music in some; and while it was crude and largely confined to the better "rags," still, it was stirring; and she wanted to see the effect of a great orchestra on them. Even the most stupid of them would like the novelty of watching the different instruments played, and this might be the opening wedge for something more another time. She felt sure they would all enjoy the sweet singer whose Irish melodies would touch and hold them from the first note; and so she smiled in anticipation of her little experiment, while they cheered and rejoiced, and made the night air ring as they hurried down the snowy path.

But just as they reached the gate Tom and Harold and Wayne turned back to the door, which still stood wide open, where Dick and his aunt stood watching their departing guests.

It was Wayne who spoke, evidently voicing the sentiments of the three.

"Miss Gracen, we thought maybe there was something else we could do over there, to-morrow or sometime. Won't Miss Bypath need things? Walks shovelled if it snows — it's beginning a little now — furnace tended to, and errands? I could look after the furnace evenings when I come from the train, before I go home to supper. The other fellows could see to it mornings."

"Yes," said Harold, eagerly drawing his fur-lined gloves over his white hands not worn with work, "I'll do the furnace mornings, and empty the ashes. I don't have to go to school. Then Tom can look after the walks after school, and run any errands —"

The tears sprang unbidden to Miss Gracen's eyes, and she put out her hands in an involuntary gesture of blessing.

"Oh, you dear boys!" she said. "You dear, dear boys! That will be beautiful! Do you know, I think you are all trying to please Him?"

They laughed a soft, conscious laugh, and called, "Good-night" as they sped down the path; and Miss Gracen turned to see the tender look of her own eyes reflected in Dick's.

"They're great, aren't they, Aunt Vic?" he said, and then after a second: "What could I do, Aunt Vic? She's an awful boob, but I want to do something, too."

Miss Gracen closed the door quickly, and, turning, folded her own boy in her arms, much to his delighted embarrassment.

"Oh, Dick, dear. You too! Oh, I am so happy! You are all so dear!"

"Well, you see, Aunt Vic," said Dick, struggling hard to explain in a matter-of-fact tone, "we had to be because you are."

21

The winter days had lengthened into spring promise, and still Miss Bypath lay and suffered — and made others suffer. Her system was in bad condition, and the bone knit very slowly, making it necessary for the cast to remain on a long time; but the rest and the forced cessation from both privation and hard work to keep up appearances were doing her good in many other ways. Her mind was more vigorous than ever, and she led the trained nurse a life of it, ordering her about from early morning till late at night, being determined, as she told her friends, to "get the worth of her money out of her," although the truth of the matter was that it was not Lydia Bypath's money that paid her — for she had no money — but Victoria Gracen's.

Faithfully all the long days had the boys taken turns in tending the furnace, emptying ashes, shovelling snow, and running errands, until they too had begun to seem to the bedridden woman like a part of her establishment, and it was nothing more than her due that they should attend to matters thoroughly.

The nurse, poor, long-suffering woman, was an imported affair from the city hospital, and knew nothing about the free gift of their service by these boys. She supposed they were paid for their work; and therefore, when Lydia Bypath sent her down with a message to them she made it fully as disagreeable as it had been originally, and even added a word or a tone now and then for the scornful silence in which her directions were always received. She had to bear such words continually from her patient, and it seemed no more than right that she should pass them on to others. Who so thick-skinned, and withal so needing them, of course, as boys? She believed that boys in general were all wrong, and that they needed constant discipline; so she gave it in full measure, as it had been measured out to her.

"Miss Bypath wishes you to be more careful about letting the ashes come up through the house in that wild fashion," she announced to Harold Constable, standing crisp and starched in her white garments on the cellar stairs, and letting her imperious eyes run over him disapprovingly, as with his brand-new blue overalls and his curly hair powdered with ashes he essayed to clean out the furnace for the first time. He looked up, his eyes dancing with fun, and, touching his plaid cap politely, said,

"Yes, ma'am, I thank you," and went cheerfully on with his work.

"He's impudent, and good-for-nothing, I think," she told Miss Bypath up-stairs, and knew not that she had been ordering about the son of the richest man in Roslyn.

Harold sinned in other ways besides sending a cloud of ashes up the registers every time he manipulated the furnace; he *would* whistle and sing. His high tenor floated up to the sick room in distinct words something like these:

> *"I never-heard-of-anybody-dying*
> *From kissing, did you?"*

for Harold continued to love rag-time for some occasions despite the fact that he enjoyed Miss Gracen's rendering of a Chopin Nocturne with as keen a delight as a musician might. Besides, rag-time just fitted emptying ashes. It suited its rhythm to the motion of the shovel excellently. So he sang. Another choice selection which came distinctly to the bed-ridden woman was:

> *"Do-you-take-this-woman for-your-*
> *lawful-wife?*
> *I do. I do."*

"Indecent and irreverent songs!" Miss Bypath declared, and sent her white starched nurse flying down the cellar stairs with the admonition that he should be discharged at once if he didn't stop, whereat Harold sat himself down on the potato-bin and laughed loud and long till the echo reached up through the pipes of the register to the indignant old lady's ears.

"All right," he declared merrily; "you may discharge me if you like, but I'm afraid you won't be able to find another as good."

However, he tried to remember not to sing when he was in the house, and succeeded in forgetting only a few times. Nevertheless, in one way or another, Miss Bypath kept her hand and her tongue on matters below stairs, and made it lively indeed for the people who were trying their best to do for her.

At last, one Saturday morning in March — the birds were out in excited groups hunting flats for the summer, and there was a smell of spring in the air — a load of wood arrived. Miss Gracen had sent it to be used in the fireplace. It would do to supplement the furnace heat morning and evening, when they wanted to keep the furnace low on account of the mildness of the middle of the day; and it would make a cheerful blaze for Miss Bypath to look at, now that she was able to sit up a little while each day. Miss Gracen sent word that some one would come that afternoon to saw and split it, and pile it ready for use.

When the wood came, it was dumped in the wrong place, of course; but it was done, and the man drove off whistling merrily, leaving Miss Bypath raging angrily at her nurse about the inadequacy of all mankind ever to do the right thing.

Immediately after lunch the boys arrived, and the sawing and splitting began. Lulled by the dreary monotony of the sawing under her window, Miss Bypath fell asleep for a few moments, but awoke to sudden alert action at the sound of sticks of wood being laid with a ringing clang one on the top of another, their ends thumping gaily against the side of the old house.

She called fretfully to her nurse, and declared that the wood must all be carried around to the other side of the house immediately and piled over again, so as to be nearer to the back stairs, so they wouldn't have to track through her nice, clean kitchen every time they wanted a stick, and wear out her kitchen oilcloth.

The nurse descended, gave her command, and there ensued an altercation. The boys were in a hurry, and were due at a basketball game at three o'clock. It would take too long to carry the wood around the house and pile it over again. The nurse went upstairs with the report, only to return with more forcible commands. The boys were standing directly under Miss Bypath's window, and every word that was said could be distinctly heard by her. Miss Bypath listened like a bird in ambush as the nurse delivered her ultimatum, turned with her rattley skirts clattering around her, and shut the door. She desired no further impudent words from those boys.

The boys stood in silent disgust, facing one another for a full minute, Wayne with his old frown growing upon his brows.

"Isn't she the limit?" drawled Tom.

"She's an old boob, that's what she is," said Harold fiercely. "I'm about sick of this."

Then Wayne, with a sudden lighting of his eyes and a comical lifting of his eyebrows:

"The poor stew doesn't know we're not

paid for it, perhaps. Anyhow, what's the difference? We're not doing it for her. We're doing it for Miss Gracen and for — something else," he added softly. "Come on, here goes, boys. It won't take much longer if we hurry."

"Yes," drawled Tom as he rose with his arms full of wood. "You know Miss Gracen said last Sunday we'd got to love one another, or nothing else we do would go down. I s'pose we've got to love this guy, even if we *don't* like her. Gee! if she was like Miss Vic, we could love her all right, but Lydia Bypath is another kind of a proposition. Well, here goes; only I kind of wish Miss Vic could know what we're up against. It might count for more."

"It strikes me she generally knows, even if nobody tells her," declared Wayne as he picked up a great pile of wood and strode off around the back of the house.

They worked silently and swiftly, and in a short time had their work done, and departed whistling cheerily down the street, light-hearted because they had conquered.

But somehow Lydia Bypath did not feel quite comfortable in her mind, and when an hour later Miss Gracen came in to bring her a new book, and see how she was feeling, she burst out with:

"Victoria Gracen, who were those work-men you sent here to saw that wood? Were they any of those ridiculous, bad boys of yours?"

Miss Gracen's cheeks grew rosy, but she looked at the poor, little, sharp creature on the bed steadily.

"Yes, they are some of my boys," she said gently; "they offered to do it for you."

"They *offered* to do it *for me!*" said the invalid sharply. "That's a very likely story. How much do you pay them for doing it?"

"Oh, I don't pay them anything. They offered to do anything they could for you while you were laid up. They suggested it themselves. Harold Constable has been attending to your furnace mornings and Wayne Forrest evenings. Tom Atterbury did the walks and the errands, and sawed wood. They were all here this afternoon piling the wood, I think. They have been very thoughtful about you, asking me almost every day if I knew of anything else you needed."

"Harold Constable attending to my furnace! That stuck-up, stylish, Constable woman's son emptying my ashes! Victoria Gracen, I never knew you to tell lies; but really I can't believe that."

"It's quite true," said Miss Gracen gently. She wasn't sure how the irascible little creature would take the news; for there was fire of some kind in her voice, and two bright red spots had come out on her cheeks; but, when she came back from lowering the window-shade to shut out a sunbeam that was dancing daringly on Miss Bypath's counterpane, she saw that there were tears slowly running down the sharp little face.

"Why, what's the matter, Lydia, dear?" she asked tenderly.

But Lydia Bypath was weeping excitedly into her handkerchief.

"They called me a booby," she sobbed; "right under my own window they called me a booby! I used to go to parties in my young days, and I always got the booby prize in any game I ever played. Oh, I know very well what they meant. And they called me something else, too. They called me a poor s-s-st-*ew!*"

The words came out with a jerk and the poor, upset suffering woman turned her wrinkled face to the pillow and sobbed aloud.

Victoria Gracen, as she leaned over to try and comfort her, could not refrain from a smile and a merry glinting of her eyes, as she instantly knew just how those boyish young voices of disgust had sounded; but she struggled to control her own voice.

"They didn't mean anything wrong by it, Lydia; indeed, they didn't. They are dear boys. They didn't like the way the nurse spoke to them; that was all."

"Oh, I'm not blaming them," blurted out Lydia. "I s'pose I deserved it. I sent a lot of disagreeable messages down to them. I never knew that they were doing it for nothing."

"Well, never mind," said Victoria, smoothing out the crumpled pillow. "I'll tell them you didn't know they were doing it for you."

"They weren't," snapped Lydia in much her accustomed way. "They were doing it for you! They said so. They said it didn't matter what I said, so they pleased you. They called me an old guy, too; and then they called me Bydia Pylath! Oh, they didn't do it for me in the least, but I don't know as they had any reason to, either. I guess I've been all wrong"; and she wiped her eyes, and blew her sharp, red nose, and looked pitifully repentant for such a respectable, little, old fighter as she had always been.

"Well, I guess I've wronged you too, Victoria," she snapped out, again emerging from her sopping handkerchief. "I hope you'll forgive me. I guess my nerves are pretty well upset by this nasty broken leg of mine. I don't feel very pleased with what those boys said about me, but I s'pose you can tell them I'm obliged."

It was, indeed, grudging thanks, but it was almost as hard for Lydia Bypath to thank or to praise anybody as it is for a boy to tell the tender thoughts that come into his heart, and Miss Gracen had acquired much wisdom in dealing with human hearts during her winter's work; so now she only smiled and, pressing her friend's hand understandingly, said gently:

"I'll tell them," and went away singing a song of triumph in her heart. She would tell her boys. Oh, wouldn't she tell them?

And when she did, putting the grudging words through the lovely spectrum of her own imagination, or perhaps, more strictly speaking, through the clear analysis of what she knew to be Lydia Bypath's true meaning, the boys stood back astonished, awed, and slightly incredulous, it must be owned, among themselves.

"She never said it like that," said Harold, "not on your life! She couldn't! But Miss Gracen saw that in it, and that's what she wants us to see. Gee! you could almost love her if you could see her through Miss Gracen's eyes every day."

There came a day in early June when Lydia Bypath went to church.

It was communion Sabbath, and the windows were all wide open, letting in the breath of the June roses that garlanded the parsonage in lavish display, and the song of ravished birds as they exulted in the day.

Lydia came in a wheeled chair, and it was Wayne Forrest who wheeled it and who helped her up the steps and down the aisle to her seat, and then went on to Miss Gracen's seat; for Wayne and Dick and Tom and Harold were to unite with the church that day, and Miss Gracen wanted them all to be together.

Mrs. Constable was there, having arrived home the night before, and sailed into the church with smiling condescension, attended by her portly husband, a look of unusual interest on his florid countenance. He had never expected Harold to do anything so altogether respectable as to unite with the church, and he was openly pleased. Not that he knew much about religion himself; but he felt that a connection with a church would keep a boy from doing anything that was really out-and-out disreputable.

Mrs. Atterbury was there with all the little

Atterburys and turned a loving smile toward Tom, well content that he should be with his friends on this day of all days. Just before the service began Miss Gracen's carriage drew up before the side door of the church, and there slipped out of it and into the back seat of the church a quiet little woman in black with a long, thick veil, who was attended by a handsome blue-eyed girl with thick, yellow hair and an extremely simple white dress and a small straw hat. Few saw them come in, and they went before anybody had an opportunity to speak to them. They were Wayne Forrest's invalid mother and his sister, and Wayne did not know until he reached home that day that they had been there.

The solemn, simple service was wonderfully impressive. It seemed as though the coming of these four strong young men into the church had stirred the hearts of all present; and, when they marched quietly, embarrassedly up together to the front, and stood with bowed heads and earnest mien, more than one handkerchief was hastily taken out to dry a furtive, unexpected tear. And "Isn't it wonderful!" one whispered. "That Wayne Forrest! I always thought he looked as if he had a great deal of character." They had never said anything in favor of his character before. "And that handsome Harold Constable! I heard he was real wild. I wonder if it will last. And Tom Atterbury! Mrs. Atterbury looks too happy to live. I'm sure I hope it's genuine. He does seem to have changed a great deal this winter. I wonder how Miss Gracen did it. That nephew of hers is a fine-looking fellow. It must have been his influence."

And so went the comments softly, or flashing from mind to mind, and finding their way eventually to the dinner-tables of the town. There were a few whose hearts were stirred with a deep, glad joy, knowing the work of the Holy Spirit, by the power of prayer, to change lives; and knowing the drawing power of the Lord Jesus Christ. These believed in the young converts and had faith that they would conquer temptations through Him who is able to keep such from falling and to present them to His Father blameless at the last day.

Among these sat Victoria Gracen, too filled with deep joy to do aught but smile and thank her heavenly Father; for she had learned to love every one of these four boys as if he had been her very own.

Sitting with her four boys later, during the communion service, Victoria Gracen beheld as it were the gate of heaven opened, and caught a glimpse of her Saviour's face. There were others present of the boys who frequented her house; but they had not presumed to sit with her that day, not counting themselves to have yet attained to the privilege, but sitting thoughtful, wistful, half-decided; trying to make out what had come over their comrades to make them willing to surrender their lives, their fun, their liberty, everything, thus, before the world, to an idea. They had not as yet seen the whole vision.

When church was over, and the boys went solemnly, shyly down the aisle, it was Lydia Bypath's hand that came out to greet them first, to welcome them into the wonderful new life; and her sharp little face was wet with tears and much softened with smiles.

"I haven't been much of a Christian, I know you think," she said softly; "but I'm glad you've started, and I want to ask you" — turning to Wayne — "to forgive me for the mean things I said to you that day on the hill."

And Wayne, the hardness and blackness all gone out of his fine face, stooped and took her hand, and in giving his hand forgave forever the thing he had struggled to forgive, and thought he never could.

Standing on the church steps with the

minister, the senior elder watched Miss Gracen going down the street with her escort, following closely behind the wheeled chair containing Miss Bypath.

"It is wonderful, wonderful!" said the senior elder, brushing a film from his eyes and clearing his throat. "How did she do it?"

"She did it by giving *herself*," said the minister softly. "She never saved herself for anything else but those boys. They said she was 'obsessed' by boys." He smiled reflectively; he had never told of Lydia Bypath's visit except to his wife. "They said she was 'obsessed by boys,' and do you know I've been thinking that, if the whole church could have such an obsession, we should be able to gather them all into the Kingdom?"

"Amen," said the senior elder, and went reverently, thoughtfully down the street behind the little procession.

The employees of Thorndike Press hope you have enjoyed this Large Print book. All our Large Print titles are designed for easy reading, and all our books are made to last. Other Thorndike Press Large Print books are available at your library, through selected bookstores, or directly from us.

For information about titles, please call:

(800) 257-5157

To share your comments, please write:

Publisher
Thorndike Press
P.O. Box 159
Thorndike, Maine 04986